The Spanish-American War
1898

THE SPANISH-AMERICAN WAR

1898

Albert A. Nofi

COMBINED BOOKS
Pennsylvania

PUBLISHER'S NOTE

Combined Books, Inc., is dedicated to publishing books of distinction in history and military history. We are proud of the quality of writing and the quantity of information found in our books. Our books are manufactured with style and durability and are printed on acid-free paper. We like to think of our books as soldiers: not infantry grunts, but well dressed and well equipped avant garde. Our logo reflects our commitment to the modern and yet historic art of bookmaking.

We call ourselves Combined Books because we view the publishing enterprise as a "combined" effort of authors, publishers and readers. And we promise to bridge the gap between us—a gap which is all too seldom closed in contemporary publishing.

We would like to hear from our readers and invite you to write to us at our offices in Pennsylvania with your reactions, queries, comments, even complaints. All of your correspondence will be answered directly by a member of the Editorial Board or by the author.

We encourage all of our readers to purchase our books from their local booksellers, and we hope that you let us know of booksellers in your area that might be interested in carrying our books. If you are unable to find a book in your area, please write us.

For information, address:
Combined Books, Inc.
1024 Fayette Street
Conshohocken, PA 19428

Library of Congress Cataloging-in-Publication Data
Nofi, Albert A.
    The Spanish-American War, 1898 / Albert A. Nofi.
       p. cm. —
    Includes bibliographical references and index.
    ISBN 0-938289-57-8
    1. Spanish-American War , 1898—Campaigns. I. Title.
    E717.N64 1996   95-53006
  973.8'9—dc20   CIP

Printed in the United States of America.
Maps by Beth Queman

For Marilyn J. Spencer
and Lori Fawcett,
in loving memory.

Contents

Acknowledgments 11

Note to the Reader 13

I "A Splendid Little War" 15

II The Beginning 57

III The Santiago Expedition 107

IV The Naval Campaign of Santiago 155

V The Fall of Santiago 191

VI The Campaign in Puerto Rico 227

VII The Philippines 263

VIII "A Bully Fight" 299

Warships—General Information 318

Warships—Statistical Profile 322

Warships—Armament 326

Order of Battle: The Santiago Campaign 331

Order of Battle: The Puerto Rican Campaign 334

Order of Battle: The Manila Campaign 337

Guide for the Interested Reader 339

Index 345

Sidebars

Why did the USS *Maine* Blow Up? 46

Funding the Fight 53

The Leap to Arms, A Case Study: New York 91

USS *Oregon* Rounds South America 93

The U.S. Army 98

The Army Corps   101
The Spanish Army   102
The Rough Riders   150
Escario's March   153
The American People Answer the Call   216
Civil War Veterans in the War   218
Black Personnel in the Armed Forces   220
American Women in Medical Service   224
The Cuban Army   224
The Press   261
The Philippine Army   292
The Siege of Baler   296
The Annexation of Hawaii   297
Some Notable Spanish-American War Alumni   306
The Spaniards   308
Spain's Strategic Options   310
Battles, Combats, and Skirmishes   313
Naval Gunnery Effectiveness   315
The Medal of Honor   318

Biographies

George Dewey   48
Patricio Montojo y Pasaron   48
Valeriano Weyler y Nicolau   49
Maximo Gomez   50
Jose Martí   51
Antonio Maceo y Grajales   52
Nelson Appleton Miles   96
William Rufus Shafter   97
Joseph Wheeler   148
Leonard Wood   149
Arsenio Linares y Pombo   151
Joaquin Vara del Rey y Rubio   152
William T. Sampson   186
Winfield Scott Schley   187

Pascual Cervera y Topete   188
Fitzhugh Lee   214
José Toral Vasquez   215
José Profansio Rizal y Alonso   291
Wesley Merritt   293
Arthur MacArthur   293
Frederick Funston   294

Maps

The Battle of Manila Bay   18
Naval Movements in the Caribbean   84
Cuba: Military Organization and
   Principal Operations   117
The Battle of Las Guasimas   124
The Battles of El Caney and the Heights of San Juan   134
The Blockade of Santiago   164
Naval Battle of Santiago: Outline Track Chart   174
The Siege of Santiago   194
Operations in Puerto Rico   234
Battle of Coamo   245
Operations in the Philippines   272

Acknowledgments

Thanks are in order to Patrick Abbazia, Richard L. DiNardo, MAJ Vincent Katinas, New York Guard, LTC Leonid Konradtiuk, Historical Section, National Guard Bureau, Kay Larsen, Stephan Patejak, Dr. Richard Somers, U.S. Army Military History Institute, and Brian Sullivan for their advice, suggestions, and comments.

Edward Ablon, Dale R. Ritter, and Gregory Urban provided considerable help with their expertise in small arms, as did Dan Whiteman, the director of the Rock Island Arsenal Museum.

César Borrero, Philip Melfi of the Harbor Defense Museum, Fort Hamilton, New York, and David Schwartz provided access to unusual old materials on the war.

LTC Luis A. de Casenave, Puerto Rico State Guard, and A.B. Feuer kindly provided access to their works on the war.

Institutions which proved of considerable help were the Alabama Department of Archives and History, the Library of Congress, the Mina Rees Library, Graduate School, CUNY, the National Archives and Records Service, The New York Public Library, and the United States Army Center of Military History.

Particular thanks are in order to my old friend Juan Francisco Serna Jorda, who provided useful materials from Spain, and who, with his family, is an ever gracious host.

And as always, very special thanks to Mary Spencer Nofi, who had to suffer through it all.

Albert A. Nofi
18 October 1995
Brooklyn

Note to the Reader

For convenience, Spanish military formations have been rendered in italics, and the 24-hours military system of keeping time has been used.

Spanish military terms have generally been translated into English for the reader's convenience. Those who are aware of the proper Spanish terminology will forgive me for the occasional forced translations in this regard.

As Titivilius, the demon of academic error, is ever active, it is likely that a few mistakes have been made, perhaps grievous ones. The author would appreciate hearing from any readers who have questions concerning statements in the text, or who have suggestions or observations they think may be of value.

CHAPTER I

"A Splendid Little War"

Save for an occasional moonbeam breaking through the cloud cover or periodic bolts of tropical lightning, signaling intermittent rain squalls which from time to time swept across the sea, the night of 30 April-1 May 1898 was warm, calm, and dark over the South China Sea. Shortly before midnight a small squadron approached the entrance to Manila Bay. There were nine vessels in line ahead, four protected cruisers, an unprotected cruiser, a gunboat, a revenue cutter, a collier and a supply ship. The protected cruiser USS *Olympia*, largest of the ships, wearing the broad pennant of Commodore George Dewey, a 60-year old veteran of the Civil War. The nearly ten-mile wide mouth of the bay had two practical entrances. That on the left—the north— lay between the rugged, jungle covered Bataan Peninsula and Corregidor Island, and was barely two miles wide. Boca Grande, the broader channel, lay on the right, the south, stretching three miles between little Caballo Island, nestled just southeast of Corregidor, and tiny El Fraile, a rocky islet separated from the mainland of Luzon by two miles of foul ground. Spanish coast defense installations covering these passages included 17 serviceable pieces of artillery. An ancient rule of the sea was that warships dueled with coastal batteries to their loss. Worse, there were rumors of mines.

Pondering his options, Dewey had chosen to run into Manila Bay through the Boca Grande. His information suggested that only six of the guns covering that entrance were modern pieces, three 4.7-inch breech-loading rifled cannon on El Fraile and

The protected cruiser **USS Olympia,** *Dewey's flagship at Manila Bay, proceeding at a moderate speed. Her two 8-inch turrets, one each fore and aft, can be plainly seen, as can some of the 5-inch and 3-inch guns sponsoned into her sides.*

three 5.9-inch breech-loaders on Caballo. At worst these guns would be dangerous only within a radius of about 1.5 miles, in which space, if well served, they might give his ships "a very unpleasant quarter of an hour." Nor did he think much of the rumored mines. A veteran of Mobile Bay—where David Glasgow Farragut had dismissed the presence of mines with a profane phrase—he considered the depth of the channel unsuited for moored mines, and reasoned that in any case mines which had been long in such seas would have been rendered inoperative by the tropical conditions.

The squadron slipped into Boca Grande just after midnight, with all guns manned and all lights dark, on a course that would take it to within a half-mile of El Fraile, more than two miles south of Caballo. The order of sailing was *Olympia*, the flagship, in the van, followed by *Baltimore, Raleigh, Petrel, Concord, Boston,* and *McCullough*, with the two merchantmen bringing up the rear. On a slightly northeasterly course, one by one the ships slipped into the bay, changing course to northeast by north as they did so, to avoid shoals further ahead. Finally only three vessels remained in the channel, the revenue cutter *McCullough*, and the colliers *Zafiro* and *Nashan*. Suddenly, just as *McCullough* came abreast of El Fraile a tall plume of flame shot up from her smokestack. The Spanish gunners on El Fraile cut loose with a single round. It sped over the ship, whistling past to fall harmlessly into the waters beyond. *McCullough* fired back. Her little 6-pounder made but a feeble response, until seconded by heavier rounds from the cruisers *Boston, Concord*, and *Raleigh*, just ahead. The Spanish fired again, two more rounds which went over and into the sea. But then a round from *Boston* landed in the Spanish position, and no more fire was returned. As the last of the ships slipped out of the channel the moon set. The U.S. Navy's Asiatic Squadron had successfully slipped into Manila Bay without loss. Some 25 miles ahead lay the city of Manila, bastion of Spanish power in the Philippines. Preferring to avoid a night action, Dewey reduced speed to 8 knots.

Although relatively small, Dewey's squadron was a compact and powerful force. Leaving aside the revenue cutter and the two unarmed merchantmen, which he held off as a subsidiary squadron, Dewey had over 19,000 tons of warships, armed with 53 guns of 5-inch to 8-inch caliber, plus about 135 smaller pieces. All his ships were of iron or steel construction, and four of them had some armor protection to vital areas. Although two of his ships were at best capable of only 10 knots, the four best could easily make 19. His men—some 1700 officers, sailors, and Marines—were well trained and eager for a fight. Dewey had trained—and waited—sixty years for the opportunity to lead a fleet into action, and that was what he was now going to do against the Spanish squadron of Rear Admiral Patricio Montojo y Pasaron.

In contrast to Dewey's squadron, Montojo's flock—to call it a squadron would be generous—was a grab-bag collection of mostly obsolete vessels, lying in Cañacoa Bay, just under the lee of the Cavite Peninsula, about eight miles southwest of Manila. Anchored in an irregular line stretching eastwards from Sangley Point, the northernmost tip of the peninsula, he had seven warships displacing slightly more than 11,000 tons. Although several of them were classified otherwise, two of Montojo's ships were unprotected cruisers and the rest were gunboats, two of which were under repair. One of his ships had a wooden hull,

PRINCIPAL SPANISH COAST DEFENSES			
no.	Name	Pieces	Type of Cannon
1	Punta Gorda	3	7-inch MLR
2	Punta Lassisi	2	6.3-inch BLR
3	Corregidor	3	8-inch MLR
4	Caballo	3	5.9-inch BLR
5	El Fraile	3	4.7-inch BLR
6	Punta Restinga	3	6.3-inch MLR
7	Sangley Point	2	5.9-inch BLR
8	Cañacao	1	4.7-inch BLR
9	Manila	4	9.4-inch BLR

Numerous very old and obsolete pieces have been omitted. Although nine of the 25 guns indicated were muzzle-loading rifles (MLRs), the particular pieces shown were by no means obsolete by the standards of the day, albeit that they had a much lower rate of fire than the breech-loading rifles (BLRs).

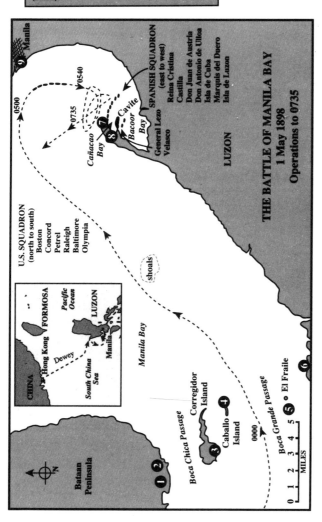

THE BATTLE OF MANILA BAY
1 May 1898
Operations to 0735

SPANISH SQUADRON
(east to west)
Reina Cristina
Castilla
Don Juan de Austria
Don Antonio de Ulloa
Isla de Cuba
Marquis del Duero
Isla de Luzon

U.S. SQUADRON
(north to south)
Boston
Concord
Petrel
Raleigh
Baltimore
Olympia

Rear Admiral Patricio Montojo y Pasaron, commander of the Spanish squadron destroyed by Commodore George Dewey at Cavite on 1 May 1898. Given the quality of his ships, Montojo ought to have considered dispersing his fleet, thereby forcing Dewey into a protracted game of cat-and-mouse.

all the others had iron or even steel hulls, and several had some armor protection. On paper all of Montojo's ships could make at least 12 knots, but most were in poor repair and had fouled bottoms. His firepower was embodied in 37 guns of 4.7-inch to 6.4-inch caliber, plus about 110 smaller pieces. His crews, some 1100 officers and men, were fairly well trained, but their morale was poor. Although the squadron lay close inshore, it was not well covered by coastal defense batteries, only three modern pieces being able to bear, two 5.9-inch pieces and one 4.7-inch.

As his squadron steamed across Manila Bay, Dewey assumed Montojo would offer battle under the coastal batteries of Manila proper, which, along with a goodly number of obsolete pieces, included four modern 9.4-inch guns, more powerful than any in his squadron. Much to Dewey's surprise, when the squadron arrived off Manila, it found only a few merchantmen lying at anchor. Concluding that Montojo had to be at Cavite, Dewey altered course southwestwards. Keeping a couple of miles off the coast, his lookouts raised the Spanish squadron shortly before 0500 The first shots of the battle were fired within minutes.

At about 0505, while still off Manila, Spanish shore batteries opened up. Their shells whistled over the American ships to fall harmlessly into the bay behind them, while two Spanish mines went off harmlessly just ahead of them. Arguably, had the coast defense personnel activated them just a few minutes later the entire mission might have been put at risk. The last two ships in Dewey's squadron, *Concord* and *Boston*, fired a couple of rounds each in reply, but then both shore batteries and ships fell silent. Minutes went by, as the American ships, steaming at 8 knots, formed on a line which converged at an angle with the Spanish, to permit as many guns as possible to bear, while Dewey ordered "Take her close along the five fathom line."

Montojo's ships opened up at about 0515, supported by the coastal batteries, even those at some distance, despite the fact that the range was too great. Dewey kept on steadily, maintaining 8 knots on a southerly bearing. Finally, at about 0540 Dewey turned to Capt. Charles V. Gridley, skipper of *Olympia*, saying "You may fire when you are ready, Gridley." The battle was joined.

The American fire was deliberate, but steady. That of the Spanish was erratic, and much slower. Almost from the first rounds the Spanish began taking damage. As the American squadron bore westwards, to maintain the five fathom line and run parallel to the Spanish squadron at about 3000 yards, Montojo's flagship took two hits in rapid succession, knocking out several light guns and causing some small fires, which were rapidly put out. A Spanish torpedo boat sortied from Cavite. When it was brought to Dewey's attention by Joseph Stickney, a journalist serving as a volunteer aide-de-camp, the Commodore said, "You look after her, I have no time to bother with torpedo boats." As he turned his attention back to the main event, the interloper was taken under heavy fire by the fleet's rapid fire guns, and even by rifle-toting Marines. Within minutes the torpedo boat was severely damaged and driven ashore.

As the squadron steamed on, it soon left the Spanish ships behind, off its port quarter. When abreast of Sangley Point Dewey ordered a 180-degree turn to starboard, and the squadron was soon steaming eastwards, a little more than 3000 yards from the enemy, with its starboard batteries now engaged. Although the American fire was heavy, more than one observer noted that it was not very accurate. Lt. C.C. Calkins, the flagship's navigator, observed, "We noted a large percentage of misses." But quantity told. Despite an overall abysmal accuracy rate, the American guns were scoring hits, numerous hits, in rapid succession. On the Spanish ships the damage was heavy. Aboard *Reina Cristina*, Montojo's flagship, American rounds began causing numerous casualties, starting fires which forced Montojo to order the flooding of the after magazine. In contrast, the Spanish fired with less effect. Although *Olympia*, *Baltimore*, and *Boston* all took numerous hits, none proved vital, and casualties were light.

The squadron passed once more beyond the Spanish ships, having made about 5,000 yards on its easterly bearing. With his ships steaming through geysers of water from Spanish shells, and enveloped in clouds of smoke from their own guns, Dewey again ordered a 180-degree turn to starboard, closing the range somewhat, and then began steaming westwards again. By now many of the Spanish ships were afire, sending thick clouds of black smoke reaching into the sky. Yet still the enemy fired back, erratically and inaccurately, but defiantly. The squadron completed its third pass, and Dewey ordered another turn to starboard. Even as this was being executed, Montojo ordered his flagship to sortie.

Reina Cristina steamed slowly out of the Spanish line, on a course bearing directly for *Olympia*. Dewey ordered the squadron to bear down on the Spanish crusier, and opened up an intensive fire. The range closed to about 1200 yards, and the Americans could see their shells bursting on the enemy ship. *Reina Cristina* was soon in desperate straits, afire in several places, with most of her guns disabled, and her steering engine shot away. Montojo later wrote, "The ship now being beyond saving, with the hull, smokestack, and mast pierced repeatedly, with the cries of the wounded echoing, with half the crew—including seven officers—down, I gave the order to scuttle her before the magazines went off." As the gunboats *Isla de Cuba* and *Isla de Luzon* came alongside to take off the wounded, the slaughter continued. *Reina Cristina*'s skipper, Capt. Luis Cadarso, although seriously wounded, refused to be evacuated until the last of his men were safely away, and was himself killed directing the abandonment of the ship.

It was then about 0735, and the American squadron again turned 180-degrees to assume a westerly course once more, beginning its fifth pass by the Spanish squadron. Then suddenly, Dewey was confronted with discomfiting news: Capt. Gridley reported that the flagship was quickly running out of ammunition, with but a few minutes supply of 5-inch shells left. Although it was clear that the Spanish had been dealt a serious blow, the enormous pall of smoke which covered their vessels made it impossible to determine the condition of the remaining ships. The enemy was still firing, and Dewey could not be certain that they had been broken. With ammunition low, and no possibility of resupply for weeks to come, he decided to break off the action. He ordered firing to cease and the squadron to proceed northwards into the bay, to redistribute its ammunition and await developments. As the squadron began changing course, the Spanish broke off the action as well. As the smoke of battle cleared, the extent of the damage to the enemy became evident. As Dewey later wrote, "It was clear that we did not need a very large supply of ammunition to finish our morning's task."

Nevertheless, the squadron rendezvoused in the heart of Manila Bay. Dewey ordered the damage assessed and the ammunition inventoried, while the crews had breakfast. Although four vessels had been hit—*Olympia, Baltimore, Boston,* and *Petrel*—he learned to his surprise that the damage was light. Only two officers and six men were injured, and only one 6-inch gun had been put out of action, all aboard *Baltimore*. Moreover, it turned out that Gridley had been misinformed about the shortage of ammunition: He had been told there were only 15 rounds of 5-inch ammunition left, when in fact the message ought to have read that each 5-inch gun had only fired 15 rounds. Meanwhile, Dewey informed the Spanish authorities in Manila that if any further fire was received from the city's coast defenses he would shell the town, a statement which they took at face value. As the Americans were steaming northwards,

Montojo ordered whatever of his ships as could still steam to fall back into Bacoor Bay, there to make a final stand, with orders to scuttle rather than surrender.

Dewey ended the squadron's breakfast break at about 1100, setting it on course for Cavite once more. The end of the battle came quickly. The Americans reopened fire at 1116. The Spanish had little with which to reply. The gunboat *Don Antonio de Ulloa* was quickly put out of action. The pair of 5.9-inch guns at Point Sangley took longer, not falling silent until 1230. Well sited, they were difficult to hit, albeit that they could not fire at targets closer than 2000 yards. At about 1215 a white flag went up over Cavite, but the firing did not end until about 15 minutes later. By then, the Spanish shore batteries had been silenced, and all their ships were sinking and burning. Dewey ordered *Petrel* and *Concord* to finish off the abandoned vessels, which they did with boarding parties. The final reckoning was not difficult. In a few hours Dewey had destroyed the Spanish Navy in the Philippines: *Reina Cristina*, *Castilla*, and *Don Antonio de Ulloa* had been sunk in action, the other six vessels scuttled or burned. No American ship had suffered significant damage. Casualties were equally one-sided: The Spanish had suffered 161 men killed and 210 wounded, the Americans only nine wounded, *Boston* having taken a hit in the final phase of the battle.

At 1400 Dewey anchored his squadron off the Paseo de Luneta, a waterfront park in Manila, named for the shore batteries around which it was built. Notifying the Spanish authorities that he would destroy the city if the coast defense batteries fired on his ships, he requested permission to use the underwater cable connection with Hong Kong to communicate with his superiors. While the Spanish officials pondered this request, the American fleet passed the night off the city, its seawall covered by numerous residents curious to see the American ships. Dewey offered them a serenade: *Olympia*'s band played various Spanish tunes until well into the night.

Little more than a week into the Spanish-American War, the United States had secured a smashing victory. Meanwhile, now master of Manila, Dewey was also seven thousand miles from home, a home which knew nothing of his decisive victory.

23

*　　　*　　　*

The Spanish-American War occurred between two countries which had but lately indulged in a rather spectacular bout of mutual admiration, on the event of the quadricentennial celebrations of Columbus' voyage, just six years earlier. The occasion had initiated a fad for things Spanish in the United States, crowned by visits of Spanish warships to American ports, and a Spanish delegation to the Columbian Exposition in Chicago. But the good will that these events had generated soon faded. It had been an anomalous trend, the Americans temporarily throwing off their English-rooted suspicion of the "Dons" in the glory of the moment. However, if traditional American views of the Spanish were by no means complimentary, there were few matters at issue between the two powers. Relations between the countries had generally been on correct, if not friendly terms, for some 75 years. There had, however, been occasional problems marring that relationship. Or rather, one problem, a place called Cuba.

The general collapse of her empire which occurred in the aftermath of the Napoleonic Wars (a collapse from which the United States had benefited through the annexation of Florida) had left Spain with only a remnant of the enormous territories which she had won in the *Siglo de Oro* that had followed Columbus' discoveries. In the distant Pacific there were the Philippine Islands and Micronesia, in the Caribbean Cuba and Puerto Rico. Of these, it was Cuba which was at once the most emotionally and financially profitable, and the most restless. Between 1821 and 1868 there were nearly a dozen conspiracies, insurrections, or filibustering expeditions intent on separating Cuba from Spain. Some of these had their origins in liberal nationalist desires for independence, while others were sparked by the convergence of interests of Cuban and American slaveholders, who wished to build a slave-owning empire, one which would include the southern U.S. and the Caribbean littoral, the so-called "Golden Circle," radiating out a thousand miles from Havana. All of these came to nought, as Spanish power was too firmly rooted in Cuba to be ousted by a coup. Nor was Spain inclined to reliquish control peacefully, turning down an Ameri-

24

can offer of $100 million in 1848, an extraordinary sum for the time. The most serious threat to Spanish power came in 1868, when the motherland itself erupted in civil war. In that year a nationalist uprising began in Cuba which spread rapidly, sparking what came to be known as "The Ten Years' War."

The Ten Years' War was the first modern guerrilla insurrection. It began modestly. A small, poorly armed band of whites and free men of mixed blood took to the hills in Oriente Province, proclaiming emancipation and independence. Within a month perhaps 12,000 rebels were under arms, and the towns of Bayamo and Holguin had gone over to them. As time passed, the rebellion spread further, infecting much of eastern Cuba. Spain woke slowly to the threat, preoccupied at home with its own complex internal struggle. But gradually forces in Cuba were built up, a blockade imposed, and repressive measures undertaken. Still the rebellion persisted. From New York, representatives of the insurgents poured out a steady stream of atrocity stories, collecting sympathy, funds, and even men for the struggle, but not what it wanted most: American recognition. The U.S. government maintained a diplomatically correct attitude towards the insurrection, enforcing its laws on neutrality and foreign recruitment. Despite this, the U.S. and Spain were on a collision course. In 1873 the steamer *Virginius*, wearing an American flag, attempted to land a large quantity of munitions and some 200 volunteers—Cubans, Americans, and Canadians. At about 1400 on 31 October, while still some 20 miles off the southern coast of Cuba, *Virginius* was spotted by the Spanish blockader *Tornado*, which gave chase. *Virginius* shaped course for Jamaica. It was a stern chase with a dash of irony, as both vessels had begun life as Confederate blockade runners. *Tornado* caught *Virginius* just 18 miles off the Jamaican coast. Brushing aside protests that *Virginius* was an American vessel on lawful occasions on the high seas, the skipper of the Spanish vessel seized the ship and brought her into Santiago harbor the next day. Faulty communications prevented the government in Madrid from learning of the seizure for several days. Although the republican government of the moment (it had been in office only a few months, and would last only a few more) ordered that there were to be no executions, these orders came even as the passengers and crew were being sentenced to death. Within days some 50 men had been shot, among them a number of Americans.

The U.S.—and Britain—protested vigorously. Not only had the ship been seized on the high seas, but men had been executed without their governments being advised. Not even the arrival of a British cruiser prevented the execution of a number of British subjects, as the local Spanish commander, Maj. Gen. Juan Burriel, ignored the implied threat, and the orders which he had by now received from Madrid. On 12 November the U.S. consulted with its minister in Madrid. The minister, one-legged Civil War veteran Dan Sickles, proposed that Spain, not having authorized the executions, could resolve the problem by issuing an apology, paying reparations to the families of the dead men, and punishing Burriel. Finding this reasonable solution distasteful, the Spanish government dithered. With mass meetings all across the nation calling for war with Spain, on 14 November President U.S. Grant instructed Sickles that if the Spanish did not accede to the conditions he had proposed by 26 November he was to close the legation and leave the country, effectively severing diplomatic relations. Madrid continued to temporize, perhaps hoping to call the American bluff. In response, Sickles began making arrangements to close up shop. This seems to have brought the Spanish government to its senses, and on the afternoon of 26 November it acceded to the American demands, effectively defusing the crisis.

With the momentary threat of U.S. intervention gone, the Cuban insurgents lost their only chance of victory. As Spain put its domestic house in order, it dispatched 25,000 reinforcements, increasing the garrison in Cuba to something like 70,000 men, who were supported by tens of thousands of loyalist volunteers. An able young general, Arsenio Martinez Campos, a veteran of the civil wars, took command. Under Martinez Campos' able leadership, the insurgents, who never numbered more than about 25,000, were given no rest, Spanish columns pursuing them wherever they went. The end came in 1878, when, in the town of Zanjon, the rebels, by then totalling at most 7000 combatants, and with their political leadership rent by social and racial tensions, agreed to lay down their arms in return for safe conduct into exile for their leaders, liberation of slaves who had borne arms, and representation in the Cortes. Although some rebels still held out for a time, the war was effectively over. It had cost Spain nearly 3700 men killed in action or dead of wounds, as well as perhaps 55,000 dead of disease; Cuban casualties were never tallied, but including civilian deaths from disease and privation, easily surpassed 150,000.

The Ten Years' War did bring some reforms in its wake, including the eventual abolition of slavery. However, on the whole, the situation in Cuba improved but little. For nearly two decades there was peace, punctuated by two or three abortive attempts at insurrection. By the Columbian quadricentenary in 1892 it seemed as though Spanish power was once again secure in the island. Nevertheless, despite the peace, Cuba languished. Economic recovery proved slow. Thousands of Cubans sought employment abroad, among them many who were inclined to the nationalist faction. Among the exiles support for a new revolution grew. Beginning in 1884, Maximo Gomez, former minister of war in the revolutionary government and despite his 61 years still a physically tough warrior, and Antonio Maceo, the best of the revolutionary commanders, a tall, handsome mulatto nicknamed the "Bronze Titan," began canvassing Cuban exiles throughout the Americas to see how strong was their support for a new try at independence. In New York they encountered the fiery young José Martí. At first Gomez and Martí clashed, the one a tough, authoritarian man-of-action, the other an intellectual and liberal ideologue. Gomez thought that success was purely a technical matter, men, money, munitions. Martí saw the need for an ideology to strengthen the cause, not merely indpendence, but liberalism, racial equality, social justice. Out of the clash between the two men there grew mutual respect, and ultimately cooperation.

In 1892 Martí and many other exiled Cubans created the *Partido revolucionario cubano* in New York. Martí personally undertook a trip to Santo Domingo, where Gomez was living more or less in retirement, and brought the old man into the party. The leaders of the *Partido revolucionario* planned carefully, and organized well. They drew spiritual and financial support not only from Cuban exiles, but also from sympathizers in the United States and throughout Latin America. Under Gomez' guidance, a covert network of agents and cells was developed that reached all over Cuba. Planning for the new insurrection bore fruit in 1895, by which time things were hard indeed in Cuba, a depression in the U.S. having led to the imposition of heavy tariffs, not the least on Cuban sugar, with disastrous repercussions in the already depressed local economy.

The insurrection was set for 24 February 1895. Rebel cells all across Cuba were supposed to rise simultaneously, thereby overwhelming the small Spanish garrison of no more than 16,000 men. But the Spanish authorities got wind of the preparations. Moving swiftly, they arrested the leaders of the insurrection in Havana. This broke the back of the uprising in the western part of Cuba. But in the east, it was different. On schedule on 24 February the revolt began in Baire, a small village some 50 miles from Santiago de Cuba. Soon rebel bands were active throughout the eastern end of the island. Antonio Maceo, his brother José, another able commander, and a band of other rebels landed near Baracoa on 31 March. Ten days later, on 10 April, Martí, Gomez, and four other rebel leaders battled their way through heavy seas to come ashore in a small boat. Over the next year 40 more expeditions landed in Cuba. The Cuban Revolution was now well underway.

Spanish reaction to the new insurgency was swift. Within days officers in Spain were volunteering for duty in Cuba, as fresh troops were ordered shipped to the island. By August there were over 50,000 Spanish troops on the island, by January of 1896 over 80,000. General Arsenio Martinez Campos, architect of the Spanish victory in 1878, was sent to Cuba as well. But Martinez Campos had trouble dealing with the new war. Unwell, he was also unable to cope with a devastating new strategy adopted by the Cubans. At Gomez' insistence, the insurgents adopted a scorched earth policy. Anything of economic value was to be destroyed, in keeping with Gomez' motto "Blessed be the torch!" This strategy had several objectives. It would further worsen the island's already poor economic plight, creating greater misery, while depriving Spain of any possible profit from the island's resources. Moreover, it would force everyone to chose between the rebels and the Spanish, a point he made brutally clear in a general order issued on 6 November 1895:

1. Plantations are to be completely destroyed, the canefields and buildings burned, the railroads cut.
2. Persons working for the sugar refineries … are to be considered traitors.
3. Persons caught in the act of, or proven to have violated item 2, shall be shot.

The scorched earth policy would also exacerbate Spain's relations with the United States, whose citizens had invested heavily in Cuba, by some accounts as much as $50 million. This was precisely what the Cuban revolutionaries wanted, for ultimately Gomez believed that the route to victory lay through American intervention.

A hard and brutal war was the result. In the traditional manner of the guerrilla, the Cubans avoided battle, and the war was primarily a series of little actions, ambushes, engagements, and skirmishes. Anxious to avoid the errors of the Ten Years' War, Gomez pressed for a "western offensive," to bring the richer and more heavily populated western provinces of Cuba into the war. This offensive began in November of 1895. By 22 January 1896 a column of 1500 rebel troops under Antonio Maceo had reached the westernmost point in Cuba, the village of Mantua in Pinar del Rio. The rebels seemed to be everywhere. The Spanish seemed unable to cope with them. In fact, this was not the case. Rather, it was that Martinez Campos knew what had to be done, but was unwilling to do it. Outlining a winning strategy, "reconcentration" of the rural population into secure areas, thereby depriving the rebels of supplies and support, would win the war, the old general concluded. But it would cause enormous suffering, and he could not bring himself to implement such a plan. On 7 January 1896 Martinez Campos tendered his resignation. His replacement, the one man in the Spanish Army whom he considered capable of implementing such a policy, arrived in Havana early the following month. He was Lt.-Gen. Valeriano Weyler y Nicolau, a young, brilliant officer with a distinguished record both in the field and as an administrator. A great admirer of William Tecumseh Sherman,

Valeriano Weyler y Nicolau, "Butcher Weyler," Captain General of Cuba, 1896-1897. A brilliant commander and disciple of William Tecumseh Sherman, Weyler's reconcentrado *policy and* trochas *broke the back of the Cuban revolution, but did much to stimulate American support for the insurgents.*

whom he had met while a military attache in Washington during the Civil War, Weyler believed that the best way to end a war was to do so quickly by whatever means necessary, that being the most merciful course.

Almost as soon as he arrived in Cuba Weyler ordered the rural population "reconcentrated." The rural populace was given eight days to move into designated camps in fortified towns, bringing with them all foodstuffs and cattle which could be moved. Anyone disobeying the order would be treated as a rebel and shot. Weyler, a notorious liberal, ordered elaborate arrrangements to house, feed, and care for the *reconcentrados.* Unfortunately, there was little time for such preparations, and no resources, nor much inclination on the part of Weyler's subordinates to bother with the matter. The peasantry were already suffering greatly from the war, and reconcentration merely made things worse. Indeed, in a sense the reconcentration of the rural peasantry had been started by the insurgents. Gomez' policy of economic warfare had already driven many of them off their land and into Spanish garrison towns, where they were suffering from hunger and disease. Reconcentration had a devastating effect on the Cuban population, the number of dead being variously estimated at between 200,000 and 400,000. Although much of the suffering was caused by the insurgents, it proved an enormous political asset in their struggle for American intervention.

By the end of the first year of the Cuban Revolution sympathy for the rebels was widespread throughout the U.S. Support for the rebels cut across class, ethnic, regional, and religious lines. Rallies and fairs in many cities raised funds and supplies for the revolution, and individual Americans volunteered their services as organizers, medical workers, and combatants. These activities were frequently in violation of American law. Formally, the U.S. considered Cuba Spanish territory, and thus the insurgents had no formal status as combatants. President Grover Cleveland and his administration worked to enforce U.S. neutrality and foreign enlistment laws. Nevertheless, although several people were sent to jail for aiding the Cuban rebels in ways that violated American neutrality, support for the rebels grew. The Cuban exile community took great care to cultivate American sympathy, going so far as to assist the police in hunting down Cuban malefactors. They also undertook a highly effective propaganda campaign to strengthen their support. The information staff of the *Partido revolucionario* emited an endless stream of often extremely imaginative atrocity stories, which the more sensational newspapers of the day, the "Yellow Press" snapped up. As the stories boosted circulation, unscrupulous journalists like Joseph Pulitzer and William Randolph Hearst demanded more, sometimes creating their own. American reporters who went to Cuba usually never left Havana, and relied heavily on covert ties to the Rebels for their stories. Weyler's reconcentration policy was grist for these mills, as the suffering of the Cuban people helped generate yet more sympathy for the revolutionary cause, while the Cuban insurgent role in creating the rural devastation which did much to fuel that suffering went unreported. The political consequences were considerable.

President Cleveland could not ignore the substantial public support for the Cuban rebels, which found its way into Congress. Nor was he insensitive to the plight of the Cuban people.

Although more or less sympathetic to the notion of an independent Cuba, he did not want to do anything that might lead to war. He was also quite concerned that some other power might acquire Cuba should Spain abandon it. Recognition of Cuban independence, or open assistance to the rebels, would have resulted in instant war with Spain. While Cleveland did not necessarily consider Spain a significant threat, there were tensions with other countries, notably Britain over the Venezuelan-Guiana boundary dispute, and Germany over Samoa, which might lead to a larger war. Granting the Cubans the rights of belligerents, which could be done without recognizing their independence, had some unpleasant side effects as well. Although recognizing Cuban belligerency would permit them to purchase arms in the U.S., it would also relieve Spain of its obligation to protect American lives and property in Cuba. Cleveland tried a different tack, attempting to end the war by mediating some sort of compromise settlement. But no plan the president suggested received much of a hearing in Madrid, and did little better among the Cubans. Meanwhile the war went on, and by no means went unfavorably for Spain.

Reconcentration was not the only card up Weyler's sleeve. Even as it began paying dividends in terms of weakened support for the rebels, he began a campaign to deprive the rebels of another of their assets, their mobility. During the Ten Years' War, one of the most effective devices adopted by the Spanish was the *trocha*, a fortified zone extending all across Cuba from San Fernando, near Moron on the north coast, to Jucaro on the south, a distance on the ground of about 50 miles. This zone, 150 to 200 yards wide, was entrenched on both sides and garnished with a broad belt of wire obstacles, cheveux-de-frise, punji sticks, and land mines. At more or less half-mile intervals there were large strongpoints, forts or blockhouses; between these were smaller fortified posts. The larger installations were connected by telegraph. Down the middle ran a single track railway to facilitate the rapid movement of troops. In a sense, the *trocha* foreshadowed the continuous front of World War I. Although it tied down a large number of troops, about 16,000, the *trocha* effectively prevented the rebels in Oriente Province from breaking out into the rest of Cuba, or anyone moving the other way, thereby keeping Cuban mobile columns from operating in the field. It was the *trocha* which during the Ten Years' War had confined most of the fighting to eastern Cuba. Weyler restored the *trocha* from Jucaro to Moron and built a second, much further west between Mariel, on the north coast not far from Havana, and Majana, on the south coast, across the narrowest part of Cuba, some 25 miles on the ground. He went beyond the original concept to add searchlights and light artillery to the defenses. Altogether the two *trochas* tied up some 30,000 troops, a force greater than that possessed by the rebels. But Weyler had a lot of troops, over 100,000 by the end of 1896, not counting some 35,000-40,000 Cuban volunteers and levies, who themselves outnumbered the rebels. Even deducting additional forces to garrison the larger towns still left Weyler with a considerable pool of troops for mobile operations. And he intended to use them. Weyler's first objective after completing the *trochas* was to go after the best commander the rebels had, Antonio Maceo, the "Bronze Titan." The military situation was favorable, for the Mariel-Majana *trocha* confined Maceo to Pinar del Rio, the westernmost province of Cuba.

Shortly after the outbreak of the revolution, its leaders had held a convention in Jimaguayi, a small village in Camaguey Province. They established a provisional government, with Salvador Cisneros Betancourt as president, a full cabinet including a war minister, under whom Maximo Gomez served as general-in-chief. This was intended not only to give the revolution a firm political base, but to further the rebels' cause with the U.S. by demonstrating the democratic nature of their movement. Unfortunately, the political leadership of the revolution was flawed. It quickly became immersed in petty political and administrative details, leaving most of the hard work of organizing the peasantry to the military forces. Moreover, Cisneros was on very poor personal terms with Gomez, an animosity going back to the Ten Years' War. Worse still was that Cisneros and most of the rest of the political leaders were creoles—Cuban-born whites—interested in maintaining white domination of Cuba, while most of the troops and two of the best rebel generals, the brothers Maceo, were black or of mixed race. In the autumn of 1896 Cisneros basically ordered Gomez, himself a

José Maceo, one of the most effective Cuban commanders, and brother of Antonio, "The Bronz Titan," the best of the rebel leaders, whom he greatly resembled. The racially mixed background of the Maceo brothers was a cause of political tension within the Cuban revolutionary movement.

creole, to get rid of the Maceo brothers. The crusty old guerrilla refused, and was promptly removed from command.

In a written message Gomez urged Antonio Maceo to return to the east to help him cope with political problems which had developed, probably intending to stage a coup. To do so Maceo had to escape from Pinar del Rio. On 9 November Maceo and 200 followers attempted to cross the *trocha* by way of the Tapia Valley, near its northern terminus. They ran into trouble immediately. Weyler, probably alerted to Maceo's intentions by an informer, was present with 6000 mobile troops, and Maceo's little force was cut to pieces.

Maceo decided that since he couldn't cross the *trocha*, he would go around it. On 4 December, with a small party, he managed to get around the northern end of the *trocha* in a small boat. He had eluded Weyler's trap. At this point his best course would have been to proceed immediately to join Gomez in the east. Instead he chose to tweak Weyler's nose by making a surprise attack virtually at the very gates of Havana itself. Gathering up a sizable body of local rebels, apparently several hundred, he intended to raid the town of Mariano, just five miles southwest of the main square of Havana. On the appointed night, 7 December, Maceo and his men gathered in the nearby village of San Pedro de Hernandez. Suddenly a small force of Spanish infantry, apparently on a routine patrol, came upon them. The Spanish attacked. The rebels took to their horses and charged their attackers. The outnumbered Spaniards retreated, with the rebels in hot pursuit. In the lead, Maceo cried out to one of his comrades, "This is going well!" Suddenly he was hit in the face by a bullet, and fell from his horse. Young Francisco Gomez Toro, son of Maximo Gomez, rushed to Maceo's side, only to be shot in the leg. Gamely the young man tried to drag Maceo away, but was struck again and killed. The rebels won the little skirmish at Lomo del Gato, but in doing so suffered the greater loss. Gomez would later write, "The army grieves, and with it its general-in-chief."

Militarily, by the end of 1896, it could safely be said that Weyler had turned the tide of war in Spain's favor, with his *trochas* and his reconcentration policy. The rebel forces had been split into three non-mutually supporting bodies; they had been more or less separated from the peasantry, and their best field commander had been killed. Over the next year Rebel activity would plummet. In 1895 there had been 83 serious encounters with the Rebels, a figure which rose to 191 during 1896. However, during 1897 there were only 49, a drop due to the combined effects of the *trochas*, the reconcentation of the rural populace, the death of Maceo, and the internal problems which beset the rebels. By the end of 1897 the rebellion was strong only in the east, in Oriente Province. So Weyler had put Spain on the road to victory. But by the time his policies were paying off, he was no longer around. For although Spain may have been winning militarily, it was still losing politically.

All though 1896 the Cleveland administration worked to convince Spain to grant some measure of political reform or even autonomy to Cuba. Fully aware that the Rebels' hands were no less bloody than Spain's, the president sought to end the conflict through mediation, leaving Spain in control of a more or less autonomous Cuba, a course he thought more stable—and more achievable—than independence for the island, which carried with it the danger of intervention by a third power. Carefully separating himself from the sometimes strident positions of the more vocal segments of the pro-Cuban elements in American society, Cleveland offered to mediate the dispute between Spain and the rebellious Cubans. His proposal implied that should Spain accept such mediation the U.S. would support continued Spanish control of Cuba, even if the Rebels rejected reform. Behind that there lay the suggestion that if Spain rejected mediation, the U.S. would eventually act on its own to resolve the crisis in Cuba. These efforts came to nought in Madrid. Like all Spanish governments of the period, that of Conservative Antonio Canovas del Castillo, was a relatively feeble one, the product of the *turno pacifico*, in which more or less liberal and more or less conservative governments alternated in power on a regular basis, to keep radical elements at both extremes of the political spectrum out of power and thus maintain domestic peace. Liberals and Conservatives differed on numerous issues, but on that of the remnants of the Spanish empire there was general unanimity. Although Liberals might suggest some degree of autonomy for Cuba, while Conservatives thought in terms of a more direct relationship with the motherland, neither was willing to relinquish complete control. Cuba was of powerful symbolic value to a Spain reduced to relative unimportance from its former state of global primacy. Moreover, by the end of 1896 it appeared that Spain was winning the war. Suggestions from Washington concerning Cuba were not welcome. Meanwhile, a new administration was coming to power in Washington.

Cuba had played little role in the presidential campaign of 1896, domestic issues such as economic recovery and free silver being uppermost in the public's mind. Although the new president, William McKinley, came from the more expansionist-minded Republican party, he was very much cut from the same cloth as his Democratic predecessor, Cleveland. McKinley, who had seen four years of hard service during the Civil War, had no romantic notions about war. In a private conversation shortly before the inauguration, McKinley expressed a desire to be as successful as Cleveland in avoiding a conflict over Cuba.

Shortly after the inauguration, McKinley had the State Department dispatch a note to Spain setting forth his thoughts on Cuba. He urged an end to the *reconcentrado* policy, an armistice, and massive relief measures, while hinting that some degree of autonomy for the island might be in order, all backed up by a veiled suggestion that if Spain did not resolve the issue in a timely fashion the U.S. might find it necessary to take action, basically a restatement of Cleveland's position. For months there was no response. Meanwhile McKinley appointed a new U.S. minister to Spain, Stewart Lyndon Woodford, who had commanded the 103rd U.S. Colored Infantry during the Civil War. Before he took up his post, Woodford consulted with American ministers in several European countries. The consensus was that most European powers would not object to American intervention in the Cuban problem if it were undertaken for humanitarian and progressive purposes. Then, just as Woodford was about to go to Spain a surprising development occurred. On 8 August 1897 Canovas was assassinated by an anarchist. A caretaker government was installed. As a result, Woodford did not present his credentials until mid-September. Shortly after that, he had a conversation with Spain's foreign minister, the Duke of Tetuan. Woodford repeated the long-standing offer that the U.S. mediate the dispute between Spain and Cuba. Tetuan replied that the war would have ended long-since were it not for American support, hinting that such support was condoned by the government. At that Woodford said Spain had until November to make "such assurance as would satisfy the United States that early and certain peace can be promptly secured" or the U.S. would "consider itself free to take such steps as its Government should deem necessary to procure this result...." In effect, Woodford delivered an ultimatum. Only a few days later Queen Regent Maria Cristina appointed a new government. Praxedes Mateo Sagasta, the new prime minister, was a Liberal already committed to autonomy for Cuba. Sagasta moved quickly to take control of the Cuban problem. He dispatched Lieutenant General Ramon Blanco y Erenas to replace Weyler in Cuba, thereby signaling a less draconian military policy, while pushing the idea of autonomy. By late October the government had decided to grant autonomy to Cuba and Puerto Rico as well, decisions which were communicated to the U.S. through Wood-

Fitzhugh Lee, a notably successful Confederate cavalryman, U.S. Consul General in Cuba from 1896 until the outbreak of the Spanish-American War, whereupon President McKinley made him a major-general of volunteers. One of the best of the re-treaded Civil War generals, Lee's appointment to command the expedition to Havana was made for political reasons, but proved sound.

ford. At the time it appeared to many that Woodford's ultimatum was the driving force behind Sagasta's decision, but this was in fact not the case. Sagasta's wing of the Liberals was already committed to autonomy before the ultimatum, seeing it as the best way to end the war, which was severely straining Spain's resources. Since the virtually empty treasury was serving to fuel the more extremist political forces in the country, the Carlists on the far right and the republicans and anarchists on the far left, the offer of autonomy was widely hailed as offering a solution to the war in Cuba. Everywhere, that is, save in Cuba. The Rebels wanted no part of the deal, preferring to continue to press for complete independence, while the Cuban Loyalists saw it as being abandoned to their enemies and joined with disaffected army officers to riot in the streets of Havana. Nevertheless, to many the Spanish initiatives appeared to have laid the groundwork for an end to the war in Cuba.

There were, of course, still issues to be resolved. In his State of the Union message, delivered on 6 December 1897, President McKinley reviewed the history of the Cuban problem. Although he once again rejected recognition of the Rebels, or direct U.S. intervention, he concluded by observing that the reconcentration policy and other practices that violated the laws of war and of basic human dignity were still in force, and suggested that Spain needed to bring these to an end "in the near future," a broad hint that Spain's words would have to be followed by deeds. And in fact, despite the proferred autonomy and the new captain general, little had changed in Cuba. The American consul general in Havana, former Confederate cavalryman Fitzhugh Lee, regularly reported on the local situation, about which he was pessimistic. Lee clearly saw that the Cuban Rebels were serious in their rejection of autonomy, and he believed that Spain was losing the war. Moreover, he saw no end to the human suffering, as Spanish resources were woefully inadequate to the task: more than half of the 100,000 *reconcentrados* in Havana Province had died. Lee urged that if Spain proved unable to begin a major relief program within 30 days, the U.S. undertake the effort. This sparked considerable interest in Washington, and, after an exchange of telegrams with Madrid, there too. In a surprisingly short time Spain granted the American Red Cross the right to bring supplies into Cuba duty-free and to administer a relief program. Meanwhile, apparently in an effort to improve relations, McKinley accepted a Spanish suggestion that the two countries conclude a new commercial treaty. Such measures obscured the serious problems which still remained. The most important of these was the refusal of the Cuban insurgents to accept autonomy. Until they did so, there would be no peace. Although by the end of 1897 the Rebels had been reduced to insignificance outside of Oriente Province, some of them were still in the field, still pressing for independence. This was the great flaw in American policy, beginning under Cleveland and continuing under McKinley. An end to the war through a grant of autonomy was acceptable to the U.S. and even Spain, but not to the Rebels. So the war went on. And with it the inevitable attainment of Maximo Gomez' primary criteria for Cuban victory, American intervention.

On the afternoon of 12 January Havana broke out in disorder. Spanish officers and local Loyalists rioted for well into the next day. U.S. Consul General Fitzhugh Lee telegraphed Capt. Charles D. Sigsbee, of the second class battleship USS *Maine*, then lying at Key West, for possible movement to Havana to protect

American lives and interests. But the situation in Havana calmed down, and so *Maine* remained at Key West, where the fleet was to gather for its annual winter maneuvers. Meanwhile, German naval activity in the Caribbean was causing some concern in Washington. A German squadron had turned up at Port-au-Prince, in order to press certain claims against the Haitian government. This had prompted McKinley to dispatch the cruiser *Marblehead* to call at the Haitian capital to show the flag. Meanwhile, other German ships were paying regular calls in the Danish West Indies. German naval officers and politicians had made no secret of their desire to acquire coaling stations in the Caribbean, a matter which did not go unnoticed in Washington, particularly since there had of late been rumors that Spain was secretly negotiating to turn Cuba over to Germany or some other European power. When consulted, Fitzhugh Lee notified the State Department that several German ships were due to visit Havana in late January, and suggested that an American warship call at the same time. On 24 January, in response to an inquiry from the State Department, the American consul at Port-au-Prince reported that there were four German warships in Haitian waters. A similar inquiry addressed to Lee elicited the reply "One German vessel in port—two others expected." That evening, after securing the reluctant assent of the Spanish ambassador, McKinley ordered *Maine* to Havana. Although Lee urged that the ship's arrival in Havana be postponed a few days, his telegram crossed the orders for the ship to move. *Maine* raised Havana harbor on the morning of 25 January. Although her arrival was unexpected, and thus technically a violation of international etiquette, the Spanish authorities permitted the ship to enter, and assigned her an anchorage.

The arrival of the American warship began a surprisingly friendly round of receptions, parties, and social calls. Over the next two weeks Captain Sigsbee entertained various Spanish dignitaries aboard his ship, while he and many of the ship's company took in the sights, saw some bull fights, and generally seemed to have had a good time. The overall effect of the visit was to greatly calm the local political situation, stimulating friendlier relations between Spain and the U.S. than had been the case for some time. Indeed, the visit went so well that when

Secretary of the Navy John D. Long suggested that the ship might have to be withdrawn due to the danger of fever, Lee not only explained that the fever season was still months away, but went on to say that the effect of *Maine*'s visit was so beneficial that when the ship departed another ought to take her place, lest the more vociferously anti-Americans in Cuba suggest that the ship had left under pressure from the Spanish government. So *Maine* remained firmly at anchor. While she lay in Havana harbor another American warship, the unprotected cruiser *Montgomery*, made a number of port calls in other parts of Cuba, and the Spanish cruiser *Vizcaya* was ordered to pay a similar courtesy call at New York. Superficially, these courtesies suggested a considerable easing of tension. But, in fact, they represented a mere lull in the friction between the two countries. By the end of 1897 a war between the U.S. and Spain over Cuba was virtually inevitable. The U.S. had committed itself to ending the suffering—and financial castastrophe—which afflicted the island, a matter which could only take place if the insurrection came to an end. But that was not going to happen, for Spain would not grant the island independence, nor would the Rebels accept anything less. Two events in February brought things to a head.

Late in December of 1897 Enrique Dupuy de Lome, the Spanish minister in Washington, wrote a letter to a friend, Jose Canalejas, editor of *El Heraldo* of Madrid and a politician of some influence. It was an extremely frank missive. In it, Dupuy de Lome suggested that the offers of autonomy and of negotiations with the Rebels were insincere. He went on to call McKinley "weak" and a "low politician." The letter had been sent to Canalejas in Havana, but it never reached him. Rebel agents in the Havana post office purloined it. Through Rebel channels, the letter was offered to the principal New York dailies. On 9 February all the morning papers in New York carried the letter, William Randolph Hearst's *New York Journal* supplying a facsimile as well as a translation. As the papers hit the streets, Horatio Rubens, a Cuban attorney, and John J. McCook, a prominent sympathizing American politician formerly close to McKinley, presented the original to the Assistant Secretary of State. Although there was some hesitation in the

An artist's impression of the destruction of the USS Maine *in Havana Harbor at approximately 2145 hours on 15 February 1898. Although less lurid than many of the artistic renditions of the disaster (most of which show bodies flying in the air), it is only slightly more realistic.*

State Department as to the authenticity of the letter, this was confirmed by Dupuy de Lome himself, who had already tendered his resignation, and was shortly replaced by Luis Polo de Bernabé. The public outcry over the letter was extraordinary. Despite the fact that it was a private letter, and had been obtained through theft, McKinley felt pressured to demand an official apology from Spain. This put Spain in an awkward position, for to offer an apology was to accept responsibility. Nevertheless, one was forthcoming on the 14th. The very next day an even more serious crisis arose.

At approximately 2145 hours 15 February 1898 the USS *Maine* blew up. The ship rapidly settled to the bottom with most of her upperworks above water. More than two-thirds of ship's company were killed or mortally injured, 268 officers and men out of 374.

The destruction of *Maine* set off a orgy of speculation. Much of this pointed an accusing finger at Spanish perfidy. Tensions

The wreck of the USS **Maine** *on the morning of 16 February 1898, only hours after the ship had been blown up.*

rose rapidly. By early March McKinley was convinced war could no longer be averted. On 9 March both the Senate and House of Representatives enacted the "Fifty Million Dollar Bill" without a single dissenting vote, the peace faction in Congress largely looking to its political future and not choosing to register its opposition. The bill provided $50 million for defense, and gave the president remarkable flexibility in spending it. In fact, McKinley chose to invest money primarily in defensive arrangements, spending most of it on enhancing coast defense, with only a small portion going to the navy to procure additional ammunition and a number of vessels suitable for conversion into cruisers. Then, on 21 March, even as the more vociferous segments of the "Yellow Press"—and war hawks such as Assistant Secretary of the Navy Theodore Roosevelt—were calling for war, a U.S. Navy board of inquiry concluded that an external explosion caused by persons unknown had detonated one of the ship's magazines. Despite a contrary conclusion by a Spanish board of inquiry, which held that the blast had been sparked by the spontaneous combustion of coal which had been overlong in the ship's bunkers, this bolstered those who argued that the ship had been destroyed by Spanish agents, although Spain had the least to gain from so overt an act. During the many weeks between the destruction of *Maine* and the publication of the conclusions of the U.S. Navy's investigation, Spain rejected a renewed proposal to sell Cuba to the U.S. Meanwhile, the U.S. rejected a Spanish proposal that the "autonomous" Cuban legislature be given until mid-September to come up with a formula to resolve Cuba's domestive problems. The U.S. suggestion that Madrid accept the idea that the alleged mine might have been placed by misguided Spaniards, and hence was not the work of the Spanish government at all, got nowhere. Meanwhile, an attempt by the Queen Regent to get the European powers to intervene likewise got nowhere. Finally, on 29 March Ambassador Stewart L. Woodford presented the final U.S. proposal on Cuba, requiring Spain to:

1. Abandon the *reconcentrado* policy.
2. Proclaim an immediate armistice, to last until 1 October.
3. Accede to Cuba's independence if arbitration so required.

Spanish reaction was mixed. Two very real concessions were that a start was made on ending *reconcentrados* in the western parts of Cuba, where the rebellion had been broken, and an armistice was proclaimed to begin 10 April. But Spain rejected the possibility of independence for Cuba. In fact, from the Spanish perspective the war in Cuba seemed won. During the first three months of 1898 there were only 28 encounters with the rebels. Of course the Rebels had not necessarily quit, merely gone underground to await American intervention. This came on 11 April, when McKinley asked Congress for specific permission to intervene directly in Cuba, albeit still withholding recognition of the Rebels, a move he made as much because of the rising interventionist sentiments on Capitol Hill as the international situation. The debate in Congress was surprisingly heated, as ultra-interventionists clashed with anti-expansionists (including not only anti-imperialist northeastern Progressives but also Southern white supremacists). In the end, Democratic Senator Henry M. Teller of Colorado provided the key to getting the president's request through Congress, in the form of an amendment to the proposed joint resolution disclaiming any intention of annexing Cuba. At 0300 on 19 April 1898—the 123rd anniversary of the outbreak of the American Revolution—Congress passed a joint resolution "for the recognition of the independence of the people of Cuba... and directing the president of the United States to use the land and naval forces of the United States to carry these resolutions into effect." McKinley signed the joint resolution the next day. On the 21st, even before the American ultimatum had been delivered, Spain recalled Minister Luis Polo de Bernabé, and broke off diplomatic relations. The U.S. Navy put Havana under blockade the next afternoon. On the 23rd Spain formally declared war, to which the U.S. reciprocated two days later.

Why did the USS *Maine* Blow Up?

The USS *Maine* was destroyed by an explosion of ammunition stored in the 6-inch reserve magazine, which set off ammunition stored in adjacent magazines. There is no question about that. But there is considerable debate as to what caused the magazine to explode.

There are essentially two theories:

1) Due to spontaneous combustion in coal bunker A-16, a fire began which heated the wall of the adjacent magazine sufficiently to detonate the ammunition stored there, which in turn detonated adjacent magazines.

2) A mine detonated beneath the ship's keel about 60 feet from her bow, just under frame 18, touched off the magazine, which in turn detonated adjacent magazines.

Despite several investigations the actual cause of the ship's loss can never be known.

The U.S. Navy performed two investigations. The first was in 1898 shortly after the ship was destroyed. The second took place nearly a decade later when the ship was raised from the bottom of Havana harbor. Although both commissions considered the question of spontaneous combustion, in the end both concluded that the ship had been sunk by a mine placed under the hull by an unknown hand.

Many voices objected to the conclusions reached by the formal U.S. Navy inquiries, holding out for the spontaneous combustion of coal. This was a relatively common occurrance. There had been several instances of spontaneous combustion in the Navy over the years, and indeed, at least two during the war: Aboard the battleship *Oregon* on 27 March, and on the auxiliary cruiser *St. Paul* on 16 May. Spontaneous combustion occurs when relatively fresh bituminous coal is exposed to air in hot conditions.

The official inquiries rejected spontaneous combustion as the cause for several reasons.

1) Compartment A-16 was on a commonly used companionway, and men passing by regularly put their hands on its bulkhead. Indeed, one of the ship's engineers recalled having done so only an hour or so before the explosion, and it did not feel hot to the touch.

2) The fire detector in Bunker A-16 was unusually sensitive, and had several times sounded an alarm due to elevated temperatures when there was no fire, so would have responded to a real fire.

3) There were over 20 cases of spontaneous combustion known, and in none of them had an explosion resulted.

4) Beneath Frame 18 of the ship's hull divers found a hole in the bottom mud approximately seven feet deep and 15 feet across.

5) The keel in the vicinity of Frame 18 was folded sharply upwards by several feet, suggesting external force upwards, rather than an internal blast.

In addition, they cited the evidence of a number of witnesses, including men of the ship's company and people aboard several vessels anchored nearby that they heard two explosions, a small one which was followed almost immediately by a larger one, a blast so powerful that ships anchored near *Maine* were damaged by flying debris.

Opponents of the official conclusion observe that there had been neither a plume of water accompanying the explosion nor dead fish around the ship, both of which commonly accompany underwater blasts. They also argue that planting a mine would have been impossible, given that the ship maintained a double watch at night. Unfortunately, these arguments do not help explain the bent keel or the hole under Frame 18.

In the 1970s, intrigued by the case, Admiral Hyman Rickover arranged for inquiries. He concluded that the villain was spontaneous combustion, arguing that the fracturing of the keel occurred when the ship settled to the bottom, the bow striking hard. However, Rickover's reasoning does not explain the hole under Frame 18, and his explanation for the bent keel seems unlikely.

As a result, despite objections the official conclusions remain more or less intact. Indeed, eyewitness accounts seem to support these conclusion. Sigmund Rothschild, a passenger aboard the liner *City of Washington* anchored nearby, happened to be on deck that evening. He heard an explosion, and

> I looked around, and I saw the bow of the *Maine* rise a little, go a little out of the water. It couldn't have been more than a few seconds... [later]... that there came in the center of the ship a terrible mass of fire and explosion... the whole boat lifted out, I would judge, about two feet. As she lifted out, the bow went right down.

But who would benefit from such an act? The Spanish government would hardly have been likely to have committed so foolish an act. But there were individual Spaniards who were extraordinarily hostile towards the United States. Indeed, the Governor-General of Cuba had been forced to place an armed guard on the U.S. consulate after several menacing demonstrations by army officers, with Cuban volunteers prominent among them. During the ship's visit, fiercely anti-American leaflets had been circulated, some including the ominous line "Death to the Americans!" And in the immediate aftermath of the blast, even as most Spanish military personnel were working to save the survivors, some Spanish officers were heard to cry "¡Viva España!" So a Spanish or Creole nationalist might have committed the deed.

Then there were the Cubans. The insurgents would have had the most to gain from blowing up the ship. And in fact, they had acquired considerable skill in the use of mines. Insurgent agents had acquired sample mines abroad and they had learned to make their own. On several occasions the Spanish had lost ships to insurgent mines, planted in rivers and harbors. The gunboat *Relampago* was mined in the Rio Cauto in January of 1897. So a Cuban radical might have done the deed as well. In fact, just days before the explosion, the U.S. consul at Matanzas received a warning that Cubans were plotting to blow up the ship, but thought nothing of it.

So the question of what caused the destruction of the USS *Maine* remains open.

George Dewey

George Dewey (1837-1917) was a native of Vermont. After attending Norwich University for a time, he entered the new United States Naval Academy, graduating in 1858. He saw extensive service during the Civil War, aboard the frigate *Mississippi* when Farragut captured New Orleans in April of 1862, aboard USS *Colorado* on blockade duty in the Atlantic, and in the naval brigade which helped storm Fort Fisher in January 1865. After the war Dewey held various assignments both ashore and afloat, rising to commander, captain, and commodore by 1896, while becoming an advocate for the "New Navy."

Dewey received the Asiatic Fleet command in late 1897. As war with Spain loomed, he presciently undertook a number of important measures, including procuring auxiliary vessels, buying extra coal, and even detaining a ship due for rotation home, while arranging for agents to reconnoiter the Spanish fleet and installations in the Philippines.

Dewey's performance in the opening days of the war was superb, handing the nation a major victory at the very start of hostilities by boldly slipping into Manila Bay despite apparent heavy defenses and annihilating the Spanish squadron at Cavite. His actions over the next weeks were equally valuable, as he maintained control of the military and political situation until ground troops could arrive to permit the capture of Manila and begin the occupation of the islands.

Promoted rear admiral for his victory, and subsequently "admiral of the navy," the only man ever to hold that rank, in late 1899 Dewey finally returned to the U.S. to a tumultuous welcome in virtually every major city in the nation. His service thereafter was in various staff positions, as president of the General Board of the Navy, on various joint Army-Navy commissions, as a representative of the U.S. at diplomatic functions, and as an advisor to the President on naval matters. A brief suggestion that he make a bid for the presidency came to nothing, partially because Dewey himself did not seem serious about the matter.

A man of considerable talent and courage, Dewey's achievements have tended to be obscured by the assumption that they were made against an inept, ill-equipped foe. But when he led the Asiatic Fleet into Manila Bay he was leading it into what was believed to be a well defended harbor.

Patricio Montojo y Pasaron

Patricio Montojo y Pasaron (1839-1917), commander of the Spanish squadron destroyed by Dewey at Cavite, came from an old naval family. He entered the service as a cadet in 1852, going to sea as a midshipman in 1855. His career included both line and staff assignments, with a good deal of war service. In 1860, by then an ensign, he was serving against the Moros in the Philippines, earning a merit promotion to lieutenant. In 1866 he served in the "Guano War," against Peru, earning a promotion to lieutenant commander. After several years of staff duty, in 1873 he went to Cuba, serving on blockade duty and in support of the army during the latter portion of the Ten Years' War. He rose to captain during the many years of peace—both domestic and colonial—which followed the end of the Cuban insurrection, and in 1891 was promoted rear admiral. A few years later he was assigned command of the squadron in the Philippines, in which post the war found him.

Although at Cavite—at which two of his sons fought, one being seriously wounded—Montojo put up about the best fight he could have, given his resources and lack of imagination. Dispersing his weak squadron among the many islands of the Philippine Archipelago would have presented a serious obstacle to an American occupation.

After the war he was subject to a court martial and briefly imprisoned before being retired.

Valeriano Weyler y Nicolau

Valeriano Weyler y Nicolau (1838-1930), known to Americans as "Butcher Weyler," was born into a Spanish military family of German ancestry. He entered the infantry academy at Toledo when he was 15, was commissioned a second lieutenant when he was 18, and was a full lieutenant by age 20. Meanwhile in 1857 the brilliant young officer entered the staff college. Weyler graduated in 1860, first in his class and a year ahead of schedule, having meanwhile been promoted to captain (at age 21). After some years on staff duty, including a tour as an attache in the U.S. during the Civil War, in 1863 he was promoted to major (at 24) and sent to Santo Domingo (which briefly returned to Spanish control after its war for independence from Haiti in 1844), where he served in the cavalry with some distinction against insurgents, earning a merit promotion to lieutenant colonel (at 25) and making the acquaintance of Maximo Gomez, then in Spanish service, who would later become the generalissimo of the Cuban revolutionary forces. Weyler served in Cuba more or less continuously from 1864 to 1872, garnering great distinction not only as an organizer and trainer of troops, but also as a field commander, capturing Bayamo from the rebels. For his efforts he won merit promotions to colonel and brigadier general, and was twice awarded the Cross of San Fernando, the Spanish equivalent of the Medal of Honor.

Weyler returned to Spain in 1872 to fight in the complex civil war among Burbon Monarchists (whom he supported), Carlist Monarchists, Secessionists, and Republicans, which had by then been raging for some years. Promoted to major general, in 1875 his division fought the last important action against the Carlists. In 1878 he was promoted to lieutenant general, and was made a senator for life by royal appointment. Over the next 15 years he served in various administrative and command assignments, including the captain generalcies of the Canary Islands and the Philippines.

Early in 1896 Weyler was sent to Cuba, where his implementation of the *reconcentrado* policy caused a storm of international protest. Although his strategy succeeded in turning the tide of war in Spain's favor, Weyler was recalled. This had little impact on his career. Over the next decade Weyler was three times minister of war and once minister of marine, helped suppress an anarchist uprising in Cataluña, was promoted to Captain General (effectively a field marshal), and was made a duke and grandé of Spain.

A noted liberal (among other things, during his tours of duty in the colonies he favored racial inte-gration of the army), Weyler supported progressive tendencies in Spanish politics, taking full advantage of his political status as a Senator and his military status as a Captain General, while also favoring colonial expansion in Morocco. Although initially a supporter of the dictatorship of Miguel Primo de Rivera (1923-1930), he soon became disenchanted and helped engineer an abortive coup designed to overthrow the regime in 1926. He thereafter lived in retirement until his death.

Weyler's reputation as a brutal thug stems largely from the enormous suffering caused by the *reconcentrado* policy, one which, he frankly observed, emulated some aspects of Sherman's "March to the Sea" during the Civil War. Moreover, Weyler's responsibility for the suffering should be shared by his erstwhile comrade and friend Maximo Gomez, who, by undertaking a deliberate strategy of total destruction of rural resources, had had much to do not only with beginning the vast shift in population from the countryside to urban areas, but also with the destruction of Cuba's food production. An outstanding soldier, Weyler, who was quite short, was not only a skilled organizer and administrator, but also a good field commander.

Maximo Gomez

Maximo Gomez (1836-1905) was born in Santo Domingo, then under Haitian rule. His family was pros-perous, and provided him with an excellent education. At the age of 16, much against his mother's wishes, he joined the cavalry to fight against the Haitians, who were attempting to reconquer the Dominican Republic after having been expelled in 1844. In 1862 Gomez transferred to the Spanish Army, when the Dominicans voluntarily returned to Spanish rule (originally abandoned in 1821, whereupon Haiti invaded). An anti-Spanish uprising in 1864 led to a renewal of Dominican independence, whereupon Gomez was made commander-in-chief of the army. A civil war followed, in which Gomez' faction lost, forcing him to flee, eventually to settle at Bayamo in Santiago Province, Cuba, where he became a farmer.

When the Cuban Revolution of 1868 broke out, Gomez enlisted as a sergeant, but his experience and demonstrable skill led to a rapid rise, so that he became a general within a year. By 1872 Gomez was the principal Cuban field commander, and for the last few years of the revolution, he was secretary of war in the revolutionary government (serving under him was Thomas Jordan, a former Confederate general who joined the Cuban rebels in 1869 and eventually rose to become chief-of-staff and then commander-in-chief

of the revolutionary force, with a $10,000 price on his head). With the Pact of Zanjon in 1878 Gomez fled to Jamaica. Later living in Honduras and the United States, Gomez immersed himself in Cuban revolutionary politics, which often involved more hostility between the various revolutionary factions than towards Spain. Jose Martí secured his adhesion to the 1895 revolutionary conspiracy, which he served as military commander. After Cuban independence Gomez lived quietly until his death, writing his memoirs and tending his farm.

Gomez, a small, physically very rugged man, was single-mindedly dedicated to the cause of Cuban independence, in which one of his sons lost his life. A guerrilla commander of some ability, Gomez was by no means a brilliant one, and by late 1897 Spain was having considerable success in suppressing the insurgency. A realist, from the onset of the 1895 revolution he foresaw that U.S. intervention was essential to Cuban victory. This was the principal reason he advocated total destruction of Cuba's economy, a move designed specifically to spark American intervention.

Jose Martí

Jose Martí (1853-1895) was born in Havana of Spanish parentage (his father was from Valencia and his mother from the Canary Islands). Well educated, he became a life-long advocate of Cuban independence. Despite his age—fifteen—he was al-

ready a published journalist and poet when the Ten Years' War broke out in 1868. The extreme revolutionary character of his writings soon led to his arrest and exile to Spain, where he continued his studies while under partial arrest. Released upon the proclamation of the Spanish Republic in 1873, for a time he remained in Spain to press for Cuban independence in word and print, but then travelled through Europe to press his case. In the mid-1870s he settled in Mexico, where he published a newspaper, later removing to Guatemala, to take up a university post.

Martí returned to Cuba after the Peace of Zanjon in 1878, but was again exiled to Spain for taking part in the abortive insurrection of 1879. Escaping from jail, he spent the next few years living in Paris, New York, Caracas, and New York once again. In New York he made a living as a journalist, working for *The Sun* and several Spanish-language newspapers, as a translator, and as consular representative for Argentina, Uruguay, and Paraguay, while continuing to write poetry and work for Cuban independence.

The final Cuban Revolution was probably due more to Martí's work than to that of any other. From 1891 to 1895 he worked tirelessly to create a unified revolutionary party, traveling extensively in Latin America to reconcile the differences among the often feuding revolutionary leaders. He himself put aside his personal feelings about Gomez' authoritarian and militaristic streak for the cause. In 1895 Martí was one of the handful of men who, one stormy night in April rowed ashore with Gomez in Santiago Province to begin the revolution. He was killed in action at Dos Rios on 19 May 1895.

A small, rather frail man, Martí possessed enormous energy. A poet of considerable talent, he was the author of *Guantanamera* and the poem which inspired the Spanish Falangist hymn "Cara al Sol."

Antonio Maceo y Grajales

Antonio Maceo y Grajales (1848-1895) was a *mulatto*, a person of mixed black and white racial background. Born on Bastille Day, from 1868 his life was closely identified with the Cuban national liberation movement. Of modest, but by no means impoverished origins, Maceo, a tall, well-built, handsome man nicknamed "The Bronze Titan," joined the revolutionary forces at the outbreak of the Ten Years' War and quickly proved to be a capable guerrilla cavalry commander, specializing in lightening mounted

raids and ambushes, and quickly rose to general. Among those who refused the Zanjon settlement, Maceo fought on into 1879, when he was forced to leave Cuba.

The next 16 years Maceo spent in exile in Costa Rica when not visiting Cuban *emigres* elsewhere, including the United States. Meanwhile he maintained close ties to Maximo Gomez and made the acquaintance of José Martí. Deeply involved in the preparations for the 1895 Cuban revolution, Maceo landed in Santiago Province in late March of that year with a band of 20 others, among the first of many exiles to return to the island.

Late in 1895 Maceo's mounted columns ravaged Matanzas Province, and then proceeded westwards, reaching the westernmost tip of Cuba on 22 January. So feared was he by the Spanish that Valeriano Weyler devoted much of 1896 to his destruction, a feat which he achieved on 7 December 1896, when Maceo was killed in a skirmish on the outskirts of Havana. With his death the insurgents lost their most capable commander.

The entire Maceo family died in the cause of Cuban independence. The general's father was killed during the Ten Years War, and he and his six brothers died in that war or the war of 1895-1898. One brother, José, was also a guerrilla warrior of some ability, rising to general and commander of Matanzas Province before being killed in 1896. The racial background of the Maceo brothers had some importance in Cuban revolutionary politics. The political and intellectual leaders of the movement were overwhelmingly *creole* (i.e., Cuban-born whites), and they were rather hostile to non-whites, a matter which was one of the causes of the failure of the Ten Years' War, and one which ultimately led to the death of Antonio Maceo, and could easily have ruined the chances for victory once more but for the intervention of the United States.

Funding the Fight: The U.S. Finances the Spanish-American War

The U.S. was already a rich country in 1898, and one with an insignificant national debt. The per capita debt was about $11.40 (about $180 in 1995 dollars), for a total of some $850 million, left over from the Civil War. Recognizing that the war could not be paid for out of current revenues, Congress enacted a variety of special measures. The very first was to float a $50 million bond issue. This was necessary to pay for the "Fifty Million Dollar Bill," which called for the immediate procurement of munitions and equipment and the purchase of ships for conversion into auxiliary cruisers.

Of course, this was just the beginning. With the experience of the Civil War—which cost slightly less than $100 million a month—more or less fresh in memory, Congress recognized that the final cost of the war would be enormous. And indeed, this was the case. By the end of hostilities in August, the cost of the war totalled about $400 million, a tremendous sum for the day (about $6.3 billion in 1995 dollars). This was about $5 for every one of the approximately 75 million Americans. Congress chose to finance the war through a combination of taxes and borrowing.

Various bond issues brought the total borrowed up to about $200 million, mostly in the form of 3 percent bonds with 10 or 20 year maturations. These sold well, quickly exhausting the issue. Trading in the bonds was brisk. Almost as soon as the issue was exhausted they were selling at about 5.3 percent above par, by mid-1899 at about 8 percent above par, and by mid-1900 they were at about 9.75 percent above par.

The balance of the cost of the war Congress chose to finance through taxation. Since it was the Progressive Era, with its concern for the growing power of the monied classes, special taxes were imposed on banks, brokerages, checks, stocks, bonds, legal documents, and, for the first time in American history, legacies. These, of course, primarily effected the upper classes. The lower classes got to pay their share in other ways.

As the Progressives also were concerned with uplifting mankind to a higher and more moral state, various "sin" taxes were increased and new ones created. The rates on tobacco, beer, and liquor were increased, as—in a further blow at the upper crust—were those on wines.

In addition, taxes were imposed on circus tickets, bowling alleys, billiard parlors, and even chewing gum.

The war with Spain ended quickly, little more than four months after it began, but the one in the Philippines dragged on into 1901. As a result, many of the levies imposed during the war remained in force. This was partially because governments find it difficult to relinquish power once secured. America's newly won power status had to be sustained, so that the armed forces expanded considerably, and not merely to provide for the security of the new colonial territories.

It's also worth noting that the $400 million cost of the war does not include the hidden costs. Pension benefits for the veterans would continue until 1993, when the last veteran—Nathan E. Cook, 102, of Tempe, Arizona, who had enlisted as a drummer boy—died. And the country will probably be paying survivor's benefits for another generation.

Relative Cost of the War

Conflict	Cost in $Billions	
	Current	1990s
The Revolution (1775-1783)	10	1.2
War of 1812 (1812-1815)	.09	0.7
Mexican War (1846-1848)	07	1.1
Civil War (1861-1865)	3.20	27.3
Spanish American War (1898)	40	6.3
World War I (1917-1918)	26.00	196.5
World War II (1941-1945)	288.00	2,091.3
Korea (1950-1953)	54.00	263.9
Vietnam (1964-1972)	111.00	346.7
Gulf War (1990-1991)	61.00	61.0

The table compares the cost of America's principal wars since 1775 on the basis of then current and 1990s dollars. Current dollars are the actual numbers spent at the time. Thus, a 1775-1783 dollar had the equivalent purchasing power of $10.75 in 1990. Actually this conversion is only a very rough guide, but at least gives some idea of the relative costs of the ten wars on an adjusted basis. However, it is not possible to take into account the increasing relative affluence of American society over the two centuries covered by the table.

Civil War figures exclude Secessionist expenditures, about $2 billion in then current terms. For the Gulf War it is worth noting that various members of the allied coalition reimbursed the U.S. for 88-percent ($54 billion) of the amount shown, so the actual cost to the taxpayer was only about $7 billion, roughly the same as for the Spanish-American War.

Chapter II

The Beginning

Even before the passage of the joint resolution which effectively began the Spanish-American War, both sides had undertaken tenative steps to prepare for the coming struggle.

Mobilization and Strategy: Spain

Spain, of course, was already mobilized due to the war in Cuba. Between regular troops and volunteers, Spain had nearly 200,000 men under arms in Cuba, about 45,000 in the Philippines, and some 15,000 in Puerto Rico, as well as another 100,000 or so in Spain proper, for a total of around 350,000. This was slightly more than a third of the 1.2 million men in Spain's mobilization pool. The troops were recruited from the peasantry, and were hardy and dogged men, serving under a professional officer corps which contained many good men, but also a lot who were more interested in their rights and privileges as a caste than in the profession of arms. Many of the troops in Cuba, and to a lesser extent those in the Philippines, were seasoned veterans, the toughened survivors of battles with rebels and tropical diseases. Although some expansion of the army was undertaken when the war began, there were already more than enough troops under arms for the coming fight. A war between Spain and the United States would have to be decided by navies not armies.

In the 1880s the Spanish Navy had begun to emerge from a long period of neglect caused by the civil wars of 1868-1875. By

The Spanish armored cruiser Vizcaya *coaling during her courtesy call on New York, in February of 1898. She was still there when the USS* Maine *blew up, and special security measures were taken by both her commander and the U.S. Navy to prevent any incidents. The ship's forward single 11-inch gun is clearly visible.*

the late 1890s it had undergone considerable expansion and modernization. But fiscal restraints had kept it small, poorly trained, and badly supplied. Although small squadrons were based at Cavite in the Philippines, Havana in Cuba, and San Juan in Puerto Rico, the heavier ships of the fleet were kept in Spanish waters. Early in 1898 the Spanish Navy began to take steps to prepare for war. An effort was made to improve the gathering of intelligence about the U.S. Navy. The battleship *Pelayo*, refitting in a French shipyard, and the just completed armored cruiser *Emperador Carlos V*, were rushed into commission, and repeated requests were made for more ammunition and spare parts for the ships already in service. Two heavier ships in American waters, the armored cruisers *Almirante Quendo* and *Vizcaya*, fresh from a courtesy call on New York, were summoned across the Atlantic to join the 1st Squadron, which had been ordered to concentrate in the Cape Verde Islands under Vice Admiral Pascual Cervera y Topete, a seasoned seaman and the senior naval officer. During the weeks of tension preceeding the outbreak of war, Cervera several times importuned the Ministry of Marine for instructions. The best the ministry could do was propose a preposterous plan whereby the fleet would be divided into two major squadrons: the 2nd Squadron, based at Cadiz, would be committed to the defense of the motherland, and 1st Squadron would steam for Havana, where, in cooperation with the locally based ships, a motley collection of older ships dubbed the 4th Squadron, it was to blockade the east coast of the United States. In a series of communications with the ministry Cervera responded that the plan was "a dream," for the ships based at Havana consisted of obsolete vessels of no value, while two of the most powerful ships—*Pelayo* and *Carlos V*—earmarked for the offensive squadron, would almost certainly not be available in time. Cervera was not optimistic about the probable outcome of a naval war with the United States. This was not because of any lack of courage or brains on his part. Indeed, he was remarkably clear headed. What was lacking was support from the government. Despite his repeated requests to the Ministry of Marine, Cervera had been unable to secure a clear definition of his mission. He was fully aware of the physical limitations of his ships, and clearly understood the odds which confronted him, having repeatedly noted that the U.S. Navy had more major warships (nearly 116,500 tons to some 56,600), which were newer, better, and more heavily gunned than all of Spain's fleet taken together. Cervera believed that Cuba was as good as lost, but that a defensive strategy, to protect the Canary Islands and the Spanish mainland, might salvage something from the disaster. He urged that such a strategy be adopted, or that war be averted by diplomatic means, perhaps a subtle suggestion that Cuba be given up without a fight. These arguments proved fruitless. The government wanted a "decisive battle," and it wanted one quickly. To Cervera and many others, the strategy laid down by the ministry suggested that the government was convinced the war was as good as lost, and that all that could be done was to sacrifice the fleet in a "Trafalgar" in order that the defeat—and the inevitable loss of Cuba—might at least be a glorious one. Obedient to orders, he could do little more than make what

Vice Admiral Pascual Cervera y Topete, a fine officer who understood the problems which his squadron faced better than anyone in Spain, but who was never given a mission compatible with his resources.

preparations were possible. Meanwhile, with a clearer understanding of its mission, the U.S. Navy had quickly gone into action.

Mobilization and Strategy: The U.S.

It can hardly be said that the United States was ready for war in the spring of 1898. The decades following the Civil War had been characterized by a profound neglect of the armed forces. Not that international peace was a foregone conclusion. During the period there had been occasional crises which might have led to war with Mexico, Spain, Britain, Germany, and even Chile and Italy. These had helped spark some attention to the Navy in the 1880s, but the Army was so little affected that most European powers considered the U.S. militarily insignificant. And in a European sense, it was. However the nation did have some strengths which were not readily apparent at the time. It has been customary to deride the military policy of the United States during the nineteenth century. Indeed, it occasionally has been said that the United States had no military policy in that period. Citing the experience of the Civil War, some authors have suggested that the nation was woefully unprepared for war. This is unreasonable. In fact, quite the reverse is true. The nation had a realistic and intelligent military policy, albeit one that developed perhaps more by accident than by deliberation. The only expected war was a conflict with an overseas power, specifically with Britain, which was, after all, the only country in the world having the wherewithal to seriously threaten the United States. For most of the nation's history national defense rested on four pillars: the Regular Army, the Navy, the coast defense system, and the militia. A foreign attack on the United States would require a prodigious effort. Indeed, probably only Britain had the capability of undertaking such a venture, and even then with some strain. Such an attack would certainly take months to mount. During that grace period the U.S. Navy would harass enemy merchant shipping while the militia of the citizenry would have time to turn out and, leavened by the Regular Army, be brought to a reasonable degree of efficiency. By the time a potential enemy was in a position to assault American shores, considerable forces would be available for service either in the field or behind the most elaborate coastal fortifications in history, a defense system liberally garnished with some 3,000 pieces of artillery. Given the war which was expected, this was a reasonable strategy. Indeed, it more or less worked, as demonstrated by the experience of 1812-1814, 1846-1848, 1898, 1917-1918, and even 1941-1945. The only time it didn't work was in the Civil War, but that was hardly the sort of conflict for which much preparation could have been made.

During the long period of rising tension between Spain and the United States, few preparations were made to strengthen the nation's land forces. The Regular Army was a hardy, highly-trained, and well equipped professional force, but, at slightly less than 28,000 men, hardly sufficient for a major war. Moreover, it was scattered in nearly 100 posts, none larger than a regiment. If war came, the Regular Army would have to be supplemented. The quickest way to do this was to call the militia—which by 1898 was generally known as the National Guard—into federal service. There were about 115,000 National Guardsmen in the several states and territories. Subject to considerable neglect after the Civil War, the National Guard had undergone something of a renaissance during the latter portion of the nineteenth century, as much for its utility in natural disasters and public disorders as for its potential in the event of foreign war, and several contingents—those of New York and Pennsylvania in particular—were quite good. However, the Regular Army was rather hostile to the National Guard. To the Regulars, the National Guard seemed an amateur force. Their concept of a proper force in time of war was an expanded Regular Army, with the National Guard limited to internal security and home guard duties. The earliest War Department proposals for the expected war, issued on 17 March, envisioned adding several regiments and expanding existing companies, troops, and batteries from about 70 men to about 200, raising the total strength to about 104,000. This proposal ran into immediate resistance from the National Guard, which was politically quite powerful. A number of prominent senators and representatives were Guardsmen. Several weeks later, Maj. Gen. Nelson A. Miles, the general-in-chief, proposed that the Regular Army be expanded to 62,000 men, to which would be added a federally recruited volunteer army of 50,000 men, available for overseas service, and an auxiliary army of 50,000 National Guardsmen, to secure the nation's coasts from a possible enemy attack. This plan also ran afoul of Congress.

Meanwhile, the Regular Army began to mobilize. On 17 April four initial concentration areas were created: at New Orleans, Mobile, and Tampa for the infantry, and at the Chickamauga battlefield park—redesignated Camp Thomas for the duration—for the artillery and cavalry. With commendable speed 22 infantry regiments, six cavalry regiments, and most of the army's field artillery were soon on the move, converging eventually into two large cantonments, at Tampa and Camp Thomas. As this movement got underway, the War Department finally began to take the National Guard into its confidences. Negotiations with governors, prominent Guardsmen, and the National Guard Association led to a compromise which satisfied all parties. The Regular Army would be expanded to about 65,000 men. There would also be a Volunteer Army, with the initial calls for troops restricted to the National Guard of each state, in proportion to their populations, with entire regiments being

Troopers of the 9th Cavalry (Colored), having already made the move from the high plains to Chickamauga, pack up for the journey to Tampa, in preparation for joining V Corps. All four of the Regular Army's black regiments took part in the Santiago Expedition, and African-Americans totalled approximately 10-percent of the troops involved.

permitted to enter federal service. Governors would be able to appoint all officers up to colonel, subject to a review of their qualifications by a panel of regular and National Guard officers. In addition, the War Department would have the right to assign one regular officer as an advisor to each unit, while the president would retain the power to appoint generals and staff officers in the Volunteer Army. This seemed to satisfy everyone.

The president's first call for 125,000 volunteers, on 22 April, was followed by additional calls, until the total number of men recruited for the Army reached nearly 270,000. In hindsight, McKinley has often been criticized for calling up so many men, not the least because of resultant pension costs. However, he was erring on the side of caution. His Civil War experience was at work. While the reputation of Spanish troops was not high at the time, historically Spanish armies had often proven tenacious in the defense. It was worth recalling the almost casual way in which the nation had assumed that the Civil War would end with one or two battles. No one could predict how long the war would last. Recalling the nearly disastrous recruiting problems caused by Lincoln's inadequate manpower call in the spring of 1861, McKinley wanted enough troops on hand before the shooting started; once the casualty lists began to grow the supply of enthusiastic volunteers might well dry up. Of course, it would take some time—at least six weeks—for the Army to be ready. Until then, the burden of the war would have to be borne by the Navy.

After the Civil War, the Navy had been subject to even more neglect than the Army. By the 1880s it was an obsolete force; most ships were of wooden construction, propelled primarily by sail and armed mostly with smooth bore guns. The few ironclad vessels left over from the Civil War were neglected, and in any case almost as obsolete as the ships in commission. This was a situation which was embarassing to many naval officers, and the intellectual elite of the Navy pressed for modernization. The epicenter of all this intellectual and technical ferment was the Naval War College, created in 1884. During the 1880s their efforts began to bear fruit, when increased public awareness of the importance of sea power (a trend which manifested itself most notably in the publication in 1890 of Captain Alfred Thayer Mahan's *The Influence of Sea Power Upon History, 1660-1783*). As a result, in the late 1880s Congress approved the construction of a series of modern, steam powered iron and steel warships. Although many mistakes were made, by 1898 the fleet, although small, was impressive, with four modern first class battleships, two new second class battleships, including USS *Maine*, and two powerful armored cruisers, as well as several smaller cruisers, and six modern monitors. Although the fleet lacked destroyers—a new category of warship—and was weak in auxiliary vessels, it was a powerful force. Moreover, unlike the Army, the Navy had begun to look ahead, developing what would today be called "contingency plans" in the event of wars with various other powers. In the mid-1890s the Naval War College prepared such plans for wars with those countries with which the potential for war was greatest—Britain, Germany, Japan, and Spain—either singly or in various combinations, even assuming

A session of the Naval Strategy Board, in Washington. From left to right, the men are Captain Alfred Thayer Mahan, Captain A.S. Crowninshield, Secretary of the Navy John D. Long, and Rear Admiral Montgomery Sicard.

the possibility of alliances with France and other powers.

The Naval War College developed several plans for a war with Spain in the period 1895-1897. All concentrated on operations in the Caribbean, envisioning a naval blockade of Cuba and Puerto Rico, followed by elimination of the Spanish fleet, and a series of expeditions to land troops in support of the Cuban insurgents. Most of the plans included the use of American naval forces in the Pacific and Far East to seize the Philippines, which was thought would be a relatively easy operation. Virtually all of the plans rejected the notion of an expedition against Spain itself, although several did suggest raiding operations against Spanish commerce. One plan assumed an aggressive Spanish stance might require deploying the fleet to defend the East Coast. When the *Maine* disaster occurred, these plans were dusted off.

The president offered surprisingly little strategic guidance to the Army and Navy in their plans for war. A joint planning committee hammered out most of the details. It was clear that the Army would be subordinate to the Navy, which had to win command of the seas. In any case, the Navy was much readier for war than was the Army, which would take several weeks at least before being able to undertake offensive operations. And as General Miles, supported by most senior officers, observed, until the autumn, when the "fever season" ended, the Army's role had to be limited to undertaking a small landing on the east coast of Cuba in order to supply the insurgents.

In a sense, the first orders for offensive action went out on 25 February 1898, almost two months before war was declared, when, taking advantage of the temporary absence of his superior, Assistant Secretary of the Navy Theodore Roosevelt, Jr., ordered Commodore Dewey, commanding the Asiatic Squadron, to "see that the Spanish squadron does not leave the Asiatic coast, and then [undertake] offensive operations in [the] Philippine Islands." While many have read conspiratorial intent in this order, it in fact merely reiterated long standing policy in the event of war with Spain. A more important development occurred on 7 March, when, under instructions from Secretary of the Navy John D. Long, the battleship *Oregon* sailed from Bremerton, Washington, to San Francisco on the first leg of what would become an epic voyage around South America to join the North Atlantic Squadron off Florida.

Meanwhile, the Navy Department was procuring ships wherever it could find them, expending $21.4 million of the "Fifty Million Dollar Bill" on this alone. Two cruisers being built for Brazil were procured in England. Other purchases included a gunboat and two torpedo boats. Several liners were bought and converted to auxiliary cruisers. Other vessels, including multimillionaire financier J.P. Morgan's yacht *Corsair*, were converted to scouts or gunboats. Altogether, from the passage of the "Fifty Million Dollar Bill" to the end of the war, the Navy acquired 131 vessels, raising the number of vessels in commission to 196, of which 73 were combat ships.

At the same time, the State Department, the Army, and the Navy began to improvise intelligence networks. As additional personnel were hastily sent to Europe by passenger steamer— among them Lieutenant William S. Sims, who would later command the U.S. Navy in European waters during World War

I—American diplomatic officials and militiary officers abroad were pressed into service collecting information from open sources, such as the press, as well as from friendly diplomats and military personnel from other nations and from corrupt or careless Spaniards. Considering the short time in which they had to work, the networks proved surprisingly extensive, reaching into high Spanish diplomatic, military, and political circles. A number of these novice agents proved highly capable. The U.S. Consul at Sao Vicente in the Cape Verde Islands cleverly arranged to buy up most of the available coal, leaving little for the Spanish fleet which was concentrating there. The Cuban insurgents made their own intelligence network available to the Americans, a most valuable source, since one of their principal agents was Domingo Villaverde, a telegrapher in the cable office in Havana, which was located in the captain general's headquarters, where he was privy to most official Spanish military communications. Meanwhile, at Hong Kong, Commodore Dewey arranged for a junior officer to surrepticiously interview recent arrivals from Manila, while an unknown American made several intelligence gathering trips between the British colony and the Philippines under the guise of business.

The Opening Moves

By 19 April, when President McKinley signed the joint congressional resolution on Cuban intervention, the Navy was ready. Aside from Commodore Dewey's squadron at Hong Kong, and the battleship *Oregon*, threading her way eastwards through the Straits of Magellan, the North Atlantic Squadron, comprising most of the fleet—two battleships, an armored cruiser, three monitors, several protected cruisers, five gunboats, and seven torpedo boats—lay at Key West, under Rear Admiral William T. Sampson. Its mission was to support a blockade of Cuba and Puerto Rico, which would actually be imposed primarily by smaller vessels, and to deal with the Spanish fleet in the event it turned up in Caribbean waters. At Hampton Roads lay the Flying Squadron under Commodore Winfield Scott Schley, with the balance of the fleet's heavy ships, two battleships, an armored cruiser, and two speedy protected cruisers, as well as several fast auxiliary cruisers, with the mission of defending the east coast. Most naval officers, and the entire public, were confident of victory. At 0630 hours on Friday 22 April the North Atlantic Squadron, by then reduced to about half its original strength due to political complications, formed up in two columns off Key West and steamed for Havana. Late that day it lay off Havana, which was declared under blockade.

In the Far East, Commodore George Dewey's Asiatic Squadron lay at anchor in Hong Kong harbor. Dewey had spent the weeks leading up to the final American break with Spain profitably, procuring additional supplies locally and purchasing two colliers. On 23 April Dewey received a communique from Major General Wilson Black, governor of the Crown Colony of Hong Kong. In formal diplomatic language, Black informed him that since a state of war now existed between the United States and Spain, a conflict in which Britain had declared its neutrality, Dewey had until 1600 hours on Monday 25 April to leave British waters. He added at the bottom, in his own hand, "God knows, my dear Commodore, that it breaks my heart to send you this notification." It was a message which Dewey had been expecting for several days. Late on the afternoon of 24 April, his squadron stood out to sea, amid cheers of good wishes from the sailors of the British warships anchored nearby. Dewey did not go very far, slipping into Mirs Bay on the Chinese coast, only about 30 miles southwest of the British colony. Although in Chinese territorial waters, Dewey rightly reasoned that the ineptitude of the Imperial government would permit him to remain there unnoticed for several days. There he had agreed to rendezvous with Oscar F. Williams, U.S. Consul in the Philippines, who would bring last minute information of value, while awaiting further orders from Washington, which would arrive at the consulate in Hong Kong and be forwarded by courier aboard the chartered British tugboat *Fame*.

Fame raised Mirs Bay late on the morning of 25 April. By 1215 hours Dewey had his orders:

> War has commenced between the United States and Spain. Proceed at once against Spanish fleet. You must capture vessels or destroy. Use utmost endeavors.

These essentially confirmed Dewey's prewar instructions. But he was not yet ready to sail, preferring instead to await Consul Williams' arrival from Manila. The latter turned up two days later, on the morning of the 27th, aboard the little *Fame*. His information proved interesting. Montojo apparently intended to offer battle off Subic Bay, about 30 miles north of Manila Bay, supported by mines and coast defense guns. Dewey accepted the challenge, and by 1400 hours the Asiatic Squadron was steaming out of Mirs Bay in two columns, *Olympia* and the large warships to the fore with the revenue cutter *McCulloch* and two merchantmen about 1200 yards behind. The squadron steamed at a steady eight knots, while the crews cleared for action. Aboard *McCulloch* were notable Filipino nationalist leaders. In the evenings *Olympia*'s band serenaded the sailors with patriotic airs and popular tunes. During the nights the squadron maintained a blackout, save for dim stern lights. The coast of Luzon was raised shortly before dawn on 30 April. Some fishermen were intercepted and interviewed, but proved to know nothing. The protected cruisers *Concord* and *Boston* were sent ahead to scout. Meanwhile *McCullouch* landed the Filipinos at Lingayen Gulf, on the northwestern coast of Luzon. Shortly after dawn several officers thought they heard gunfire to the south, and the protected cruiser *Baltimore* was dispatched to support the two scouts, while the main body maintained eight knots. At 1530 hours the main body arrived off Subic Bay, where the three cruisers were standing. Montojo was nowhere to be found.

Admiral Montojo had departed Manila Bay at 1100 hours on 25 April with his six best ships, believing that he would be better off at Subic Bay, where he could offer battle behind a minefield, supported by four 5.9-inch coast defense guns. The short voyage to Subic Bay proved unfortunate, however. One of his better ships, the wooden-hulled unprotected cruiser *Castilla*, had begun taking water through her propeller shaft housing. The only way the leak could be stopped was with cement, which immobilized the propeller shaft, and left the ship dependent on rudimentary sails or towing. Worse still, Montojo soon learned that only five of the fourteen mines in the planned mine barrier had been emplaced, and that the four coast defense guns had not yet been mounted. On the morning of 28 April, Montojo was apprised of the fact that Dewey had sailed from Mirs Bay on the 27th. After a council of war with his principal subordinates—a reed upon which inept commanders frequently lean—he decided to return to Manila Bay and offer battle off Cavite, where he might secure some support from shore batteries and where the water was shallow, so that although his ships might be sunk the loss of life would be minimized. Montojo's squadron, with *Castilla* in tow, departed Subic Bay at 1030 on 29 April, and dropped anchor in a few hours off Cavite. It was there that Dewey found him on the morning of 1 May.

While Dewey was smashing Montojo's squadron off Cavite, half a world away in the Caribbean, the Gulf of Mexico, and the Atlantic other American sailors were busy tightening the U.S. Navy's blockade on Cuba and Puerto Rico. Havana had been locked up on 22 April. The first shots of the war occurred earlier that day in the Gulf of Mexico, when the gunboat *Nashville* captured the Spanish merchantman *Buenavista*, bound from Pascagoula, Mississippi, to Rotterdam with a cargo of timber. She was brought to a halt with the traditional round across her bow. Over the next few days the blockade was extended across much of the north coast of Cuba and portions of the southern coast, as well as San Juan, in Puerto Rico. On 26 April President McKinley proclaimed a formal blockade, although with various restrictions, limitations, and exceptions (for example, Spanish ships in American ports had until 21 May to depart for home, and would be immune from seizure while en route). A shortage of ships prevented the complete sealing off of all ports in the two islands until quite late in the war, but the Navy deployed its resources carefully, and was able to effectively cut maritime trade to a fraction of its prewar levels. In all, dozens of ships were stopped, although only 30 were actually seized, sold and the proceeds awarded as prize money to the lucky crewmen of the ships which effected their seizure, a practice abolished in the United States Navy only in 1899. The blockade was quite effective. Less than three dozen ships are known to have made it into Cuba (c. 12) and Puerto Rico (22) during the war (half entered through ports not yet under blockade). Even fewer ships managed to escape from the two islands.

The "Coast Defense Battleship" Indiana, *at full steam. Although a compromise design, by relatively inexperienced naval architects,* Indiana *and her two sisters,* Oregon *and* Massachusetts *proved surprisingly successful warships.*

On Blockade

The U.S. Navy's blockade of Cuba and Puerto Rico was an active one. The fleet did not merely lay off shore waiting for things to happen. On several occasions coastal batteries were deliberately engaged. For example, on 27 April, shore batteries at Matanzas were engaged by Sampson's flagship, the armored cruiser *New York* and the monitors *Amphitrite* and *Puritan*; the flagship momentarily came under small arms fire from some Spanish cavalry. On 12 May, the bulk of Sampson's squadron (battleships *Iowa* and *Indiana*, armored cruiser *New York*, and monitors *Amphitrite* and *Terror*, supported by two smaller cruisers and a torpedo boat) bombarded the defenses of San Juan, suffering two men killed and seven wounded in action, while inflicting six deaths and about 50 wounded on the defenders and citizens of the town. In addition, landing parties from the fleet undertook several raids to destroy various installations ashore. Two of the most notable occurred on 11 May.

Cienfuegos, on the south coast of Santa Clara Province, was the terminus of two underwater cables. On the morning of 11 May a boat party from the cruiser *Marblehead* attempted to cut the cables. Supported by cannon fire from *Marblehead*, the gunboat *Nashville* and the revenue cutter *Windom*, as well as two steam launches full of Marines, one with a 1-pounder Hotchkiss automatic cannon and the other with two Colt machine guns, joined by two ship's boats under Lieutenant Cameron Winslow, put into Cienfuegos harbor shortly after 0700 hours on 11 May. As the ships' cannon swept the Spanish installations, including the cable house, Winslow's bluejackets rowed into the shallow water near the cable landing. When the boats neared the shore, the bombardment let up, but the Marines in the accompanying steam launches began a steady rifle and automatic weapons fire, which was answered by Spanish troops—probably from the Galician volunteers battalion—in rifle pits and fox holes about 50 yards behind the shore. When the boats were within 100 yards of the shore, where the bottom—five to seven fathoms— could be seen, Winslow ordered the grapnels out. Under fire, the bluejackets hauled the first cable aboard, stretching it about 150 feet between the two boats, an arduous task, for it weighed about six pounds per foot and was thick around as a man's wrist. After attempting to cut it with axes and chisels, the men found that hacksaws worked better, if slowly, requiring nearly a half hour to cut through. As the severed section was dropped to the bottom of one of the boats, the men began grapelling for the second cable, further to the east.

This proved a more dangerous proposition, for they had to pass close inshore under galling fire from Spanish troops. The warships fired shells close to the heads of the cutting party. The sailors, already tired, managed to haul aboard a piece of the second cable, and laboriously cut out about 90 feet. As they completed the work, Winslow located a third cable, smaller than the others, apparently a local line, linking the cable house with the city of Cienfuegos proper. He decided to cut that as well. As the men worked, the Spanish troops ashore, apparently reinforced, resumed their fire. As Winslow put it, "We saw the splash of the bullets in the water about us.... Now the bullets began dropping so fast that the little sheets of spray where they struck the water could be plainly seen by the ships... . " The steam cutters and the warships resumed a voluminous fire as the cable was finally hauled aboard the boats. Despite this, the Spanish fire intensified. A Marine in one of the steam launches was shot through the head and killed, the first American killed in the war. Another was mortally wounded, several less seriously so. Deeming the task too risky, Winslow, himself among the wounded, abandoned the attempt to cut the third cable. By 1015 the dead and injured were being lifted aboard *Marblehead*. The whole operation had taken about three hours.

Later that same day a more famous action occurred at Cardenas, about 80 miles east of Havana. On 11 May Commander Chapman C. Todd, of the gunboat *Wilmington*, was on blockade duty on the northeastern coast of Cuba, in company with the revenue cutter *Hudson*, actually an armed tug commanded by First Lieutenant Frank H. Newcomb, and the torpedo boat *Winslow* under Lieutenant John B. Bernadou. *Hudson* and *Winslow* were taking soundings near the harbor entrance when shortly before 1400 hours the Spanish shore batteries opened a desultory fire on them. As the shells whistled overhead, Todd ordered his squadron into the harbor to take on the Spanish guns. *Winslow* took the lead to scout out the channel for the deeper draft vessels, nosing into the port at about 1405 hours. A hot fight developed, with surprisingly little effect. Then at about 1435, a 6-pounder round disabled the steering mechanism from *Winslow*'s forward conning tower, while a second smashed the after steering mechanism, jamming her rudder hard over. Supported by fire from the two larger American vessels, *Winslow* opened up with three 1-pounder guns, while Bernadou attempted to steer by alternately using the boat's port and starboard propellers. This succeeded, and within a few minutes Ensign Worth Bagley and four sailors (John Barberes, John Daniels, George B. Meek, and E.B. Tunnell) managed to secure a towline from *Hudson*. But Spanish fire was heavy and accurate, and *Winslow* was struck several more times. As the five were securing the tow line, a shell landed in their midst, killing Bagley and Daniels instantly, as the other three fell mortally wounded. Another shell parted the tow, and yet a third damaged *Winslow*'s starboard engine, while severely wounding

Bernadou as well. Maneuvering with one engine, *Winslow* attempted to close again with *Hudson*, which was itself the object of very heavy fire. Another line was passed and made fast, and *Hudson* managed to tow *Winslow* out to sea. It had been a hot little engagement, with five men killed and five wounded. Spanish losses had been severe; two of three small gunboats in the harbor had been set afire, along with a number of buildings along the waterfront, and several deaths were reported.

The loss of Bagley and his comrades at Cardenas created a much greater impression upon the American public than the deaths of the marine and bluejacket at Cienfuegos several hours earlier. That the 25-year-old officer was handsome, a former Naval Academy football hero, and came from a North Carolina Confederate family probably fueled a misunderstanding. Details of his life and excerpts of his last letters to his mother were widely circulated in the newspapers, so that his loss gradually overshadowed that of the seamen who died with him, and he became known as the "first" American casualty of the war.

There were many other incidents during the blockade. U.S. ships several times engaged in shoot-outs with Spanish vessels attempting to run the blockade, actions in which Spanish warships often sortied from blockaded ports to lend a hand. Several times Spanish gunboats attempted to ambush blockaders, and there were numerous instances in which Spanish coastal batteries engaged U.S. vessels. On a number of occasions the Navy conducted landings to disable or destroy lighthouses. Most of these actions were virtually bloodless, but casualties were surprisingly high, especially during the aborted Navy attempt to seize the lighthouse at Fisher's Point, Cuba, on 11 June, which resulted in six American dead and 16 wounded. There was a particularly hot fight at Manzanillo on 18 July, when several U.S. gunboats ran into the harbor and were engaged by six Spanish gunboats and some field guns ashore. All six Spanish gunboats were sunk or run aground, and two or three transports damaged, while several of the U.S. ships were hit, though none seriously. The Spanish suffered several dead and wounded, but surprisingly no Americans were reported injured.

The blockade was also punctuated by repeated attempts, mostly successful, to land personnel and supplies in support of the Cuban insurgents. The most famous was Lieutenant Andrew S. Rowan's mission to Garcia. Rowan, attached to the Army's Military Information Division, which passed for an intelligence service in those days, began his mission to Cuba early in April before the war started. By a circuitous route, he made his way to Jamaica in the guise of an English gentleman. From Jamaica, agents arranged to smuggle him into Cuba, where he landed near Mount Turquino on 24 April. From there he was escorted through the countryside to Bayamo in Oriente Province, where he met wtih General Calixto Garcia y Iñiguez on 1 May. Garcia briefed the young man on the military situation in eastern Cuba, supplied him with maps and documents, and sent him home again with some of his staff to serve as advisors to the U.S. Army. Rowan's rather uneventful mission—one of several undertaken by various officers and even journalists—caught the public's attention when it was fictionalized as "A Message to Garcia" by an imaginative magazine editor who got most of the details wrong.

A more eventful mission was that of Captain Joseph H. Dorst of the 4th Cavalry. Dorst was supposed to land supplies for the Cuban insurgents in Pinar del Rio, Cuba's easternmost province. On 10 May the old sidewheel steamer *Gussie* departed from Tampa with Dorst, two companies of the 1st Infantry, several Cubans, and a considerable load of arms, ammunition and other supplies, escorted by the armed yacht USS *Wasp* and another small warship; several journalists followed on two chartered tugboats. The voyage south was moderately eventful, punctuated by a rain squall which left many of the men sea sick. As she approached the Cuban coast, *Gussie* and her escorts were several times challenged by U.S. Navy blockaders, no one involved in dispatching her having had the foresight to notify Admiral Sampson of her mission. Fortunately, although several shots were fired, *Gussie* was able to elude injury. Early on 12 May she was steaming westwards within sight of Havana. Thus alerted, the Spanish flashed word by heliograph to their garrisons along the coast. Spanish troops at Mariel attempted to take the ship under fire without success, as she continued on her way unscathed. Later that morning *Gussie* put in at a small bay some 30 miles west of Havana. Dorst sent two boatloads of infantrymen ashore to establish a bridgehead. *Guadia Civil* posted at the site opened fire. When Dorst put his men into a skirmish line, they became the first American troops to fight on Cuban soil. As newspapermen blundered about their lines, the troops exchanged fire with the Spanish. A Cuban scout dispatched through the enemy lines returned shortly with the surprising news that they were within two miles of the considerable Spanish garrison at Cabañas, where the *Cuba Infantry Regiment* was posted. Dorst ordered a hasty withdrawal under covering fire from the escorting naval vessels. By remarkably good fortune, the little expedition suffered only one casualty, James F. J. Archibald, a reporter from the San Francisco *Post* who was slightly wounded in the left arm.

The setback did not deter Dorst from attempting to complete his mission. *Gussie* steamed westwards yet again, looking for signs of the Cuban insurgents. None were found, and on 13 May Dorst decided to return to Tampa, which he reached without incident on the 15th. Two days later, Dorst set out again, this time in the steamer *Florida*. After an uneventful voyage and a more careful reconnaissance of the coast, Dorst was able to land at Port Banes without incident. There he disembarked over 400 armed Cubans and 7500 Springfield rifles with a million rounds of ammunition, plus a large supply of rations, uniforms, and other equipment, as well as more than 100 horses and mules. Similar missions were not as successful. An attempt to run supplies into Tayabacoa on 30 June resulted in several casualties in an action so heated that four men from the 10th Cavalry were awarded the Medal of Honor for rescuing their injured comrades under fire.

The first American plans for full scale operations in Cuba were essentially upscale versions of Dorst's mission. As early as 29 April, Major General William R. Shafter, commanding the V Corps concentrated at Tampa and comprising the bulk of the Regular Army, was ordered to prepare an expedition of 6,000-7,000 troops to effect a landing at Cabo Tunas, near Cienfuegos on the southern coast. His orders indicated that the expedition would remain ashore only a few days, its mission being " ... a reconnaissance in force, to give aid and succor to the insurgents, to render the Spanish forces as much injury as possible, and

Secretary of War Russell A. Alger. Although a Civil War veteran, Alger was a poor administrator and planner, who seemed more interested in interservice battles with the Navy than in fighting the Spanish.

avoiding serious injury to your own command." Although this expedition was scrubbed the next day, by 2 May it had been replaced by a plan to land Shafter's expeditionary force at Mariel, about 26 miles west of Havana, where there was a fine harbor relatively easy to reach from the main fleet base at Key West. This expedition was more than a "reconaissance in force." Working together, Army and Navy brass—Secretary of War Russell A. Alger, Secretary of the Navy John D. Long, Major General Nelson A. Miles, and Rear Admiral Montgomery Sicard—planned for Shafter to establish a fortified camp which could serve not only to supply the Cubans, but also, when suitably reinforced, as a base from which to launch an offensive against Havana itself. But the undertaking had to be held in abeyance, whenr Washington learned that the Spanish fleet had sailed from the Cape Verde Islands.

"Where Is the Spanish Fleet?"

The Spanish fleet had been concentrating at Sao Vicente in the Portuguese-owned Cape Verde Islands for several weeks before the war broke out. The first contingent to arrive was a flotilla of three torpedo boats, bound for the Caribbean but held in the islands when war seemed unavoidable. On 14 April Vice Admiral Pascual Cervera, the senior Spanish naval officer afloat, arrived at Sao Vicente with the armored cruisers *Infanta Maria Teresa* and *Cristobal Colon* and three destroyers, six days after leaving Cadiz. The ships had experienced mechanical troubles and burned excessive amounts of coal, which proved extremely difficult to replace since the U.S. Consul in the islands had bought up much of the available supply. Five days later the armored cruisers *Quendo* and *Vizcaya* arrived from the Caribbean. On paper this gave Cervera a substantial force: four armored cruisers, three destroyers, and three torpedo boats. But there were many difficulties. All of the larger ships and two of the destroyers were experiencing engine trouble, while *Vizcaya's* bottom was extremely fouled. There was also a shortage of trained stokers, those indispensable men who heaved coal into the ships' boilers. As if these problems were not enough, there were worse. *Cristobal Colon*, theoretically the most powerful ship in the squadron, lacked her 10-inch main gun, while the 5.5-inch secondary guns of the three sister armored cruisers—*Maria Teresa*, *Quendo*, and *Vizcaya*—had defective breech mechanisms, and in any case had been supplied with faulty ammunition. Cervera was well aware of these problems. Indeed, much of his time during the final weeks of peace was spent in trying to convince the Ministry of Marine in Madrid that the material problems of his vessels constituted a definite handicap to the development of a rational war plan. On 3 March, for example, he wrote " ... the lack of resources, the absence of organization, in a word, the want of preparation, is readily apparent." Nor were material wants his only problem, for the Ministry was wholly unwilling to provide any strategic directions to be followed in the event of war. From Cadiz on 4 April, he wired the ministry, "Having no instructions, it would seem well that I proceed to Madrid to obtain them and to determine a plan of campaign." Minister Segismundo Bermejo y Merelo, a serving admiral, replied, "In the midst of this international crisis, it is impossible to formulate anything definite." Having received orders to depart for Cape Verdes on 8 April, preparatory to sailing for the Caribbean, Cervera responded, "Allow me to insist upon the necessity of agreeing upon a general plan of campaign, in order to avoid fatal vacillation. The government doubtless has its plan, and it is indispensible that I should be informed of it, so as to be able to act according to it efficiently." The ministry replied, "The urgency of your departure prevents for the moment making known to you the plan for which you ask. You will have it in all its details a few days after you arrive at Cape Verde, by a steamer loaded with coal which will follow you." The denouement came a few days later when the collier reached the Cape Verdes with the promised coal but without the promised instructions. Cervera wired, "I request precise instructions for the contingency of war not having been declared upon my departure," to which Bermejo replied, "I am unable to give you more precise instructions." Even an appeal to the ministry on 20 April by his principal subordinates, urging that the squadron be based in the Canary Islands, was rejected by the Minister on 23 April, who went on to order Cervera to depart for Puerto Rico as soon as possible. Even last minute attempts to appeal directly to Prime Minister Praxides Sagasta, through a conservative politician friendly to the navy and through a naval officer who was also a member of the *Cortes*, brought little change to his orders and indeed only served to deepen the conviction that the government did not know what the condition of the fleet was. Sagasta actually argued that Cervera's ships possessed "superior speed" over their American opponents, which was not even true on paper. Cervera's final message before sailing from the Cape Verdes ended with the line " … disaster is upon us."

The total absence of strategic direction from Madrid makes understandable the perception which Cervera and many other Spanish naval officers had that the government had given little thought to strategic planning beyond the notion of sending the fleet westwards in order to lose it in a "Trafalgar," so that the war would end quickly with a "glorious" defeat. Shortly after war was declared, Portugal proclaimed its neutrality. Cervera was given 24 hours to leave Portuguese territorial waters. On 29 April, ostentatiously dispatching a message to the Minister of Marine that he was sailing north, Cervera departed Sao Vicente, shaping course westwards for Puerto Rico in compliance with the only clear instructions he had ever received. He had with him the armored cruisers *Colon*, *Quendo*, *Maria Teresa*, and *Vizcaya*, plus the destroyers *Furor*, *Terror*, and *Pluton*, having wisely chosen to send his three torpedo boats, which he deemed too small to make a trans-Atlantic crossing, and two supply ships home. Word of his departure was immediately dispatched to Washington.

Had Cervera remained in the Cape Verde Islands, or had he shifted his base to the Canary Islands, his squadron would have constituted what American naval strategist Alfred Thayer Mahan termed a "fleet in being," that is an inferior force which, because of its location and readiness for action, imposes certain restraints upon the activities of a considerably stronger fleet. To cope with the ever-present potential threat posed by a fleet in being, the dominant fleet must restrict its operations in order to be ready at all times to deal with a surprise move on the part of the smaller one. The initial effect of Cervera's departure from the Cape Verdes was to temporarily heighten the value of his squadron, as the U.S. Navy had to be prepared to meet the Spanish fleet wherever it might turn up. The U.S. Navy maintained that the best way to cope with any threat from Cervera's squadron—which in fact was greatly inferior in every way—was to keep the fleet united in anticipation of a decisive action. This was a sound idea on paper, but ran afoul of political realities.

Even before Cervera sailed from the Cape Verdes, panic had begun to infect elements of the population on the East Coast. Fanned by hysterical reporting of the devastation which the Spanish fleet might inflict if it made a sudden descent upon New York, Boston, or other populous area on the Atlantic seaboard, local politicians demanded protection. As Assistant Secretary of the Navy Theodore Roosevelt recorded (shortly before resigning to proceed to San Antonio in his Brooks Brothers lieutenant colonel's uniform, to join the new 1st Volunteer Cavalry) "... Chambers of Commerce and Boards of Trade of different cities all lost their heads for the time being, and raised a deafening clamor and brought every species of pressure to bear on the Administration ... " to secure special protection from the dreaded 'Cape Verde Fleet.'" The outcry forced both armed forces to take measures which neither actually considered necessary. Many newly enrolled volunteer regiments found themselves manning coast defense installations. Army engineers planted minefields to defend ports, including New York. The Navy hauled out of reserve eight old monitors, corroding relics of the Civil War, hastily refurbished them and distributed them, along with three newer monitors, among the principal harbors along the East Coast, to reassure the locals. But that was not sufficient to calm the nervous. Even before the war broke out, the Navy was forced to divide the fleet into four squadrons, two of them quite substantial.

Rear Admiral William Sampson's North Atlantic Squadron, based at Key West, was reduced to the battleships *Iowa* and *Indiana* with *Oregon* momentarily expected as a reinforcement. The armored cruiser *New York* was flagship, and the new monitors *Puritan*, *Amphitrite*, and *Terror*, as well as three protected cruisers, five gunboats, and seven torpedo boats, plus an increasing number of smaller warships were to impose and defend the blockade of Cuba. The ships taken from Sampson were formed into the "Flying Squadron" under Commodore Winfield Scott Schley. Based at Hampton Roads and comprising the battleships *Texas* and *Massachusetts*, the armored cruiser *Brooklyn*, and the very fast protected cruisers *Columbia* and *Minneapolis*, the Flying Squadron was to protect the East Coast from a potential Spanish raid. Commodore John A. Howell was given the Northern Patrol Squadron, a collection of smaller warships—gunboats, yachts, tugs—with the mission of providing protection to the East Coast north of the Delaware Capes. The fourth squadron was comprised of small vessels and officially designated the Auxiliary Naval Force, but was more commonly known as the "Mosquito Fleet." Manned mostly by naval militiamen, the Mosquito Fleet's mission was harbor patrol, maintenance of minefields, support of coast defense installations, and performance of duties normally carried out by the Revenue Cutter Service.

This "division" of the fleet did not please the Navy brass, which wanted to concentrate everything at Key West. Mahanian mindset aside, the Navy had good reason to believe that a Spanish raid on the U.S. mainland was highly unlikely. With some inkling of the poor quality of Cervera's ships and some notion of Cervera's instructions, top level naval officers believed that the Spanish squadron would most likely make for San Juan, which was, in fact, its actual destination. The only real concern the Navy had regarding Cervera's activities was the possibility that he might intercept the battleship *Oregon* on the last leg of her voyage around the Americas. In fact, although Spanish consular officials had been telegraphing word of the battlewagon's progress to Madrid, their fears proved groundless. Cervera was having enough troubles on his voyage westwards without taking on *Oregon*, which in any case could outgun his entire squadron.

Cervera's departure from the Cape Verde Islands had done more than spark a panic along parts of the East Coast. It had also brought about a serious inter-service clash at the highest levels. Citing the difficulties of maintaining the blockade and remaining prepared to cope with Cervera at the same time, the Navy urged an immediate landing in Cuba. The Army, citing the need to train large numbers of volunteers, the imminent fever season, and the potential threat from Cervera, demurred. The Navy retorted that delaying until the fever season was past would not only mean that the fleet would have to suffer prolonged wear and tear on tedious blockade duty, but would result in undertaking operations during the hurricane season. These were irreconcilable differences. General Miles, with the backing of Alfred Thayer Mahan, urged a compromise, an early invasion of Puerto Rico. They advanced several arguments in favor of such an operation. Seizing Puerto Rico would deny Spain the use of San Juan—generally regarded as Cervera's objective—as a base for action against the United States, and it could become a valuable base for the Navy. Puerto Rico was a much healthier place than Cuba, even in the fever season. The garrison, at most 14,000 men including local volunteers, was so small that even an improvised invasion force—say 30,000 men with partially-trained troops—would have little difficulty securing the island, while gaining valuable experience in the process. Such a victory would also bolster morale and support for the war. With Puerto Rico secured, the expedition, reinforced by fresh well trained troops from the U.S., could then move on to Cuba, avoiding both the fever season and the hurricane season. Although Miles' proposal was well-reasoned, President McKinley rejected it and came up with the 2 May plan for a descent by 6,000-7,000 men on Mariel within three or four weeks.

Within days the Mariel plan began to come apart. On 6 May Secretary of the Navy Long reported that the Navy had concluded the Army could not possibly be ready for action by the end of the month. Taking personal offense at this critical, if accurate, observation, Secretary of War Alger told Long the Army's affairs were none of his business. Then on 9 May, Alger got sweet revenge on the Navy by ordering Miles to prepare an immediate expedition of 70,000 men to Mariel for operations against Havana, thereby forcing the Navy to admit it could not undertake such an operation in so short a time. But in making his grandiose proposal, Alger had failed to consult Miles. By-passing official channels, the general went directly to McKinley and detailed the reasons that such an operation was impossible, citing not only the lack of trained manpower, but a shortage of ammunition, the need for time to concentrate transports, and other legitimate objections. McKinley postponed the operation until 16 May. But before that date arrived, the operation had to be scrapped, for on 10 May the Spanish fleet suddenly turned up at French-owned Martinique in the Caribbean.

Since departing the Cape Verde Islands on 29 April, Cervera's squadron had maintained a steady course of roughly west-by-southwest, reaching Martinique in 11 days. It was an uneventful voyage of some 2,150 miles. Since coal supplies were low, *Vizcaya* had a fouled bottom, and virtually all of the ships had experienced engine problems of one sort or another—the destroyers had to be towed part of the way—the squadron had been able to maintain an average speed of only 7 knots. By the time Cervera arrived off Martinique, his fuel situation was perilous, greatly limiting his options. He could make for San

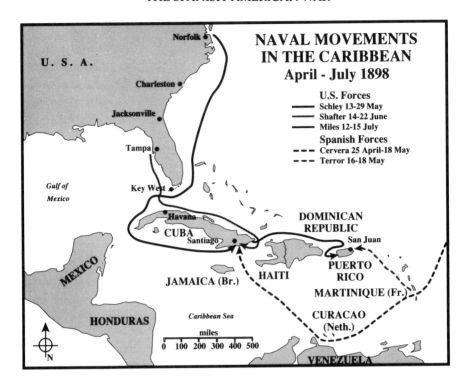

Juan, which lay some 400 miles to the northwest. That voyage would require more than two days, considering his best sustainable speed, but would at most consume only about a third of his precious remaining coal. At San Juan, a well defended harbor, he would find not only coal but a valuable strategic location only about 1400 miles from New York, a little more than 1200 miles from Chesapeake Bay, and a little less than that from Havana. However, San Juan was under blockade and he might have to fight his way in. Alternatively, he could make for Santiago de Cuba, some 1200 miles to the northwest, which had not yet been placed under blockade. But that voyage would consume virtually all his coal, and there was little to be had upon his arrival. He had to find fuel. Maintaining the bulk of his squadron in international waters, late on 10 May Cervera sent Captain

Fernando Villaamil, leader of his destroyer flotilla, into Fort de France, Martinique, with *Terror* and *Furor*, to inquire about coal supplies and to obtain information from the Spanish consulate. The French gave Villaamil a hard time. Citing their neutrality, they refused to supply any coal. Worse, since the USS *Harvard*, an auxiliary cruiser, had just departed the port, they informed him that he was subject to the "48-hour rule," which requires a neutral to detain warships of a belligerent for 48 hours after those of its opponent have left port. Villaamil did what he could, securing dispatches from the Spanish consul, and, after fruitless arguments with the French, pretended to accede to their enforcement of the 48-hour rule while preparing to slip out of port. On 12 May, under the the pretext of testing her engines, Villaamil took *Furor* out into the harbor, leaving *Terror*, which *was* having severe engine problems at dockside. When the French authorities let down their guard, Villaamil ordered *Furor* to put on all steam, and dashed out of the harbor into international waters. It was a skillful ruse. At the cost of abandoning the damaged *Terror*—which shortly was released by the French and made her way to San Juan—Villaamil managed to get out of Fort de France about a day before the 48-hour limit.

Most of the dispatches Villaamil brought to Cervera proved routine. But one was disturbing, which informed Cervera that even as he lay off Martinique, San Juan was being subjected to a naval bombardment by a substantial portion of the American fleet. Under the circumstances, proceeding there might prove fatal. Prior to leaving the Cape Verdes, Cervera had been assured by the Minister of Marine that special arrangements were made to station a collier loaded with 5000 tons of quality coal at Curaçao in the Netherlands Antilles. If Cervera could put that coal in his bunkers, his options would improve. Cervera set out for Curacao, about 500 miles to the southwest. When he arrived there on 14 May, the collier was nowhere to be found. Worse, the Dutch authorities were strictly enforcing their neutrality. *Vizcaya* and *Maria Teresa* were allowed to enter the port for no more than 24 hours to take on 600 tons of coal. The next evening the squadron shaped course to the northwest, bound for Santiago de Cuba.

A "fleet in being" is a threat only so long as its intentions cannot be discerned. Once Cervera was in the Caribbean, the threat value of his squadron rapidly diminished. Cervera's stop at Martinique prompted the U.S. Navy to order the Flying Squadron to shift its base from Hampton Roads to Key West. Then, shortly after Cervera sailed from Curacao, the Navy received confidential information from Havana that Cervera had a number of cargo ships carrying ammunition and other supplies. Concluding that the most likely place for Cervera to land was Cienfuegos, a decent port connected to Havana by rail, on 18 May the Navy ordered the Flying Squadron to concentrate on blockading that port. The Flying Squadron sailed from Key West on this mission at 0700 hours on 19 May. But Cervera did not have any supply ships with him, and his intentions were different. Upon leaving Curacao he had four options: Proceed to San Juan, which, based on the last information he had received—about Sampson's bombardment of the 12th—might already be in enemy hands; make for Cienfuegos or Havana, both under blockade, and therefore probably necessitating a fight before reaching safety; or make for Santiago de Cuba. He chose Santiago, which, although lacking in supplies, was not under blockade and from which he could continue on to San Juan, according to his orders, or consider other alternatives. As a result, Cervera reached Santiago undisturbed at 0900 hours on 19 May.

Cervera's arrival at Santiago had telegraph cables buzzing. Word was quickly flashed to Havana by land line—the Cuban insurgents never cut the principal overland cable—and to Madrid via Cap Haitien. The U.S. Navy had never been able to sever that underwater cable to Haiti. From Havana, the Cuban agent Domingo Villaverde quietly passed word on by cable to Key West, from where it was forwarded to Washington, where it was greeted with considerable skepticism by high officals in the Navy Department, some of whom, including the Secretary, did not know of the existence of the secret intelligence conduit from the Captain General's palace in Havana. Still unaware that Cervera did not have cargo ships ladened with war materiél, several senior officers doubted the message, particularly since the auxiliary cruiser *St. Louis* shortly reported that she had reconnoitered Santiago on the morning of the 19th and seen no evidence of the Spanish fleet, which was true enough as she departed the area an hour before Cervera arrived. Fearful of a ruse, no orders were issued based on the information. Not until the next morning, by which time additional telegrams had come in from Havana confirming the presence of Cervera's squadron at Santiago, was Secretary Long let in on the secret of the Havana cable office.

Long immediately cabled Key West, and by 1230 Admiral Sampson was reading, "The report of the Spanish fleet being at Santiago de Cuba might very well be correct, so the Department strongly advises that you ...send orders to Schley by your fastest dispatch vessel." Sampson, however, still believed that Cervera was seeking to unload military supplies, and that therefore his objective was Cienfuegos. Since Secretary Long's cable was an advisory rather than an order, he instructed Schley to remain off Cienfuegos, leaving Santiago uncovered, and thus giving Cervera considerable freedom of action. But Cervera's options were quite limited. His ships were in terrible shape, all of them in need of engine overhauls and boiler cleanings, both time consuming undertakings given the limited resources at Santiago. There was a little coal available, albeit of poor quality, but a shortage of lighters and coaling equipment made it impossible to load more than about 150 tons a day for the entire fleet, which had a bunker capacity of over 4250 tons. There was also a shortage of food and other supplies. Nevertheless, on 20 May Cervera telegraphed Captain Ramon Auñon y Villalon, newly appointed Minister of Marine after a shakeup of the Sagasta Cabinet on 18 May, "Intend to refit ships in shortest possible time; I believe Santiago will soon be in difficult straits ...." The next day followed a warning that if Santiago were invested before the fleet could finish coaling the squadron would be locked up in port. On the 22nd the Ministry wired that a collier loaded with 3000 tons of anthracite was on its way.

Meanwhile, on 21 May the Navy Department received definite confirmation that Cervera was at Santiago in the form of intercepts of Cervera's exchange of messages with the Ministry of Marine, courtesy of an agent in the French cable station at Cap Haitien in Haiti. Word was promptly wired to Sampson at Key West, who immediately sent a dispatch boat to Schley, nearly

600 miles away off Cienfuegos. Even at high speed, the dispatch vessel required nearly 24 hours to make the journey. In any case, Sampson's instructions to Schley were very ambiguous, "Spanish squadron probably at Santiago ... . If you are satisfied that they are not at Cienfuegos, proceed with all dispatch ... ." In fact, Schley was by no means certain that Cervera was not at Cienfuegos. The blockade of the latter place had been intermittent, and the Spanish squadron might have slipped in before he arrived on the afternoon of 21 May. Confirming his suspicions was a report received from a neutral ship that Cervera had entered Santiago on 19 May, which was true, but had left on the 20th, which was false. So the Flying Squadron remained off Cienfuegos, leaving Cervera free to leave Santiago if he could.

Actually, although he seemed ready to undertake further operations, by the time he reached Santiago, Cervera's options were severely limited. No course of action was likely to produce desirable results. Proceeding to Cienfuegos, or Havana, or San Juan would most likely provoke an engagement with superior American forces. Even if the squadron survived such a clash, upon reaching its objective it would immediately be blockaded, the same fate which awaited it if it remained inactive at Santiago. In fact, Cervera's squadron had already lost any ability it ever possessed to control the course of the war once it left the Cape Verde Islands for the Caribbean rather than for the Canaries. Even though the U.S. Navy failed to act swiftly to seal off Santaigo, the final bottling up of the squadron could not long be delayed.

On the night of 23 May lookouts aboard Schley's ships observed repeated displays of three white lights from the hills near Cienfuegos. Captain Robely D. Evans of the battleship *Iowa* was the only man in the squadron who recognized them as signals from Cuban insurgents. Evans, nicknamed "Fighting Bob" for his salty tongue and belligerent manner, assumed that Schley must also be aware of their purpose and did nothing. As a result, it was not until the following morning that a parley with the Cubans was arranged after Commander Bowman H. McCalla, skipper of the newly arrived cruiser *Marblehead* who was also in on the secret, learned of the nocturnal signals. After several hours ashore, McCalla returned and informed Schley that Cubans confirmed Cervera was at Santiago, not Cienfuegos. Although Schley was still not fully convinced, he ordered a look at Santiago. At 0755 the Flying Squadron steamed east at a surprisingly modest speed, in order to allow its slowest vessels to maintain station. The Flying Squadron wended its way slowly westwards for all of 25 May and most of the 26th as well. At 1725 hours, some 25 or 30 miles south of Santiago, the squadron hove to in order to receive reports from scouting cruisers. The most important report was that of Captain Charles D. Sigsbee, formerly of the unfortunate *Maine* and now skipper of the auxiliary cruiser *St. Paul.*

Sigsbee reported that on the previous day he had intercepted the collier *Restormel*, loaded with 3000 tons of coal for the Spanish fleet. Although he had interviewed the captain of the captured vessel, the latter had apparently misinformed him as to the ship's destination. As a result, Sigisbee reported, "They are not here. I have been here for a week, and they are not here." Schley, who already had doubts about the presence of the Spanish squadron at Santiago, ordered the Flying Squadron to reverse course and return to Key West for coaling, bypassing Cienfuegos once again. Meanwhile he sent a dispatch boat to Jamaica to cable the Navy Department of his decision. But then he had second thoughts. Beset by conflicting emotions, his belief that the Spanish were at Cienfuegos conflicting with his orders to the contrary, at about 2000 hours, some two hours after altering course, he ordered the squadron to halt. And there it remained, through the night and the following morning, drifting slowly westwards with the current, some of his ships using the respite to take on coal from a collier. At about noon on 27 May the squadron resumed steaming westwards with occasional halts. Then suddenly at 1325 hours, Schley ordered the squadron to proceed to Santiago. At 1940 hours the Flying Squadron finally arrived off the entrance to Santiago harbor. It remained there through the night. As dawn broke on 28 May, Captain Evans and Lieutenant Commander Raymond P. Rogers oberved the harbor entrance through their binoculars. Rogers, former naval attache in Madrid, suddenly cried out, "Captain, there's the *Cristobal Colon.* Evans quickly confirmed the observation, seeing the ship clearly moored in a position to cover the harbor entrance in support of the shore batteries. Word was immediately dispatched by signal flag to the armored cruiser *Brooklyn*. Although several times over the previous few days Cervera had discussed making a sortie from Santiago in order to reach the greater security of Cienfuegos, a course of action from which he was dissuaded by his captains, he no longer had any options in the matter. The Spanish fleet was definitely bottled up.

The Leap to Arms, A Case Study: New York

McKinley's calls for volunteers met with enthusiastic response throughout the nation. Hundreds of thousands of men answered the call, including about 90 percent of prewar militiamen, and some 95 percent of prewar militia officers. The case of New York State was typical.

Including the Naval Militia, and some 3,000 men recruited for U.S. Regular and Volunteer units, New York State contributed about 30,000 troops to the war effort, over 10 percent of the almost 300,000 who served.

New York Units Mustered into Federal Service, 1898-99

Unit	Locale	Enlistment	Assignment
A Trp	N.Y.C.	1 May-28 Nov	I Corps
C Trp	Brooklyn	2 May-25 Nov	I Corps
4th Bty*	N.Y.C.	19 Jul-21 Oct	Camp Black
5th Bty*	N.Y.C.	15 Jul-24 Oct	Camp Black
7th Bty*	Rochester	15 Jul-30 Nov	Camp Black
1st Rgt*	Albany	2 May-26 Feb	VIII Corps
2nd Rgt*	Troy	1 May-2 Nov	IV Corps
3rd Rgt*	Rochester	29 Apr-30 Nov	II Corps
8th Rgt	N.Y.C.	2 May-3 Nov	III Corps
9th Rgt	N.Y.C.	2 May-15 Nov	III Corps
12th Rgt	N.Y.C.	2 May-20 Apr	III Corps
13th Rgt	Brooklyn	2-7 May	Camp Black
14th Rgt	Brooklyn	2 May-28 Nov	III Corps
22nd Rgt	N.Y.C.	9 May-23 Nov	IV Corps
47th Rgt	Brooklyn	3 May - 31 Mar	I Corps
65th Rgt	Buffalo	1 May - 1 Nov	II Corps
69th Rgt	N.Y.C.	2 May-31 Jan	III Corps
71st Rgt	N.Y.C.	2 May-15 Nov	V Corps
201st Rgt*	N.Y.C.	5 Jul-3 Apr	II Corps
202nd Rgt*	Mixed	5 Jul-15 Apr	II Corp
203rd Rgt*	Mixed	15 Jul-25 Mar	Camp Black

In New York, as in many other states, the number of men who volunteered exceeded the state's quota under the President's calls, and this despite the fact that an enormous percentage of the men who presented themselves for service were rejected as "lacking in legal, mental, moral, or physical qualifications" (the army accepted only 23 percent of the nearly one million men who tried to enlist, and only 10 percent of those who tried to secure a commission). As a result, only the fittest men and the "best" National Guard units were taken, the latter condition determined as much by political expediency as by military efficiency. Since in many of the very rural upstate areas there were no organized regiments in the National Guard, merely numbers of independent companies or separate battalions grouped into brigades, and since there were a lot of volunteers with no ties to the National Guard, the state raised several new units for the war, denoted on the table by an asterisk. The 202nd Regiment was raised mostly from volunteers and individual guardsmen from New York City and Buffalo, while the 203rd was raised on a statewide basis, and never completed formation. The oddly high numbers of the 201st, 202nd, and 203rd were dictated by the need to avoid using regimental numbers from the Civil War, lest members of their veterans' associations take offense (several other states resorted to the same expedient, which is why there was a 27th Indiana Battery). Although many of the men accepted into these new units had no prior military service, the adjutant general, Frederick Phisterer, a Civil War Medal of Honor winner, gave preference to men who had militia experience when commissioning officers. As a result, most of the officers in these outfits were from militia units which were not mustered into Federal service, in particular men from the 7th Regiment.

The 7th Regiment, the state's most famous and arguably best militia unit, did not volunteer. There were a number of reasons for this. It being a very fashionable regiment, many of the officers, non-commissioned officers, and enlisted men were older than the norm for the positions they held (it was not unusual for company commanders to have 25 years in grade), so that some were not in the best physical condition and would probably have been rejected for federal service. In addition, the regimental commander and many of the other officers and men were unwilling to serve under Regular Army officers, whom they considered martinets and militarists. Despite this, many of the regiment's men volunteered on an individual basis, serving as officers and NCOs in other regiments, most notably in the newly raised units.

The 13th Regiment spent only five days in Federal service. When it arrived at Camp Black, the state's muster ground on the Hempstead Plain on Long Island, it was found to be considerably understrength. As the 22nd Regiment was also understrength, albeit much less so, four companies were raised from individual volunteers from the 13th, which were incorporated into the 22nd as its 3rd Battalion.

As was the case for a majority of the men under arms during the war, most Empire Staters never went overseas. The only New York units to see combat during the war were the 71st, which took part in the Santiago Campaign, and had a difficult time during the Battle of San Juan Hill, and Troops A and C, which were involved a number of skirmishes in Puerto Rico. A few units also managed to go abroad on occupation duty.

Overseas Service of New York Volunteers

A Troop	Puerto Rican Campaign, 31 July-10 September 1898
C Troop	Puerto Rican Campaign, 31 July-10 September 1898
1st Regiment	Occupation of Hawaii, 6 August-6 December 1898
12th Regiment	Occupation duty, Cuba, 1 January-20 March 1899

22nd Regiment	Ordered to I Corps for Puerto Rican service, a movement that was cancelled upon conclusion of the Armistice
47th Regiment	Occupation duty, Puerto Rico, 15 October 1898-4 March 1899
71st Regiment	Santiago Campaign, Cuba, 23 June-10 August 1898
202nd Regiment	Occupation duty, Cuba, 9 December 1898-15 March 1899

In addition to its contribution to the army during the war, New York also sent about 475 members of its naval militia into the service. New York naval militiamen provided the crew for the appropriately named auxiliary cruiser USS *Yankee*, the large, speedy former merchantman *El Norte*. *Yankee* saw service on blockade duty and was in action on several occasions. Many other New York naval militiamen served with those from other states in other naval vessels, and in some of the Navy's coastal signal stations.

New York State suffered 436 men dead in the service, only 15 of whom were killed or mortally wounded in action, all in the 71st Infantry.

U.S.S. *Oregon* Rounds South America

The battleship *Oregon* was built at Union Iron Works in San Francisco, one of only two major warships ever built for the U.S. Navy on the West Coast (the other being the battleship *California*, the famous "Prune Barge" of World War II). Laid down in 1891 and launched two years later, *Oregon* was commissioned in 1896. Along with her sister ships, *Indiana* and *Massachusetts*, she was officially rated as a "coast defense battleship" to assuage the fears of isolationists, and as a result had a rather low freeboard for so powerful a vessel, her main deck standing only a little more than 11 feet above the water, which made her difficult in heavy seas.

One of the most powerfully armed ships of her day, *Oregon* was the principal American warship in the Pacific Ocean when war broke out with Spain. As a result, the Spanish discounted the possibility that the U.S. Navy would attempt to bring her the 16,000 miles to the East Coast, considering that she would most likely be used against the Philippines. In fact, the decision to bring the battleship to the Atlantic was made shortly after the *Maine* disaster. On 7 March Secretary of the Navy John D. Long ordered *Oregon* to San Francisco from Bremerton, Washington. On 12 March, shortly after she arrived at San Francisco, her skipper, Captain Charles E. Clark, a tough 55-year-old veteran of the Civil War, received orders to proceed to Callao, Peru, preparatory to taking the ship to the

East Coast. In a flurry of activity, the ship was readied for sea. On Saturday, 19 March, riding rather low in the water due to the 1640 tons of coal in her bunkers, 500 tons of ammunition in her magazines, and almost 150 tons of stores in her food lockers—enough to feed the nearly 470 officers and men aboard for about six months—she stood out into San Francisco Bay, passed through the Golden Gate onto the broad bosom of the Pacific, and shaped course southwards. Although heavily laden, her engines soon brought her up to 12 knots, running easily on three boilers. Her voyage became almost legendary, but was actually uneventful, and rather routine. Captain Clark imposed, and the sailors cheerfully accepted, a rather spartan regime; To reserve fresh water for the boilers he placed limitations on the consumption of drinking water.

Few incidents marred the journey, but on 27 March smoke was detected emerging from one of the ship's coal bunkers. Working furiously in ten minute shifts, hundreds of sailors dug down through the coal seeking the source of the smoke. After four hours the fire was discovered and put out; the cause, spontaneous combustion. On 4 April the ship reached Callao, Peru, having made 4,112 miles in 16 days from San Francisco, at an average speed of about 9.3 knots, consuming 900 tons of coal in the process, an overall excellent performance.

Fearful of sabotage by Spanish sympathizers among the Peruvian populace, Clark kept the ship anchored in the harbor, rather than bring her alongside. He maintained tight security, with double watches and a round the clock patrol by the ships' steam launches. While the ship coaled from lighters, a tedious, filthy process, her engineers—including Passed Midshipman William D. Leahy, who would eventually wear five stars—did maintenance on her boilers and engines. Having been out of communiction with the rest of the world since departing San Francisco, Clark found a bundle of dispatches awaiting him. One of them, dated 26 March, warned that the Spanish torpedo gunboat *Temerario*, a station ship at Montevideo, Uruguay, had left that port for places unknown, and suggested he take care when negotiating the Straits of Magellan. On the 6th Clark received orders to proceed to Montevideo or Rio de Janeiro. Refueled, with her stores replenished and her boilers and engines fine tuned, *Oregon* left Callao the next day, continuing on her southerly course. On 9 April speed was increased to 14 knots. A few days later *Oregon* overtook the U.S. gunboat *Marietta*, also bound for the Caribbean on orders from Washington, but soon left the slower vessel behind. Late on 15 April, in heavy seas, *Oregon* reached the western entrance to the Straits of Magellan. Rather than attempt to enter the waterway at night, she anchored in a protected inlet. The next morning, after taking on a Chilean pilot, she began the delicate task of negotiating the treacherous first half of the straits. *Oregon* reached Punta Arenas, more or less midway through the 330 mile long straits on 18 April, after completing the most difficult part of the passage. Captain Clark paused there for a few days to refuel and check the ship's machinery. There she was joined by little *Marietta*, which had caught much better weather. At 0600 on the 21st, the two ships steamed eastwards, then headed north in the Atlantic.

At 1500 hours on 30 April *Oregon* reached Rio de Janiero, a few hours ahead of the plodding *Marietta*. There Captain Clark received formal notice that the U.S. and Spain were at war, and was again warned about the Spanish torpedo gunboat *Temerario*. The two American warships spent several days at Rio, where they were joined by the cruiser *Buffalo*, purchased from Brazil just weeks earlier. On 4 May the three American vessels sailed. When it became evident that neither of her consorts could keep up, Captain Clark decided to go it alone at full steam, rather than reduce speed, and thereby delay joining the fleet. On 8 May *Oregon* reached Bahia in northeastern Brazil. Although he informed the local authorities that he was going to remain at Bahia for several days, Clark took his ship out of the port on the evening of the 9th.

On 14 May, as she was steaming hard just north of the equator off the Brazilian coast, the 38-foot long American sailing yacht *Spray*, also headed northwards, was sighted. After the usual exchange of pleasantries, Captain Clark informed the vessel's captain that war had broken out between the U.S. and Spain, and inquired as to whether Slocum had seen any warships about. *Spray*'s skipper, Joshua Slocum—America's most famous old salt—replied that he had not, and then hoisted the signal "Let us keep together for mutual protection." Unamused, Clark and his battleship proceeded, while Slocum sailed on to complete what was the first solo around-the-world trip in history.

The battleship arrived at Bridgetown, Barbados, on 18 May. Obedient to the 24 hour rule, Clark loaded coal and steamed away the next evening. After a little deceptive maneuvering, in case Spanish agents were reporting his movements, she reached the coast of Florida on 26 May, where the revenue cutter *Hudson* greeted her. Her unheralded arrival at Key West two days later caused a momentary panic among some U.S. Navy lookouts, who spotted her looming monstrously out of the morning haze, until they saw the Stars and Stripes streaming from her foretop. *Oregon* had taken 66 days—including several layovers—to travel nearly 16,000 miles, for an average speed of nearly 12 knots, at the time a world's record for so large a warship. She arrived at Key West in excellent condition, and within days was taking her turn on blockade and patrol duties.

The war with Spain provided *Oregon*'s only taste of combat. Within a few years she and her sisters were eclipsed by bigger, faster, more powerfl vessels. In the ten years following the Spanish War the U.S. battlefleet went from five ships to 26, with more abuilding. She saw limited service during World War I, and in 1925 was designated as a museum. In December 1942, in a moment of panic over steel shortages, the veteran warship was ordered scrapped, with surprisingly little protest. The work had reached the point where the superstructure and most of the interior fittings had been removed, when the Navy requisitioned her for use as an ammunition transport. Loaded with ammunition, the hulk was towed to the Central Pacific in July 1944, where she helped keep the modern battleships supplied during the liberation of Guam and the conquest of the Marianas. She remained derelict at Guam until long after the war. Sold to a ship wrecker in 1956, she was scrapped in Japan.

Nelson Appleton Miles

Nelson Appleton Miles (1839-1925) was born and raised in Massachusetts. On the outbreak of the Civil War he was commissioned a captain in the 22nd Massachusetts Volunteers. He shortly transferred to Maj. Gen. Oliver O. Howard's staff, earning a promotion to lieutenant colonel of volunteers for distinguished conduct at Seven Pines (31 May 1862). Returning to his regiment, during the Battle of Antietam (17 September 1862) he took command after the colonel became a casualty, and was promoted to colonel himself, once again for distinguished conduct under fire. His abilities as a regimental commander were again demonstrated at Fredericksburg (13 December 1862), where he was severely wounded, and Chancellorsville (2-4 May 1863), for which he was later (1867) breveted to brigadier general in the regular army and still later (1892) awarded a Medal of Honor. Meanwhile, in May of 1864 he was promoted to brigadier general of volunteers, fighting from the Rappahannock to Petersburg, where he commanded a division. Shortly after the war ended he was promoted to major general of volunteers and given a corps command on occupation duty in Virginia.

In 1866 Miles was made a colonel in the regular army. After the reorganization and reduction of the post-war army, in 1869 he ended up commanding the 5th Infantry. His career over the next 25 years saw him rise to major general, while serving variously against the Cheyenne, the Comanche, the Kiowa, the Arapaho, the Sioux, the Nez Perce, the Bannocks, the Apache, and the Pullman Strikers. In 1895 he was named general-in-chief.

Miles played an important role in overseeing the expansion of the army for the war with Spain, albeit hampered by not having direct authority over the various staff departments or even operational forces in the field. Although he had hopes of commanding troops in Cuba, he had to be satisfied with command of the expedition to Puerto Rico, a mission which he performed superbly. After the war Miles, continued as general-in-chief and was promoted to lieutenant general in 1901. Following a tour of the Philippines, Miles was openly critical of the conduct of some American commanders there, arousing considerable controversy. He retired in

1903. Despite rumors that he might run for president, he lived quietly until his death.

A fine administrator and good tactician, Miles never had the opportunity to command an army in battle. His conduct of the campaign in Puerto Rico was excellent, suggesting that he may well have proven a fine commander. He was certainly a controversial one, being involved in the bitter arguments over the Battle of Wounded Knee, butting into the Sampson-Schley dispute, and so forth.

William Rufus Shafter

William Rufus Shafter (1835-1906) was a teacher when the Civil War broke out. He volunteered for service and was commissioned a 2nd lieutenant in the 7th Michigan. His Civil War record was varied and honorable, if not spectacular. Initially serving in the East (Ball's Bluff and the Peninsula Campaign, during which he particularly distinguished himself at Fair Oaks, for which he was eventually awarded a brevet), in late 1862 he was promoted to major and sent to the 19th Michigan in the Western Theater (Thompson's Station, where he was captured, to be exchanged shortly afterwards, and Nashville). Promoted colonel early in 1864, he was given command of the 17th U.S. Colored Infantry. Mustered out late in 1865 with a brevet as brigadier general of volunteers, Shafter secured a lieutenant colonelcy in the Regular Army in 1867. From 1869 to 1879 his service was with the black 24th Infantry, mostly on the frontier. Promoted colonel in 1879, he commanded the 1st Infantry until made a brigadier general in 1897 and assigned command of the Department of California, in which post he was serving on the outbreak of the Spanish-American War.

Appointed major general of volunteers in May of 1898, Shafter was assigned command of the V Corps, organizing at Tampa. The corps, which comprised the bulk of the Regular Army, was intended for limited operations, to effect short term landings in Cuba for the purpose of supplying the revolutionary forces to strengthen them towards the day when a full scale invasion of the island could be undertaken. The arrival of Cervera's squadron at Santiago led to a hasty revision of the corps' mission, so that on 14 June Shafter sailed with some 15,000 men with the object of seizing the Cuban port.

Shafter's Santiago Campaign (22 June-16 July) was successful, but attended by much mismanagement, not a little bungling, and considerable privation among the troops, leading to the virtual disintegration of the corps as an effective fighting force. Although some of this was Shafter's fault, much of the blame should be laid to the haste with which the expedition was undertaken.

Late in 1898 Shafter was named commander of the Department of the East, but within days was transferred to the Department of California. Retiring from the Regular Army as a brigadier general in 1899, he continued on duty as a major general of volunteers until 1901, when he retired, whereupon he was promoted to major general on the Regular Army retired list.

Shafter was a tall man. An imposing figure in his youth, by 1898 he was quite heavy, over 300 pounds.

In Cuba the heat combined with his weight and his various ailments, including gout, to limit his effectiveness as a commander. By no means a good organizer, much of the success of the Santiago Expedition was due to his good fortune in having a number of fine staff officers. Nevertheless, he appears to have had a sound idea of the general shape of the operation, and as capable a man as John J. Pershing, then a captain with the black 10th Cavalry, considered him a good officer.

The U.S. Army

In 1898 the Regular Army was quite small, with an authorized strength of only 27,858 officers and enlisted men, of whom only 27,146 were actually on active service. The end of the Indian Wars led to reorganization of the army, and many small posts were abandoned, permitting whole regiments to train together on a regular basis. Standards were high, for although the Army was by no means an attractive profession there were more than enough volunteers for it to be selective. There were seven to eight million men of prime military age in the country, and the Army needed only a couple thousand recruits a year to sustain its numbers.

In many ways the troops of the Regular Army were superior to those of the other major powers. The men were well trained with stress placed on physical fitness. In addition, they were intelligently equipped. The experience of the Indian Wars had taught the American soldier to travel light, and in 1898 his equipment weighed less than that carried by most foreign troops, though, interestingly, the Spanish veterans in Cuba were even more lightly equippped. Great stress was still placed on individual marksmanship, and the newly issued Krag-Jorgensen, a bolt action breechloading magazine rifle, was one of the most modern pieces available. Most U.S. equipment was good, but the uniforms were not. U.S. troops went into action clad in felt campaign hats, blue flannel shirts, brown woolen trousers, and brown canvas leggings, with heavy, high top shoes, an outfit hardly suited to a tropical climate. The first cotton khaki uniforms did not reach Cuba until after the armistice. Of course, the Regular Army was not big enough to undertake a war on its own. Backing was provided by the National Guard, as the militia had come to be known.

The history of the militia was one in which long periods of neglect were followed by short spurts of great interest. On the eve of the Spanish-American War the nation had 115,627 active National Guardsmen, almost precisely the number that had been on hand on the eve of the Civil War, thirty years earlier, when there had been only half as many Americans. It was a poorly funded body. Annual Federal expenditure on the militia was a mere $400,000, just recently increased from the $200,000 allocated since Jefferson's presidency. The states threw in another $2.8 million, for a total of $3.2 million, or about $27.50 per militiaman, perhaps $750-$1000 in money of 1996. Despite this neglect, in most states the National Guard had excellent manpower. In fact, by the late 1890s the National Guard was undergoing a renaissance. Associations of officers and interested citizens were promoting greater professionalism and lobbying for increased support. Many units raised money through fairs and the like, and some—such as New York's affluent 7th—levied cash contributions on their officers to provide extra equipment. Training was becoming more realistic. In addition to regular drills and headquarters nights, most state militia units engaged in periodic summer camp training, sometimes in cooperation with Regular Army units or National Guard units from other states, engaging in parades, drills, rifle matches, and sham battles. On several occasions U.S. militia units even confronted the Canadian militia in rifle matches. And, of course,

the militia turned out as needed to support the civil authority in natural disasters, labor disputes, and public disorders. Although its role in suppressing labor unrest and urban rioting received the most attention, much of it exaggerated, in fact the National Guard's most frequent use was to enforce the law in situations where local authorities were unable—or unwilling—to do so. For example, during the 1890s the Alabama militia was most often called out to prevent lynchings; in 1896-1897 it did so on eleven occasions, all but once successfully. Although the quality of each state's contingent varied considerably, by 1898 the National Guard consituted a moderately well trained, somewhat experienced, reserve army. To be sure, the National Guard was not trained up to the standards of the Regular Army, nor was it so well-equipped. It was also an unbalanced force. Virtually all National Guardsmen were infantry. Only about 10,000-12,000 of the Guardsmen belonged to the artillery or cavalry, and there were very few signal, engineer, or medical personnel. Nevertheless, without the National Guard, mobilization for the war would have been much more difficult.

Of course the concentration of the army in 1898 was extremely muddled. The War Department and the army had been "thinking small" for 30 years, since the Civil War, during which their principal focus had been on the Indian Wars. Organization, deployment, leadership, training, routines, procurement, and stockpiles were all geared to this small war viewpont. At best, the Army had stockpiles suitable for a force of about 35,000 for no more than three months. The supply of Krag rifles, for example, was so limited that the Army had to resort to issuing the obsolete Springfield '73 rifle to the volunteers. Had the mobilization been effected with less haste, many of the problems would have been avoided. Certainly, the Regular Army mobilized with commendable efficiency. On 15 April the War Department ordered 22 of the 25 infantry regiments to concentration areas at New Orleans, Mobile, and Tampa, as well as six of the ten cavalry regiments and most of the Army's field artillery batteries at Chickamauga Battlefield Park. Within a week virtually all of these troops had reached their concentration areas, fully equipped for war service. A few days later the troops at New Orleans and Mobile were distributed to Tampa and Chickamauga, again quickly and ef-

ficiently. But on 22 April the President issued a call for 125,000 volunteers (the War Department had planned for 60,000) to serve for two years, which met with enthusiastic response from National Guardsmen, almost all of whom entered service. This measure was followed on 26 June by legislation authorizing the addition of nearly 37,000 men to the Regular Army, while subsequent legislation and calls over the next few weeks amounted to nearly 90,000 more men, on paper a tenfold increase in manpower. Although the recruiting goal for the Regular Army was never met, the growth in manpower was spectacular: on 1 April 1898 there were slightly more than 27,000 officers and men on active duty, by 1 July there were almost 265,000, and by 1 August about 272,000, of whom nearly 45,000 were overseas or at sea.

Strength of the Army

Date	Regulars	Volunteers	Total
1 Apr	27,146	—	27,146
1 May	36,715	124,804	161,519
1 Jun	46,026	160,474	206,500
1 Jul	52,617	212,100	264,717
1 Aug	56,012	216,034	272,046

Further complicating the mobilization was the desire of the Regulars to get the volunteers under their control as quickly as possible. Volunteer regiments were mustered at their respective armories. They then moved to their state National Guard camp. Many states had long maintained such camps, so that the troops could spend a week or two each year in training. Some of these camps, such New York's Camp Black on Long Island, or the Texas

Camp Mabry near Austin, were well laid out and quite well appointed. Rather than leave the volunteers in their respective state mustering grounds until all preparations had been made to receive them, the War Department ordered volunteers to concentrate in one of the corps training grounds. But few of the camps were well sited with regard to rail communications and port facilities, and none of the camps were ready for use when the first troops arrived. Moreover, the fact that most of the corps commanders had little or no experience handling masses of men made matters worse, and there was considerable suffering and disease among the volunteers as a result. It is interesting to note that the best run camp was that of the VII Corps. Major General Fitzhugh Lee, a Confederate veteran with extensive experience of high command, did an excellent job of sorting out the administrative muddle, made easier because the corps' location at Jacksonville, Florida, was well served by rail lines. The VIII Corps, which began concentrating at San Francisco in May, benefited from the fact that it was organized piecemeal with regiments shipping out quickly in a series of convoys, so that there never was a large concentration of troops to overwhelm the available facilities.

The Army Corps

Corps	Cantonment	Operations
I	Chickamauga	Puerto Rico Campaign, elements to the Philippines
II	Camp Alger*	Elements to Puerto Rico, the Philippines
III	Chickamauga	Elements to Cuban occupation
IV	Tampa	Elements to Puerto Rico, and later Cuban occupation
V	Tampa	Santiago Campaign
VI	Chickamauga	Never raised
VII	Jacksonville	Occupation of Havana after the armistice
VIII	San Francisco	Hawaiian occupation, Philippine Campaign

* *About two miles from Dun Loring, Virginia, near Washington.*

Congress authorized the activation of as many as 18 army corps to consist of three divisions of three brigades, each of three regiments. Every corps was to have an artillery battalion and a hospital detachment, and each division a signal company and hospital detachment. In fact, only eight corps were ordered raised, I through VII in May and VIII in June. The I, II, III, and VII Corps were composed almost entirely of volunteers. The V Corps was largely regulars, seasoned with a few regiments of volunteers, while the IV and VIII Corps were mostly volunteers, plus a few regulars. The VI Corps was supposed to have been activated at the Chickamauga National Battlefield Park from volunteers, but had no units allocated to it (its commander, retread Civil War "boy general" James H. Wilson, was diverted to command a division in I Corps for the campaign in Puerto Rico). Troops selected for occupation duty were drawn from all corps, primarily as a political move, to ensure that at least some men from each state went overseas.

The Spanish Army

In 1898 the reputation of the Spanish Army was not high. And indeed, it did have many problems.

There were too many officers, an average of one for every 5.3 men, and one general for every 236, whereas in the U.S. Army, including volunteers, there was one officer for every 22 men of lower rank, and one general for every 3,600 others. The Spanish problem was a result of promotion by the "merits of war," a practice designed to reward gallantry in action. There were few officers in the infantry or cavalry who did not have at least one promotion by merit. But engineer, artillery, and even staff officers rarely had an opportunity to earn merit promotions. Most operations were guerrilla affairs, with little demand for specialized troops: Of 160,000 regulars in Cuba, only about 2,200 were field artillerymen and about 2,400 combat engineers, while of some 8,000 regulars in Puerto Rico, only 120 were field artillerymen and none combat engineers; of the 45,000 regulars in the Philippines only 600 were field artillerymen and 1,700 combat engineers. This created tensions between the arms of service. It also resulted in a scarcity of first and second lieutenants in the infantry and cavalry, with a consequent demand for new men in those grades, while there was a surplus of middle- and upper-ranking officers.

The other great rift in the officer corps was that between regular and reserve officers. The term "reserve officer" did not mean a civilian subject to be called for service. Reserve commissions were awarded to enlisted men who had particularly distinguished themselves. They remained on permanent active duty just like any other officer, but were rarely promoted above major.

The officer corps was also plagued by nepotism. In 1898 most of the 53 Spanish generals in the Philippines, Cuba, and Puerto Rico had one or two relatives under their command, often serving as aides-de-camp. Indeed, several generals had more than one kinsman serving with them. Two of Vara del Rey's sons died with him at El Caney, where his brother was wounded, and there was a nephew in the town as well. Brig. Gen. José Garcia Aldave, who commanded a brigade at Manzanillo, had both sons on his staff; one of them served eleven of his first seventeen years in the service as an aide to his father, who rose to lieutenant general. (Naval officers were similarly nepotistic, Montojo having two sons with him at Manila Bay, one of whom was seriously wounded.)

Most regular junior officers were quite young, since in the Spanish Army they entered a military academy at age 13 or 14, emerging in two or three years as second lieutenants. On the other hand, reserve lieutenants were quite often much older, in their 20s and even 30s, since they were all former enlisted men. Officers, regardless of arm or type of commission, often had their hand in the till, indeed as did NCOs. They also tended to be negligent of the well-being of their troops.

The enlisted men were almost entirely conscripts from the peasant and urban working classes, since anyone with a little money could pay commutation. Most of them were between 20 and 23, usually hardy and stubborn in combat, but not very well educated and lacking initiative. Conditions of service were harsh. Food was usually poor, barracks inadequate, and the health of the troops was frequently bad at least in the colonies, where they had to cope with malaria, yellow fever, and tropical conditions. The Spanish Army had the highest rate of death from disease of European armies: 10.93 men per thousand per year, at a time when the British Army rate was 3.6 and the German 1.5.

Despite the limitations of both the officers and the enlisted men, the Spanish Army could fight. Officers led from the front and incurred high casualties. Enlisted men were noted for their ability to endure hardship and their tenacity in defense.

Reputation aside, the Spanish Army was actually quite good at what it was called upon to do. This was not to engage in sustained conventional warfare against a major power. In fact, the Spanish Army had not been called upon to fight such a war since the Napoleonic invasion of 1808. Crushed by Napoleon, the army was reborn in a protracted guerrilla war, from 1808 through 1814, which, supported by and supporting the Duke of Wellington's British Army, arguably did as much to destroy the Napoleonic Empire as did the Russian Campaign. So the Spanish Army in the nineteenth century had its origins in an insurgency. All of its wars from then onwards were guerrilla wars, and most of them were successful. The army became quite good at counter-insurgency warfare, a tradition that continued into the twentieth century. Its swift and successful reaction to the insurgency in Cuba in 1895 and that in the Philippines the following year stand in testimony to its skill at irregular warfare.

Tactically the Spanish made very effective use of cover, rifle pits (the nineteenth century term for fox holes), and entrenched positions, both offensively and defensively. Permanent defenses were characterized by extensive earthworks and the use of barbed wire. From such bases, columns emerged to relentlessly pursue guerrilla bands.

Of course, there was a price to pay for this expertise. The Spanish Army was too light to fight a conventional war. Even the small allotment of artillery which the U.S. V Corps brought to Santiago, 16 field guns, eight light mortars, and a few miscellaneous pieces, were more numerous than the artillery available to the defenders.

Nevertheless, the army fought well. Indeed, most American troops came home from the war with considerable respect for their erstwhile opponents. One American officer later wrote:

The Spanish impressed me much more favorably than I expected. They look small beside our men, but they are generally well set up, bright and alert, and look ready for business. They wear a uniform—blouse and trousers—of a bright homespun material, without any facings, but with brass buttons and collar ornaments. For the head they wear a straw hat, wide brim and a cockade on the left side.

They are armed with the Mauser and short knife-bayonet. The cartridges are carried in a clip in bunches of five, and these are carried in small leather pouches attached to the belt, several in a pouch. The leather trimmings are all of fair or tan leather, and far superior in appearance to our black leather trimmings. For the feet the men wear sandals with rope soles. Many, however, had on black leather shoes, and some of them wore moccasins. Each man had a blanket slung over the left shoulder, and carried a fair-weather bag or haversack. I saw no tents and no wagon train. They... do not depend on mules and wagons to help them conduct a campaign.

I saw a company marching along the street, and noticed that they move with a quick, springy step, that enables them to cover ground quickly.

U.S. and Spanish Military Organization Compared

The Spanish-American War was the last between major powers in which the primary tactical units were relatively small, the regiment for the U.S. Army and the battalion for the Spanish. Despite the difference in nomenclature, these were essentially the same size.

The U.S. Army. On paper, infantry regiments had twelve companies in three battalions. However, due to peacetime economies, the 25 infantry regiments of the Regular Army had only ten active companies, plus two in cadre, with their officers assigned as what would today be called R.O.T.C. instructors. In theory, on mobilization the cadre companies would be filled out and the regiment would then form three battalions. However, since the Regulars went to war so quickly in 1898, they usually shipped out with only ten companies, forming a single battalion. National Guard units usually had twelve companies in three battalions, and when they volunteered for service the Army tried to get them to reorganize on a ten company basis, with no success. Volunteer regiments were also usually much stronger then Regular Regiments, even though they too were usually short of authorized strength, 1,428. The 18 Regular infantry regiments with V Corps in Cuba had an average strength of only 518 officers and men, while the six volunteer regiments averaged about 860. The situation in Puerto Rico was somewhat better. The 19th Infantry was virtually at full strength and the 11th Infantry had about 1,100 men, while the eight volunteer regiments averaged about 900, but then the expedition to Puerto Rico got underway nearly a month after that to Cuba. Also, the many regiments had "unofficial" members: For example, the commander of the 6th Massachusetts brought his 15-year-old son along, and the 8th Ohio "adopted" two orphaned African-American boys, one of whom went to Cuba as an officer's orderly.

The six cavalry regiments which fought in Cuba did so as infantry. At full strength they were supposed to have twelve companies of about 100 men, forming three squadrons. The ten Regular Army cavalry regiments consisted of twelve companies, with about 750 men on duty. But the regiments that went to Cuba did so with only two squadrons, and even then their average strength was only about 400, while the two squadrons of the Rough Riders numbered about 600.

Although on paper the army had five artillery regiments, these existed mostly to take care of paperwork and provide jobs for colonels of artillery. Each regiment had ten batteries of coast artillery and two of light artillery. At best numbers were low, most batteries having only about 50 men, whereas on paper coastal batteries were supposed to have 200 and light ones 173. By scrounging for all available manpower, the Army was able to beef up enough light batteries to accom-

pany the overseas expeditions. Nevertheless, the six batteries with V Corps averaged only about 70 men apiece. The army did better for the Puerto Rico expedition, the five regular batteries averaging about 110 men, while the four volunteer batteries were practically at full strength.

The Spanish Army. Although infantry regiments existed on paper, these were actually more administrative than tactical organizations. Typically in peacetime a regiment had two battalions of six companies. In wartime the battalions might serve together, but more likely one would remain home in Spain to support the battalion in the field and to provide cadres for the creation of additional battalions, which would eventually serve in the field, sometimes in company with a sister battalion and sometimes not. The colonial emergencies in the Philippines and Cuba resulted in a large scale mobilization. As a result, the local garrisons there, and in Puerto Rico, were augmented by troops from the motherland. Although there were slight differences among the various types of battalions—regular, colonial, peninsular, volunteer, expeditionary, provisional, and rifle—at full strength they had between 950 and 1,100 men, and were comparable to full U.S. regiments. Volunteer units were nevertheless in practice usually much weaker. The fourteen volunteer battalions in Puerto Rico averaged only 550 men. Of course combat often reduced the number of effectives, but even then the battalions rarely fell below about 500 men. In most cases, battalions in the field were reorganized to reflect the demands of counter-insurgency warfare. It was not uncommon for half-battalions to be employed. In addition, most battalions organized "guerrilla" companies by drawing volunteers from the ranks, plus a few from the local population. These were small (35-50) units specialing in irregular warfare, reconnaissance, raids, and pursuits. Usually a battalion had one mounted and one foot guerrilla company.

The organization of the other arms was not critical to the war. Attuned to the nature of counter-insurgency warfare, the Spanish forces in Cuba, the Philippines, and Puerto Rico were overwhelmingly composed of infantry. There were few cavalry, field artillery, or combat engineers, as can be seen from the accompanying table, which excludes volunteers, who were almost entirely infantry.

Distribution of Troops by Arm

Place	Cavalry	Artillery	Engineers	Infantry
Cuba	10 Rgts	18 Bttys	2 Bns	120 Bns
Philippines	1	6	1	28
Puerto Rico	-	1	-	6

Chapter III

The Santiago Expedition

The bottling up of Cervera's squadron at Santiago on Cuba's southeastern coast had a decisive effect on American strategy. During the last weeks of peace and the first of war a succession of tentative plans had been hammered out in a series of high-level conferences involving the service secretaries and the principal military and naval commanders, with the president having final approval. Like Lincoln at the onset of the Civil War, McKinley initially tended to accede to the proposals produced in this fashion. However, for a variety of reasons he began to take a more active role. McKinley was quick to recognize that the absence of a formal high level decision making mechanism, the administrative limitations of Secretary of War Russell A. Alger, the impolitic and erratic brilliance of Major General Nelson A. Miles, differences in organization and readiness between the Army and the Navy, and interservice rivalry, not to mention the demands of domestic politics, dictated greater involvement on his part. By the first week in May the president had approved a plan for an offensive against Havana to commence around the end of the month with the landing of the first of some 70,000 troops at Mariel, an operation in which Miles and other senior officers had little faith. Cervera's appearance off Martinique on 10 May caused the suspension of the operation. May 20 reports that Cervera was at Santiago resulted in the War Department proposing an expedition "within a few days," followed up on 25 May with a proposal to ship 30,000 troops to Cuba if the Navy could provide suitable escorts. The next day

Major General William Rufus Shafter, in civilian dress, which tends to minimize his bulk. A tall man, Shafter was also quite fat, some 300 pounds, and suffered from various ailments. As a result, his appointment to command the Santiago Expedition could be viewed as ill-considered. However it seems likely that few of the other senior officers in the Army would have done much better under the circumstances.

McKinley met with Secretaries Alger and Long, General Miles, and the Naval War Board, an advisory body which included several distinguished naval officers, most notably Rear Admiral Montgomery Sicard and Captain Alfred Thayer Mahan, to discuss strategy. The Havana operation was put off indefinitely, and the Army and Navy were instructed to undertake an expedition to Santiago followed immediately by one to Puerto Rico.

Orders began going out. While Miles alerted Major General William R. Shafter, commander of V Corps at Tampa, to have his 25,000 men, the bulk of whom were regulars, ready for immediate movement to Santiago, Secretary of the Navy Long informed Sampson to prepare to escort the invasion force from Tampa. They were to proceed south through the Gulf of Mexico, eastwards across the northern coast of Cuba, south again through the Windward Passage, and then west to Santiago. Definitive orders to move were issued on 31 May, when Shafter was instructed to effect a landing near Santiago, secure a lodgement that overlooked the harbor, and, in cooperation with the Navy, "capture or destroy the Spanish fleet ... ," setting the date of departure for 4 June. It was an appointment Shafter found impossible to keep.

The Expedition Sails

Shafter's inability to get the expedition underway as scheduled was due to a number of factors. He himself was part of the problem. Although intelligent and possessed of a good record in the Civil War and on the Plains, like most senior Regulars he had no experience in commanding larger formations. He was also 63 years of age, very overweight (someone once said he looked like "three men rolled into one"), and unwell, all of which tended to make him rather lethargic, although he could work with prodigious energy at times. However, Shafter was only part of the problem. The War Department and the Army were responsible for many of the problems which plagued mobilization. Procedures and resources geared to the needs of what was essentially a frontier constabulary rapidly began to show signs of strain as the number of troops under arms grew from barely 28,000 officers and men to over 260,000 in a matter of weeks. As a result, a lot of materiel was in short supply, the management of concentration areas was often faulty, and training frequently left something to be desired, matters complicated by the great speed with which the mobilization was effected. The great influx of volunteers overwhelmed the Army's capacity to care for them.

In this regard, Shafter's V Corps suffered less than the other corps in the Army, for it was composed mostly of Regular Army men, with a modest seasoning of the best of the volunteer units. By the end of May V Corps had about 25,000 men. Only about 10 percent were volunteers, comprising several infantry regiments and the 1st Volunteer Cavalry, the "Rough Riders." The preponderance of regulars at Tampa made life there much better than at any of the other concentration areas. Unlike the volunteers, even those with National Guard background, the regulars had a good grasp of camp sanitation. They pitched their tents in well drained areas, laid out drainage systems, dug proper latrines, and maintained strict camp discipline. But if Shafter's troops were an asset, his location was not.

Tampa had been selected as a concentration area when

Troops of Companies M and K, 22nd Infantry, falling in for Sunday morning inspection, at the regimental tent-city near Tampa. The simplicity of the American soldier's field kit is readily apparent.

tentative war plans envisioned the first operations against Cuba as little more than massive raids by 6,000-7,000 men. No other port in Florida with rail connections to the interior of the U.S. was closer to Cuba. When plans were changed to envision a major offensive, initially against Havana and then, after Cervera's arrival, against Santiago, the army was stuck in Tampa. Although it would have served to support the original concept of a raid on Cuba, Tampa was ill-suited to the needs of a major expeditionary force. Only two rail lines connected Tampa with the rest of the U.S.; both were single tracked and each belonged to a different company, which engaged in some remarkable petty feuding: At one point, one of the lines refused to permit freight cars belonging to the other to run on its track. Tampa had only modest marshalling facilities, limited sidings, and little warehouse space. The nine miles between Tampa proper and Port Tampa were served by a single track railroad. Such limited facilities made the management of supplies extremely difficult. By the end of May over a thousand freight cars

The V Corps embarking at Tampa for Cuba. The troops in the foreground are Regulars, as can be seen from the Krag rifles with which they are armed. The lack of dockside facilities is readily apparent.

were clogging rail facilities in the Tampa-Port Tampa area, and hundreds more were standing idle on sidings for hundreds of miles north of Tampa, some supposedly as far north as Columbia, South Carolina. Many of the freight cars had been dispatched without bills of lading, so that it became necessary to physically open them in order to determine what they contained. As if this was not confusing enough, the army had chosen to ship rations in bulk directly from the contractors. So although V Corps was supplied with some ten million rations, these were not neatly packaged and ready for distribution, but rather in scores of freight cars, each loaded exclusively with preserved meat, bread, coffee, sugar, salt, or other item. Shafter's supply staff had to locate the appropriate freight cars, prepare packaged rations, and then crate them up so that they could be loaded aboard ship, no easy task.

Port Tampa had one wharf, which could take nine transports alongside. The rail line from Tampa ran not along the wharf, but some 50 feet inshore of it, much of the intervening space being loose sand. Since there was a shortage of wagons, goods had to

Loading heavy artillery at Tampa for the Santiago Expedition. The V Corps had eight of these 5-inch siege guns. The lack of port facilities at Siboney—which was even less well provided than Tampa—caused them to be left aboard ship when the corps landed in Cuba.

be manhandled from the boxcars to the wharf. As the wharf lacked even the simplest facilities, loading had to be accomplished by ships' hoists.

Given time, the muddle could have been sorted out. But time was in short supply. On 26 May V Corps, which had not even existed a month earlier, began loading its equipment and supplies aboard transports, under orders to proceed to sea on 4 June. The Army Quartermaster Department had managed to charter 31 small freighters. These had been partially fitted out as troop transports, with rough bunks, simple kitchens, and improvised latrines. There were also a collier, two water tankers, a sea going tug, three steam lighters, and two barges. The freighters were brought alongside the wharf in groups of nine and loaded rather willy-nilly with whatever equipment and stores were available. They were then sent out to anchor in the harbor, as the next nine vessels came alongside. The last freighter did not complete loading until shortly after midnight on 7 June, by which time the 4 June sailing date had been long passed. Then

*A company of the 25th Infantry (Colored) marches into Key West.
They would later be transferred to Tampa. The troops are in full
field kit, but their elderly-looking officer is wearing a rather more
formal uniform. Note the children "marching along" beside the men.*

it was the troops' turn.

By 7 June it was clear that the available transports were only
going to be able to lift about 17,000 of Shafter's 25,000 men. As
the transports once again came alongside, regiments were
brought up from their camps in the vicinity of Tampa. These
movements were badly managed. Shafter's chief quartermaster
had made only the simplest preparations, and many regimental
commanders learned only by accident which ship their men
were to board, and the time they were to do so. As everyone was
anxious to go to Cuba, what little organization that did exist
soon broke down. Regiments competed with each other to board
trains and transports. The Rough Riders, camped outside
Tampa, had waited all night for their train. When a locomotive
pulled up, towing a number of empty coal cars, Lieutenant
Colonel Theodore Roosevelt, second-in-command, seized the
train. Hastily loading the cars with their equipment, the men
climbed aboard and off they went. When they reached the
wharf, regimental commander Colonel Leonard Wood and
Roosevelt searched for the chief quartermaster through the
swarming mass of troops while the Rough Riders remained in

Men of the 71st New York Volunteers entraining for Tampa. The 71st was one of New York's more fashionable regiments, and while most of the men in the photograph are wearing Army issue, the one in the upper left appears to be wearing the regimental uniform.

the cars. Within a few minutes Colonel C.F. Humphrey, Shafter's chief quartermaster, erroneously informed them that their regiment was assigned the steamer *Yucatan*, still anchored in the harbor, and suggested that they should "seize her instantly, if you hope to keep her." Wood commandeered a launch to get *Yucatan*, while Roosevelt remained at dockside. As he waited for *Yucatan* to come alongside, Roosevelt learned that the ship was actually assigned to the 2nd Infantry and the 71st New York. Acting quickly, he roused his troops from trackside and raced them to where *Yucatan* was coming alongside. As the Rough Riders began swarming aboard, the 71st arrived, having themselves just seized a train at bayonet point, with the 2nd close behind. With his men laughing and jeering at the latecomers, Roosevelt smiled, greeting them, "Hello, What can I do for you?" "That's our ship!" came the angry response. Roosevelt's reply was, "Well, we seem to have it." Rather than debate the issue, the 71st ran off to seize a transport of its own.

Thus did V Corps prepare for the largest overseas movement of American troops that had ever been attempted. Loading of men and equipment was completed by the morning of 8 June.

Nearly 17,000 men, some 1000 horses and 1300 mules, 34 pieces of artillery, and four Gatling guns were aboard the dangerously overloaded transports ready to put out to sea. And then they waited. Secretary of War Alger and President McKinley had both wired Shafter more than once to advise him to get going immediately. Then on the morning of the 8th, just as Shafter had dispatched word that the expedition was about to sail and was boarding his own ship, *Segurança*, the War Department wired, "Wait until you get further orders before you sail." Within hours, as the transports lay at anchor near the harbor entrance, Shafter was informed that several ships on patrol had reported the presence of Spanish warships. What came to be known as the "ghost squadron" totally disrupted the Santiago expedition. While the Navy detached heavy ships to search for the reported interlopers, V Corps remained at anchor off Tampa in the semi-tropical heat. The Navy quickly determined that the reports had been in error, the scouts having mistaken distant American ships for those of the enemy. But Admiral Sampson, who by now had brought the North Atlantic Squadron to support the Flying Squadron's blockade of Santiago, wanted to be sure none of Cervera's ships were still at large. He ordered Lieutenant Victor Blue to personally reconnoiter Santiago Harbor. To get Blue ashore and then escorted to a point from which he could observe the interior of the harbor safely, and then back to make his report—that all of Cervera's ships were indeed at Santiago—and inform Washington required four days. Aboard the idle transports, the troops began to suffer. Only very crude arrangements had been made to support the troops, as it had been assumed they would be aboard for no more than 36 hours. Surprisingly, despite the heat, bad food, and increasing filth, morale remained high. But the delay was causing Nelson A. Miles to have second thoughts about the wisdom of the expedition. Over the next few days he suggested changing its objective to Puerto Rico or to Nuevitas on the northern coast of Cuba, and proposed changing its route around the eastern end of Cuba to sailing around the western end. All of which suggestions were shot down by the Secretary of War and the President, both of whom were losing patience with him. On 12 June Shafter was informed that all was clear, and he arranged for the transports to rendezvous with the naval escort on the 14th. The expedition—some 16,300 men with 30 pieces of artillery and 6 machine guns, plus 2295 horses and mules, 200 wagons, and seven ambulances, not to mention about 89 journalists—was finally underway.

Off the Dry Tortugas, a small island group west of Key West, the transports met their escorts, the battleship *Indiana* and nine smaller warships, auxiliary cruisers, and armed yachts. The transports formed up in three columns on a front of about 1600 yards, with the ships about 300 yards apart in line ahead. The escorts were posted about 1600 yards ahead of and around the sides of the convoy. The voyage on "a sapphire sea, wind rippled, under an almost cloudless sky," as Theodore Roosevelt put it, was uneventful and on 20 June the expedition arrived off their objective, Santiago de Cuba.

The Spanish Preparations

Although one of Cuba's larger cities, Santiago was a sleepy colonial town of some 15,000 people, swollen by refugees to perhaps 25,000. It lay at the northern end of a broad, roomy, well sheltered harbor about four miles from the sea through a narrow, difficult channel. The harbor entrance is dominated by heights in excess of 230 feet on both sides, the Socapa on the west and the Morro on the east, both in turn overshadowed by the even higher Punta Gorda, looming over the channel behind them. In addition to a large number of obsolete pieces—some dating back to 1724—the harbor mouth was covered by eleven more or less modern coast defense guns and howitzers of 3.5-inch to 8.2-inch caliber, distributed in five batteries. The city was the headquarters of Lieutenant General Arsenio Linares Pombo, who commanded *V Corps*, which encompassed all Spanish troops in Oriente Province, some 35,000 officers and men. In and around Santiago itself Linares had only about 10,500 troops, comprising thirteen infantry battalions, four squadrons of cavalry, one battalion of field artillery, three companies of engineers, two transportation companies, a reinforced telegraph company, and a section of the *Guardia Civil*. The force was organized as a provisional division under Major

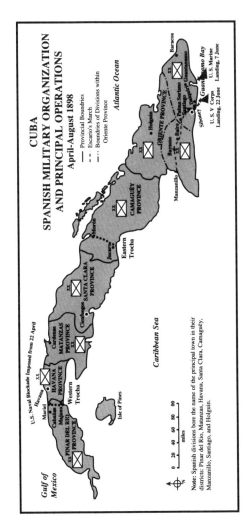

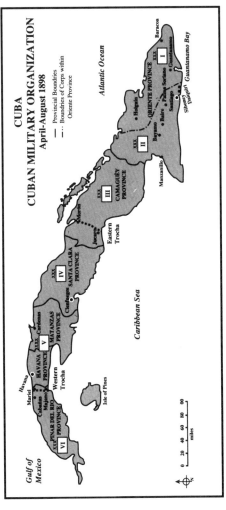

General José Toral Vasquez, with Brigadier Generals Joaquin Vara del Rey y Rubio and Antero Rubin as his principal subordinates.

As early as April Linares had been alerted by the Governor-General of Cuba, Captain General Ramon Blanco y Erenas, that Santiago was likely to be the object of an American attack. Security in Washington was so lax that newspapers regularly published details of high level decisions. That Santiago would be attacked became a certainty with the arrival of Cervera's squadron on 19 May. By then Linares had taken measures to enhance the defense of the city. Beyond strengthening existing defenses, and emplacing thirteen electrically detonated mines in two rows across the harbor entrance, there was little that could be done. Although a battalion of infantry had been called into Santiago from Guantanamo, and on 22 June Linares had ordered some 3700 troops brought in from Manzanillo, it was impossible to substantially strengthen the garrison, despite the presence of some 25,000 troops scattered across Oriente Province. Doing so would have meant abandoning vast areas to the insurgents. Nor could such a host have been fed. In normal times, Santiago was supplied by the farms, ranches, and orchards of its hinterland, but these had been devastated. Only one shipload of food had reached the city since the war broke out, and that on 25 April. In this regard, Cervera's arrival was actually beneficial; the ships had more than sufficient rations for their crews, and their guns could be used to support the defense. About a thousand sailors formed a naval brigade and entered the trenches under Captain Joaquin Bustamante, Cervera's chief-of-staff.

Linares prepared several defensive lines. The first was a mere outpost line, stretching along the coast from Daiquiri, nearly 20 miles southeast of the city, westwards for about ten miles across the most likely landing sites. Lightly held, its purpose was to harass American invaders, giving Linares time to identify the principal landing site and take action accordingly. The second line lay along a ridge running about eight miles southeast of the city, roughly parallel to the coast, and covering the only practical lines of advance from the coast to the city. Although there were a few fortified positions along the ridge, its principal

A contemporary engraving showing part of the Spanish lines at El Caney with surprising accuracy. The troops appear to be some of the Cuban volunteers who formed part of the garrison. They are wearing the Spanish Army's standard light weight uniform, with a straw hat. The black soldier in the foreground appears to be wearing leather shoes, rather than the more common rope-soled military sandal.

strength was natural. Relatively strong forces here would impede the American advance, inflict what casualties they could, and then pull back. On the northern and eastern sides of the city, running for about eight miles, was another outer line of defenses. Based on a series of *fortins*—entrenched blockhouses surrounded by barbed wire—and a number of fortified villages and hamlets, this line was designed to protect a railroad running north from Santiago and cover the city's water supply from attacks by Cuban insurgents. Its eastern terminus was the fortified town of El Caney, about five miles northeast of Santiago's outskirts, from which a thinner line comprising several *fortins* stretched southwards. The inner line of defense consisted of a series of trenches and blockhouses stretching from the harbor just northwest of Santiago in an arc curving eastwards and then southeastwards back to the harbor. Most of the works were within a half-mile or so of the outskirts of the city, but to the east they were nearly a mile-and-a-half distant on the banks of the San Juan River. Many of the larger works were linked by telephone to headquarters.

These works generally made good use of terrain, with positions laid out to provide mutual support and with an eye on maximizing fields of fire. Well constructed, mostly out of earth and timbers, the trenches and *fortins* were protected by barbed wire. The system capitalized on the traditional doggedness that characterized the Spanish infantryman. It had been developed through long experience and had repeatedly proven effective against Cuban insurgents and Moroccan tribesmen, who lacked the numbers and the artillery—not to mention the newly invented automatic weapons—to attack them effectively. Against a more modern foe they had not been tested.

The Landings

The convoy carrying V Corps arrived off Santiago on 20 June. As the ships lay off the coast, Captain French E. Chadwick, chief-of-staff to Admiral Sampson, boarded *Segurança* to explain Sampson's ideas as to how the troops should be employed to General Shafter. These were quite simple: Sampson wanted the army to seize the coast defense batteries on the heights on either side of the harbor entrance, so that the mines could be removed from the channel and the fleet could go in and destroy the Spanish squadron. Although Shafter was non-committal, Chadwick had the impression that he agreed with the plan. Actually, a direct assault on permanent fortifications did not appeal to the corpulent general. Shafter had already made his plans. He was familiar with the disaster which had attended British Admiral Edward Vernon's 1741 attempt to seize Santiago. Disease laid low so many of Vernon's troops that the expedition had to be abandoned before it reached the city. As Shafter later put it, "whatever we did at that season had to be done very quickly." He would attack Santiago from the east.

Later that same day Shafter and Sampson went ashore at Aserraderos, about 18 miles west of the harbor entrance, to confer with local Cuban commanders Generals Calixto Garcia and Jesus Rabí, in a thatched hut not far from the beach. Garcia commanded the II Corps, the largest and most important of the six insurgent army corps, in southwestern Oriente Province, where the rebellion was strongest. Although he probably had 15,000 men under his command, most of them were occupied in tying down Spanish garrisons all over the province, so that there were only 6500 men in the general vicinity of Santiago. Garcia recommended a landing at Daiquiri, 15 miles east of the harbor entrance. Shafter agreed, setting 22 June as the landing date. A simple plan was adopted. About a thousand Cuban insurgents would create a diversion by attacking Spanish troops in the vicinity of Daiquiri, while an additional 500 Cubans attacked Cabañas, three miles west of the entrance to Santiago Harbor, and the Navy made diversionary bombardments at other likely landing spots, and supported the troops at Daiquiri. Once the landings were completed, the Navy agreed to transport large numbers of Cuban troops from Aserraderos to Daiquiri and near-by Siboney to support the American expedition. Surprisingly, the Aserraderos conference did not disabuse the Navy of its belief that Shafter planned to attack the harbor forts. Although this had no serious effect on the outcome of the campaign, in other circumstances such lack of communication might readily have had disastrous consequences.

Daiquiri was a poor place. Little more than a village, its most substantial structures were corrogated iron huts. It lay on a modest cove and was endowed with a steel railroad pier and a small wooden dock which served to load ore from a nearby mine. There were some simple defenses, including several obsolete cannon, manned by about 300 troops of the *1st Talavera Peninsular Battalion*. As the transports dropped anchor off Daiquiri, the fleet laid down a heavy artillery fire, which quickly convinced the Spanish defenders to leave. As the Army was but ill-supplied with small craft to undertake a landing—V Corps brought with it only a small tug, three steam launches, and a barge—a second barge had broken its tow and been lost on the voyage to Santiago—the Navy lent its ships' boats and steam launches to aid in the landings. The first man to "hit the beach"— Midshipman Halligan of the armored cruiser *Brooklyn*—did so at about 1000 hours, and was greeted by a lone

Cuban waving a white flag. The debarkation of the expedition was if anything even less well-organized than had been its embarkation two weeks earlier.

The sea was choppy with strong swells running onshore, so the transports stood well off the coast. As the longboats were brought bobbing and rolling alongside the transports the troops jumped in, carrying their equipment. Steam launches took several boats in tow at a time, and brought them to the pier, which rose well above sea level. There the troops had to jump to the pier as the boats rose and fell in the sea. It was a dangerous business, and Corporal Edward Cobb and Private John English, of the black 10th Cavalry, missed their footing. As they fell into the sea, Captain William "Bucky" O'Neill, of the Rough Riders, who had landed earlier, jumped from the pier after them, followed by several others. It was to no avail. Weighted down by their rifles and accoutrements, the two sank quickly, drowning before they could be pulled to safety. They were the only casualties of the day, among the troops. Losses among the Army's animals were more serious. It being impossible to bring the transports alongside the pier, the Army's horses and mules were merely thrown overboard to swim ashore. Some of the animals panicked, and swam for the open sea. A quick thinking bugler sounded "right wheel," which brought many of the animals around, a number were lost, including Theodore Roosevelt's Rain-in-the-Face, drowned by a breaker while being lowered into the water. His Texas—or Little Texas—made it safely ashore. By 1800 hours, with night beginning to come on, a halt was called to the landing. Nearly 7000 men had gotten ashore, plus many tons of supplies, hundreds of animals, and several guns. Meanwhile, Brigadier General Henry W. Lawton, commanding the 2nd Division, had begun to push westwards towards Siboney, eight miles away, supported by Brigadier General John C. Bates' small Independent Brigade, while the balance of the troops ashore passed an easy night camped on the beach, with pickets out, and with the searchlights of the warships playing on the surrounding hills.

Guided by the insurgents of Cuban General Demetrio Castillo Duany's brigade, Lawton's column approached Siboney in the small hours of 23 June. The 600 Spanish troops there, who included fugitives from Daiquiri, pulled out without a fight, falling back northwestwards. The Americans quickly occupied the town, forming a defensive line around it. By mid-morning the balance of V Corps began to land, some at Siboney and the rest at Daiquiri. By late evening Shafter had ashore 17,000 men, 26 pieces of artillery, and four Gatling guns. But if the troops were ashore, much of their equipment was not. With only one barge suitable for the movement of bulk items, eight heavy siege guns had to be left aboard ship, as well as much tentage, many wagons, a good deal of ammunition, most of the Army's engineering equipment, and a lot of medical supplies. Making matters worse, the troops already ashore had begun discarding "unnecessary" pieces of their kit, like blankets and ponchos, items which would be needed later. It took some time to sort out the corps' supply situation. It seems clear that, although anxious to get the operation over with as soon as possible in view of the imminence of the fever season, Shafter wanted to delay offensive action until the balance of his supplies and equipment had been landed.

Las Guasimas

Shafter's instructions to Lawton were to entrench at Siboney if he encountered any opposition, and to cover the landing and concentration of the remaining troops and equipment. However, with Shafter still at Daiquiri, technically speaking the senior officer at Siboney by the afternoon of 23 June was not Lawton, but Major General Joseph Wheeler. A 62-year-old former Confederate lieutenant general with a considerable reputation as a cavalryman, Wheeler commanded the 2700-strong dismounted cavalry division. Upon arriving at Siboney, Wheeler learned from Castillo that there appeared to be a considerable force of Spanish troops—perhaps 2000 men well dug-in with some artillery—on the heights of Las Guasimas, which ran roughly parallel to the coast about three miles to the northwest, but suggested that the enemy might be preparing to pull out. Pressing forward to conduct his own reconnaissance, Wheeler decided that there were indeed Spanish troops at Las Guasimas. Brigadier General Samuel B.M. Young, commanding

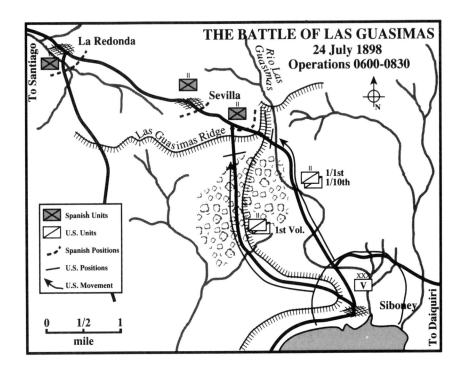

Wheeler's 2nd Brigade, proposed a reconnaissance in force for the next morning to feel out the Spanish position. Although such a movement was contrary to Shafter's instructions, that the troops entrench if they encountered resistance, Wheeler decided to undertake the operation. Although it is generally assumed that he did so in order to gain the distinction of being the first to encounter the Spanish on Cuban soil, a case could be made that he feared the consequences of a Spanish concentration so near to the beachhead. With Castillo agreeing to support the reconnaissance in force with 800 men, Wheeler ordered Young to take his brigade of Regulars of the 1st and 10th Cavalry Regiments, plus the "Rough Riders" of the 1st Volunteer Cavalry, about 1300 men, to attack the ridge. Young formed the troops into two columns, each about 500-550 men strong. The right hand column under his own command consisted of a squadron each from the

1st and 10th Cavalry, plus four 3.2-inch field guns; while the left consisted of two squadrons of "Rough Riders" with two Colt machine guns under Colonel Leonard Wood. In reserve Young held the remaining squadrons of the 1st and 10th Cavalry, as well as both squadrons of the 9th, borrowed from the 1st Brigade. Young's column was to advance along the main road from Siboney to Santiago, called the Camino Real, though little more than a country lane, while Wood's was to pass along a forest trail paralleling the Camino Real roughly a half-mile to the west. Young's intention was to unite the two forces before Las Guasimas and then use the Regulars to pin the attention of the Spanish to their front, while the Rough Riders struck on their right flank. Although called a "reconnaissance in force," the undertaking was actually an attack intended to throw the Spanish out of their positions.

The troops were quietly roused at 0300 hours. After a breakfast of hardtack and bacon, washed down with black coffee, they checked their equipment and formed in ranks. The attackers moved out at about 0600 hours on 24 June. During the advance, the Rough Riders with Roosevelt at their head on Little Texas, found the going tough. It was hot, the troops were more used to riding than walking, and numerous biting insects swarmed about them. Despite the slow going and the hardships, morale was good, and the men joked and laughed.

Spanish Brigadier-General Antero Rubin had some 1500 men available to defend the ridge of Las Guasimas. His mission was to impede the American advance for as long as possible to give the Spanish Army time to prepare Santiago for defense. He planned a delaying action, intending to fall back when things grew too hot. Accordingly, he deployed in three successive lines: the first on the crest of the ridge, the second a bit less than a mile behind that by the village of Sevilla, and the third about two miles further to the rear before the town of La Redonda. There were six rifle companies in the first line; three in the second plus one of engineers, one of guerrillas and two field pieces; and four rifle companies in the third, plus some mounted guerrillas. The companies in the first line had scouts well forward. The Americans, moving through the thick woods, failed to realize that some of the bird calls were made by human lips and not all of

*Leonard Wood, an army sur-
geon with a taste for combat,
parlayed his position as physician to the President and
personal friend to Theodore
Roosevelt to rise from captain to brigadier general in
the Regular Army—via com-
mand of the "Rough Riders"—
in only 22 months.*

the rustlings in the underbrush were made by land crabs.

About 0730 hours, the pointman of the Rough Riders, Sergeant Hamilton Fish, Jr., scion of a distinguished New York
family, came upon a corpse lying across the trail, a "landmark"
which the Cuban insurgents said would indicate proximity to
the Spanish lines. Fish passed word back to Captain Allyn K.
Capron, Jr., commanding the advanced guard and halted the
column. Colonel Wood ordered the officers to dismount and the
troops to load their rifles. Quite suddenly from out of the east
came the sound of a cannon, followed by a second blast, as the
Regulars went into action. Almost instantly Spanish troops on
the Heights before them opened a voluminous fire. The Rough
Riders, under fire for the first time, hesitated, then took cover as
Wood shouted, "Deploy!" As the firing grew heavier, Wood
ordered Roosevelt to take three troops into the woods to the
right and make contact with the Regulars. "In theory, this was

excellent," Roosevelt later wrote, "but as the jungle was very dense the first troop that deployed to the right vanished forthwith, and I never saw it again until the fight was over." Rather than lose the entire regiment in the dense growth, Wood formed the men under cover along the trailside and began moving forward. Within a short distance, the column came upon a clearing covered with high grass, and the troops took cover. Men began to fall. With the Spanish using smokeless powder, it proved difficult to locate them in the underbrush. Then one of the troops spotted them. With the enemy located, the troops began to fight back in an orderly fashion. As half a troop laid down covering fire, the other half advanced. When the moving half-troop went to ground, it in turn gave covering fire as the first half advanced. The regiment was deployed on a front of five troops, with three in reserve. Casualties mounted as bullets flew. Firing his pistol—salvaged from the USS *Maine*—Roosevelt took shelter behind a palm. Sticking his head out for a moment to have a look at the action, he was surprised by a Mauser round through the trunk of the palm that showered him with splinters. The Spanish began pulling back. By about 0830 hours, the Rough Riders had advanced several hundred feet, and found the bodies of Capron, Fish, and other members of the advance guard.

By this time the Rough Riders had gained the edge of the forest, with seven troops now deployed in line. Before them lay more open ground, sloping upwards to the heights of Las Guasimas. Above them a ruined farm house was being used by the Spanish as a strong point. Almost simultaneously, Wood, on the left of the Rough Riders' line, and Roosevelt, on the right, concluded that the farm must be taken. Snatching up a rifle from a wounded trooper, Roosevelt personally led the charge up the slope. By this time Spanish General Rubin, who had supported his first line with elements from the second and third, had decided to begin pulling his troops back to Sevilla. As the Rough Riders swept upwards, out of the woods to their right burst the lead elements of the 10th Cavalry with Captain John J. Pershing among them, and to their right the head of the 1st Cavalry.

The Regulars had also been surprised by the Spanish and suffered some casualties. But, well trained—many of the Rough

Riders had not fired their Krag rifles before the battle—and with more experience, they had handled the situation better. With the Regulars pouring on an enfilading fire, the Rough Riders were able to drive the Spanish rearguards from the vicinity of the farm. It was during this attack that Joe Wheeler, having learned that the heads of his columns were heavily engaged, rushed forward himself, and is alleged to have shouted, "Come on! We've got the damned Yankees on the run!," an incident which is almost certainly apocryphal, particularly considering that among the troops were the black regulars of the 10th Cavalry, the "Buffalo Soldiers." Although the two squadrons of the 9th Cavalry, another black outfit, soon came up the main road in response to an earlier request from Wheeler for support, the latter chose not to pursue the retiring Spanish. By about 1000 hours the action was over.

At Las Guasimas the Spanish conducted a very successful rearguard operation. Aided by a combination of sound tactics, favorable terrain, and American errors, General Rubín had inflicted a modest reverse on the attackers at small cost to himself. Spanish losses were 9 dead and 27 wounded; American casualties were 16 killed and 52 wounded, of whom eight of the dead and 34 of the wounded were Rough Riders, about 8-percent of those engaged. Afterwards, there was some criticism from Regulars to the effect that the Rough Riders had been ambushed and about their performance under fire. However, there had been no ambush, both the Regulars and the Volunteers had merely run into the Spanish outpost line. Moreover, considering the state of their training, the fact that many of the men had never had a chance to test fire their Krags, and that the regiment had never before been under fire, the Rough Riders had done pretty well. Surprisingly, although Shafter soon gave him instructions severely limiting his freedom of action (" ... do not try any forward movement until further orders."), little criticism was levied on Wheeler for disobeying orders. At the time, the action at Las Guasimas was not seen as a reverse, but rather as a victory: An apparently inferior force of American troops—men from all parts of the country, of all races and faiths, fighting together under a former Confederate commander—had driven an apparently superior force of Spanish troops from prepared positions. That the Spanish never intended to hold the heights of Las Guasimas (named after a clump of palm trees where the Camino Real crests the ridge) was unknown at the time, and generally ignored afterwards. Of course, the Spanish could have done more. Had Linares chosen to make a stand at Las Guasimas, concentrating a more substantial force than Rubin's 1500, he might have inflicted a severe reverse on the attackers, who would have found it difficult to get troops forward quickly, through the dense growth between the heights and Siboney. Although attempting a stand at Las Guasimas would have exposed the defenders to the fire of Sampson's warships, lying just offshore, the effectiveness of a naval bombadment at the ranges involved—7000 to 9000 yards—might not have been very great. As it was, after Las Guasimas the Spanish pulled back, not merely to Sevilla, the next possible defensive line, but beyond it, to El Pozo, and then beyond that to occupy defenses along the line of the San Juan River. That Linares did not chose to act in a more aggressive fashion on this day or any other during the campaign was fortunate for the Americans, who might otherwise have been seriously discomfited.

Las Guasimas boosted high American morale even higher. Shafter—still spending most of his time aboard the transport *Segurança*—ordered the corps to advance the three miles to El Pozo, a small, hilltop village just south of the Camino Real a little more than a mile from the main Spanish defenses along the San Juan River. It was an easy march, unhampered by Spanish resistance. In his diary Leonard Wood, colonel of the Rough Riders, wrote that the countryside was "as beautiful as a dream—great mountains green to their tops, valleys filled with coconut and great royal palms and all kinds of superb trees. Water is fine and at night you want two blankets over you." He added that the people and their dwellings were dirty. As V Corps settled into the Pozo position, its outposts forming an arc from the northeast around to the southwest, Shafter tried to clear up his increasingly serious logistical problems, and informed Sampson that he would move on Santiago "as soon as the command is all ashore, with sufficient rations and ammunition." There was much to be done, as most of the corps' heavy equipment and supplies still remained aboard ship. Unfortunately, facilities at Siboney and Daiquiri were so limited that little could be landed each day beyond basic rations and ammunition stocks, and what was landed could not be moved forward efficiently due to a shortage of transport and the inadequacies of the Camino Real. When the rainy season began the Camino Real turned into a muddy track, further impeding the movement of equipment and supplies. The troops at the front experienced shortages very quickly. In an effort to secure something besides bacon and hardtack, on 26 June Theodore Roosevelt took a detail of the Rough Riders and several pack mules down the muddy Camino Real. At Siboney they located 1100 pounds of beans. When informed by the quartermasters that the beans were reserved for officers' messes, Roosevelt wrote a request from the officers' mess of the Rough Riders for 1100 pounds of beans, and presented it to the quartermaster. After further dickering ("Colonel, your [30] officers can't eat 1100 pounds of beans!" "You don't know what appetites my officers have."), Roosevelt secured the beans.

Although logistics was the main impediment to resuming operations, there were others. Soon after the last of V Corps' troops were landed, the Navy began the transfer of Cuban insurgents from the west side of Santiago harbor to the east. The movement involving some 3000-3500 men was complex because the troops had to be brought off the beaches at Aserrados in small boats, then loaded aboard transports, which then had to steam out to sea, so as to give Sampson's blockading squadron off Santiago plenty of sea room, then steam back to Siboney, where the men had to once more transfer to small boats to be put ashore. Shafter also had to deal with the Navy. As late as 26 June, Admiral Sampson was still laboring under the mistaken assumption that Shafter had accepted his 20 June proposal that V Corps attack the harbor forts. Needless to say, he was surprised when Shafter informed him that was not his plan. Shafter envisioned using the bulk of the corps in a frontal attack against the defenses of Santiago, and that not before all of his supplies had been landed, a matter which would take some time. However, Shafter soon discovered that he had little time. On 28 June Shafter was informed that "General Pando, with 8,000 Spanish regulars, ... with an abundance of supplies in the way

Maj. Gen. William R. Shafter and his personal staff surveying the opening of the fight for El Caney, on the morning of 1 July 1898. The corpulent general can be readily seen on the right of the photograph. Behind him, in order to the left, are his staff engineer, an aide-de-camp, his orderly, and another aide.

of pack trains and beef on the hoof" was marching hard for the relief of Santiago. Such a reinforcement would give Linares more troops than Shafter had, a potentially disastrous development. So on the 28th Shafter issued orders to attack Santiago.

Shafter's plan included several separate operations. The battle was to open with an attack on El Caney, conducted by about 6500 men under Brigadier General Henry W. Lawton. El Caney, a fortified town, was well situated to enfilade an attack against the main Spanish lines on the Heights of San Juan, about three miles to the southwest. This operation was expected to take about two hours, whereupon Shafter would launch the main effort. The main attack would begin with 8000 men directly under Shafter attacking across the San Juan River to secure the Heights of San Juan so that, reinforced by Lawton's troops from El Caney, the whole corps could immediately continue on to capture Santiago. Two ancillary operations were planned to support these attacks. An hour before Lawton's assault on El Caney, Brigadier General Henry M. Duffield with 1200 men of the 33rd Michigan Volunteers, supported by several hundred Cuban troops, would undertake a feint across the Aguadores River, as if preparing an attack on the Morro Battery, covering the eastern side of the harbor entrance. Meanwhile about 3000 Cuban troops would cover the northern flank of the army to protect it from interference by the Spanish column reported to be on the march from Manzanillo. Aside from three troops of the 1st Squadron, 2nd Cavalry (mounted on some captured Cuban horses), and two batteries of 3.2-inch guns, there was no reserve. The only other U.S. troops available were about 1200 in the newly arrived 34th Michigan Volunteers, plus a few hundred engineers, quartermasters, and medical personnel at Siboney. Although Shafter admitted that the plan lacked finesse (it was, he said, "simply going straight at them"), there did not seem to be any alternative. Santiago was well-entrenched and there were no other options. A protracted siege was out of the question given the imminence of the fever season. A frontal attack might be costly, but would certainly be cheaper than the price which the fever would exact. At 1500 hours on 30 June Shafter set the attack for the next morning. The troops would have plenty of time to get into position, take a meal, and get some rest before dawn.

The Aguadores River

Brigadier General Henry M. Duffield got the 33rd Michigan aboard the light coastal railroad at about dawn on 1 July for the eight mile ride to the left bank of the Aguadores River, a small stream running through a deep gorge. Their mission was to capture the 700-foot long railroad bridge across the river and feint an attack on the Morro, about two miles further west, with the intention of drawing Linares' attention away from the main front. The attack was scheduled to begin at 0600, with a bombardment by Sampson's flagship, the armored cruiser *New York* and two lighter warships. However Duffield detrained his men more than a mile and a half from the river, forcing them to march through the densely wooded countryside. The troops finally arrived in position about 0900 hours when the Navy obligingly opened fire in response to the pre-arranged wig-wag flag signs. A skirmish developed, as the 400 Spanish defenders began firing on the approaching Americans. The Spanish had taken the precaution of destroying about 40 feet of the span near the western—their—side of the river. Although the firing continued for several hours, and Duffield tried to maintain the pretense of serious intent, the operation had clearly failed. The only serious injury inflicted on the Spanish appears to have been when a round from USS *Suwanne* knocked the flag from a small fort. U.S. losses were two killed and ten wounded. By 1330 hours Duffield pulled back his troops and entrained for Siboney. The impact of the day's efforts was slight.

El Caney

The small town of El Caney comprised a few score buildings and a couple of streets arranged around a central square. To the north, west, and southwest of the town was a series of six heavy timber blockhouses, while to the southeast was El Viso, a small stone fort which, with a stoutly built stone church, was the keystone of the defensive system. These positions were connected by trenches and covered by barbed wire. There were about 520 Spanish troops in El Caney, mostly regulars from the *29th Infantry Regiment*, plus a company of volunteer guerrillas. The garrison was commanded by Brig. Gen. Joaquin Vara del Rey. To reduce El Caney, Brig. Gen. Henry Lawton had available about 6500 men comprising his own 2nd Division, plus the Independent Regular Brigade under Brig. Gen. John C. Bates; D Troop, 2nd Cavalry, and Battery E, 1st Artillery under Captain Allyn K. Capron, Sr., father of the young Rough Rider officer killed at Las Guasimas. On the night of 30 June-1 July Lawton's troops bivouaced in three brigade camps, each about a mile southeast of the other. The first was less than a half mile east of El Caney, with the Independent Regular Brigade further back, between Sevilla and El Pozo on the Camino Real. Lawton roused his troops quietly before dawn, so that they could move into position for an attack at 0700 hours. Brig. Gen. Adna R. Chaffee's 3rd Brigade was to attack from the northeast and east, while Brig. Gen. William Ludlow's 1st Brigade would attack from the south and southwest, incidentally cutting El Caney off from Santiago. The attack would be supported by Capron's battery, firing from a height nearly a mile south of El Viso through the half-mile gap between Chaffee's left and Ludlow's right, and

THE BATTLES OF EL CANEY AND THE HEIGHTS OF SAN JUAN

1 July 1898, Situation about 1300 hours

(For clarity, units and command symbols have been simplified).

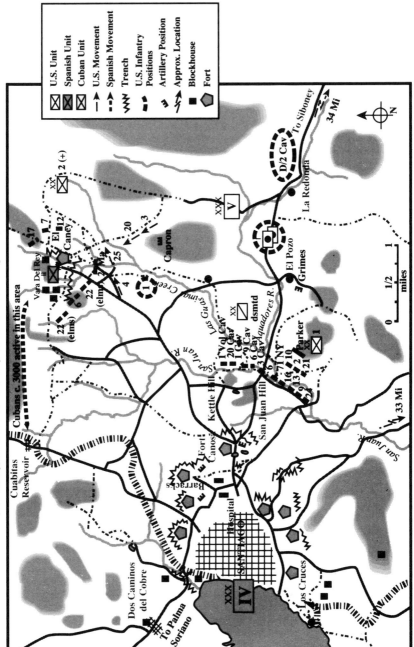

Legend:
- U.S. Unit
- Spanish Unit
- Cuban Unit
- U.S. Movement
- Spanish Movement
- Trench
- U.S. Infantry Positions
- Artillery Position
- Approx. Location
- Blockhouse
- Fort

some Cuban insurgents, who would close off El Caney from the north. Colonel Evan Miles' 2nd Brigade and Bates' Independent Regular Brigade would be held in reserve,

Capron's battery, four 3.2-inch field guns, opened fire at 0630 hours even as infantrymen were still moving into position. Although not at first clear, their fire did not prove effective. Not only was the range too great for such light pieces, but the rate of fire was too low. In addition, the black powder which the guns used generated clouds of thick smoke that blocked visibility. Nor did Capron direct fire efficiently. Many of the rounds were aimed at the town, rather than the works, and there were many "overs," rounds which fell beyond their targets. Meanwhile the infantry were within 600-800 yards of the Spanish works. At 0700 hours Lawton's infantry opened fire. The Spanish promptly replied, and very shortly a major firefight developed. It very quickly became apparent that El Caney was not going to fall easily. Since the operation was supposed to end quickly, in order for him to go to the support of the main attack on the Heights of San Juan, Lawton should have called off the attack. By screening El Caney with one brigade, he could neutralize it and still support the main attack with most of his division. Instead he persisted, committing his reserves.

The battle soon became a slugging match. None of the Americans—commanders, officers, or soldiers—had thought there would be much of a fight. Some had even supposed that the Spanish might flee. Instead, the Spanish proved tenacious in a desperate encounter. They maintained a constant, well-aimed fire, as the American troops—virtually all Regulars—got nowhere as they tried to advance through the tall grass. Hours went by, the stalemate continued, and casualties mounted.

The situation in the Spanish lines was little better, but their defenses offered somewhat more protection. Vara del Rey seemed to be everywhere, moving among the Spanish positions, constantly exposed to fire. He might easily have pulled out his garrison after bloodying the Americans' noses. But, he was aware that by pinning down as many of the enemy as he could at El Caney he improved the chances of victory on the Heights of San Juan. Vara del Rey fell at noon, his legs shattered, but resistance continued. At about the same time, Shafter, then

Spanish troops captured at El Caney on 1 July 1898. They appear to be regulars from the 1st Battalion, Regiment of the Constitution No. 29, *which formed the backbone of the defenders of the town.*

heavily engaged against the Heights of San Juan, realized his mistake in attempting two operations at the same time, and sent a courier to Lawton with orders to break off the attack. But an hour later when Captain J.C. Gilmore, Jr., reached Lawton, the latter objected. In a quick reply to Shafter, Lawton claimed that his troops were too heavily engaged to withdraw. Having no choice, Shafter withdrew the order. Meanwhile, Capron moved his battery forward about a quarter mile to shorten the range. When the bombardment resumed, over the heads of the men in Bates' brigade, it proved much more accurate, and El Viso took a serious pounding. At about 1500 hours Chaffee's left hand regiment, the 12th Infantry, stormed the ruins with support from the 3rd and 20th Infantry of Bates' Brigade and the 25th of Miles', breaking the back of the resistance. By 1600 hours El Caney was secured, although some snipers held out for nearly an hour more.

It was a bloody fight. Of the 520 defenders, only about 185 escaped, fleeing northwards through the Cuban troops, who had maintained only the slightest pressure on El Caney during the battle. There were about 38 dead, including five officers, among them not only Vara del Rey (who was awarded Spain's highest decoration, the *Cruz Laureado de San Fernando*), but also two of his sons, while at least 138 men had been wounded, among them Vara del Rey's brother and nine other officers. About 160 men had been taken prisoner, including many of the wounded. U.S. losses were higher, 81 killed and 360 wounded. It was a heroic fight, but an unnecessary one. El Caney could easily have been neutralized by a single brigade, with minimal casualties, while the balance of Lawton's force supported the main attack on the Heights of San Juan, making victory in that action more certain. By diverting nearly half his command to a secondary mission, Shafter had risked a disastrous defeat.

San Juan Hill

The Heights of San Juan lie nearly 3000 yards east of Santiago. The larger mass, usually called San Juan Hill, is about 1300 yards long on a north-south axis, and 200 yards wide. The smaller mass—later called by the Americans "Kettle Hill"—is about 650 yards by 200 yards. The area between the two masses varies from 200 to 400 yards with the intervening space partially taken up by a small lake. Although not very high, the heights dominate the most practical approach to the city from the east. Anyone attempting to attack Santiago would be forced to deploy in the open country in front of the San Juan River, a minor stream running roughly northwest to southeast, just east of the heights. Linares integrated the heights into his defense system with trenches and entanglements. Anticipating action on several fronts—the northwest where Escario's column was expected, the northeast at El Caney, and the east across the San Juan—Linares was forced to adopt a cautious plan of deployment. He committed only about 1700 men to the defense of the heights: 521 in the trenches on Kettle Hill and San Juan Hill supported by a few light cannon; with a further 400 or so supported by two guns, a 6.3-inch and a 4.7-inch, in reserve further back; and about 800 sailors at Fort Canosa, his headquarters halfway between the heights and Santiago. Most of the troops were from the *Talavera Battalion*, with three companies each from the *San Fernando* and the *1st Puerto Rico Battalions*, plus three companies of militia, a company and a half of sappers, 50 artillerymen, and the sailors from the fleet. In the town proper, available for use on whichever front they seemed most necessary were a further 3000 troops.

The 8000 American troops committed to the attack were from the Cavalry Division (now under Brig. Gen. Samuel S. Sumner since Wheeler had taken ill) and the 1st Division (under Brig. Gen. Jacob F. Kent). They spent the night of 30 June-1 July in bivouac, the cavalry near El Pozo and the infantry at Los Mangos. The troops were roused from their tents at dawn on the 1st. By 0700 hours Sumner's men were on the march, followed shortly by Kent's, with the four Gatling guns of 2nd Lt. Charles F. Parker's Battery L; 2nd Artillery brought up the rear, while Capt. George S. Grimes got his battery (A, 2nd Artillery) of four 3.2-inch rifled cannon into position on a rise just south of El Pozo, some 2500 yards from the Heights of San Juan. The plan was simple. Upon reaching Las Guamas Creek, a tributary of the San Juan, the Cavalry Division was to deploy on the right facing Kettle Hill, and the 1st Division on the left facing the Heights of San Juan from the southeast; the 1st Division's 2nd Brigade would constitute the reserve. When deployed, the two divisions would have a front of about 1500 yards facing the San Juan Heights. Then, with Parker and Grimes offering fire support, the troops were to assault the Spanish lines. While the bulk of the 1st Division attacked across the open ground southeast of the Heights of San Juan, the Cavalry Division was to attack across the San Juan River through high grass, overrun Kettle Hill, and then attack San Juan Hill on their eastern side. They were to be supported on the right by Lawton's Division, which would presumably have finished with El Caney and arrived in time for the 1000 hours jump off. While given the situation the plan was not necessarily the worst possible; there were a number of things which could have been done to improve the chances for success. None of the commanders involved, from generals on down to company commanders, had been given an opportunity to reconnoiter the line of march or the Spanish positions. In addition, the plan failed to commit all of Shafter's resorces. Two of his batteries, Capt. Clement L. Best's G, 1st Artillery, and

Capt. Charles D. Parkhurst's E, 4th Artillery, had been bivouacked so far in the rear that they could not possibly reach the
battle area until noon. Moreover, the assumption that Lawton
would arrive in time to support the second phase of the Cavalry
Division's attack was optimistic at best. And Shafter's timetable
was even more so.

The battle began at about 0800 hours when Grimes opened
fire on the Spanish trenches. Linares' artillery soon replied. The
Spanish guns, more modern than the American pieces, quickly
had the range of Grimes' pieces, whose position was betrayed
by great clouds of smoke generated by black powder charges.
Spanish shells began inflicting casualties on the American and
Cuban troops gathered about Grimes' position. By about 0900
Grimes ordered a cease fire. As the clouds of gunsmoke cleared,
the Spanish, deprived of their aiming point, ceased firing as
well. Meanwhile, the American troops struggled along the
narrow road.

At about 0930, accompanied by Lt. Col. Joseph Maxfield of the
Signal Corps, Lt. Col. George McC. Derby, of Shafter's staff went
aloft in a hot air balloon. (On the cutting-edge of nineteenth
century military technology, the 15,000 cubic foot rubberized
cloth bag required eight wagons and a crew of 32 to service and
operate.) From about a thousand feet, Derby had a panoramic
view of the unfolding battle. After he dropped several notes to
Shafter outlining his observations, Derby made a serious error.
When Maxfield suggested that they descend, lest they attract
enemy fire which could fall among the troops below, Derby
overruled him and ordered the balloon towed forward along the
line of march so that he could continue to observe the operation.
The Signal Corpsmen below winched the balloon down to about
100 feet and began hauling it along the crowded road, impeding
the passage of troops. By this time the operation was already
considerably behind Shafter's schedule. Lawton was still tied
up at El Caney with no end in sight, while the movement of the
troops of the main body to the front was already an hour late.

At about 1100 hours the troops finally were reaching the
planned line of departure, as the Cavalry Division deployed to
the right off the road. Firing was general. Spanish troops on
Kettle and San Juan Hills were engaged in blind firing on the

road based on their knowledge of the terrain, and exchanged fire with the Americans as they took up positions. The Signal Corps balloon was also attracting enemy fire. The Spanish were using the balloon, only 600 yards from their lines, as an aiming point. When their artillery opened up, shells landed among the troops crowding the narrow way. Meanwhile the punctured balloon sank to the ground. Derby, having observed a trail splitting off southwards from the main road just behind Las Guamas Creek, jumped out, located General Kent, and advised him of it. With congestion on the main road seriously disrupting his schedule, Kent promptly ordered his troops to use this trail. The 71st New York was his leading regiment. It was almost noon when the first battalion of the regiment successfully negotiated the narrow trail, some 800 yards long and in places only wide enough for one man. As the battalion deployed along the San Juan River, it came under heavy artillery fire. Within seconds more than a dozen men were killed or lay mortally wounded, with scores more less seriously injured. The troops took cover in adjacent forest. What happened next would be the subject of controvery ever after: Regular Army men claimed the regiment panicked, National Guardsmen claimed it performed well. Richard Harding Davis, the famous war correspondent who was present, later wrote, "The regiment did not run away, but it certainly did not behave well," observing that some of the officers—but not the men—"funked the fight." Whatever the case, the problem involved only the 1st Battalion, for even General Kent, its severest critic, wrote that to get the "panic-stricken" troops off the trail he "ordered them to lie down in the thicket and clear the way for others of their own regiment, who were coming up behind." In any case, the 71st was ordered off the trail into the thicket, and the balance of Kent's division marched past it. Finally, at about 1220, more than two hours behind schedule, the troops were in position.

The Cavalry Division lay to the right of the Santiago road. Its 2nd Cavalry Brigade, now under Col. Leonard Wood, was on the extreme right, which was held by the Rough Riders, who had their flank in the air (anticipating that Lawton's Division would arrive there shortly). Moving back towards the road were the 10th and 1st Cavalry Regiments. To their left, and slightly in

A fanciful depiction of the attack of the 71st New York Volunteers on San Juan Hill on 1 July. In fact the 71st advanced slightly to the right and rear of the 6th Infantry, and the troops were much less tightly deployed. The engraving reflects traditional depictions of Civil War tactics—early Civil War tactics.

front of the 1st Cavalry, was the 1st Cavalry Brigade, with the 9th, 6th, and 3rd Cavalry Regiments in line. To the left of the Santiago road lay Kent's division, its 1st Brigade having the 6th and 16th Infantry Regiments in line (the 71st New York being somewhat to the rear), and, still further to the left was Kent's 3rd Brigade, with the 13th, 9th, and 24th Infantry Regiments. In Kent's rear was his 2nd Brigade, still getting into position, accompanied by Parker's battery. The two other batteries that were to support the assault, Best's and Parkhurst's, were still struggling along the main road some three miles to the rear. The approach march had taken much longer than planned. And from their positions on the heights the Spanish had been laying down a heavy fire, with only a sporadic response from the Americans. The Spanish fire was primarily unaimed, but it was considerable and casualties were becoming heavy. In addition to the scores of men killed and wounded in the 71st New York, there had been other losses as well. In Kent's 3rd Brigade alone, commanding officer Col. Charles Wikoff had been killed shortly after noon while directing his troops into line. He was replaced by Lt. Col. William Worth, who was wounded within ten minutes (c. 1215) and replaced by Lt. Col. Edward H. Liscum, who was himself wounded within five minutes and replaced by Lt. Col. Ezra P. Ewers. Popular Rough Riders captain William "Bucky" O'Neill, who had tried to save the drowning men at Siboney just days earlier, was hit in the mouth as he walked the line and died instantly. But now that the American troops were virtually all in line, they began a sustained response to the enemy's fire. And they waited for Lawton to come up.

By 1230 hours, however, it was becoming increasingly clear that Lawton was not coming. And it was becoming just as clear that the position in which they lay was untenable. As Richard Harding Davis later wrote, "The situation was desperate. Our troops could not retreat, as the trail behind them was wedged with men. They could not remain where they were, for they were being shot to pieces. There was only one thing they could do—go forward and take the San Juan Hills by assault." But no orders had been received to do so. Roosevelt, commanding the Rough Riders since Leonard Wood had been jumped to brigade command, sent back a number of requests for permission to advance, as did several other officers. On the Santiago Road, General Sumner, several brigadiers, and a small herd of other officers anxiously awaited word from Shafter. With them was John D. Miley, Shafter's aide. In conversation with Sumner, Miley—whose regular army rank was that of lieutenant—agreed that, as Shafter's eyes and ears on the spot, the decision was his. Finally shortly before 1300 hours, he turned to General Sumner and said, "The heights must be taken at all hazards." The knot of generals and field officers broke up, as the men raced to pass the word.

The Rough Riders, at the "post of honor" on the far right of the V Corps' front, were deployed more or less under cover in several lines. Theodore Roosevelt was thinking that "in the absence of orders I had better 'march toward the guns.'" He had just made up his mind to do so when Lt. Col. Joseph F. Dorst, who in May had twice landed in Cuba on missions to supply the insurgents, came riding up "through the storm of bullets," as Roosevelt put it. Dorst brought "the welcome command" to attack in conjunction with the Regulars. Quickly mounting Little Texas, Roosevelt now began what he later called his "crowded hour." It was a little before 1300 hours

The American attack actually began in the center, as Kent's 1st Brigade under Brig. Gen. Hamilton S. Hawkings, just to the left of the Santiago Road, began advancing through the 300 yards of high grass that separated its line of departure from the base of the San Juan Hill. At the top there was a Spanish blockhouse. On the far right the Rough Riders, slightly to the rear of their brigade, were the first to get moving. Roosevelt, one of the few officers to take part in the attack mounted, began the charge behind the lines. His men passed forward through the regiment's successive lines, getting each moving, until they were in front of the others. Roosevelt at first rode back and forth across the front to urge the men on. In a quick conversation Roosevelt urged a confused lieutenant of the 10th Cavalry to get moving. When the latter hesitated, Roosevelt snapped "Then let my men through, sir!" The Rough Riders pressed on, joined by the 10th and then the 1st Cavalry, while further to the left the 9th Cavalry had already jumped off, to be joined by the 6th and 3rd. Initially the attack was across the flat bottom of the valley. Then, with Roosevelt waving his hat, the troops began sweeping up the slopes. From nearby Richard Harding Davis observed the attack.

> They had no glittering bayonets, they were not massed in regular array. There were a few men in advance, bunched together, and creeping up a steep, sunny hill, the top of which roared and flashed with flame. The men held their guns pressed across their breasts and stepped heavily as they climbed. Behind these first few, spreading out like a fan, were single lines of men, slipping and scrambling in the smooth grass, moving with difficulty...slowly, carefully, with strenuous effort. They walked to greet death at every step, many of them, as they advanced, to sink suddenly or pitching forward and disappearing in the high grass, but others waded on...a thin blue line that kept creeping higher and higher up the hill.

The charge was somewhat confused. As the two cavalry brigades overlapped, elements became intermingled. When the colorbearer of the 3rd Cavalry went down, that of the 10th took up the colors, bearing those of two regiments as the troops swept forward. By this time the troops were ascending the slope, some cheering. About 40 yards from the crest Roosevelt encountered a wire fence. Dismounting, he turned Little Texas loose and went ahead on foot, pistol in hand. Within minutes the hilltop was covered with troops, black and white, regulars and volunteers. As Spanish troops on the northern end of San Juan Hill, just to the west, began firing on them, Roosevelt got the men into a rough firing line, some taking shelter behind a huge iron kettle used in sugar processing, for which the hill was soon dubbed "Kettle Hill." It was a glorious moment. Rough Rider Sergeant Frank Knox later wrote that it "would live in my memory forever."

Despite the loss of Kettle Hill, the Spanish were doing well. Although heavily outnumbered, initially by some 16 to one, the terrain and their entrenchments greatly favored the defenders. During the fight, defending companies of the *1st Provisional Battalion of Puerto Rico* and some volunteers were reinforced by elements of the *1st Talavera Peninsular Battalion*, bringing the total to about a thousand. Linares himself had come forward to sustain the men on San Juan Hill, who had Hawkins' brigade pinned down in the jungle growth and tall grass to their southeast.

From Kettle Hill Roosevelt had "a splendid view" of Hawkins' brigade as it attacked San Juan Hill, about 500 yards off to the southwest. The brigade was having a rough time under heavy fire from the blockhouse on the lower end of the hill. He was the men pinned to the valley floor. In support, Roosevelt had his troops lay down volley fire on the Spanish positions for some minutes. Then, suddenly, at about 1315, the troops heard a "peculiar drumming sound." A momentary panic over "Spanish machine guns" quickly passed when it was realized that Parker's Gatlings were finally in action, sweeping the Spanish positions. It was Parker's fire which proved decisive.

Lt. Jules G. Ord, of the 6th Infantry jumped up, shouted

"Come on! We can't stop here!" and charged forward, with pistol and sword in hand. Hawkins' troops charged behind him. Surprisingly, the Spanish had dug in on the topographic crest of the heights, rather than the military crest (that line just below which offers the widest field of fire and no "dead ground" in which attacking troops can seek cover), and that, coupled with the supressive effects of the Gatlings and the Rough Riders' rifle fire, enabled Hawkins' men to sweep up the slope. As the attacking infantry reached the crest, the Rough Riders and the Gatlings lifted their fire. At ranges of about 700 yards, Parker's guns had swept the Spanish lines with thousands of rounds for just 8.5 minutes, enough time for the 16th and 6th Infantry to begin climbing the slope, with the 71st New York close behind. The rush of the attacking infantry, coupled with the beating they had taken from the covering fire, broke the will of the Spanish defenders, who abandoned their positions as the Americans crested San Juan Hill at about 1330. Ord—son of Civil War hero Maj. Gen. Edward Ord—was the first to reach the crest, and the first to fall.

Witnessing the storming of the southern end of San Juan Hill, Roosevelt decided to lead an attack on the northern end. Shouting an order, he leaped a barbed wire fence and started across the valley between Kettle Hill and San Juan Hill. He had covered about a hundred yards when he realized that only five men had followed. Believing that the regiment had chickened out in the face of the Spanish fire, he angrily raced back, only to discover that the troops "were quite innocent," not having heard the order. At that moment General Sumner came up. With the general agreeing that the attack was a good idea, Roosevelt once more leaped the fence, this time with the mass of troops, black and white, regular and volunteer, following behind. They quickly crossed the little valley, taking few casualties, for the Spanish were already abandoning the northern end of San Juan Hill to fall back on their prepared reserve line in front of Fort Canosa. As the Americans swept up into the Spanish trenches there was some brief fighting, with Roosevelt in the thick of it. The troops pressed on to occupy the crest of the hill at about 1400 hours.

Atop San Juan Hill, the American troops, described by

Roosevelt as "being completely intermingled—white regulars, colored regulars, and Rough Riders," began to dig in, occupying and adapting the positions just abandoned by the enemy in anticipation of a Spanish counterattack. But this never came.

Arguably, had the attack continued, the Americans might well have swept into Santiago. To be sure, the Spanish reserve positions about Fort Canosa were strong, indeed, better than those on San Juan Hill. However, in the case of an immediate assault, they would have to be held by the tired survivors of the fighting on the Heights reinforced by perhaps 300 fresh soldiers and many of Bustamante's seamen, no more than 1200 men, many lightly wounded. But the American troops were not in much better condition. Casualties had been heavy. The attackers had suffered 124 men killed and 817 wounded. Officers had suffered particularly, with 22 killed—including 11 in the 10th Cavalry, half the regiment's complement—and 94 wounded, even without counting such minor injuries as Roosevelt incurred when a Mauser bullet grazed his elbow. Spanish losses had been grave as well, with 58 killed, including 11 officers, and at least 170 wounded, among them Linares himself and Juoaquin Bustamante, Cervera's chief-of-staff, who had been commanding the *Naval Brigade*, was mortally wounded. Surprisingly, there were few prisoners, only 39. The total Spanish casualties, some 267 men, amounted to a third of the 800 troops involved in the action, a grievous loss. Although the Americans on San Juan Hill and the Spanish in their new lines traded fairly heavy fire until nightfall, the Battle of San Juan Hill was over.

The fighting on 1 July 1898 had been heavy and bloody. Taking all three actions together, Aguadores, El Caney, and San Juan Hill, the V Corps had suffered over 200 men killed in action and nearly 1100 wounded, almost 10 percent of the forces engaged. Spanish losses had been severe as well, about 35 percent of the forces engaged, including 215 killed and some 375 wounded, many of whom became prisoners.

The day had gone well for the U.S., but not by much. The ferocity of Spanish resistance had been very underestimated, and that had nearly led to disaster. Shafter's plan of operations was poorly conceived and certainly too optimistic. Rather than commit Lawton to two separate operations on the same day,

Shafter ought to have postponed the assault on Santiago by a day, until El Caney had been cleared up. The Spanish too had made errors. Certainly Linares should have put more troops on the Heights of San Juan. And he could have committed more artillery than the four or five pieces. As it was, he barely held on to the city. In the end, for the Spanish disaster was averted by the pluck of their troops in the defense, while the Americans gained a marginal victory, more by luck and courage than by skill. And even then, their objective had not been attained, for Santiago remained in Spanish hands. But the day's fighting did have an important strategic consequence. Even the limited success which Shafter's troops had gained threatened the security of the Spanish squadron in Santiago harbor. Shortly before midnight on 1 July Cervera began issuing orders for the men of the *Naval Brigade* to return to their ships. He was ready to run the American blockade.

Joseph Wheeler

Joseph Wheeler (1836-1906) was born at Augusta, Georgia, and graduated from West Point in 1859. Commissioned a second lieutenant in the Regiment of Mounted Rifles (now the 3rd Cavalry), Wheeler served on the frontier for a time before resigning in that rank on 22 April 1861 to accept a first lieutenantcy in the Confederate artillery. That September he became colonel of the 19th Alabama.

Wheeler led his regiment at Shiloh in April of 1862, and distinguished himself while covering the Confederate retreat on the 7th. He shortly thereafter transferred to the cavalry and in July was made chief of cavalry in the Army of Mississippi. He served in this capacity during Braxton Bragg's invasion of Kentucky, fighting at Perryville, where he covered Bragg's retreat, for which he was promoted to brigadier general. He again did well at Murfreesboro, which earned him a major generalcy in January of 1863. Wheeler led his cavalry with considerable skill during the Tullahoma and Chickamauga Campaigns, and conducted a spectacular cavalry raid after Union forces under Maj. Gen. William S. Rosecrans were bottled up in Chattanooga, virtually destroying Rosecrans' lines of supply in a nine day sweep (1-9 October 1863), though himself incurring heavy losses. Wheeler was again active during the Atlanta Campaign in 1864, conducting several important raids with the object of disrupting William Tecumseh Sherman's operations, and during the "March to the Sea" in late 1864, Wheeler's cavalry continually harassed Sherman's columns.

In February of 1865 the 28-year-old Wheeler—known as "Fighting Joe"—was made a lieutenant general, and served under Gen. Joseph E. Johnston in the Carolina Campaign, during which the lack of discipline in his command caused him to be superseded by Lt. Gen. Wade Hampton. Wheeler tried to make his way west after Johnston's surrender, but was captured near Atlanta in May. After the war he settled in New Orleans for a while, and then in Wheeler, Alabama, where he practiced law and raised cotton. He was several times elected to Congress, rising to chairman of the Ways and Means Committee.

On the outbreak of the War with Spain in 1898 Wheeler was made a major general of volunteers, as part of McKinley's conscious policy of using the new war to help heal the wounds of the old. He commanded the cavalry division in V Corps during the Santiago Campaign, with considerale courage but little distinction, doing poorly at Las Guasimas (24 June 1898) and being ill much of the time. After the war he continued in the service, retiring in 1900 as a brigadier general in the Regular Army. He held only two ranks in the regular army, second lieutenant and brigadier general. A dashing cavalryman, one of the best of the Civil War, Wheeler was by no means a great commander.

Leonard Wood

Leonard Wood (1860-1927) received an M.D. from Harvard in 1884, and was commissioned an assistant surgeon (medical first lieutenant) in the Army two years later. He served in a number of Indian Wars, including the Geronimo Campaign, during which he won a Medal of Honor for services as a combatant. In 1895, as a captain, he was appointed White House physician by Grover Cleveland, retaining the post when McKinley became president. He was a close friend of Theordore Roosevelt, who recommended him for command of the 1st Volunteer Cavalry on the outbreak of the war with Spain. Commissioned a colonel of volunteers, Wood organized and trained the regiment and led it to Cuba. He commanded it in the Battle of Las Guasimas, but shortly afterwards assumed acting command of the 2nd Cavalry Brigade, a post soon made permanent with a promotion to brigadier general. Appointed military governor of the city of Santiago, largely because of his medical credentials, he quickly brought order to the city's chaotic public services, greatly reducing the death rate from disease, and was shortly made a major general of volunteers and military governor of Santiago province.

In 1899 he was promoted to brigadier general in the Regular Army, and made military governor of Cuba. He performed his duties energetically, greatly improving public health on the island, while overseeing the demobilization of the Cuban insurgent army, a task made difficult by the fact that some of the former rebels preferred brigandage to peace. Relinquishing control of Cuba to an elected government in 1902, over the next few years he served as military attache to Germany and as a district commander in the Philippines, was promoted major general in the Regular Army, commanded the Philippine Department, and in 1910 was appointed chief of staff of the Army. His tenure in this post was acrimonious, as he pressed to strengthen the power of the chief at the expense of the bureaus, a battle which he ultimately won. After his term as chief of staff he held various administrative posts, helped organize the Plattsburg Program, in which upwards of 40,000 young men voluntarily underwent officer's training, and became a major advocate for preparedness.

When the U.S. entered World War I, Wood—by then the seniormost officer in the army—and Roosevelt proposed raising a volunteer division, an idea that was vetoed by John J. Pershing with the enthusiastic support of Woodrow Wilson. Although he tried repeatedly to get overseas, Wood spent the entire war stateside, first as commander of the 89th Division and then, when it shipped out, as commander of the 10th Division.

After the war he attempted to secure the Republican nomination for the presidency in 1920, losing to Warren Harding. Harding gave him the civilian post of governor of the Philippines, which he still held at the time of his death.

Wood was an excellent soldier,

both administratively and in combat. He actually walked through Spanish fire to the top of San Juan Hill, pausing now and again to tend the wounded while directing the bat-

tle. In action he wore khaki breeches with a gray shirt and no insignia, carrying no weapon except a riding crop, and his medical kit. He rode a horse named Charles Augustus.

The Rough Riders

One of the most famous military organizations in American history, the Rough Riders—more formally the 1st Volunteer Cavalry Regiment—had its origins in the President's first call for volunteers. No quota was assigned to the western territories, Arizona, New Mexico, and Oklahoma. The governor of Arizona objected, saying there were men aplenty willing to volunteer in the territories, each of which had a National Guard. As a result, legislation was passed authorizing the raising of three regiments of volunteer cavalry. Knowing that Theodore Roosevelt was looking for a commission, Secretary of War Russell A. Alger offered command of the first of the three regiments to him. Roosevelt, in an uncharacteristically modest gesture, refused on the grounds of lack of experience, suggesting that Leonard Wood, an army surgeon with a hankering for serious soldiering, be given command, with himself as lieutenant colonel. This was done. Almost immediately Wood departed for San Antonio to begin organizing the regiment, while Roosevelt remained behind in Washington to take care of bureaucratic infighting.

Recruiting for the regiment proved remarkably easy. As soon as

word went out that Wood and Roosevelt, both already well known figures, were raising a regiment, the men poured in by the thousands. Over 2300 volunteered in the first 48 hours, of whom 1,200 were accepted. More than a quarter of the men—362—were from the territories. A handful were eastern dudes, college athletes, professors, playboys, and the like (Roosevelt took them aside and lectured them about pitching in and getting dirty). There were miners, soldiers, cowboys, sailors, lawyers, preachers (seven of them), physicians, and farm boys, plus about 60 Indians. They came from all 45 states, all three territories, and ten foreign countries. Remarkably for so hastily organized a collection of rugged individualists, there was not a single discipline case in the regiment from its activation in San Antonio to its deactivation at Camp Wikoff at Montauk Point, N.Y.

At Wood's urging, Roosevelt procured for the regiment Krag carbines and the army's standard fatigue uniform, so that it would be armed and equipped in conformity with the regular cavalry regiments, and thus be more likely to be brigaded with them, and to see action. While Roosevelt scrounged up this equipment, the men drilled with wooden sticks—some did not receive their carbines until they were aboard the transport *Yucatan*, and many were issued machetes rather than sabers, which proved more useful anyway. Only about half of the regiment went overseas, and aside from the senior officers none of them had horses.

In Cuba the regiment fought at Las Guasimas and on the Heights of San Juan, at the latter under Roosevelt's command, Wood having been given the brigade. The Rough Riders incurred higher losses than any other American unit in the war. Of approximately 600 men who went to Cuba, 23 were killed or mortally wounded and 104 were less seriously wounded, a casualty rate of 21 percent, while casualties from disease numbered nearly as many. An extraordinary record for a regiment which had an active life of only 133 days!

Arsenio Linares y Pombo

Arsenio Linares y Pombo (1848-1914) entered the army as a sub-lieutenant in 1860 at the age of 12. He attended the artillery academy from 1863-1866, graduating as a lieutenant of infantry. His next four promotions were all gained through merits of war. From 1867 through 1870 he was involved in operations against republican separatists and Carlists in Cataluña, La Mancha, and the Basque region. He spent most of 1872-1874 fighting insurgents in Cuba, returning to Spain in 1874 to fight in the closing campaigns of the civil wars, and was made an aide-de-camp to the Minister of War. In 1875 he went to Cuba, where he served in the field until 1878, earning a merit promotion to colonel for the battle of Arroyo del Gato.

As good an organizer and administrator as he was a field commander, over the next few years he held a series of important special assignments, including command of the Guardia Civil in the Philippines (1883-1885), membership on a commission to reform the military justice system (1887), as a section chief at the war ministry (1887), and as chief of the commission reorganizing the recruiting service, meanwhile rising to brigadier general. In 1893 he commanded a brigade with some distinction in an otherwise lackluster campaign in Morocco.

Linares was sent to Cuba early in 1895. He held various commands, and was generally successful against the insurgents, helping to clear them out of Pinar del Rio province and earning a promotion to major general. In May of 1896 he was assigned command of the division holding Santiago. Promoted lieutenant general in April of 1898, he was shortly named commander of the corps, responsible for all operations in eastern Cuba, in which post the war found him.

During the Santiago Campaign Linares acted with considerable caution. Although he conducted an energetic defense, he undertook no initiatives, which might seriously have discomfited the American invaders. The fighting on 1 July, caused him the loss of an arm, and he was forced to relinquish command to Maj. Gen. Jose Toral. This kept his reputation free of the stain of having surrendered in the field, and he thus avoided a court martial.

After the war Linares continued in service for many years, holding a variety of increasingly important posts, including director general of the Guardia Civil (the Spanish national police), president of the Supreme War Council, and minister of war, while being promoted to captain general and appointed a senator.

One of the best officers in the Spanish Army, Linares was brave and hard-working rather than brilliant.

Joaquin Vara del Rey y Rubio

Joaquin Vara del Rey y Rubio (1840-1898) was born into an old military family from Ibiza in the Balearic Islands. He entered the infantry academy at Toledo at the age of 15, and emerged in 1858 as a second lieutenant. He spent the next few years in garrison, meanwhile rising to first lieutenant. Vara del Rey participated in the complex series of insurrections and civil wars which plagued Spain from 1868 through 1876, rising to major. Promoted to lieutenant colonel in 1884, he was sent to the Philippines, where he spent six years and earned a merit promotion to colonel in action against Moro tribesmen. Returning to Spain in 1890, he spent five years as chief of a recruiting zone. He apparently did not like this duty, for when the Cuban Revolution broke out Vara del Rey was one of the first four officers to volunteer for service.

Vara del Rey, who was rather short, quite thin, and had a scraggly white mustache and goatee, greatly distinguished himself in action in Cuba, winning notable acclaim for the Battle of Lomo del Gato, in which Antonio Macías, the best Cuban commander, was killed. Promoted to brigadier general, he was given a brigade under Linares in Santiago Province. Scheduled to be rotated home due to illness when the Spanish-American War broke out, he voluntarily returned to active duty and met his death conducting the heroic defense of El Caney on 1 July 1898, holding off far superior numbers for most of a day, an action in which two of his sons also perished and his brother was severely wounded. The only general on either side in the war to garner any personal glory, he was so hated by the Cubans that they attempted to hide his body when the Spanish Army requested that it be returned to Spain, yielding it up only after First Lieutenant M.E. Hanna, an American staff officer, applied considerable pressure ("Lead us there or I'll blow your head from your shoulders.").

Escario's March,
22 June - 3 July 1898

One of the most extraordinary feats of arms during the Spanish-American War was the cross-country march of some 3,750 Spanish troops from Manzanillo to Santiago.

Anxious to reinforce Santiago before it was invested by the Americans, on 20 June Linares ordered the commander of the Manzanillo Division to send a relief column. The division commander in turn ordered Col. Federico Escario Garcia, a veteran infantry officer on his staff, to organize and lead the column.

Escario quickly put together a column comprising five infantry battalions, three companies of mounted guerrillas, and a section of two 80-mm (3.15-inch) guns, plus some engineer, medical, and transportation troops, the latter leading 198 mules heavily ladened with ammunition and rations. Wise to the problems of campaigning in a tropical environment, Escario adopted a pattern of resting his men during the heat of the day, preferring to march for several hours each morning and evening. The column set out in the early evening of 22 June. Catching the insurgents by surprise, the column had a good march that day, suffering no casualties. But that was only the beginning.

Escario's March

Date	Events
22 Jun	Departed Manzanillo at 1700 hours
23 Jun	Harassment by Cuban guerrillas
24 Jun	Harassment by Cuban guerrillas
25 Jun	Rain showers; harassment by Cuban guerrillas
26 Jun	Bayamo reached, amid skirmishes with the Cubans
27 Jun	Continuous skirmishing along the line of march
28 Jun	Very heavy fighting, including a sharp combat at the Rio Jiquani, which Escario crossed by means of a double envelopment, and skirmishes at Yarey and Baire, which was occupied
29 Jun	The column rested at Baire, under some harassment
30 Jun	The march resumed; combats at the Rio Contramuestre and La Mantonia
1 Jul	Very sharp combat at Aguacate (7 Spaniards killed and 43 wounded, with 17 known Cuban dead)
2 Jul	A sharp hot combat at Palma Soriano, where the column spent the night
3 Jul	Considerable harassment along the final stretch into Santiago, the advanced guard arriving at 0400 hours, and the rear guard at 1000.

Altogether the column clashed with the Cubans between 40 and 45 times, firing a total of 24,000 rounds of rifle ammunition and 38 of artillery. During the march Escario lost 27 men killed, 71 wounded, and about 250 missing, many of them troops who dropped out from physical exhaustion and illness, usually to an uncertain future. Cuban casualties are unknown, but at Bayamo and Aguacate, Escario made a "body count," totalling 22 Cuban dead and nine wounded and captured.

Despite its heroic character, the military consequences of Escario's march were mixed. On the one hand, poor American intelligence attributed to the column about double its actual numbers and so caused Shafter to move up his timetable for an assault on the defenses of Santiago by several days to 1 July, which resulted in inadequate preparations and problems during the assaults on El Caney and the Heights of San Juan. On the other hand, Escario—who was immediately promoted to brigadier general—arrived just too late to bolster the defenses of Santiago during the crucial battles, and

his arrival merely strained the logistical resources of the garrison. Although the Cuban insurgents are usually credited with slowing Escario down long enough to prevent his arrival at Santiago before the critical fighting on 1 July, it is difficult to see how his rate of advance could have been much greater given the physical obstacles he had to confront.

Escario's column marched some 205 miles, considering what Napoleon referred to as "the minor sinuosities of roads." The march was across mountainous terrain, often requiring a trail to be cut through dense growth, all the while under almost continuous harassment by Cuban forces. Excluding the day of rest at Baire on 29 June, and considering that the column departed Manzanillo at 1700 hours on 22 June and reached Santiago at 0400 hours on 3 July, the troops maintained a sustained rate of march of nearly 20 miles a day. An impressive feat by any standard.

Chapter IV

The Naval Campaign of Santiago

Confirmation of the presence of the Spanish fleet at Santiago on the morning of 28 May 1898 (received in Washington on the 29th) brought about a major change in the character of the naval campaign, as the fleet began moving to reinforce the blockade. On the 30th Schley received orders from Secretary Long to "hold on at all hazards," and informing him that Sampson was en route. On 31 May there was a brief clash, as Schley belatedly decided to engage *Cristobal Colon*, still lying in the channel, under the harbor forts. At about 1400 the battleships *Iowa* and *Massachusetts* and the cruiser *New Orleans* steamed into range to engage the Spanish cruiser and the forts. The American ships opened up at about 7000 yards, an enormous range, and the Spanish promptly responded. Although the Americans ceased firing after only ten minutes, the Spanish kept it up for nearly an hour. There were no casualties on either side. Sampson arrived off Santiago the next evening, with the battleship *Oregon*, the armored cruiser *New York*, the yacht *Mayflower*, and the torpedo boat *Porter*. This brought the American fleet off Santiago to four battleships, two armored cruisers, three cruisers, and several small warships, plus two colliers—a force far superior to Cervera's. However, perhaps even more valuable than the additional ships was the presence of Sampson. Where Schley had been overcautious and hesitant (a postwar inquiry concluded he had shown "vacillation, dilatoriness, and lack of enterprise" during those last days of May), Sampson proved himself able to act with decision. He quickly decided that an attempt to run past the forts in order to get into Santiago harbor was too risky. Not only would the squadron have to negotiate a narrow and tortuous channel while subject to heavy fire from the Spanish coast defense installations, but the way was known to be mined. He also preferred not to have to lie off Santiago for the weeks and possibly months that it would take for an army to land, invest the city, and reduce it by storm or siege. Such were his conclusions even before arriving off Santiago. Instead, he had a simple, elegant, and dangerous solution to the problem of eliminating the Spanish fleet: he would sink a blockship in the harbor entrance, thereby preventing the Spanish from coming out even if the fleet were not lying just off shore. Even before Cervera's presence at Santiago had been confirmed Sampson had begun making preparations for the operation.

The *Merrimac* Affair

Richmond Pearson Hobson, a 27-year old assistant naval constructor, was entrusted with the task of sinking a blockship in the Santiago channel on 29 May. Hobson made meticulous plans for his mission. At the bow and stern of the ship anchors were set lashed over the sides with ropes so that they could be dropped in an instant with one or two blows from an axe. Along the port side of the ship ten 78-pound explosive charges were affixed, each two fathoms below the waterline, at approximately 30 foot intervals. Hobson's plan was simple. With a small volunteer crew, he would run the ship into the channel by moonlight, when there was a running tide. At the narrowest point—and the channel was only 350 to 450 feet wide—the bow anchor would be cut loose and the engines stopped, so that the ship's stern could swing around until she was athwart the channel, whereupon the stern anchor would be dropped and the charges exploded electrically, ripping open the ship's side. As the ship settled to the bottom the crew would make its getaway in small boats or by swimming to shore.

Hobson arrived off Santiago with Sampson on 1 June. Although he originally intended to attempt blocking the channel around 0330 on the 2nd, just after moonset, this proved impossible, as there was insufficient time to prepare the blockship, the collier *Merrimac*. Some 200 sailors had worked through the day and well on 'til dawn getting her ready, but by then the moment had passed, so Sampson ordered the attempt made for 0300 on the 3rd. The delicate question of who could go along on the dangerous mission created problems, as everyone wished to go. Aboard the battleship *Iowa* every one of her 34 officers and 646 men volunteered, but only one was allowed to go, chosen ultimately by the toss of a coin, and he refused an offer of $50.00 from someone to take his place. In addition to Hobson, six men were chosen: Daniel Montague and George Charette, petty officers off the armored cruiser *New York*; Osborn Deignan, coxswain, John F. Philips, machinist, and Francis Kelly, water tender, all off *Merrimac*; and J.C. Murphy, coxswain and lucky winner of the coin toss aboard *Iowa*. Caught up in the fervor of the moment, Coxswain Rudolph Clausen of *New York* stowed away, becoming thereby the seventh member of Hobson's crew, all old Navy hands and all older than Hobson.

Merrimac began her run into the Santiago Channel at about 0300 from a position 2000 yards off the entrance. Bringing her speed up to the maximum 9 knots, Hobson steered right for the entrance. At about 500 yards a Spanish picket boat opened fire on the ship's rudder. Two rounds missed, then a third hit the ship's superstructure, causing slight damage. Other Spanish guns began firing. With the Morro just two ship lengths ahead, Hobson ordered the engines stopped and relied on momentum to bring the ship into position. As she glided beneath the cliffs, *Merrimac* was subject to increasing light artillery and machine gun fire. At just 30 feet Hobson ordered the bow anchor dropped. As Coxswain Murphy chopped through the line to drop the anchor, Hobson ordered the first charge detonated, then the second, and ordered the wheel put hard over to port. But there was no response. The rudder having been shot away. Then the stern anchor was shot away. The bow anchor line parted. Hobson ordered other charges detonated, but they failed to go off, after Spanish fire had apparently cut the wires. The ship was sinking, but too slowly and at too poor an angle to block the channel. She drifted on. The Spanish detonated a mine

An artist's impression of Lt. Richmond Hobson's attempt to scuttle the collier Merrimac *in the channel into Santiago Harbor on 3 June 1898. Among the more obvious inaccuracies is the fact that the attempt is depicted as occurring in daylight.*

close by, but it only shook the ship; several others had no effect. The *Merrimac* drifted on, target of numerous bullets and shells. Further up the channel, cruisers *Vizcaya* and *Reina Mercedes*, and the torpedo boat *Pluton* took her under fire. Then, quite suddenly, the ship gave a lurch, fell off to port, and her bow angled downwards in a final plunge. Hobson and his men—all miraculously uninjured—abandoned ship, jumping overboard and swimming to floating debris. Within minutes *Merrimac* had settled on the bottom, with her upperworks just above water, in the center of the channel, about where it broadened into Santiago harbor, offering only a minor hazard to navigation. From the start of his run into the channel, to the moment when he abandoned ship, Hobson's mission had taken little more than a half hour.

The Spanish shoved off from shore in small boats, searching for the crew with lanterns. When Hobson gathered his men around a raft, amazingly, they were all there and none had suffered any injury, despite the intense fire from enemy ships and batteries, fire which had inflicted numerous casualties among the Spanish. They drifted quietly for more than an hour, until dawn. Then Hobson hailed a passing Spanish launch. In a coincidence so remarkable a novelist would be embarrassed to use it, the launch was Cervera's own gig, and the old admiral himself helped Hobson and his men out of the water, crying "¡Valiente!—Heroic!" Indeed, so impressed was Cervera by the deed that he took the unprecedented step of sending a ship under flag of truce to inform the Americans that Hobson and his men were all safe. But as heroic as the mission had been, it had failed.

The failure to block the channel into the harbor doomed the American fleet to a long blockade of Santiago. On the morning of 12 June, escorted by Cuban insurgents, Navy Lieutenant Victor Blue confirmed that all of the Spanish ships were indeed present at Santiago by the simple expedient of counting them from a vantage point northwest of the city. This meant that every American ship had to be available off Santiago, in the event of a sortie. Thus, the presence of the Spanish squadron inside Santiago Harbor kept the American one outside just as firmly as the Americans kept the Spanish inside. It was tedious, wearing, and dangerous work. One of the most dangerous aspects of the work, the possibility of engaging the enemy aside, was coaling.

To take on coal at sea required a collier to come alongside, so that heavy sacks of coal could be manhandled from one ship to the other. In the best of circumstances it was a lengthy, difficult process, fraught with danger, as men might easily fall overboard in the process, to be crushed between the two hulls. What was needed was a safe anchorage. Even before the presence at Santiago of the Spanish fleet had been confirmed, Captain Sigsbee—formerly of the ill-fated *Maine* and now of the auxiliary cruiser *St. Paul*—wrote the Secretary of the Navy that Guantanamo Bay, about 45 miles east of Santiago, a broad, well protected inlet "should be seized, and the shores garrisoned by United States troops," to serve as a coaling station and supply base. On 3 June the Navy Board approved the capture of the bay, issuing instructions for the 1st Marine Battalion at Key West to undertake the mission.

Guantanamo

The 1st Marine Battalion, five rifle companies and one battery of four 3-inch guns, was organized at the Brooklyn Navy Yard on 20 April from Marines collected from East Coast navy yards. It shipped out for Key West on 22 April, 653 men strong (20 percent of the entire Marine Corps) under Lt. Col. Robert T. Huntington, a Civil War veteran and the second ranking man in the corps. At Key West the Marines remained quartered aboard the transport *Panther* until 23 May, when the ship was assigned other duties. Each morning the Marines had been ashore for several hours of intensive drill and training, since many of the enlisted men were new recruits. Now they established a proper camp and training was intensified. Finally, on 7 June came orders to embark for duty. The men reboarded *Panther*, and shaped course for Guantanamo. That same day, the cruisers *Marblehead* and *Yankee* steamed into Guantanamo Bay. They had a brief skirmish with the feeble coast defenses and the gunboat *Sandoval*, which quickly withdrew into the inner bay to the town of Guantanamo. Then a party of Marines and sailors landed at Playa del Este to destroy the cable station. With Marine Capt. M.C. Goodrell in command, they performed this duty and then conducted a brief reconnaissance of the area. The two cruisers then lay off the harbor to await the Marines. *Panther* arrived off Santiago early the next day. Lt. Col. Huntington was given his orders by Admiral Sampson, who placed Commander Bowman H. McCalla of *Marblehead* in command of the expedition. The Marines rendezvoused with *Marblehead* that afternoon. Later the Marines came ashore on the east side of the harbor entrance. As the 1st Company formed a skirmish line, the balance of the battalion made camp on a site selected by Capt. Goodrell on a hill rising 150 feet. Aside from an old blockhouse and a few muzzle-loading coast defense guns, all of which showed signs of having been hastily abandoned, there was no evidence of the Spanish. Surprisingly, although there were several battalions of Spanish troops based at Guantanamo, 12 miles distant, the Marines spent a quiet night. Huntington later wrote, "We went ashore like innocents and made a peaceful camp and slept well on the tenth." The next morning the Marines off-loaded their

An artist's impression of the defense of the Guantanamo beachhead by Lt. Col. Robert T. Huntington's 1st Marine Battalion, 10-14 June 1898. The Leathernecks are using the Navy's standard Winchester-Lee Model 1895 6mm rifle.

heavy equipment. Meanwhile, Huntington expressed doubts about the camp site, which was surrounded by dense underbrush and forest, dominated by a much higher ridge just 1100 yards to the northwest. Surprisingly, Huntington did not move to occupy the ridge. The Spanish made their presence known late that afternoon.

At about 1700 two Marines on outpost duty were killed by sniper fire. Huntington sent out a patrol, but it was unable to locate the enemy. Despite the danger, Huntington remained confident. Over the next few hours there were five skirmishes with the Spanish, all minor affairs. Then, at about midnight, the Spanish undertook a more energetic campaign of harassment, touching off nearly four days of intensive skirmishing punctuated by occasional attacks. Surprisingly, despite often intense fire, which rose and fell in random fashion for nearly 100 hours, Marine casualties were low; the Navy surgeon was mortally wounded shortly after midnight on the morning of the 12th, and a Marine was killed and three wounded around dawn. As the

Marines entrenched their hilltop, Huntington seems to have taken counsel of his fears, suggesting to McCalla that a withdrawal might be necessary. The latter is reputed to have replied, "You were put there to hold that hill and you'll stay there. If you're killed, I'll come and get your dead body." Meanwhile a company of Cuban insurgents, about 60 men, reinforced the Marines. Spanish harassment continued through the day and into the night, once again with surprisingly light casualties. That night the Cubans did some reconnaissance and informed Huntington that the Spanish numbered only 400 to 500 men, based at the village of Cuzco, six miles to the south near the coast, which had the only good well in the area. On 14 April Huntington dispatched Capt. George F. Elliot (a future commandant) with two companies—about 200 Marines—and the Cubans to destroy the well.

Guided by the Cubans, and accompanied by Stephen Crane, correspondent for the *New York World*, who had arrived on the 12th, Elliot's men struggled through the dense undergrowth. The column encountered the Spanish on a hillside about a mile north of Cuzco, and a sharp engagement began. Supported by gunfire from the dispatch vessel *Dolphin*, the Marines and Cubans formed a firing line and engaged the Spanish. As the Marines moved forward, their advance was threatened by naval gunfire. Sgt. John Quick, a signalman who had been using wig-wag flags to direct ship fire, jumped to a prominent location to issue a warning. Already exposed, he was fired upon repeatedly, so that, as Crane put it, "His society was sought by none." The ship did notice Quick, and lifted its fire, but over the next hour he had to signal it several more times, as the Marines' advance could not be observed from *Dolphin*. Fortunately, none of the Marines were injured by friendly fire; Quick was awarded a Medal of Honor for his daring under fire. It was a sharp skirmish which the Spanish finally broke off, when they fled to the rear. The Marines and Cubans took Cuzco and blocked up the well. They were back within the Marine lines by nightfall. The mission had cost one Cuban killed, plus three Marines and several Cubans wounded. Spanish losses were a number of men killed and an equally indeterminate number wounded, as well as 18 men taken prisoner, including one officer. The next day, supported by gunfire from the battleship *Texas*, some Marines went ashore at Caimanera on the west of Guantanamo Bay, which the Spanish had abandoned.

The destruction of the well at Cuzco and the capture of Ciamanera effectively put an end to the fighting in the Guantanamo area, forcing the Spanish to fall back on the city proper. A more energetic Spanish commander might have done more, considering the forces available, but it was not to be. At the cost of six American dead the fleet gained a secure forward base for the rest of the war.

For other reasons, Guantanamo was also an extremely important operation for the future of the Marine Corps. Not only had the Corps proven its ability to seize forward bases for the fleet, but, aided by favorable publicity from the pen of Stephen Crane, Marines suddenly became popular. As one Marine put it, the girls no longer mistook him for a Salvation Army officer.

The Long Vigil

For the first few days on blockade off Santiago the duty was novel, especially after the seemingly endless weeks spent searching and waiting for Cervera's elusive squadron. Now the fleet knew where the enemy was, and might see some action soon. And indeed, action came quite soon. On the morning of 6 June, concerned that the Spanish might be trying to remove *Merrimac* from the channel, Sampson undertook a bombardment of the defenses and the inner harbor, hurling shells over the high bluffs that shielded it from the sea. The Spanish responded, not only with the half-dozen modern pieces, but also with several great muzzle-loaders left over from the eighteenth century. Although the exchange lasted from about 0740 hours to about 1000 hours casualties were entirely on the Spanish side with nine killed and 33 wounded, many aboard *Maria Teresa*, which took 35 hits. Horribly mutilated, her second-in-command Cdr. Emilio Acosta died crying "This is nothing. Long live Spain!" After all those weeks on patrol, this was exciting work for Sampson's bluejackets. But the novelty soon wore off.

The fleet very quickly settled into a standard routine. The heavy ships stood about three to four miles off the entrance to

BLOCKADE OF SANTIAGO
Schematic Diagrams to Illustrate Deployment of U.S. Ships
(not to scale)

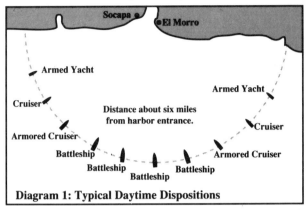

Diagram 1: Typical Daytime Dispositions

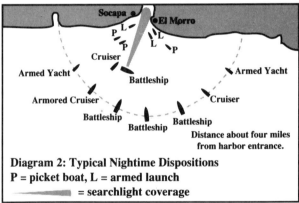

Diagram 2: Typical Nighttime Dispositions
P = picket boat, L = armed launch
= searchlight coverage

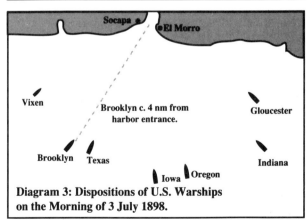

Diagram 3: Dispositions of U.S. Warships
on the Morning of 3 July 1898.

The "dynamite cruiser" **Vesuvius,** *a highly experimental vessel armed with three forward-firing 15-inch pneumatic guns, which used air pressure to fire dynamite-filled shells. Although much was expected of this radical technology, neither the ship, the guns, nor the dynamite shells worked very well, and* **Vesuvius** *was eventually relegated to service as a harbor defense ram, another role for which she was poorly suited due to relatively low speed, only 20 knots.*

Santiago harbor in an arc about eight miles long, while several lighter vessels stood about two miles out from the Morro, and three small launches were stationed just a mile off the Morro. During the night the ships moved in a little closer, a dangerous business, but necessary lest the Spanish attempt a sortie under cover of darkness. Every few days ships had to go to Guantanamo Bay to coal, while the remaining vessels moved to cover the gaps. On 8 June Sampson ordered his battleships to take turns each night keeping the harbor entrance in the beam of their searchlights from about a mile's distance, while other vessels used their searchlights to scan the coast on either side of the harbor entrance.

On 14 June one of the most unique warships in the world arrived to reinforce the blockaders, the dynamite cruiser *Vesuvius.* The ship mounted three 15-inch pneumatic cannon that fired shells containing dynamite charges. A full 15-inch round was 980 pounds, including 500 pounds of dynamite, but smaller rounds could be fired to greater ranges. The three guns were fixed to the ship's forward deck at an angle of 18-degrees, and could only be aimed by moving the vessel itself. Much had been expected of her, but *Vesuvius* proved a failure. Using full-sized shells her guns fired about 1700 yards. The range could be increased, but only at the cost of using special shells of small size and much less effect. Another problem was that while in theory aiming was simply a matter of pointing the ship's bow in the right direction, in practice the range was so short that maneuvering the ship made it virtually impossible to perfect her aim in a timely fashion.

But the arrival of *Vesuvius* and her failure in action barely ruffled the increasingly familiar routine of the fleet. The daily habit of patrol was broken only occasionally. On 16 June, reacting to information that suggested the Spanish were trying to strengthen coastal defenses, several ships fired on the Socapa and Morro batteries, inflicting some casualties while again suffering none. Less than a week later on the 21st and 22nd, several ships bombarded Daiquiri and Siboney in support of the landing of V Corps. And on 1 July, the armored cruiser *New York*, Sampson's flagship, and two lighter warships supported a feint across the Aguadores River.

Of course, the entire U.S. Navy was not off Santiago. Several monitors and cruisers maintained the blockades of Havana and San Juan, while other cruisers and smaller warships stood off smaller ports, and cruisers patrolled in search of blockade runners. Several vessels skirmished occasionally with Spanish warships which emerged from the blockaded harbors. Two clashes occurred off San Juan. It was not subject to a permanent blockade until 18 June, when the monitors *Amphitrite* and *Terror*, the cruiser *New Orleans*, and the auxiliary cruisers *St. Paul* and *Yosemite* took up station off the harbor entrance. Four days later, the old Spanish cruiser *Isabel II*, the gunboat *General Concha*, and the destroyer *Terror* (which had come up from Martinique on the 17th, after being left there by Cervera on the 14th), sortied from the harbor in order to test the blockade. *St. Paul*, under Capt. Sigsbee, and *Yosemite* moved to intercept. A short running fight ensued. With their two larger vessels able to make no better than

10 knots, the Spanish broke off the action quickly. As the larger ships retired towards the harbor entrance, *Terror* attempted a torpedo attack to cover the retreat. She ran in against *St. Paul*, but at 5,400 yards the cruiser took her under fire, striking her repeatedly with small caliber rounds, and put a 5-inch round through her starboard side. Having suffered two men killed (the only casualties on either side in the engagement), *Terror* retired. Just two days later, the Spanish again essayed a sortie, with *Isabel II* and *General Concha* being joined by the small gunboat *Ponce de Leon* (*Terror* was still under repair), in an effort to help the steamer *Antonio Lopez* run the blockade. The three ships engaged *New Orleans*, *St. Paul*, and *Yosemite* at long range, with no damage to either side. While the shooting was going on, there being no chance that the merchantman could make it into the harbor, the Spanish ran *Antonio Lopez* aground up the coast and began offloading supplies and arms. It was several hours before the American vessels arrived. They quickly sent a few rounds into the ship, and she burned on the beach. Naval skirmishing of this sort took place on a number of occasions off several of the ports blockaded by the U.S. Navy. These affairs may have been small, and virtually bloodless, but they had a deadly purpose: to keep or break the blockade.

Although Cervera's squadron included the bulk of Spain's modern warships, there were a few powerful vessels which had not accompanied him across the Atlantic. Towards the middle of June these began to have an important influence on naval operations. The Spanish Ministry of Marine had proposed and rejected a variety of plans for the use of these ships. One envisioned using the fast new armored cruiser *Emperador Carlos V* and several speedy auxiliary cruisers for a raid on the East Coast of the United States, while a squadron of auxiliary cruisers pillaged American commerce, and a third squadron defended home waters. That was a good plan, and one which might have paid considerable dividends, but it was rejected. Meanwhile, the remaining modern vessels were concentrated at Cadiz: the battleship *Pelayo*, ten years old but newly emerged from a refit, the new *Emperador Carlos V*, several auxiliary cruisers, and several destroyers. The U.S. Navy's improvised intelligence service in Europe, under Lt. William S. Sims, tried to determine the Spanish intentions, a task made difficult by the inability of the Spanish Ministry and Naval high command to settle upon a strategy.

None emerged until mid-June. On 15 June the Ministry of Marine ordered Rear Admiral Manuel de Camara, commanding the 2nd Squadron of the fleet at Cadiz, to prepare to sail for the Philippines with *Pelayo*, *Carlos V*, several auxiliary cruisers, and three destroyers, plus 4000 troops in two transports and several colliers. The squadron sailed almost immediately. On 17 June Sims cabled the Navy Department that Camara had definitely passed through the Straits of Gibraltar bound for Suez at ten knots.

Camara's departure for the Philippines created a problem for the U.S. Navy. If Camara reached the Philippines Dewey was doomed. Two monitors at San Francisco, *Monterey* and *Monadnock*, were ordered across the Pacific to reinforce Dewey, but that was not enough. The voyage would be dangerous, for monitors were slow and had a very low freeboard, no match for heavier Spanish vessels. The best way to deal with the threat to the Philippines was to undertake a strategic diversion. On 18 June Secretary Long instructed Admiral Sampson that, "in the event of the Cadiz division passing Suez" he was to form an "Eastern Squadron," consisting of three of his best and heaviest ships, battleships *Iowa* and *Oregon*, the armored cruiser *Brooklyn*, and the auxiliary small cruisers *Dixie*, *Yankee*, and *Yosemite*, for a raid against the coast of Spain, in the belief that such an attack would prompt the Spanish to recall Camara. As a consequence of the assignment of these ships to a trans-Atlantic mission, the entire fleet was reorganized. Old squadrons were abolished. The fleet was redesignated the North Atlantic Fleet, with two active components: the First and Second North Atlantic Squadrons, plus the Eastern Squadron to be formed from the other two as the situation warranted. One consequence of this reorganization was that Commodore Schley, commanding the Second North Atlantic Squadron, fell from second-in-command of the fleet to fourth. Of these developments the average sailor on the blockade knew little. For him, the daily routine continued. Until the 37th day.

Cervera's Squadron

The pressures of the blockade were not confined to the American sailors who imposed it. Inside Santiago harbor, Cervera and his crews faced an assortment of difficulties. To remain at Santiago linked the fate of the squadron to Linares' ability to hold the city. If the city could be held, then the squadron would survive; if not, the whole would be lost. On the other hand, if the squadron essayed a sortie, it would inevitably clash with the far superior American fleet, with results that were probably equally predictable. As Cervera put it, "The blockading fleet is four times larger, so a sortie would be without doubt certain destruction." The U.S. ships were more numerous than the Spanish, and larger and more heavily armed as well. And, although there could be no certainty on this point, the American ships were likely more ready for action than the Spanish ones. Cervera did know the condition of his squadron, and it was not encouraging. In a poor state when they left the Cape Verdes, the long voyage across the Atlantic had done nothing to improve the situation. *Vizcaya's* bottom was still fouled, reducing her speed considerably, and two of her 5.5-inch guns were inoperable, as was one of *Almirante Quendo's*. And *Cristobal Colon* still lacked her main battery. Worse, nearly 80-percent of the 6000 rounds of ammunition for the squadron's 27 serviceable 5.5-inch guns were unreliable, while most of the fuzes were defective. So if the squadron sortied, at best some of the ships might get away despite the odds, while at worst all would be lost. There was little to choose from between the two options.

The possibility of a sortie appears never to have been far from Cervera's thoughts from the time the squadron arrived at Santiago. As early as 20 May, just a day later and even before the U.S. Navy had imposed its blockade, Cervera wired the Ministry of Marine that he intended to leave the port as soon as the ships could be refitted. But facilities at Santiago proved inadequate. Worse, American ships were off the harbor entrance on 21 May, when the cruiser *Minneapolis* and the auxiliary cruisers *St. Paul* and *Harvard* conducted a brief reconnaissance. On 24 May Cervera proposed that the squadron leave Santiago for San Juan, Puerto Rico, but his captains argued that *Vizcaya's* slow

One of the ten 5.5-inch secondary guns on the Spanish armored cruiser Vizcaya. *Although there were 30 of these in Cervera's squadron, over 70-percent of the 52 heavy guns available, they were unreliable, three having defective breech mechanisms (two aboard* Vizcaya *and one aboard* Quendo*), and they were supplied with faulty ammunition, which caused a disastrous explosion aboard* Almirante Quendo *during the battle off Santiago.*

speed would make the move very dangerous, and given the presence of the American fleet, Cervera accepted their objections. By the next day, Cervera was convinced, erroneously to be sure, that Santiago was under blockade, when *St. Paul* was observed intercepting and capturing the collier *Restormel* not far off the harbor entrance. A proposal for a sortie on 27 May—when it appeared that the Americans had temporarily abandoned the blockade—had to be rejected because heavy seas were running into the harbor entrance, which, according to pilots, made the channel impassable for heavy ships. Although Captains Joaquin Bustamante, Cervera's chief-of-staff, and Victor M. Concas, skipper of the flagship *Infanta Maria Teresa*, urged him to make the attempt anyway, Cervera allowed himself to be swayed by others of the squadron, and decided against it. Although Cervera did not know it at the time, this was actually his last chance to leave Santiago since Schley's Flying Squadron arrived off the harbor entrance that very evening.

On 8 June Cervera convened a conference of his captains. Bustamante presented a plan for a nocturnal sortie. The destroyers *Pluton* and *Furor* would lead the way, making torpedo runs against the American battleships. They were to be followed by the heavier ships, which would scatter in different directions. As only two of the blockading ships were capable of sustaining better than 15 knots, the chances that at least half of the Spanish cruisers might get away seemed good, and perhaps if the American armored cruisers *Brooklyn* and *New York* were not present, even better. But once again only Concas supported Bustamante, and once again Cervera ruled against making the attempt. A few days later, acting under instructions from Governor-General Blanco, Cervera concluded an agreement with Linares to commit some of his sailors to reinforcing the troops ashore in the event of an American attack on the city. Thus, when V Corps began landing at Daiquiri on 22 June, Cervera sent a thousand men ashore—nearly half the squadron's complement—under Bustamante's command. Meanwhile discussions began concerning the landing of some of the squadron's lighter guns to further strengthen the defenses. The very next day, Cervera received orders from the Minister of Marine—Ramon Auñon, the third so far in the war—authorizing him to leave Santiago. By now convinced that a sortie would be disastrous, Cervera polled his captains, who not surprisingly agreed with him. This did not end pressure to attempt a sortie. Over the next few days, Cervera heard from Governor-General Blanco suggesting a sortie, as well as from the Minister again, who proposed a nocturnal attempt. The safety of the squadron was not the principal concern of either Blanco or the minister. A sortie was necessary, as Blanco put it, because "it is better for the honor of our arms that the squadron perish in battle ... ." Since Cervera did not take the hint, on 28 June, after conferring with the government in Madrid, Blanco ordered him to make a sortie as soon as possible, or if the city appeared likely to fall. Obedient to this command, Cervera asked Linares if he could provide reasonable warning of the fall of the city. When Linares indicated it may not be possible, Cervera requested the immediate return of Bustamante's *Naval Brigade*. Linares said he couldn't do that, either. Cervera referred the matter to Blanco. By this time it was 1 July. Within hours of the American capture of San Juan Hill Cervera convened a meeting of his captains, with Concas now chief-of-staff since Bustamante had been mortally wounded in the fighting ashore. The consensus was that a sortie was suicidal, and that the resources of the fleet should be expended in prolonging the defense of Santiago. Cervera communicated this decision to Blanco, who objected in the strongest terms. The Governor-General instructed Maj. Gen. Jose Toral, who had assumed command of the defenses after Linares had been wounded, to give the admiral all possible support even at the risk of hastening the loss of Santiago. Then he told Cervera, "Your Excellency will reembark the ships' crews as quickly as possible and sortie immediately." Shortly before midnight on 1 July Cervera issued orders for the sailors to return to their ships.

The officers and men of the squadron spent 2 July returning to their ships and putting everything in readiness. In the afternoon when the ships raised steam, the dark smoke rising from their stacks into the clear sky was observed by lookouts on the American ships offshore. That evening Cervera issued his orders. He rejected a nocturnal sortie, as urged by both Blanco and the Minister of Marine (and many a critic since), because he believed the squadron might have difficulties negotiating the narrow, torturous channel in the dark. In any case, night would offer few advantages, since the harbor entrance was illuminated by American searchlights, and the blockaders were close in. So the squadron sortied at about 0900 hours the next morning. It would be led by *Maria Teresa*, which would fire on the nearest American vessel, while boldly holding course directly for the armored cruiser *Brooklyn*, the fastest American ship, in an attempt to ram her, thereby taking her—and *Maria Teresa*—out of the fight, thus increasing the chances that the other Spanish ships might escape. In quick succession behind *Maria Teresa* would come the cruisers *Vizcaya*, *Colon*, and *Quendo*, followed by the two destroyers, *Pluton* and *Furor*, under orders to avoid action and use their superior speed to escape.

The ships' crews stirred on the morning of 3 July, making final preparations for the sortie. As it was a Sunday, chaplains held mass including communion. Shortly after dawn, Concas made a final reconnaissance of the blockading squadron. He noted that *Brooklyn*, the most dangerous of the American ships, lay further out than usual, leaving a gap near the western end of the semicircle of ships. Acting on this information, Cervera instructed his ships to flee westwards towards Cienfuegos, as *Maria Teresa* rammed *Brooklyn*. At 0800 the flagship hoisted the signal "Clear for Action." The ships made their final preparations, breaking out their great red and gold battle ensigns and, as ordered, getting their boilers up to full pressure. About a half hour later the flagship hoisted "Sortie in the prescribed order." Moments later Cervera ordered a final hoist, "¡*Viva España!*" run up the flagship's signal mast. It was about 0845 when *Maria Teresa* proceeded into the channel, followed by *Vizcaya, Cristobal Colon*, and *Almirante Quendo*, with the destroyers *Furor* and *Pluton* bringing up the rear. As the ships got underway Concas cried out "¡*Pobre España!*—Poor Spain!"

"The Enemy's Ships Are Coming Out!"

After several weeks blockade duty off Santiago, the U.S. fleet had settled into a predictable routine. As darkness turned to twilight, and twilight to dawn, the ships pulled back from their nighttime positions to assume day stations. The number of warships off Santiago was less than usual. The battleship *Massachusetts*, the cruisers *Newark* and *New Orleans*, and a small armed tender had departed for Guantanamo Bay during the night to take on coal and stores. Shortly before 0900 the armored cruiser *New York*, escorted by an armed yacht and a torpedo boat, steamed eastwards at about 12 knots, Admiral Sampson having agreed to confer with General Shafter at Siboney. So rather than the normal complement of five or six battleships and armored cruisers, plus two or three cruisers, a couple of armed yachts, and one or two torpedo boats maintaining the blockade, there were that morning only five heavy ships and two armed yachts. Deployed in an east-to-west arc two and four miles from

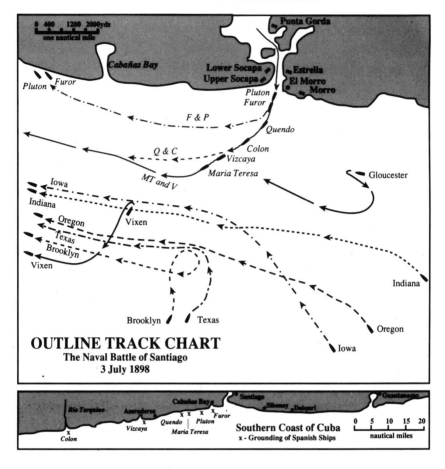

OUTLINE TRACK CHART
The Naval Battle of Santiago
3 July 1898

Southern Coast of Cuba
x - Grounding of Spanish Ships

the harbor mouth were the armed yacht *Gloucester* (Robber Baron J.P. Morgan's *Corsair*, on loan to the Navy for the duration), the battleships *Indiana, Oregon, Iowa,* and *Texas,* the armored cruiser *Brooklyn,* most valuable ship in the fleet, and the armed yacht *Vixen.* Surprisingly, the ships had not adjusted their positions to compensate for the absent vessels. As a result, while the eastern side of the harbor entrance was covered by *Gloucester, Indiana, Oregon,* and *Iowa,* there was a two-mile gap between *Iowa* and *Texas,* which was only about 600 yards to starboard of *Brooklyn.* Between *Brooklyn* and the coast to the west of the harbor entrance, a distance of some four miles, there was only the armed yacht *Vixen.* It was this gap which Concas had observed in the early hours of 3 July, and for which the Spanish ships had been ordered to make. Further complicating matters was the fact that Sampson had not bothered to impart word of his departure to Commodore Schley, his second-in-command. So by chance, the very day on which Cervera decided to attempt his escape from Santiago was probably the most favorable.

The American squadron began 3 July just as it did every Sunday. The men had risen early, had breakfast, and dressed in whites in anticipation of inspection, the reading of the Articles of War, and divine services. While ships had all boilers lit, they were maintaining pressure suitable for only about 12 knots, and were actually steaming at less than that. Aboard *Brooklyn*, Schley had settled into a deck chair near the afterbridge. It was 0930. About six miles to the east *New York* and her escorts could be seen steaming away towards Siboney. Behind the headlands on either side of the harbor entrance were plumes of heavy smoke, as had been the case on the previous day. From his position on *Brooklyn*'s bridge the ship's quartermaster, Petty Officer Anderson, observed the smoke carefully. At about 0935 he turned to the ship's navigator, Lt. Hodgson. "That smoke looks as if it were moving toward the entrance, sir." Hodgson took Anderson's binoculars, gave a quick look, turned, and called out "Afterbridge, there! Report to the commodore! The enemy's ships are coming out!" Almost simultaneously a 6-pounder aboard *Iowa* rang out, her lookouts having just spotted a ship in the channel, while aboard *Texas* the duty officer had also seen the enemy, and set the ship's alarm bells ringing. Within minutes all the American ships were busy with activity as sailors cleared for action, still in their Sunday finery. Among them was Commodore Schley, who rushed to the bridge to take a position on the wooden platform just alongside *Brooklyn*'s conning tower. His first act was not to look at the Spanish ships, but to search eastwards. "Can you see the flagship?" he asked Lt. Hodgson. "No sir. The *New York* is out of sight," came the quick response, a pleasing one, for there was bad blood between Schley and Sampson. Then Hodgson called out, "Commodore, they're coming right at us!" Schley snapped back, "Go right for them!" Meanwhile, the American ships had begun firing, the sounds of which chased *Iowa*'s warning shot as it echoed eastwards to alert Sampson that a battle was underway off Santiago. The admiral ordered the flagship to turn about and make full speed.

The Spanish ships came out of the channel at about ten knots, then quickly raised speed. They emerged from the harbor entrance about 800 yards apart, at four to six minute intervals— not ten, as some American obervers would later report. As ordered, they peeled off in three echelons. Destroyers *Furor* and *Pluton* headed eastwards as soon as they cleared the shoals about the harbor entrance. The armored cruisers at first continued in line ahead, but then *Colon* and *Quendo* altered course eastwards, while *Maria Teresa* and *Vizcaya* made right for *Brooklyn*, threatening to ram. The flagship at first took most American fire, but as additional ships emerged, the Americans took them under fire as well. The Spanish replied in kind, supported by fire from the Morro and Upper Socapa coastal batteries. As the Spanish came out, the American ships began to shape course towards them, while increasing boiler pressure in an attempt to raise speed. Closely followed by *Vizcaya*, *Maria Teresa* drove right on *Brooklyn*. At 1005 hours the two ships were on a collision course and only about 600 yards apart, less than a minute's steaming. Suddenly *Brooklyn* put her helm hard over to starboard—at a time when the other American ships were turning to port—and began circling eastwards to avoid being rammed. As she did so, she came close to—or appeared to come close to—*Texas*, just off her starboard side. Fearing a collision, the skipper of *Texas* ordered full astern and the ship lost way. *Brooklyn* continued on hard to starboard, making practically a fully circle, while *Texas* went full ahead again. Meanwhile, *Brooklyn*'s turn increased the Spanish chances of escaping. *Maria Teresa* and *Vizcaya* altered course to the west, as *Iowa* came up about 2600 yards to their starboard, with *Oregon* and *Indiana* close behind. Save for little *Vixen*, which promptly went hard over to port and steamed to the southwest, the Spanish squadron was now to the west of all the American ships. If the Spanish ships could sustain their speed, they might well escape. For the Americans to win they would have to win a stern chase.

The two squadrons were soon on roughly parallel courses, the Americans about a mile to the port of and a little behind the Spanish. The Spanish were in line ahead, *Maria Teresa* and *Vizcaya* having caught up with *Colon* and *Quendo*, which fell in

An excellent view of the famed battleship **Oregon,** *apparently taken in San Francisco Bay some time before the war. The simplicity of the design is quite evident. Note the disposition of the 8-inch wing turrets, to either side and somewhat astern of the main 13-inch turret, the simple bridge and "military mast," and the prominent ram bow with torpedo tube.*

behind. The Americans were in a less orderly formation, each ship more or less on its own course, all more or less running parallel to the Spanish. Firing was general now, as the Americans opened up with everything that could bear, and the Spanish responded in kind. But the weight of metal was distinctly favorable to the Americans. They had more and heavier guns, and more and better ammunition. The Spanish ships began taking hits. One of the very first rounds from *Iowa* hit *Maria Teresa* in her stern turret, killing or wounding most of the crew, and knocking the heavy gun out of action. The Spanish scored hits as well. *Colon* put two rounds into *Iowa*, one wrecking the ship's dispensary, but causing no casualties and no harm to the ship's integrity. The second was more serious,

The **USS Iowa***, America's first proper full scale battleship. Although superficially similar to the somewhat older ships of the* **Indiana** *Class, Iowa's lower freeboard—the height of her main deck above the water—made for greater stability.*

striking along the waterline. Taking water, *Iowa* had to reduce speed, falling somewhat behind but maintaining fire, in which she had been joined by the rest of the fleet.

Although she was making good speed, *Maria Teresa* had taken many hits, particularly during the opening minutes of the battle. The two leading American ships, *Brooklyn* and *Texas*, had hit her repeatedly. There were uncontrollable fires aboard, the flames threatening the magazine. At about 1020 Cervera decided that there was no hope and ordered the ship to run to shore in order to save as many lives as possible. Even as ammunition began cooking off in her magazines, *Maria Teresa* was run aground on a small beach just west of Punta Cabrera, striking her colors as the crew desperately flooded her magazines. At 1035 hours; the battle had been raging for just under an hour.

Quendo had also been badly hit. The tail end ship in the Spanish squadron, she was subject to the concentrated fire of three pursuing battleships, *Iowa*, just 1600 yards off her port quarter, plus *Oregon* and *Indiana*, while *Brooklyn* had come up off

The Naval Battle of Santiago, 3 July 1898: The armed yacht USS Gloucester *finishes off the Spanish torpedo boats* Furor, *to the left center, afire, wracked by explosions and sinking, and* Pluton, *in the center aground just off Cabañas Bay. The armored cruiser* Maria Teresa *is beached and burning to the far left of the engraving.*

her starboard bow. Worse, during the action a defective 5.5-inch shell exploded prematurely in the breech, blowing out the block and killing an entire gun crew. Yet the ship fought on. "Fighting Bob" Evans, captain of *Iowa*, watched in admiration as round after round struck the ship, while she "pluckily held on her course and fairly smothered us with a shower of shells and machine-gun" fire. But the cruiser was hurting badly. A fire in her after torpedo rooms spread rapidly. With the fire raging out of control and threatening a disastrous ammunition explosion, the captain decided to run her ashore, beaching her a few hundred yards to the west of where the flagship had grounded just five minutes earlier. Now there were only two Spanish vessels left, *Vizcaya* and *Cristobal Colon*, for the Spanish destroyers had already been accounted for.

As the destroyers *Furor* and *Pluton* emerged from Santiago harbor, the heavier American ships had taken them under fire, but then pressed on in pursuit of the Spanish cruisers. The destroyers had both been hit repeatedly, but still had a chance for escape. However, the armed yacht *Gloucester* came after them. Although the destroyers were more heavily armed, *Gloucester* was bigger, faster, and undamaged. Closing rapidly on the destroyers, *Gloucester's* men worked their guns. Wisely taking advantage of the ship's relatively large crew (over 80 men), her skipper Lieutenant Commander Richard Wainwright, who had been aboard the battleship *Maine* when she blew up in February, had organized them to work in relays, so that no one was on duty for more than a few minutes at a time. The two destroyers were hit rapidly and repeatedly, while *Gloucester* suffered not at all. At 1045 *Pluton* ran up on the beach a little west of Cabañas Bay. Within five minutes *Furor* went down in deep water close to the bay. Both ships had fought to the last.

Thus, by about 1050 hours only *Vizcaya* and *Colon* remained of the six Spanish ships which had emerged from Santiago Harbor. They pressed on westwards, the latter drawing ahead of her consort. *Brooklyn* had begun to outstrip the other American ships. As *Quendo* ran aground she was nearly abreast of *Vizcaya*. Schley called out to her commander, Captain Francis Cook, "Get in close, Cook, and we'll fix her." Cook closed the range to some 950 yards. *Brooklyn* sent numerous 8-inch and 5-inch rounds into the Spanish cruiser. Although further away, the other U.S. ships, battleships *Texas*, *Iowa*, *Oregon*, and *Indiana*, were striking the Spanish cruiser as well. Her energetic reply had some success. One of *Vizcaya's* 5.5-inch shells tore into *Brooklyn*, cutting through a 5-inch sponson. Amazingly, although the compartment was wrecked, only one of the twelve men in it was injured. Another shell took the head off Yeoman George Ellis, a 25-year old Brooklynite, who had been calling off the range from the signal bridge. When two officers picked up Ellis' body to heave it overboard, Schley called out for them to stop, so that Ellis could have a Christian burial. They laid the body out of sight under a canvas. It was just about 1100 hours. Unable to see through the thick gunsmoke which hung about the ship, Schley called up to a Marine in the ship's fighting top, asking if the Spanish were being hit. The man replied that he could see the enemy ships, and that they did indeed seem to be taking hits. *Vizcaya* began a turn to port, as if attempting to come about to

The armored cruiser **USS New York,** *flagship of the North Atlantic Squadron, at full steam in pursuit of a blockade runner.*

ram or torpedo *Brooklyn.* Suddenly an 8-inch round from *Brooklyn's* forward turret cut into the Spanish cruiser's bow. In an instant there was a tremendous explosion; the shell had apparently detonated a torpedo in one of *Vizcaya's* forward tubes. The blast blew out a large piece of the ship's bow. Another 8-inch round brought a portion of her bridge down. The fire spread, fed by the wooden paneling common to ships of the day—even American ships. Ready ammunition for the ship's secondary guns began exploding amid the flames. At 1106 she turned hard to starboard and ran for the beach, as her battle ensign was struck. Cheers went up aboard the American ships, at which Captain J.W. Philip of *Texas* cried out, "Don't cheer, boys! Those poor devils are dying," and ordered a ceasefire.

Now only *Colon* was left, steaming hard to the west. She was making nearly 15 knots, and had opened up a considerable lead. *Brooklyn,* the fastest American ship, was some six miles astern of her, with her black gang working hard to get every knot out of the engines, rated at 20 but now in need of overhaul after the long months at sea. Not far behind *Brooklyn* was little *Vixen,* which had hung on the fringes of battle, and now joined the pursuit. Coming up hard was *New York,* which had missed most

The Spanish armored cruiser Maria Teresa, *aground off Punta Cabrera. The first of the four Spanish armored cruisers to succumb, she shows the extent of the damage inflicted on her by American shellfire and internal explosions.*

of the battle, but by dint of her powerful machinery had laid on nearly 20 knots in her effort to take part. *Texas* and *Oregon* were coming up behind these ships, making their best speeds, *Oregon* helped along by burning Cardiff coal, a higher quality than that used aboard the other American ships. The chase was long, and for a time it seemed *Colon* would win. An hour passed. *Colon* began to falter. Her boilers, stoked with inferior coal, began losing pressure, and speed began to fall. The pursuing Americans closed in. At 1220 *Oregon* opened fire with one of the great 13-inch guns of her forward turret. The hurtling round missed, but a tall geyser erupted in the sea just astern of the fleeing cruiser. As the range closed, another round followed, as did 8-inch rounds from *Brooklyn* and *New York*, while *Colon*—lacking the 10-inch guns of her main battery—was able to respond with only the one 6-inch gun which bore. *Colon* had taken only two hits—both probably 5- or 6-inch—but the range was closing rapidly. With the Americans now just a mile astern, and no hope of escapte remaining, *Colon*'s skipper, Captain José de Paredes, decided the game was up. To save as many of his men as possible he ordered the ship to head for the mouth of Rio Tarquino, about 75 miles west of Santiago, and ran her up the beach. It was 1315 hours. The Naval Battle of Santiago was over. The Spanish squadron had been completely destroyed.

Captain Philip of *Texas* was by no means the only humanitarian present that day. Indeed, the Americans had commenced rescuing their defeated foemen even as the battle raged. And no Spanish ship had been fired upon once her colors had been stricken or she was seen to be aground. As soon as firing ceased, boats were put over. American sailors who had just minutes before sought to kill them, now pulled the burned and injured Spaniards from the sea, where some were taken by sharks before they could be rescued. Other American bluejackets bravely brought their boats alongside the still burning wrecks of the Spanish ships, to take off the remaining survivors. Those of the Spanish who made it ashore were not always safe, for there were sharks on land as well. Cuban insurgents came out of the hills to take pot shots at Spaniards who clung to drifting wreckage, and killed some of those who made shore, apparently including Captain Fernando Villamil, who commanded the destroyers. "Fighting Bob" Evans of the *Iowa* was so incensed by the Cuban actions that he sent a file of Marines ashore to protect the beaten enemy, while one of his officers sought out the local Cuban commander to inform him that "unless they ceased their infamous work" he would turn the guns of his ship on them. Likewise, Lieutenant Commander Wainwright of *Gloucester*, *Maine* survivor that he was, informed the Cubans that if they did not leave the beach he would fire on them.

It was an age when words like *gallantry* and *honor* still had meaning. When Captain Antonio Eulate of *Vizcaya* was carried aboard *Iowa*, suffering from three wounds, he struggled to his feet and presented his sword to Captain Evans. "Fighting Bob" returned it, and then, amid cheers from his men, personally helped the wounded Spaniard to his own cabin. Eulate paused for a moment to look at the burning wreck of his ship. He raised his hand in salute and cried out, "¡Adios, *Vizcaya*!" At that moment the flames aboard the stricken cruiser reached her forward magazines, and there was a spectacular explosion. Sadly, Eulate allowed himself to be led away.

The armored cruiser **New York,** *her battle ensigns prominently displayed and flying the signal flags indicating "Cease Firing" as the last of the Spanish ships runs aground. Flagship of Rear Admiral William T. Sampson,* **New York** *was out of sight more than six miles to the east of the entrance to Santiago Harbor when the Spanish squadron sortied, but by making all speed was able to take part in the final pursuit of the armored cruiser* **Cristobol Colon.**

A short time later Wainwright picked Admiral Cervera off the beach, and rendered him every courtesy. The admiral, so wet and dirty that one Spanish officer present recalled he looked "like a beggar," was transferred with great courtesy to the *Iowa*. Captain Evans greeted his defeated enemy like a victorious ally, with sideboys, a Marine honor guard, salutes, and bugle calls, once again amid cheers from the American crew for a gallant foe.

Cervera and his men were treated almost as guests, rather than prisoners. The admiral himself was taken to Annapolis and confined on the premises of the U.S. Naval Academy in company with his officers. The most severaly wounded among his men were treated aboard the hospital ship *Solace*, and later transferred to the U.S. naval hospital at Norfolk, Virginia. The other prisoners were placed aboard the auxiliary cruisers *Harvard* and *St. Louis* for transfer to Seavey's Island near Portsmouth, New Hampshire. The only unseemly incident marring the good treatment of the Spanish prisoners occurred during their transfer to New Hampshire. About 600 prisoners were aboard *Harvard*. Although given quarters below, an area of the deck had been marked for their use, and they had been instructed not to stray beyond it. The weather was very hot, and many of the prisoners spent most of their time on deck, even sleeping there. Around midnight on 4-5 July one of the Spanish prisoners either crossed the line defining the restricted area, or seemed to be about to cross it, the subsequent investigation never cleared up the matter. He was challenged by a sentry from the 4th Massachusetts. The man either refused to obey the sentry, or did not understand him, probably the latter. The sentry fired. The shot woke hundreds of men who were sleeping on deck. Someone gave the alarm. Several men from the 4th Massachusetts fired on the prisoners. Although order was restored within minutes, six of the Spaniards were killed and 13 wounded. The U.S. Navy expressed deep regret for the incident, and there were no repetitions. Indeed, from his confinement Cervera wrote that the Amerians were "vying in making our captivity as light as possible." But American courtesy and regret could not mask the bitter taste of defeat.

Spanish losses at Santiago had been enormous. Of 2,227 officers and men aboard the six ships when they sortied from Santiago harbor, 323 had died, and 151 been wounded, about 50 very seriously. Including the wounded 1,720 Spaniards had been taken prisoner: About 180 Spaniards managed to elude capture, some hiding out in the hills, others managing to make it back to Santiago overland. The losses were over 90 percent of the men engaged. On the American side, only one man was killed, the unfortunate Ellis; and only one injured by enemy action, Fireman First Class John Burns, also of *Brooklyn*, plus one man aboard *Iowa* who suffered a broken leg attempting too vigorously to negotiate a ladder. Although all the Spanish ships had been lost, not one of the American ones had suffered grievous injury, and none had taken damage that required immediate repair. Indeed, save for some vessels which continued with the work of rescuing the Spanish survivors, and securing the enemy wrecks, the American ships resumed their blockading positions off Santiago by nightfall.

William T. Sampson

William T. Sampson (1840-1902)
graduated first in the Naval Academy class of 1861. His Civil War service was mostly unspectacular. For some time assigned as an instructor at the Academy, he subsequently served on blockade duty, the high point of which was when the monitor *Patapsco* was mined in Charleston harbor on 15 January 1865. Shortly after the war by-then Lieutenant Sampson was assigned to the screw frigate *Colorado* in European waters. Promoted lieutenant commander in mid-1866 he spent the next few years at the Academy or at sea, rising to commander in 1874. In 1879 he was transferred from head of the Physics Department at the Academy to the command of the screw sloop *Swatara* on the Asiatic Station. From 1882-1897 his assignments were mostly academic, scientific, or diplomatic activities, including command of the Naval Observatory, delegate to the Prime Meridian Conference in 1884, command of the torpedo school, superintendency of the Naval Academy, and chief of the Bureau of Ordnance, though from 1890 to 1893 by then Captain Sampson was named first commander of the new cruiser *San Francisco*. In 1897 he became the first captain of the new battleship *Iowa*. Chairman of the board which investigated the *Maine* disaster, Sampson was promoted to acting rear admiral and given command of the North Atlantic Squadron in April of 1898.

On the outbreak of the Spanish-American War, Sampson commanded the blockade of Spain's Caribbean possessions, rounding up merchant ships, undertaking bombardments of several shore installations, including the defenses of San Juan, and supported the landing of supplies for the Cuban rebels. When Cervera's squadron was reported to have arrived at Santiago, Sampson moved quickly to impose a close blockade. His squadron, reinforced by Commodore W.S. Schley's "Flying Squadron" kept Cervera bottled up in Santiago while supporting the landing and operations of Shafter's V Corps. Sampson missed the Battle of Santiago on 3 July; with his flagship, the armored cruiser *New York*, he was to the east of the scene of the principal action, and arrived for only the mopping up.

A considerable controversy blew up after the Naval Battle of Santiago as partisans of Sampson and Schley argued over the credit for the victory, a controversy in which both officers quite unprofessionally took part, and which dogged the subsequent careers of both men. Sampson served for a time as one of the commissioners supervising the armistice, before returning to command his squadron. Promoted to permanent rear admiral in March of 1899, in late 1899 he was named commander of the Boston Navy Yard. He retired early in 1902, and died shortly afterwards.

A capable officer, Sampson, more than anyone, deserves the credit for the effectiveness of the blockade of Cuba and Puerto Rico, for the bottling up of Cervera's squadron, and, ultimately, for the defeat of the latter, which was as much a result of his close attention to training and his carefully detailed battle plans, as to Schley's leadership. His participa-tion in the bitter controversy over the credit for the victory ultimately denied him his due.

Winfield Scott Schley

Winfield Scott Schley (1839-1909) graduated from the Naval Academy in 1860. His initial service was in the Pacific, but upon the outbreak of the Civil War he was assigned to block-ade duty. He served on a number of ships in the Gulf and on the Missis-sippi, once earning the dubious dis-tinction of being the direct object of Admiral David G. Farragut's wrath when, before Port Hudson in March of 1863, he failed to respond promptly to a signal ("I want none of this Nelson business in my squad-ron about not seeing signals."). From 1864 to 1866 he commanded a gunboat in the Pacific. After the Civil War Schley's career was distin-guished and varied, including sev-eral tours as an instructor at the Naval Academy, service in Korea in 1871, command of various ships, command of an expedition to rescue the survivors of the Greeley Arctic exploration expedition in 1884, and bureau chief at the the Navy Depart-ment. In 1891, as commander of the cruiser *Baltimore*, his ship was in-volved in the Valparaiso Incident, which nearly led to war with Chile. The eve of the Spanish-American War found Schley as chairman of the Lighthouse Board. He was shortly promoted to commodore and given command of the "Flying Squadron," intended to counter any sudden Spanish descents on the East Coast.

Soon afterwards, Schley was placed under Sampson's command, which caused some friction, as he techni-cally outranked the latter (Schley was a commodore, while Sampson was a temporary rear admiral, with the substantive rank of captain).

As a commander, Schley proved indecisive under pressure. His fail-ure to seal off Santiago for nearly a week after Cervera had slipped in could easily have had serious reper-cussions had the Spanish squadron been in better physical condition than was actually the case. By chance in command when Cervera sortied from Santiago on 3 June, Schley and his flagship, the armored cruiser *Brooklyn*, played critical roles in the destruction of the Span-ish squadron. The resulting ugly controversy between his partisans and those of Sampson (it even took on religious overtones, the one be-ing a Roman Catholic and the other a Protestant) cast some shadow over the careers of both men.

Schley was promoted rear admi-ral in early 1899, and commanded the South Atlantic Squadron from then until his retirement in late 1901. His retirement came with some measure of disgrace. Having for some time demanded an inquiry into the Naval Battle of Santiago which would fix responsibility for the victory, in late 1901 a board headed by George Dewey was severely critical of Schley's actions during the campaign, the conclusions of which, although Dewey did not share them, President Theodore Roosevelt saw fit to approve. An outgoing, affable man, Schley had ruined what had been a rather impressive career.

Pascual Cervera y Topete

Pascual Cervera y Topete (1839-1909) was the son of a prosperous wine merchant and an admiral's sister. He entered the naval academy at the age of nine, emerging as a sublieutenant in 1851. Most of his career was spent afloat, during which he saw considerable action. Service against separatists in Murcia brought him a promotion to lieutenant in 1853. He served in the Franco-Spanish expedition to Indochina in 1862, was a naval attache in Washington in the latter portion of the Civil War, and commanded a ship late in the "Guano War" with Chile and Peru in 1865-1866. From 1868 to 1878, the years of civil war in Spain and insurgency in Cuba, he was repeatedly under fire in both theaters, and in the Philippines. Cervera particularly distinguished himself in action at Carraca and Cartagena in 1873, by which time he was a commander, and while on blockade duty in the Philippines in 1875. His reputation was considerable, and as a result in 1887, by then a captain, Cervera was appointed the first skipper of the new battleship *Pelayo*, fitting out in France and the first important ship to be added to the Spanish fleet in over 20 years.

When this plum assignment was over he was successively inspector of naval shipyards, naval aide to the queen regent, chief of the Spanish delegation to the London Naval Conference of 1891, and minister of marine, meanwhile rising to rear admiral, and in 1896 vice admiral and senior officer afloat.

In 1898, with war imminent, Cervera was named to command the principal squadron of the Spanish fleet. An intelligent man, who clearly understood the strategic situation, Cervera waged an unsuccessful struggle with this naval and political superiors to prepare the squadron for service and to develop a more realistic strategy. Despite his efforts, the squadron was forced to sail unprepared, and was ultimately lost in action off Santiago. Although in the final crisis at Santiago, Cervera might have acted with greater energy, it is difficult to see how the outcome would have differed, given the impossible circumstances.

After the war Cervera successfully defended his performance before a court martial. His reputation in the Spanish Navy remained high, if for no other reason than that it was clear the defeat had been caused by administrative incompetence and lack of vision of Spain's political leadership. He remained in the service, wrote on the war, was chief of staff of the Navy, served on the Supreme War Council, and ended his days as the captain general of El Ferrol.

Cervera, a distinguished looking man with courtly manners, was very well liked by those Americans who came in contact with him, not the least for his gallantry in going personally to the rescue of Lt. Richmond Hobson and his men after their unsuccessful attempt to block the channel into Santiago harbor. Unjustly subject to much criticism in the naval literature of his times, his reputation has been long in recovering. A capable man, he might have achieved more given better resources, or just better orders.

Chapter V

The Fall of Santiago

*T*he capture of El Caney and the Heights of San Juan by the American V Corps on the afternoon of 1 July virtually completed the investment of Santiago de Cuba. The next day General William Shafter sent General José Toral (to whom command of the city had fallen after Linares was seriously wounded on the 1st) a demand that the city be surrendered. Toral refused. At that point Shafter's options were limited: He could attempt to storm the city's final line of defenses or he could undertake a siege. The heavy casualties which V Corps had suffered on 1 July had convinced him that it would be better to besiege the city than to storm it. As a result, the American troops spread out in an arc around the city, hastily throwing up entrenchments, while Garcia's Cubans secured their right and rear. Over 2-3 July a number of firefights developed, as the Spanish harassed the Americans from the security of their defenses. U.S. casualties were rather heavy, with several men killed and many—over 100—wounded, a serious price when added to those of 1 July. Since landing on 22 June the V Corps had lost nearly 10 percent of its strength. Casualties among officers had been particularly serious: Of four officers on Leonard Wood's staff on 1 July, three had been killed or wounded by nightfall on the 3rd, as had he himself, albeit lightly. The Spanish were busy too, strengthening their defenses. They completed the work of stripping the guns from the old cruiser *Reina Mercedes*, laid up in the harbor, and emplaced them in earthworks batteries. Surprisingly, the preparations for the sortie of Cervera's squadron went unnoticed by the be-siegers, despite the fact that nearly a thousand sailors were withdrawn from the front lines.

Shafter's major concern on 2-3 July was the Spanish forces in his rear. There were nearly 5,000 Spanish troops based at San Luis, about 25 miles north of Santiago, another 10,000 in the vicinity of Holguin, about 50 miles north of San Luis, and some 6,000 at Guantanamo, some 50 miles to the east, and a relief column—"General Pando, with 8,000 Spanish regulars"—which was on the march from Manzanillo. The threat posed by this column had prompted Shafter's decision to attack the Santiago defenses before his heavy artillery had come up or his logistical problems had been resolved. In fact, the relief column numbered less than half as many men as Shafter believed, and was under the command of Col. Federico Escario Garcia. Escario's troops had left Manzanillo on the evening of 22 June. Days of hard marching and hard fighting had followed. Early on the morning of 3 July Escario's advance guard approached Santiago from the northwest. Although the Cuban troops guarding Escario's line of march into the city attempted to put up a fight, they were easily brushed aside—the column lost only two men killed and eight wounded—and by 1000 hours the last of his men had reached the security of the Spanish lines. Escario's heroic march—an average of 20 miles a day through very difficult country under almost continuous enemy harassment—had brought 3400 fine troops to reinforce Santiago. But these men were as much a liability as an asset.

From the first imposition of the American naval blockade, the food supply in Santiago had been tight. When the Americans had occupied the city's hinterland on 28-30 June, they had cut off the possibility of supply from the local countryside and seized control of the city's reservoir at Cuabitas, promptly closing down the gate valve on the ten-inch main which sup-plied the city. The city was overcrowded, with more than 13,500 troops and some 25,000 civilians—more than double its normal population.

On 3 July Shafter had been scheduled to meet with Sampson in an attempt to convince him to try to force the harbor entrance. The conference did not occur because of the sortie by the

Volunteers being subjected to a physical examination before being mustered into Federal service. Although these men are shown partially clothed, Carl Sandburg recalled standing in a group of naked men in the basement of the city hall of Springfield, Illinois, awaiting his turn to be examined. In contrast to the "physical" given volunteers in the Civil War, which basically amounted to counting arms, legs, eyes, and teeth, that given in the Spanish-American War was a very detailed examination. It was probably for this reason that, in contrast to the Civil War, no young women managed to enlist in 1898.

Spanish squadron. As soon as Shafter received word of the American naval victory he once again renewed his demand that Toral surrender. "To save needless effusion of blood and the distress of many people," he wrote, "you may reconsider your decision of yesterday. Your men have certainly shown the gallantry which was expected of them." Toral replied with a short, polite message, concluding " ... this place will not be surrendered." A truce was arranged so that civilians wishing to leave the city might do so, and from 4 to 8 July a vast number of people—estimated at 20,000—made their way to El Caney, where a makeshift refugee camp was estalished. Conditions for the people who sought refuge at El Caney were not much better

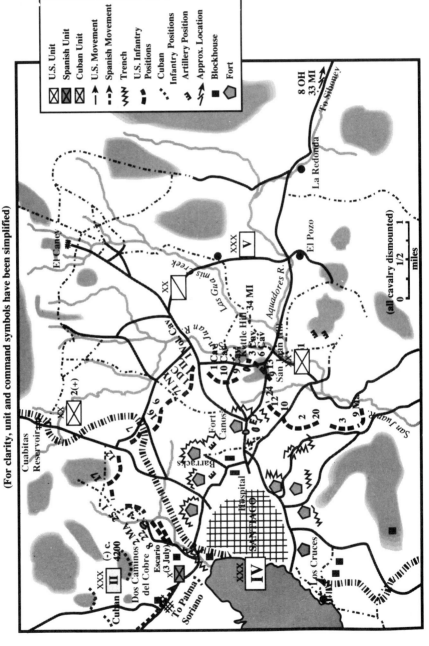

THE SIEGE OF SANTIAGO

1-14 July 1898, Situation after 3 July

(For clarity, unit and command symbols have been simplified)

194

than for those who remained behind in Santiago. The little village was extremely overcrowded, and food remained scarce, the only source being the American army, itself on short rations due to the difficulty of bringing supplies up from Siboney and Daiquiri. But at least the people at El Caney were safe from any further fighting and the threat of bombardment which Shafter had held over Toral's head in an effort to force his surrender.

Toral was not one to give up easily. He asked for and received permission from Governor-General Blanco to sink a blockship in the channel into Santiago harbor to prevent the Americans from forcing their way in. On the night of 4 July the old cruiser *Reina Mercedes*, whose guns had already been stripped off to be used in the landward defenses, made her way into the channel. As was their custom, the U.S. blockaders had moved in closer for the night, and the battleship *Massachusetts* had her main search-light pointed directly up the channel. Shortly before midnight lookouts aboard *Massachusetts* spotted *Reina Mercedes* as she entered the narrowest part of the channel. *Massachusetts* opened fire, as did *Texas*, which was serving as guardship. Although the old cruiser was struck repeatedly, her crew kept her on course, dropped her anchor, and blew out a portion of her hull. But as had been the case when the U.S. Navy tried to block the channel by sinking the collier *Merrimac*, the ship had too much way, and the current was too strong. She went down at the narrowest part of the channel, but so far to the eastern edge that she constituted no obstacle at all.

While Toral was working hard to strengthen the defenses of Santiago, Shafter was also taking steps to improve his position. Escario's arrival at Santiago forced him to extend his right flank virtually to the head of Santiago Harbor, confining the Cubans to a few hundred feet of front. From the head of the harbor the front formed an irregular semi-circle running about six miles to the left flank, which more or less stood in the air. The only Spanish forces beyond the left were those holding the Morro and coastal batteries on the eastern side of the harbor entrance, and those at Aguadores, which were numerically negligible. Shafter had about 13,000 men available, slightly less than Toral. Since he thought the relief column numbered 5,000 men (fewer than the 8,000 original estimate, but more than the actual 3,500),

A battalion of Cuban troops in combat drill under the direction of its commander, Major Estrampa, who is the mounted officer. The unit appears to be well equipped and well trained. The men are more or less uniformly outfitted, the officers all seem to have swords, and they are maintaining a disciplined formation. It is possible that this was a posed photograph, perhaps of Cuban troops training in Florida.

Shafter believed the V Corps was considerably inferior in number, so he put all eight brigades and all his artillery (sixteen field guns and four Gatlings, plus the Rough Riders' dynamite gun) into the front lines. This left an immediately available reserve of one regiment, the 34th Michigan, and a mounted squadron of the 2nd Cavalry, to which the 33rd Michigan, securing the corps' base at Siboney, could be added on a day's notice. To be sure, Shafter was supported by 4,000 to 6,000 Cuban insurgents under General Calixto Garcia. However, the Americans were fast becoming disenchanted with their ostensible allies. They had begun the war with considerable admiration for the insurgents. Not fully understanding the inherent differences between insurgency and conventional warfare, they now saw Cuban failures in combat as indications of unreliability, incompetence, and cowardice. On 1 July the Cubans had proved unable to prevent the escape of many of the Spanish troops holding El Caney and then they had been unable to keep Escario out of Santiago (a matter arguably due to Shafter's unwillingness to let Calixto Garcia commit a major portion of his forces)—both were disturbing to Americans. Shafter shared this view, and petitioned the War Department for more men, requesting "15,000 troops speedily," although conceding that it might be difficult to land them, given the limitations of the port facilities. Supported by the War Department, Shafter also urged Sampson to use the fleet in an attempt to force the channel into Santiago Harbor. Sampson refused, preferring a coordinated attack, in which the fleet would batter the harbor defenses in support of an attack by the army, a matter in which he was backed by the Navy Department. The Navy's view was cold blooded, but firmly rooted in the iron laws of war. The country had few ships but many men.

By early July the nation did indeed have many men. The president's two calls for troops had produced a flood of enthusiastic volunteers, so that by early July the strength of the armed forces was climbing above 200,000 men. So many volunteers had come forward that many had to be turned away. Those who volunteered for the first call were formed into regiments in their home states, with men from the second call going to fill out the ranks. A few of the new regiments were assigned to coast defense installations, frequently in their home states. However, after short periods of training—often no more than three or four days—most of the the volunteers were shipped to one of the five army authorized training camps at the Chickamauga battlefield park, Jacksonville, Tampa, Dun Loring, Virginia, just outside of Washington, or San Francisco. Most of the troops moved by train, many in sleeping cars. A few, notably those from the northeast, moved by ship to ports from which they entrained for their assigned encampments. When the men began arriving before camps had been prepared, they overwhelmed the facilities. By 1 June there were nearly 45,000 men at Chickamauga, 20,000 at Dun Loring, over 25,000 at Tampa, and 10,000 at Jacksonville, a total of 100,000 men housed in facilities which had not existed just a few weeks before. The situation was exacerbated by the fact that most of the troops—even the

Black recruits—possibly from the 3rd North Carolina Volunteers—learning the manual of arms at Camp Thomas, Chickamauga National Battlefield Park. The instructor appears to be a Regular, or perhaps a National Guardsman, as he is fully uniformed and wearing gauntlets. The recruits have rifles and are wearing cartridge belts, but are otherwise wearing civilian clothes. Many volunteers who did not come from the National Guard ended up wearing their civilian garb for weeks on end.

Regulars and National Guardsmen among them—had little experience living in large tented cantonments. Consequently, many of the camps lacked proper drainage, had poorly sited latrines, were short of potable water, and had inadequate messing facilities. As two of the camps—Tampa and Chickamauga—were also poorly served by rail lines, shortages of supplies and food stuffs soon developed. Since most Americans still lived in rural communities or small towns, the sudden crowding together of so many men in such large, inadequately provided communities, led to serious illnesses.

There were also severe shortages of military equipment. The army normally maintained only small stockpiles of uniforms, arms and accoutrements, and kit. Although contracts were hastily let for all sorts of materiel, it took time for the goods to be manufactured, delivered, and distributed. As in all hasty mobilizations, a good deal of shoddy material was procured. Fortunately, many of the states outfitted their own regiments. And often National Guard units brought equipment with them. But in some regiments for weeks on end men wore whatever they happened to have had on at the time they were mustered into service. Gradually this muddle was remedied, as the flow of equipment and supplies improved and as the troops learned—or relearned, in the case of the many Civil War veterans in the ranks—the tricks of camp life. Although there were many casualties from exposure and disease, morale remained high. The troops had enlisted with great enthusiasm, out of patriotic fervor or merely in the spirit of adventure (As one soldier put it, "I wanted to find out whether I would run when the shootin' began."), and public support for the war was strong. The troops were subject to constant visits by religious leaders, political figures, and famous heroes of the Civil War, many of whom were veterans of the very regiments in which the troops served, and often their fathers as well. Meanwhile training began.

The prescribed training regime required five to six weeks. It was based on Civil War experience, as modified by three decades of peace, during which the Army had had little experience training large numbers of men in haste. The troops did a lot of marching, with two and three day hikes not being unusual. This was considered necessary to strengthen discipline and toughen up the men. There was also a lot of drill, which was necessary since the established tactics envisioned the maneuver of entire brigades. Much firearms training was included, albeit mostly with the obsolete "trapdoor" Springfield rifle. An important aspect of training was the sham battle, a maneuver in which the troops "fought" each other using blank cartridges. On 28 June the 1st Brigade of the 1st Division, II Corps, held a sham battle which was more or less typical. The brigade had made a ten mile march on 27 June, from Camp Alger, near Dun Loring, Virginia, and had bivouaced on the banks of the Potomac northwest of Washington. On the morning of the 28th the 6th Massachusetts was sent ahead to establish a defensive position. Several hours later the balance of the brigade, under Brig. Gen. G.A. Garretson, moved out. The 3rd Battalion, 8th Ohio formed the advanced guard, with the balance of that regiment and the 6th Illinois following behind. The advanced guard encountered outposts of the 6th Massachusetts north of Dun Loring, where Col. Charles Woodward had assumed a position holding a prominent rise. A skirmish soon developed between the bri-

Men of the 6th Massachusetts drilling at Camp Alger. In addition to drill, the training regime included target practice, long marches, and sham battles, one of the most notable of which occurred on 28 June 1898, when this regiment "defended" Dun Loring, Virginia, against two of its brigade mates.

gade's advance guard and the 6th Massachusetts' pickets. As these forces skirmished with each other, the balance of Garretson's brigade came up, deployed and attacked. The pickets of the 6th Massachusetts fell back on the regiment's main position. A full scale "battle" developed. This lasted about a half hour, with the "fire" at times being described as heavy. Towards the end of the action the troops were fighting hand-to-hand, with a few casualties when some wielded rifle butts with too much enthusiasm as the brigade dislodged the 6th Massachusetts from its position. Some sham battles were so heated that, as one observer reported, "only the use of real ammunition" would have made it possible to determine a winner. The training was perhaps unrealistic, but in many ways more advanced than that provided in other armies, laying greater stress on marksmanship and physical training than was common at the time. Of course, the army had plans for these men.

The Santiago expedition had been forced upon the army by the movements of Cervera's squadron. The place had no strategic value, and certainly was not vital to the Spanish hold on Cuba. Havana was, as the ultimate bastion of Spanish power in Cuba, there were over 25,000 Spanish troops holding the fortress city, which had more than 100 guns in its landward defenses and 34 modern pieces in its seaward defenses, manned by some 4,000 more troops. To ensure control of Cuba, the U.S. would have to take Havana. This task was assigned to former Confederate general Fitzhugh Lee. Lee, who had last worn the uniform of the United States in 1861 and not seen any military service since 1865, was a good choice, and not merely for political reasons. During the Civil War he had proven an able commander, rising to major general. He knew Cuba, and particularly Havana, having served there as U.S. Consul shortly before the war. Lee was given VII Corps, concentrating at Jacksonville, to prepare for the Havana operation. Aided by the fact that Jacksonville had excellent rail communications, Lee, as able an organizer as he had been a field commander, proved extremely effective in sorting out the administrative problems of establishing a training camp and keeping 25,000 men well housed, well supplied, and healthy. As a result, the troops experienced fewer hardships than those at Chickamauga or Tampa, and there were fewer deaths from disease. By early July the training of VII Corps was well advanced. If all proceeded according to plan the corps would be ready for operations at the end of the summer, with over 30,000 trained troops in three divisions.

In addition to the Havana expedition, the Army's commanding general, Nelson A. Miles, had a personal project of which he was quite fond, an expedition against Puerto Rico. Miles secured the President's approval for this expedition in late June. Since VII Corps was earmarked for the Havana operation, and none of the four other army corps training in the U.S. was ready for operations, Miles decided to sift out the best units from the remaining corps to secure the 40,000 men he believed necessary for a campaign in Puerto Rico. Moving quickly he organized an expedition by taking the headquarters staff from I Corps, a division staff from VI Corps, which had not yet received any troops, plus a division each from I and III Corps and a brigade each from II and IV Corps, so that by the beginning of July he had some 20,000 troops immediately available (albeit somewhat scattered across the southeastern quarter of the United States). They were to be followed up by some 18,000 more, comprising the bulk of IV Corps. So by the beginning of July the United States Army consisted of over 150,000 troops, a six-fold increase in less than 60 days. But fewer than 15,000 of them—the men serving with V Corps at Santiago—were in action.

The lull in the fighting at Santiago as a result of the temporary truce established on 4 July to permit civilians to leave the town, permitted Shafter to try some diplomacy. On 5 July he released 28 prisoners-or-war into the Spanish lines, including four officers, in the hope of inducing Toral to consider surrender. Toral responded graciously, and the next day a more formal exchange of prisoners was arranged, in which Shafter secured the release of Richmond Hobson and his men for an equal number of Spaniards. Meanwhile the troops on both sides strengthened their defenses and looked to their wounded.

Advances in both weaponry and medicine combined to greatly improve the chances of the wounded. The Spanish Mauser fired a small, sharp bullet at great velocity, which caused relatively less damage than did Civil War-era muskets, which fired large, low velocity balls. Medical science, meanwhile, had progressed to the use of antisepsis and anesthesia, so that most wounds which were not immediately fatal could be treated with a considerable degree of success. Medical planning for the Santiago expedition had been good by the standards of the times. Regiments were authorized a surgeon, assistant surgeon, and sixteen enlisted medical aidemen, and the corps had a detachment of the army's Hospital Corps as well. As a result, there were nearly 150 surgeons and physicians with V Corps, including those who, like Leonard Wood, were serving as combat troops, as well as over 600 enlisted medical personnel. As soon as the corps arrived before Santiago, the medical corps established two facilities. A field hospital had been set up about two miles to the rear of V Corps' lines, between El Pozo and La Redonda, which provided primary care, and a base hospital had been established at Siboney, six miles further back, the two together having something like 600 beds. About half the surgeons with the corps were actually with the troops in the trenches or in the field hospital, while the rest were at the base hospital. The idea was to provide immediate care at the field hospital and more intensive treatment at the base hospital, with the most serious cases being transferred to hospital ships for movement to the United States. The concept of "triage" had been introduced, and the regimental medical personnel were trained to evaluate the condition of the wounded, and tag them appropriately: red indicated requiring immediate treatment, white indicated the less serious cases, and blue those mortally injured. This ensured that medical attention was given to those most desperately in need.

However, a high standard of medical care proved difficult to maintain. With some 1400 wounded men on hand, nearly a third of them with serious injuries, the medical facilities of V Corps were severely strained. The problem was not so much inadequate planning, as poor administration. The limitations of Siboney as a port had prevented the landing of four of the seven field ambulances, so that wounded men had to be transported in standard army wagons, which were not only unsuited to the task, but were in short supply. Left aboard transports were many tents, beds, and medical supplies. Further complicating matters was the fact that the road—the Camino Real—between Siboney and the corps' rear area was so poor that it took hours to move the wounded from the field hospital to the base hospital, a journey which proved extremely painful for many of the most seriously injured. And, of course, no matter how "adequate" the planning was, the number of wounded was always overwhelming. So serious did the situation become that Shafter requested assistance from the Navy, and Admiral Sampson sent the fleet surgeon and several other medical personnel ashore to lend a hand. Despite the difficulties, only 31 of the wounded men who were treated at the base hospital died.

The difficulties of Shafter's medical services was part of the logistical muddle in which V Corps found itself. The problem was not the number of bottoms. Indeed, there were plenty of ships. To the 31 transports which had accompanied the expedition, the War Department had managed to add nearly two dozen more, and the Navy had arranged for the loan of four of its own vessels, including the oceanliners-turned auxiliary cruisers, *Harvard*, *Yale*, and *Columbia*. By 6 June, a fortnight after the initial landings at Daiquiri, there was a large backlog of cargo ships lying off Siboney, waiting to be unloaded. Some of them had arrived with the expedition on 22 June. Neither Siboney nor nearby Daiquiri had any but the most rudimentary port facilities. All but the smallest vessels were prevented from approaching the simple piers, the water alongside being quite shallow. Ships had to stand off the beach and transfer their cargoes to lighters or barges, which came alongside the piers to offload. As there were only four self-propelled lighters, one of them lent by the Navy, and only one good tug for the barges, this was a slow, tedious process. But off-loading the ships actually proved an easier task than getting the supplies up the Camino Real to the troops, so that the troops frequently had slender rations—and occasionally none at all—while large supplies of rations were piled up at Siboney. Since the Army's field kitchens were not available, what food that did get through to the troops was often ill-prepared. The mainstay of the ration was canned roast beef, a product used by the U.S. Army and several foreign ones for many years. Under normal circumstances this was an excellent product. However, the excessive heat in Cuba often rendered it inedible when uncooked. The expedition did have field kitchens, but they were mostly still aboard ship, as was a lot of the corps' heavier equipment. One way to relieve the supply problem would have been to improve the road between Siboney and the front. There was road building equipment available, but it remained on transports, since unloading it would have impeded the landing of rations and equipment, and even if the engineering equipment was landed, using it would reduce the movement of supplies up the Camino Real. It was quite a paradox: To improve the admittedly inadequate flow of supplies that flow would have to be interrupted. Since the corps was basically living from hand-to-mouth, it could not take the risk.

For the troops in the trenches life quickly degenerated into a hard, dirty, hungry, and dangerous experience. Since the enemy proved to be excellent snipers, the besiegers had to adopt a largely nocturnal lifestyle. During daylight hours—between the intermittent heavy rains—they tried to stay out of sight, while at night they worked on entrenchments, performed fatigue duties, and brought up supplies. When supplies were scarce, there was sometimes no food for a day or two. Even tobacco occasionally ran out. Uniforms and shoes, inappropriate as they were (most of the men were wearing blue flannel shirts, wool trousers, and heavy shoes), deteriorated from constant wear in the humidity and heat. Even officers found it impossible to bathe. Since there was little that could be done to improve the flow of supplies from Siboney, officers and men tried to procure food locally. Some units were lucky enough to be able to buy a cow or some hogs from the Cuban peasantry, but this was rare. The ubiquitous land crabs (their habit of crawling about in the dark caused more than one startled sentry to open fire, occasionally resulting in a wild fusillade) proved tasty eating, until the troops observed that they fed on corpses.

The situation inside the defenses of Santiago was no better than that in the trenches outside it. There were over 13,500 troops and 5,000-7,000 civilians in the besieged city. Once the Americans arrived municipal services broke down, and neither Linares nor Toral took adequate measures to place the city under complete mililtary control. As a result, there was probably more suffering than was necessary. Despite the severing of the city's water main, there proved to be enough water available from local wells and cisterns. There was food available, but most of it was in military stockpiles. As a result, civilians had to shift for themselves. Some were able to survive by fishing in the harbor, which gradually became more difficult due to overfishing. There was also a thriving black market, and those with the means managed to purchase enough to sustain life. Those who could find nothing to eat suffered, and some died. Those who died were often left for days in their houses.

Life was somewhat better for the troops. They were fed from military stocks, which proved adequate. Better acclimated than the Americans, the Spanish troops were also more appropriately dressed in a light cotton uniform and the traditional Spanish military sandal. Their defenses were good, mostly erected before the arrival of the U.S. forces, and combined earthworks, blockhouses, and small stone forts, seasoned with about 30 guns, albeit some obsolete. As a result, they suffered less than did their American opponents. In fact, Toral believed he held the upper hand.

Late on 8 July Toral proposed an arrangement whereby he would surrender the city if the garrison were allowed to retire with the honors of war and safe passage to Holguin, over 75 miles to the north. He oberved that he had a good deal of ammunition still available and rations were sufficient to last for some time, particularly since the city was virtually devoid of civilians. He dismissed Shafter's threat of a naval bombardment of the city by pointing out that most of the casualties would inevitably be among remaining civilians, since his troops were in the trenches. He also made pointed reference to the fact that his troops were well acclimated, a veiled reminder that the fever season was almost upon them. Shafter extended the temporary truce for two days so that he could refer Toral's offer to Washington. Considering the military situation, Shafter believed the offer should be accepted. He wired Secretary of War Alger four reasons for doing so: Allowing the Spanish to march away with the honors of war would make the harbor and city immediately available to the American forces; it would permit the thousands of refugees at El Caney to return to their homes; it would prevent the further destruction of property; and that it would make possible the immediate relief of V Corps for use elsewhere, "while it is in good health." In case no one in Washington got this last point, he added that, "There are now three cases of yellow-fever at Siboney, in [the 33rd] Michigan ... no one knows where it will stop." Aside from heat-related illness, there had so far been no serious medical problems in the ranks. Although a number of people in Washington recommended accepting the proposal, including Captain Alfred Thayer Mahan, both the Secretary of War and the President were opposed. Nor were the troops in the trenches in disagreement. In a letter on 10 July to Henry Cabot Lodge, Theodore Roosevelt wrote "It will be a great misfortune to accept anything less than unconditional surrender." The truce expired that afternoon. All through the night the troops on both sides indulged in sniping at each other, with some casualties, while the Navy bombarded Santiago with 8-inch shells for an hour on the 10th and for over three hours on the morning of the 11th, causing the predicted casualties among the civilians, with little effect on the military situation, since the ships were firing with care to avoid hitting V Corps' trenches, in places within a quarter-mile of the Spanish lines.

Neither President McKinley nor Secretary of War Alger were indifferent to the danger that a prolonged siege might hold for the health of V Corps. But both saw that securing Santiago by a negotiated arrangement whereby the Spanish troops could march off with the honors of war would not constitute much of a victory in diplomatic terms. Seeking a way to induce Toral to lay down his arms, Alger came up with a clever scheme. If Toral surrendered, rather than intern his troops somewhere, the United States would return them to Spain. He reasoned that the arrangement would save Spanish military honor, while creating a very favorable impression among the Spanish troops remaining in Cuba, and possibly undermining their morale. Alger cabled his proposal to Shafter on the morning of the 11th. Once more declaring a truce, Shafter passed the communique on to Toral, adding that he had just received considerable reinforcements. The latter was accurate, for on 11 July four fresh batteries had landed, with eight field guns and eight light mortars, plus several regiments, the 1st District of Columbia, the 1st Illinois, the 9th Massachusetts, and the 8th Ohio, along with the commanding general, Nelson A. Miles. While Shafter hustled his fresh troops into the lines, Toral composed a reply to Secretary Alger's proposal.

Toral's response was confusing, made the more so by being in fractured English. He rejected the proposal, and reiterated his offer to accept the honors of war and retire to Holguin. But he went on to state that he desired only "conditions honorable for the Spanish arms." Observing that he believed Shafter a chivalrous and honorable man, he went on to say "therefore must a solution be found that leaves the honor of my troops intact." Shafter could make nothing of this. But Miles, who despite his seniority refused to usurp command, recognized the message as a plea for the Americans to come up with a face-saving arrangement. By careful reading of Toral's messages, he concluded that the Spanish general intended the withdrawal to Holguin to be made only by the troops with their personal arms and equipment, leaving behind his artillery and ammunition stocks. He cabled Secretary Alger that he concurred with Shafter's recommendation that Toral's offer be accepted, reiterating the general's reasons, and added "there are [now] a hundred cases of yellow-fever in this command, and the belief of the Chief Surgeon [is] that it will spread rapidly." Secretary Alger, who greatly disliked the general, remained adamant.

Rebuffed, Miles threw himself into a scheme to storm the harbor forts with some of the troops he had aboard ship, with the support of the Navy. Admiral Sampson had been advocating this operation since before V Corps landed in Cuba, with no response, let alone cooperation, from Shafter. A plan was quickly worked out with the Navy, which lent Lt. Richmond Hobson to Miles as a technical advisor. Covered by supporting fire from the fleet, a brigade (the former 1st Brigade, 1st Division, II Corps, which had fought the sham battle near Dun Loring on 28 June) would be landed east of the Morro on 14 July, to advance to the Punta Gorda battery, thereby isolating the Spanish troops on the eastern side of the harbor entrance. Shafter had been opposed to such an operation from the first, believing that the Navy should undertake the mission on its own. So on 12 July he wired the War Department reiterating his suggestion that the Navy should take responsibility for the mission. Observing that as the rainy season progressed it was becoming imperative that the city be taken immediately, he concluded that if the Navy did not force the harbor entrance, "we will simply have to take the town by assault, without regard to what it costs." In Washington this set off a spate of memoranda between Secretary of War Alger, who supported Shafter's proposal, and Secretary of the Navy Long, who opposed it, further exacerbating interservice tensions as members of the service took sides and as the matter spilled over into the press. At the same time Shafter repeated his recommendation that Toral's offer to withdraw to Holguin be accepted. Miles concurred, and cabled his view to Washington separately. Meanwhile, the generals arranged to meet with Toral. Extending the truce for another day, Shafter offered to meet at 0900 on the 13th at a convenient large tree between the two armies. Toral accepted, reminding Shafter that unless an honorable arrangement could be reached he would have to "make defense as far as my strength will permit."

Under flag of truce Toral and his party arrived at the appointed place precisely at 0900, accompanied by the British Vice-Consul at Santiago, Robert Mason, who had volunteered to serve as an interpreter. Meeting them there were Miles, Shafter and his aide John D. Miley, Joe Wheeler, and an interpreter. The meeting began in the formal style of the age, with salutes and introductions. Miles then took the stage, and basically repeated

Secretary Alger's surrender proposal. Toral observed that he was authorized by Governor-General Blanco to discuss American proposals. He observed that under Spanish law he could not surrender on his own authority so long as his troops had food and ammunition. Therefore, to conclude a surrender he would have to consult Madrid, a matter which might require several days. Observing that Toral had had plenty of time to consult his government, Shafter gave him until 0500 the next morning, or "I will open fire upon your works with every gun I have." Toral responded by saying in that case he would have to fight from house to house if necessary, destroying the city and blocking the harbor so that in the end the Americans "would gain practically nothing, and we would both suffer a terrible loss, for my men can fight." When Shafter agreed that Spanish troops could indeed fight, Toral repeated his request for more time. Shafter and Miles walked off a short way. They spoke briefly, then returned. Miles informed Toral that he would have until noon on the 14th, a seven hour extension. In fact, Toral was bluffing. To be sure, the garrison had enough food, 1.2 million rations, perhaps 30 days' supply. But it was fast running out of ammunition. There were less than 200 rounds available per infantryman.

Madrid was already fully aware of the desperate plight of the garrision of Santiago. The problem was not a lack of information, but one of political will. The Liberal cabinet, under Praxedes Sagasta, wanted to be sure that it not suffer adversely from the political consequences of a surrender. The loss of Santiago was likely to prove the loss of the Empire, and although the disaster had begun during a Conservative administration it was the Liberals who were now in power, and likely to bear the blame. The government also had to be sure that the Army would accept its decision. rebellion was not exactly alien to the Spanish military ethos. Even as Shafter and Toral were sending each other polite notes, the government was requesting the views of Captain-General Blanco as to what the Army in Cuba would do if Toral was authorized to surrender. Not until 14 July did Blanco respond, saying that although the Army wished to prolong the defense of Santiago, it would obey orders. That very same morning Toral received authority to negotiate a "capitulation" on the basis of the Alger plan, with the repatriation of the surrendered garrison. The American and Spanish commissioners met at 1430 hours that same afternoon. To the surpise of the Americans, Toral agreed to surrender all the troops of the Division of Santiago, not merely those in the city itself, but also those who were not in the city, another 9,000 men, who had been virtually inactive throughout the entire campaign. But they quickly ran into other problems. The Spanish had to consult with Madrid over several of the points to be negotiated. Talks had to be suspended while this took place. On the 15th the cables to both Washington and Madrid experienced heavy use. Not until 2200 hours—10:00 p.m.—was Toral able to inform Shafter that all issues had been resolved. The articles of capitulation—the word "surrender" was avoided—were signed at 1800 hours on 16 July, and the formal ceremonies were held the next day. On 17 July, amid salutes and elaborate ceremony, the Spanish troops marched out of Santiago to lay down their arms.

The surrender of Santiago probably saved the United States from a major military disaster. Although Toral's garrison was in a difficult situation—all but one of the colonels and generals had been killed or wounded, and there was little Mauser ammunition left—that of the American forces was about to become much worse. Although the food supply improved almost immediately upon the surrender, and although the flow of medical supplies increased markedly—the first ship into Santiago harbor was the Red Cross supply vessel *City of Texas*, with Clara Barton aboard—V Corps was confronted by a major medical crisis. The first case of yellow fever had been detected on 6 June. By the 8th there were three cases, by the 11th a hundred, and the number kept rising. Meanwhile malaria broke out, while many men came down with dysentery, as a result of eating bad food and drinking bad water. By 13 July plans were afoot to relocate the corps' camps to higher ground, where "infection" was known to be less. Although the role of the mosquito as a vector for yellow fever and malaria was as yet unknown, experience had shown that higher, cooler elevations greatly reduced the disease rate. On 14 July the men of the 24th Infantry, one of the Army's black regiments, volunteered to serve as nurses, it being widely believed that African-Americans had a natural immunity to yellow fever. Of the 60 men accepted, 36 eventually died of malaria or yellow fever.

Soon it seemed as though virtually the entire corps was on the sick list, and in fact only 20 percent of the troops appear to have avoided infection. Routine military tasks, such as inspections and the posting of sentries, had to be suspended in most regiments because there were few men fit for duty. Morale, which had held steady through the siege, plummeted. At first Shafter failed to properly notify the War Department that a medical crisis was at hand. But on 19 July he requested hundreds of medical personnel, hospital attendants, nurses, and doctors, as well as two "immune" regiments. Adjutant General Henry C. Corbin, who was functioning as the President's chief-of-staff, directly queried the general as to how serious the yellow fever problem was. Taking three days to reply, Shafter hedged by saying that his medical personnel were uncertain as to the number, but that there some ill in every regiment, and that he was moving the troops to higher ground as quickly as possible. Not until 23 July did he admit there was a major problem, and even then minimized it by saying there were only about 1500 sick men in V Corps, of whom no more than 10 percent were down with yellow fever. In fact the number of sick men was more than double Shafter's figure, and while most had malaria, not yellow fever, the number was growing daily. By 28 July there were over 4000 sick men in the corps. Not until 2 August did Shafter flatly inform the War Department that V Corps was confronted with a major epidemic, wiring "I am told that at any time an epidemic of yellow fever is liable to occur. I advise that the troops be moved as rapidly as possible while the sickness is of a mild type." On the advice of the Surgeon General, who was acting on the basis of contemporary medical expertise, Secretary Alger urged Shafter to move the troops to higher ground north of Santiago, "where yellow fever is impossible." It was not the response Shafter was seeking.

On 3 August Shafter convened a meeting of senior officers, among whom was Theodore Roosevelt, acting commander of the 2nd Cavalry Brigade. The general read Alger's message. They took it badly. They believed that the only way to cope with the epidemic was to get the troops out of Cuba entirely. Shafter hinted that word of the plight of V Corps be leaked to the press. But only Roosevelt, a volunteer with no career to worry about, was willing to speak openly. He expressed a willingness to be interviewed. Leonard Wood suggested that the senior officers prepare a joint message to Shafter expressing their concern. This was done. In the letter, later famous as the "Round Robin," the division and brigade commanders conceded that the corps did not yet have an epidemic of yellow fever, but suggested that one was imminent. They cited reasons to demonstrate that the solution proposed by Secretary Alger was unworkable and went on to conclude "This army must be moved at once or it will perish." Meanwhile, Roosevelt, who signed the Round Robin, prepared a much stronger letter, in which he wrote, "to keep us here ... will simply involve the destruction of thousands." To these letters, Shafter added a report by the medical staff of the corps which substantially supported the position of the senior officers in the Round Robin. Shafter forwarded all three to the War Department, to which he added "In my opinion there is but one course to take, and that is to immediately transport the Fifth Corps ... to the United States. If this is not done, I believe the death rate will be appalling." Then he leaked the Round Robin and Roosevelt's letter to the press.

On 4 August newspapers all across the United States published the Round Robin and Roosevelt's even stronger letter. The public outcry was enormous. The War Department, already under criticism for apparent failures in mobilization and for the squalid conditions at some of the training camps, came in for even heavier criticism, which naturally tarred the Administration, setting off a chain of events that would leave the careers of several distinguished soldiers in ruins and lead to major reforms in the administration of the army, while ultimately propelling Roosevelt into the White House. Yet unbeknown to the officers who signed the Round Robin, the War Department had already taken steps to withdraw V Corps from Cuba. On 2 August a contract had been concluded with the Long Island Rail Road for the use of its dock facilities at Montauk Point. Over the next few days arrangements were hastily made to erect a camp—named Camp Wikoff in honor of a brigade commander killed before Santiago on 1 August—where V Corps could recuperate. Orders to begin the evacuation of V Corps were issued on 5 August, and the first troops took ship two days later. Meanwhile fresh regiments, the so-called "Immunes," were arriving to assume occupation duties at Santiago.

The voyage to Camp Wikoff took seven days. Conditions aboard the transports were not good, for they were poorly prepared to deal with the many sick and debilitated men which they had to carry. When the men arrived at Camp Wikoff conditions were little better, for facilities were only partially completed. Literally thousands of public spirited citizens pitched in to help, sending food and clothing and even tending to the sick. Conditions gradually improved. Of the approximately 20,000 men who passed through Camp Wikoff, only 257 died, mostly from yellow fever or malaria, in contrast to the 514 who succumbed in Cuba. But while V Corps was being withdrawn from Cuba, the war went on. The blockade continued, and American troops went into action in Puerto Rico and the Philippines.

Fitzhugh Lee

Fitzhugh Lee (1835-1905) was born on a plantation in Virginia. At West Point he was almost dismissed for misconduct, but managed to convince the superintendent (who happened to be his uncle Robert E. Lee) to permit him to remain. He graduated in 1856, 45th in his class. "Fitz," as he was known, served in the cavalry on the frontier, and was severely wounded fighting Indians. When Virginia seceded he was tactical officer at West Point. Lee resigned his commission as a first lieutenant on 21 May 1861, almost immediately entering Confederate service in the same grade, and was shortly named lieutenant colonel of the 1st Virginia Cavalry.

During the Peninsula Campaign Lee at first served on Richard Ewell's staff and later on that of Joseph E. Johnston, during which he accompanied J.E.B. Stuart on his famous "Ride around the Union Army." He was made a brigadier general in July of 1862 and commanded a cavalry brigade at South Mountain and Antietam and on raids and reconnaissances in late 1862 and early 1863. His brigade covered the flank march of Lt. Gen. Thomas "Stonewall" Jackson's II Corps during the Chancellorsville Campaign and he served ably during the following Gettysburg Campaign, being promoted major general shortly afterwards. During Grant's 1864 campaign Lee led a division with particular distinction at Spotsylvania and during Jubal Early's operations in the Shenandoah Valley. In January of 1865 he assumed command of the Cavalry Corps when Wade Hampton was ordered to the Carolinas. He led his uncle's cavalry thereafter until Appomattox. After the war Lee took up farming and writing, producing a biography of his famous uncle and several other historical works. He served as governor of Virginia from 1885 to 1889. Lee was appointed U.S. consul in Havana in 1896, and served in that capacity until the outbreak of the Spanish-American War in 1898.

During the war he was commissioned a major general of volunteers and given VII Corps, organizing at Jacksonville. Although he did not see field service Lee's experience in the Civil War paid off during the War with Spain. He proved a very able organizer and trainer of troops, and his corps had few of the administrative and health problems which plagued many of the others. Shortly after the armistice, VII Corps was sent to Cuba on occupation duty.

After the war, Lee remained on active duty as a brigadier general in the Regular Army, retiring in 1902. When he died, he was buried in his U.S. Army uniform, prompting one ex-Confederate to say, "What'll Stonewall think when Fitz turns up in heaven wearing that!"

José Toral Vazquez

José Toral Vazquez (1832-1904), the scion of an old military family, had a relatively pedestrian military career. Although he entered the military academy at a young age, as was the custom in Spain at the time, and served in the several colonial, foreign, and civil wars which plagued the country from the 1840s to the 1870s, it was not until 1889 that he rose to brigadier general. For most of his military career Toral served in various administrative and staff positions, and was only occasionally in line positions, and then mostly in garrison. The outbreak of the Cuban Revolution in 1895 found him in command of the 1st Brigade of the 1st Division of the I Army Corps, an essentially ceremonial unit on garrison in Madrid. He volunteered for service in Cuba and was soon commanding a brigade holding the Guantanamo area, in southern Santiago Province. In this capacity he saw a great deal of service against the Rebels, and proved a moderately capable commander. Still at this work when the Spanish-American War broke out, he was called to Santiago by Linares, his superior, as an American invasion became more likely.

At Santiago Toral was subordinate to Linares, until the latter was wounded, whereupon command devolved upon him. It was a very difficult situation, with V Corps closely investing the city. Toral twice refused Shafter's demand that he surrender, and made strenuous efforts to bolster the defense. However, in the end, he had little choice, and he did manage to secure rather favorable terms. Arguably, he might have been able to prolong the defense. If he could have stretched resistance out for a few more weeks the effects of fever might have forced an American withdrawal, which would certainly have greatly improved Spain's negotiating position. But his own troops were suffering greatly as well, and it seems unlikely that they could have held out long enough to affect the outcome of the war. Upon repatriation in early 1899 Toral was subject to a court martial. Although he managed to clear himself of all charges of culpability or cowardice, he saw no further active service. By no means a great commander, Toral managed as well as anyone could have done in the circumstances.

The American People Answer the Call

Units Raised for the Army

Contingent	Inf Rgts	Cav	Art Bttys	Other
Alabama	3			
Arizona/New Mexico	1			
Arkansas	2			
California	4		4	
Colorado	1		1	
Connecticut	2		3	
Delaware	1			
D.C.	1			
Florida	1			
Georgia	3		2	
Idaho	1			
Illinois	9	1 rgt	1	
Indiana	5 + 2 coys		2	
Iowa	4		2	
Kansas	4			
Kentucky	4	2 trps		
Louisiana	3			
Maine	1		4	
Maryland	2			
Massachusetts	5		12 (coastal)	
Michigan	5			
Minnesota	4			
Mississippi	3			
Missouri	1		1	
Montana	1			
Nebraska	2			
Nevada	1	1 trp		
New Hampshire	1			
New Jersey	4			
New York	15	2 trps	3	
North Carolina	3			
North Dakota	1			
Ohio	10	1 rgt	4	
Oregon	2		2	
Pennsylvania	17	3 trps	3	
Rhode Island	1			
South Carolina	2		1	
South Dakota	1			
Tennessee	4			
Territories*	1			
Texas	4	1 rgt		

Contingent	Inf Rgts	Cav	Art Bttys	Other
Utah		1 rgt	3	
Vermont	1			
Virginia	5			
Washington	2			
West Virginia	2			
Wisconsin	4		1	
Wyoming	1		1	
U.S.V.	10	3 rgts		3 rgts engineers 17 coys signals
Private			1**	

Summary

Infantry:	163 regiments and 2 companies
Cavalry:	6 regiments and 9 troops
Artillery:	1 regiment and 32 batteries
Engineers:	3 regiments
Signals:	17 companies

* *Personnel recruited from Arizona, New Mexico, and Oklahoma. In addition, many men from these areas joined the U.S. Volunteer Cavalry.*

** *Recruited at John Jacob Astor's expense by Lt. Peyton March (Astor himself served as an aide-de-camp to Shafter in Cuba.)*

The Naval Militia

Before the war 15 states had a naval militia. These men volunteered for duty at the outbreak of the war. Along with newly organized contingents from Florida and Virginia, a total of about 4,500 naval militiamen served in the war, some 2,600 afloat and another 1,800 ashore, with considerable efficiency.

Militia by State

State	Naval Men	State	Men
California	385	New Jersey	365
Connecticut	165	New York	475
Florida	185	North Carolina	230
Georgia	225	Ohio	215
Illinois	525	Pennsylvania	215
Louisiana	260	Rhode Island	130
Maryland	240	South Carolina	150
Massachusetts	440	Virginia	45
Michigan	195		

In addition to providing most of the crews for the auxiliary cruisers *Yosemite* (Michiganders), *Yankee* (New Yorkers), *Dixie* and *Badger*

(Marylanders), *Prairie* (Bay Staters), and *Resolute* (Jerseyites), naval militiamen served aboard many of the other ships in the fleet, and were entirely entrusted with the operation of the navy's 36 coastal signal stations during the war.

Civil War Veterans in the War

A surprising number of those who attained some prominence in the Civil War served in the Spanish-American War. Indeed, virtually all senior officers from colonel on up were veterans of the earlier war, some of them with distinguished records. While most of these men had fought for the Union, President McKinley distributed volunteer commissions to several former Confederates, as a way of both strengthening Southern support for the war and helping to further heal the wounds of the earlier conflict.

Some Notable Union Army Veterans in the War

Maj. Gen. John R. Brooke, brigadier general of volunteers in 1865, commanded a division in Puerto Rico.

Maj. John Lincoln Clem, the "Drummer Boy of Shiloh," was in the quartermaster corps, but saw no overseas service.

Maj. Gen. Grenville Dodge, more famous as the chief engineer of the Union Pacific Railroad, held the same rank in the Civil War and served in an administrative capacity after being recalled to service in 1898.

Brig. Gen. Guy V. Henry, who commanded a column in Puerto Rico, had emerged from the Civil War as a full colonel, and later won a Medal of Honor in the Indian Wars.

Maj. Gen. Alexander McDowell McCook, one of the famous "Fighting McCooks of Ohio," ended the Civil War as a brigadier general of volunteers, stayed on in the post-war army, and held an administrative post in 1898.

Maj. Gen. Wesley Merritt, who commanded VIII Corps in the Philippines, had been a brigadier general of volunteers in the Civil War and a led a cavalry brigade at Gettysburg.

Brig. Gen. Arthur MacArthur, who commanded a brigade and later a division in the Philippines, had won a Medal of Honor for leading a regiment at Missionary Ridge in 1864.

Maj. Gen. Nelson A. Miles, the commanding general of the Army, had risen from second lieutenant to major general of volunteers during the Civil War.

Maj. Gen. William R. Shafter, commander of V Corps in Cuba, had emerged from the Civil War as a brevet brigadier general, with a Medal of Honor.

Brig. Gen. Edwin Vose Sumner, Jr., who commanded a brigade in Cuba, had won a brevet promotion to brigadier general in the Civil War.

Maj. Gen. John H. Wilson, a "boy wonder" cavalryman who was a major general of volunteers five years after graduating from West Point in 1860, was officially commander of VI Corps, which was never organized, but managed to get into action commanding a division in Puerto Rico.

Brig. Gen. Samuel B. Young, who commanded a cavalry brigade in Cuba, had a brevet in the same rank from 1865.

Some Notable Union Naval Veterans

Capt. Charles C. Clark, who took the battleship *Oregon* on her famed voyage around South America to join the fleet off Cuba, had been with Farragut at Mobile Bay.

Commodore George Dewey, the hero of Manila Bay, had been a junior officer on the Mississippi and the East Coast during the Civil War, and fought in the naval brigade at the storming of Fort Fisher.

Capt. Nehemiah H. Dyer, of USS *Baltimore* at Manila Bay, entered the Navy as a volunteer officer in 1862, served in various vessels, was commended for gallantry at Mobile Bay, achieved the highest score on the exam given volunteer naval officers who wished to enter the regular service—2274 out of a possible 2753, equivalent to 82 percent—and was commissioned a lieutenant. He retired shortly after the Spanish-American War as a rear-admiral.

Capt. Robley D. Evans, of the battleship *Iowa* at Santiago, graduated from Annapolis at the age of 17 (having lied about his age four years earlier), served on blockade duty and with the naval brigade in the storming of Fort Fisher, where he was severely wounded.

Capt. Charles V. Gridley of Dewey's flagship *Olympia*, had been with Farragut at Mobile Bay.

Rear Adm. William T. Sampson, who commanded at Santiago, had done blockade duty during the Civil War, and was aboard the monitor *Patapsco* when she was mined in Charleston harbor in early 1865.

Commodore Winfield Scott Schley, second in command at Santiago, had seen extensive riverine and blockade service during the Civil War.

Capt. Charles D. Sigsbee, of the ill-fated *Maine*, had been with Farragut at Mobile Bay.

Some Notable Confederate Army Veterans

Maj. Gen. Matthew C. Butler, who had held the same rank in Confederate service, was one of the commissioners who supervised the Spanish evacuation of Cuba.

Maj. Gen. Fitzhugh Lee had been a Confederate general. In 1898 he commanded VII Corps on occupation duties at Havana, where he would have led the attack had the war lasted longer.

Brig. Gen. William C. Oates led the *15th Alabama* up Little Round Top on 2 July 1863, only to see it shattered by the 20th Maine; a notorious segregationist, he behaved so boorishly towards the black 9th Ohio Battalion in his brigade of II Corps that he was transferred.

Brig. Gen. Thomas L. Rosser held the same rank in the Confederate Army, but saw no active service in 1898.

Maj. Gen. Joseph Wheeler, who had held that rank in the Confederate Army, commanded the cavalry division in V Corps at Santiago.

An Other

Clara Barton, who had begun her career as a nurse and relief worker during the Civil War, and gone on to found the American Red Cross, served as a relief worker in Cuba even before the Spanish-American War, organizing supplies and medical services for refugees. When the war came, she went too, taking a shipload of supplies into Santiago.

Black Personnel in the U.S. Armed Forces

The 1890s were a period of delicate balance in terms of race relations in the U.S. On the one hand, in the wake of *Plessey vs Ferguson*, Jim Crow was becoming firmly established throughout much of the country, eroding many of the gains black Americans had made in the aftermath of the Civil War. On the other hand, the Republican party still maintained some sense of obligation towards black citizens, handing out patronage to black party-stalwarts in the South, in some areas of which there still were a surprising number of black voters and elected officials.

When the nation went to war, its black citizens responded with an enthusiasm equaling that of their white counterparts. And black men offered themselves for service.

African Americans could, of course, join one of the Regular Army's four black regiments. The enlisted ranks of the 24th and 25th Infantry and the 9th and 10th Cavalry, raised shortly after the Civil War, consisted entirely of African-Americans. In these regiments almost all the officers were white. Aside from chaplains, there were only a handful of black officers in the Army, never more than two at any one time. These were among the elite units of the army. However,

regiments required few recruits. So if black men were to serve in some numbers, they would have to join the volunteer army.

Very early in the war the black press began to agitate for the recruitment of black volunteers. A delegation of notable black citizens, led by Pinckney B.S. Pinochet, a prominent black Republican and former Reconstruction lieutenant governor of Louisiana, paid a visit to President McKinley to urge the recruitment of black men. The delegation, which included a number of distinguished veterans of the Civil War and the militia, succeeded in extracting from the President a pledge that African-Americans would be accepted for service in the volunteer army, including service as officers (as one black paper put it, "No officers, no fight."), to be recruited on the same terms as white volunteers. Indeed, state quotas often specified the number of black men to be recruited. Alabama's quota, for example, specified two regments of whites and one of blacks, which created some problems since the state militia had three regiments and several separate batteries and troops of whites but only two companies of black men.

The decision to recruit black men

was widely applauded in the black community. Notable African-Americans were very active in recruiting. Ida Wells, for example, the distinguished journalist and civil rights advocate, helped raise the 8th Illinois, while organizations such as "The Patriot Colored Women of Brooklyn" organized canteens and collected funds to support the troops.

Surprisingly, there were considerable numbers of black National Guardsmen, and not only in the North. Georgia, for example, had 2,072 black men in its National Guard, 19-percent of its strength. Although Georgia was rather unique in terms of the proportion of black militiamen in its National Guard, there were black battalions or companies in the Alabama, Connecticut, Illinois, Kansas, Maryland, Massachusetts, Ohio, Tennessee, and Virginia militia, as well as in the District of Columbia. In addition, a few black men served in otherwise all-white units in several states, such as South Dakota and Ohio.

Mobilization of Black Volunteers

State	Unit
Alabama	3rd Alabama
D.C.	1st D.C. Separate Battalion
Illinois	8th Illinois
Kansas	23rd Kansas
Massachusetts	Company L, 6th Massachusetts
North Carolina	3rd North Carolina
Ohio	9th Ohio Battalion
Virginia	6th Virginia

In addition, the 7th, 8th, 9th, and 10th U.S. Volunteers—so-called "Immune" regiments—were composed of black men, many of whom were recruited by states (for example, Indiana raised two companies for the 8th U.S.V.). Of black men serving in otherwise white outfits, one man in the 5th Ohio was not accepted for federal service, while one in the 1st South Dakota was, shipping out with his regiment and seeing active service in the Philippines, making the regiment the first openly integrated U.S. Army unit since the Revolutionary War. Additional black units were the 48th and 49th U.S. Volunteers, raised after the war for the Philippine Insurrection. Although the men in some black units raised in the South were poorly educated (in Alabama about 30 percent of black recruits were unable to sign their own names, in contrast to only about 6 percent of whites), those in units raised in other areas were educationally at about the level of their white counterparts, and in some cases superior, since there were relatively fewer slots for black recruits than there were for whites. The junior officers in these units were often black men. Many former NCOs from the four Regular Army regiments accepted commissions in black volunteer regiments, while some men who had graduated from what would today be called R.O.T.C. programs at places such as Tuskegee Institute and Howard University were also commissioned. The only black volunteer unit which had no African-American officers was the 3rd Alabama. The 8th Illinois had a black commander, Col. John R. Marshall, a prosperous businessman. Although some "race" newspapers expressed the view that Marshall was merely being used as a "front" to improve recruiting, in fact he commanded the regiment throughout its time in Federal service, which included occupation duty in Cuba from 15 August 1898 to 11 March 1899.

All four black regular regiments saw extensive combat service in Cuba and in the Philippine Insurrection. The four black U.S.V. "immune" regiments performed occupation duty in Cuba after the armistice, as did the 8th Illinois, while the 48th and 49th U.S.V. saw combat during the Filipino-American War. The only black state volunteers to come under fire in the war with Spain were the men of Company L, 6th Massachusetts, an otherwise white regiment, which engaged in some skirmishing during the campaign in Puerto Rico. This regiment had a chequered career.

Upon being mustered into service the 6th Massachusetts was sent south for training. Passing through Baltimore the regiment was given a rousing reception, quite a surprise considering that the city was one of the most racially segregated in the country. Indeed, in the first days of the Civil War the same regiment had been assaulted by a secessionist mob with bloody results. The regiment was assigned to the Puerto Rican expedition. When Brig. Gen. G.A. Garretson found out he had a

black company in his command he attempted to get it transferred out to the 9th Ohio Battalion. The regimental commander, Col. Charles Woodward, successfully opposed Garretson, with the backing of the governor of Massachuetts and ultimately the President. So the regiment went to Puerto Rico with Company L. Unfortunately, Col. Woodward's views on race relations were considerably better than his abilities as a military commander. He was rather lax in the performance of his duties and clearly not attuned to the serious nature of war (he brought his 15 year old son along with the regiment, so the boy would have a taste of war). After two instances of panic in the ranks— both white and black—in less than 24 hours, during both of which Woodward was absent from his regiment sleeping aboard a transport, Garretson relieved him of command. Although the claim has been made by some journalists and historians that Woodward was relieved because of his refusal to relinquish Company L, Garretson's decision was certainly militarily justifiable.

The exact numbers of black men who served in the war with Spain are difficult to establish. About 7,000 black men seem to have served in state volunteer units, nearly 5,000 in the four "immune" regiments, and about 5,000 more in the four regular army black regiments, for a total of 17,000 men, about 6 percent of the total Army manpower.

The Navy also included many black men. In fact, nearly 10 percent of the men in the fleet were black. Over a score of those killed when

USS *Maine* blew up were African-Americans. Unlike the Army, the Navy was not segregated, at least not on the lower deck. Although there were no African-American officers, blacks served alongside whites in all enlisted positions, including such prestigious petty officer ratings as Chief Bosun's Mate and Chief Gunner's Mate. The Revenue Cutter Service—precursor of the Coast Guard—not only had black enlisted personnel, but also a few officers, some of whom served as ships' captains. Including the men in the Navy and the Revenue Cutter Service, the total number of black personnel on duty with the Armed Forces during the war with Spain was probably a little more than 20,000, about six or seven percent of those enrolled.

At the time, many notable Americans openly praised the performance of black troops. For example, although at one point he implied a lack of determination on the part of some black regulars, overall in his *The Rough Riders* memoir of the war, Theodore Roosevelt several times remarked upon the courage of the black cavalrymen at Las Guasimas and on the Heights of San Juan. Observing that black soldiers were suspicious of white officers not from their own regiments, when they had confidence in the officers over them "the colored troops did as well as any soldiers could possibly do." Commenting on the performance of the men of the 24th Infantry, an officer of the 6th Infantry said, "Those colored fellows were the lions, afraid of nothing," while a Southern-born officer observed, "They were the best, the readiest, the most

cheerful, and, I believe, the deadliest fighters in the war." Despite this, most—though not all—white newspapers played down the accomplishments of black troops, and played up their faults. Col. Robert Lee Bullard (who later commanded a corps in the Muese-Argonne) of the 3rd Alabama, hardly an advocate of racial equality, remarked that every time two of his men had a fight the press was quick to report a riot by hundreds of intoxicated blacks.

The welcome accorded black troops by civilians was mixed. In some cases, even in the South, black volunteers passing through town were greeted with as much enthusiasm as had been accorded whites. In others, however, they were greeted with sullen silence, or occasional jeers. Of course black troops were subject to most of the indignities commonly inflicted upon African-Americans in the 1890s, not always without protest, and there were a number of clashes with white troops and citizens, a few of which lead to violence and some deaths.

Interestingly, although the "color line" was drawn quite sharply with regard to African-Americans, the army was otherwise comparatively well-integrated. Jewish volunteers, prompted by memories of Spanish persecution, numbered about 4,000 and were found in many regiments. Seven served in the Rough Riders, including one officer, and nearly 100 in the 1st California. Thousands of American Indians (500 Cheyenne alone) and Mexican-Americans were accepted for service, including some as officers, and there were even some Asian-Americans in the ranks.

Overall, the war had little influence on the role of blacks in the armed forces. Although two regiments of black volunteers, including many officers, were raised for the Philippine Insurrection, the 48th and 49th U.S.V., they were discharged when the emergency was over. The number of black regulars remained unchanged, as did the number of black National Guardsmen.

American Women in Medical Service

In contrast to the experience of the Civil War, there was little acrimony when Congress authorized the recruitment of female nurses for war service. In part this was due to experience gained during the Civil War and also to the increasing status of nursing as a profession in latter nineteenth century. Nurses were paid $30 a month plus room and board, a good wage for the day. Initially they were recruited by the Medical Department through the Red Cross, the Daughters of the American Revolution, and other organizations. On 29 August Dr. Anita N. McGee was commissioned an assistant surgeon (effectively a captain) in the Army and appointed assistant to the Surgeon General in charge of the new Nurse Corps. A total of 8000 women nurses were authorized. Most served at reception camps and hospitals in the U.S., including Camp Wikoff. About 1600 women nurses served abroad, some aboard hospital ships during hostilities, but most with the post-war occupation forces in Cuba and Puerto Rico.

The successful large scale employment of women as nurses during the war with Spain—nearly three times as many as had been recruited during the Civil War—directly resulted in the creation of the Army Nurse Corps and the Navy Nurse Corps shortly after the war.

The Cuban Army

The Cuban revolutionaries created a well organized military force. They divided Cuba into six army corps districts, each responsible for recruiting and operations within its district. Combat units were small, and a corps might have no more than 2,000-3,000 men under arms. The basic unit was the company, usually recruited locally. On paper a company was supposed to number 48 to 65 men, but was often smaller. Two companies constituted a battalion, usually 100-150 men, but occasionally as few as 50. Two or three battalions made a regiment, from 100 to 500 men. Two regiments formed a brigade, two or three brigades a division. On paper cavalry regiments comprised four squadrons of 72 men each, but in fact a large portion of the Cuban infantry was also mounted.

The primary weapons were the rifle, usually a Remington '71, and the machete. There was a handful of artillery available, manned mostly by foreign adventurers like Frederick Funston.

Racially, the rebel army was completely integrated, right up to the highest ranks, the Maceo brothers being among the highest ranking Cuban commanders. However, the typical *mambi*—as rebel troops were nicknamed—was black about 70 percent of the time, out of a population that was only 32 percent black. Robert Lee Bullard, an American officer, observed that blacks were the backbone of the rebellion, "the soldier, the man behind the gun, the arm that swung the machete." This created problems, since most of the political leadership was white, as were most of the foreign volunteers, adventurers, and mercenaries.

There were few genuine battles during the insurrection, the only action really meriting the name being at Bayamo in 1895, in which a large rebel force was cut to pieces, a lesson kept in mind for the rest of the war. Hit-and-run was the principal rebel tactic, fixed ambushes and mounted machete charges the norm.

Frederick Funston, who was for a while chief of artillery in the rebel army, described the Cuban insurgent as " a ragged, unwashed individual, armed with a Remington rifle, and machete." Like all peasant soldiers, the Cuban rebel was hardy, tough, and stubborn. The insurgents claimed to have lost 5,180 men in action, plus a further 3,437 to disease, very likely understated figures. Only 53,744 veterans received pensions from the Cuban Republic after the war. So even assuming the casualty figures to be accurate, there were barely 60,000 men in the insurgent army at any time. Peak strength was probably not more than 40,000 in early 1896, and by the time the Spanish-American War broke out may have been less than 30,000.

Chapter VI

The Campaign in Puerto Rico

Although brief, the American campaign in Puerto Rico was one of the most interesting operations undertaken by the United States during the Spanish-American War. Despite this, it is practically forgotten. This is unfortunate, for the campaign was neither minor nor a walkover. U.S. forces committed to Puerto Rico totaled about 16,000 men, almost as many as served in Cuba, and nearly twice as many as those who were sent to the Philippines; Spanish forces were of comparable scale.

More importantly, certain aspects of the campaign throw some interesting light on the operational abilities of the U.S. Army. In Puerto Rico the army showed a considerable mastery of basic tactics, and it demonstrated how effectively a few months training served to turn the volunteers into reasonably capable soldiers.

Objective Number 2

The genesis of the campaign in Puerto Rico is rather confusing. Ultimately, once war had been declared, consideration of an American invasion of Puerto Rico became inevitable. There were several sound reasons for such an undertaking. After all, an invasion of Puerto Rico would liberate yet another supposedly oppressed populace from the "Spanish yoke." It would also deny the Spanish fleet the use of the port of San Juan, and eliminate an isolated but reasonably strong Spanish garrison. Then too, it would result in the acquisition of potentially profitable real estate. Of some consequence was the island's excellent geographic advantages. Not only did it possess the fine anchorage that is now known as Roosevelt Roads, but the island could serve as a base to project power into both the Caribbean and the South Atlantic. There were potential geopolitical implications as well, for it was known that the German General Staff had included the island in its contingency planning for war with the United States. Finally, the more the U.S. took from Spain, the less it might have to give back as part of a peace settlement. Nevertheless, even in view of the obvious advantages of an invasion of Puerto Rico, it is difficult to determine who precisely was the first to suggest the operation.

The Army's Military Intelligence Division (MID) had been collecting information on Puerto Rico since 1893. However, despite the charges of radical Puerto Rican nationalists, this was hardly a demonstration of an inordinate pre-war American interest in the island. After all, the MID was in the business of collecting information on potential foreign enemies, of which Spain certainly was one, and Puerto Rico was certainly a Spanish possession. In fact, one of the first clearly stated suggestions that the United States invade Puerto Rico in the event of a war with Spain came from Puerto Rican nationalists. On 14 March 1898—at a time when war seemed inevitable— Roberto Todd, head of the *Club de Borinquen* of New York, at the urging of such leading Puerto Rican exiles as Dr. Julio Jose Henna of the *Seccion puertoriqueño del partido revolucionario Cubano*, which had been organized in New York in late 1896, wrote a letter to Assistant Secretary of the Navy Theodore Roosevelt. In this letter, Todd urged an American invasion of the island in the event of war, promising that the people would rise in support of any American invasion. Whether this had any influence on subsequent American planning is difficult to determine. It did, however, create a split among the Puerto Rican nationalists. Eugenio Maria de Hostos, the most prominent of them, was adamantly opposed to Todd's initiative. The extent to which Todd's letter stimulated American interest in the island is difficult to assess. It does appear to have strengthened an otherwise vague interest. The island was omitted from the 1896 Naval War College plan for a war with Spain, which envisioned a primarily maritime campaign against Spain, with the army in a decidedly inferior role. On 4 April the Joint Army-Navy Board, the highest American military planning agency, reaffirmed the broad outlines of the 1896 plan, but added a suggestion that it might be desirable to acquire an advanced base in Cuba and to invade Puerto Rico—designated "Objective Number 2"—for the purpose of denying its use to the Spanish in the event that they attempted to reinforce their Cuban garrison.

Other voices were heard urging the invasion and eventual annexation of the island. Philip C. Hanna, American consul in San Juan, was among the most vocal. Hanna pointed out the relative prosperity and health of Puerto Rico in comparison with Cuba. Some of President MacKinley's advisors stressed that the United States accounted for 30.9 percent of Puerto Rico's exports, mostly coffee and sugar, and supplied 20 percent of the island's imports, at a profitable $4.2 million a year. These suggestions made the invasion of the island all the more probable.

Of course, an invasion of Puerto Rico immediately upon the outbreak of war was neither possible nor wise. An army had to be raised, and the Spanish fleet had to be accounted for. These tasks took time. Nevertheless, as the Army mobilized, as Dewey won his resounding victory at Manila, and as the Navy bottled up the Spanish fleet at Santiago de Cuba on 19 May, setting the stage for the Santiago Campaign, preparations for operations in Puerto Rico also began.

On 15 May 1Lt. Henry H. Whitney of the Army landed at Ponce, on the south coast of Puerto Rico, disguised as a British seaman. Over the next two weeks, Whitney carried out an extensive reconnaissance of the southern and western portions of the island, obtaining invaluable information on topography, troop strengths and dispositions, fixed defenses, port facilities, public opinion, and internal communications, even managing to locate a negotiable trail over the central mountains that was not marked on Spanish maps. Had he been caught, Whitney would probably have been shot, but he eluded capture. By 9 June he was in Washington, adding his information to that already accumulated from other sources. More information came in from Philip C. Hanna, who shifted his operation to St. Thomas in the Virgin Islands and kept up a steady stream, not all of it helpful. More useful by far was information provided by the "Porto Rican Commission," an informal body that included Roberto Todd and several Puerto Rican exiles. With their intimate knowledge of the island, they provided a vast amount of intelligence and assisted in sifting that collected by Whitney and other sources. As this information was collated and evaluated, Commanding General Nelson A. Miles began to formulate operational plans.

Nelson A. Miles Plans a Campaign

Miles had been an early advocate of an invasion of Puerto Rico. Indeed, he urged such a course in lieu of landings in Cuba. There were several reasons for this. The Spanish garrison in Puerto Rico—estimated at about 8,000 regular and 12,000 volunteer troops—was essentially on peace-time duty, while that in Cuba had been engaged in a bitter guerrilla war for some years. A green American army would be far better able to cope with the relatively less experienced Puerto Rican garrison than the battle-hardened Cuban one. Moreover, an early campaign would have to occur in the summer, which was an extremely unhealthy time in Cuba, while being considerably less so in Puerto Rico with its generally salubrious climate. Thus, Miles urged that the initial American effort in the war be made against Puerto Rico, with operations in Cuba confined to the seizure of a small port on the east or south coast through which materiel could be funneled to the Cuban insurgents. Miles' plan for a Puerto Rican operation envisioned landing 25,000 or 30,000 of the best prepared men at Cape San Juan, near Fajardo, on the eastern coast of Puerto Rico a few miles southeast of the city of San Juan. The army would have all summer to secure the island. In the process the troops would become inured to the physical hardships of protracted campaigning and would gain valuable combat experience. Then in the autumn, the Puerto Rican veterans would spearhead a massive invasion of Cuba which would probably resolve the issue within a few months at the outside. It was a well reasoned plan, taking advantage of all available information and well suited to the potentially ill-trained invasion force.

Major General Nelson A. Miles, in full uniform. Miles had a distinguished career in the Civil War and the Indian Wars, rising to Commanding General in 1895, a post which was largely ceremonial. When the war with Spain came, Miles worked hard to prepare the Army, but his poor relationship with President McKinley and Secretary of War Alger limited his effectiveness.

But the Administration had other ideas. Secretary of War Russel A. Alger, with whom Miles was on poor terms, and President McKinley desired a major offensive against Havana, the seat of Spanish power in the Caribbean, at the earliest possible moment, with an eye on ending the war as quickly as possible. Of course there was also the influence of Cervera's squadron. Nothing could be done until it was accounted for. When it took refuge in Santiago harbor, that initiated the Santiago Campaign and necessarily postponed any undertaking involving Puerto Rico. On 26 May President McKinley met with Secrtary of the Navy Long, Secretary of the Army Ader, General Miles, Captain Alfred Thayer Mahan, and several other prominent officers to review strategy in the light of these new developments. It was decided to temporarily abandon the Havana operation in favor of an expedition to Santiago, with the suggestion that upon its successful completion the veterans of that campaign, reinforced by newly trained troops from the U.S., could be used for an invasion of Puerto Rico. With that the Puerto Rican operation began to take on a life of its own.

On 4 June, even as Shafter struggled to get the Santiago expedition organized and underway, President McKinley requested Miles to detail his proposals for Puerto Rico, assuming a "worst case" situation, one in which V Corps would be unable to support the invasion. Miles replied on 6 June. He would need 30,000 men in five divisions, plus a reserve of 10,000 more, all to be drawn from among the best troops remaining in the U.S. The expedition would land at Cape San Juan on the east coast of the island. While the bulk of the army would concentrate on the reduction of the city of San Juan, which was rather well fortified, smaller contingents would secure the rest of the island. Miles optimistically estimated the expedition could sail within ten days of being ordered to do so. Surprisingly, the President approved the plan, and on 26 June Miles was formally authorized to organize and command such an expedition.

Miles moved quickly. Orders went out to I, II, and IV Corps, concentrating at Chickamauga, Camp Alger near Washington, and Tampa, to prepare specific units for service with the Puerto Rican expedition. Working with surprising speed, testimony to the increasing experience of army staffs and the increasing availablility of supplies, some units were ready for sea as early as 7 July. Of course, being ready for sea was not necessarily the same as getting to sea. The situation in Cuba was still uncertain and there was a severe shortage of transports. As Secretary Alger and the War Department worked furiously to obtain transports by any means possible, disquieting reports were coming out of Cuba. Miles went to have a look, bringing along some of the troops designated for Puerto Rico and some reinforcements for V Corps. He arrived at Siboney on 11 July and landed the reinforcements for Shafter. Since the health of V Corps was deteriorating rapidly, Miles was careful to keep his Puerto Rico bound troops aboard their transports at Guantanamo Bay, rather than permit them to mingle with the infected troops ashore. He had a hand in the surrender negotiations, and then prepared to take his expedition to Puerto Rico.

To invade Puerto Rico Miles had to get his troops there. However, the transport situation was critical. Not only were vessels required to maintain and eventually repatriate V Corps, but additional ships were necessary to lift the so-called "immune" regiments—outfits composed of men allegedly resistant to tropical diseases—to Cuba, and still more would be needed to carry his army to Puerto Rico. Further complicating matters was the Navy's abortive scheme to form an "Eastern Squadron" to strike at the Canary Islands and Spanish mainland. Despairing of getting any cooperation from the sister service, on 17 July Miles appealed to the President. Within 24 hours he had confirmation of his orders to proceed to Puerto Rico and the Navy had been instructed to render him every possible assistance. In the U.S. troops embarked at once, greatly facilitated by Alger's adoption of Maj-Gen John R. Brooke's suggestion that units take ship at ports nearest their training camps rather than at ports closest to Puerto Rico, such as Jacksonville and Miami.

Meanwhile, of course, Miles had his troops lying off Santiago. His transports there weighed anchor on 21 July. After four months of debating strategy and coping with administrative chaos; after the heartbreaking disintegration of V Corps and last minute sibling rivalry with the Navy, Miles was finally to get his wish, a fight with the Spaniards in Puerto Rico.

La Isla Bonita—The Beautiful Island

Puerto Rico enjoyed a rather unique status for a colony in 1898. Practically speaking it was the most free colony in the world, the 950,000 inhabitants even enjoyed rights not possessed by the people of Spain itself. Acting under pressure from Puerto Rican nationalists and mindful of the revolts afoot in Cuba and the Philippines, on 28 November 1897 Spain had granted the island a considerable measure of internal autonomy, including a legislative assembly. In addition, the Captain General, though a royal appointee, had power to veto legislation from Madrid which he believed injurious to the well being of Puerto Rico, so long as such legislation dealt with internal affairs. So while defense, foreign relations, customs, and other taxes remained under the control of Madrid, Puerto Rico was essentially an autonomous province, with control over internal economic, educational, and police matters to a degree which compared favorably with the status of Australia at the time. At

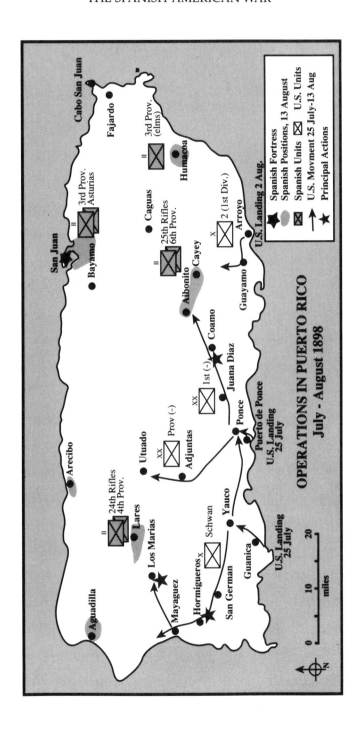

OPERATIONS IN PUERTO RICO
July - August 1898

Spanish Fortress
Spanish Positions, 13 August
Spanish Units
U.S. Units
U.S. Movment 25 July-13 Aug
Principal Actions

234

least on paper. Legislative elections were held on 27 March 1898, with the suffrage confined to wealthier classes. However, the assembly had not begun to function when the war broke out. Acting within his powers as the supreme military officer in Puerto Rico, the newly appointed captain general, Lt. Gen. Manuel Macias Casado, exercised his right to suspend portions of the colonial charter. On 12 May, after an American squadron bombarded San Juan, Macias suspended the balance of the charter, and declared martial law. Meanwhile he ordered defensive preparations.

The military situation of Puerto Rico was not totally bleak. Although about half of the 4,000-man permanent garrison of the island had been sent to help put down the Cuban insurrection, additional units had been raised locally, reinforcements had arrived from Spain, and on 15 May troops had landed from Cuba, despite the American blockade. This gave Macias about 8,000 regular troops, mostly in six infanty battalions with a sprinkling of artillery and services. These troops were well-equipped and reasonably well-trained, and they could be relied upon if well-led. Since most of the ancient militia companies of Puerto Rico, several dating back to the sixteenth century, had been abolished by the Spanish some years earlier for fear they might become the focus of an insurgency, in late May the captain-general authorized the establishment of a new volunteer militia. Response to the call for volunteers was commendably enthusiastic; some 9,000 men came forward to form fourteen infantry battalions and six guerrilla columns. But these troops were less well-equipped and less well-trained than were the regulars, and the units they formed were of very uneven quality. Nevertheless, they might be expected to stand up to the equally inexperienced American volunteers.

The basic defensive plans for Puerto Rico had been worked out in 1897. One regular battalion, in some cases supported by artillery, was stationed on each coast, with one in a central position, and a sixth held near San Juan. These battalions garrisoned the coast and provided stiffening for the volunteers. When an invasion came the idea was not to attempt to defeat it on the beaches, but to harass the invaders, delaying them so that the troops in other parts of the island could concentrate athwart their line of advance on terrain favorable for a defensive action. Should such an action prove successful, the army could assume the offensive and destroy the invaders. If unsuccessful, the troops could fall back toward San Juan possibly trying conclusions again, if necessary retiring into the fortress city to stand siege while irregular forces harassed the enemy's rear. It was a realistic plan, taking into account the vulnerability of Puerto Rico's long coastline and the lack of experience of most of the troops. Given a little luck it might have worked. But Macias' position was seriously flawed.

The majority of the inhabitants of Puerto Rico were no longer committed to Spanish rule, despite their newly won autonomy. Reform had been promised before and by suspending the charter and imposing martial law, Macias was acting in a suspicious fashion. Moreover, Puerto Rican conscripts were fighting in Cuba against a kindred people and a cause with which many sympathized. Save for the resident Spaniards, the clergy, and elements of the upper and middle classes, the war was not popular. The lower classes were largely indifferent; the intellectuals were more or less nationalistic; and much of the middle class largely inclined to independence or American annexation.

Invasion

Miles' invasion plan remained substantially that which he had outlined in his communication to the President on 6 June. His initial contingent, some 3,550 men, would effect a lodgement at Cape San Juan and secure the town of Fajardo. Within days Maj. Gen. James H. Wilson's 3,800 reinforcements would arrive. In fact, they embarked at Charleston even as Miles sailed from Santiago. A few days more and additional forces already taking ship at Newport News, Tampa, and New York would arrive, bringing forces up to about 18,000 men, while more troops would soon follow. With the troops at hand, the plan was for Miles to immediately move against San Juan and seize the city before Spanish forces in the south and west of the island could retire into its defenses. Such was the plan at least. Or at least the plan as Miles explained it to everyone. However, he appears to have feared a leak. Word of the expedition got out. The President and Secretary Alger might be above reproach, but there were others in the Army and the government who might have leaked information to the press. Carl Sandburg, a private in the 6th Illinois, recalled seeing details of the plan, including mention of the Cape San Juan landing site, in newspapers. Moreover, Miles had held extensive meetings with the Porto Rican Commission, pumping them for information on the defenses of San Juan and the eastern end of the island. The suggestion that the expedition's objective had been compromised by a leak was strengthened by last minute intelligence that suggested the Spanish had begun to concentrate strong forces in the vicinity of Cape San Juan. So Miles appears to have decided to use the Cape San Juan operation as a cover plan, and land elsewhere. There is no direct evidence for this. However the way in which events unfolded strongly suggest that this was indeed the case. Strengthening this view is the fact that Miles was quite aware there were neither port facitilies nor a sheltered anchorage at Cape San Juan. A landing would have to be supported across the beaches, a situation which had contributed greatly to the disintegration of V Corps at Santiago. Miles' new objective, which he communicated to no one before putting out to sea, was Guanica, a small port on the southwest coast of Puerto Rico. In contrast to Cape San Juan, Guanica was almost ideal for Miles' purposes. Henry H. Whitney, by now a captain on Miles' staff, had visited it during his reconnaissance and reported favorably on both the harbor and its facilities, indicating that it had good communications to the north and east, noted that there were no coast defenses of any sort, and observed that the inhabitants were highly dissatisfied with Spanish rule.

The first contingent of the expedition put to sea from Guantanamo Bay, Cuba, on 21 July, while Miles sailed from Santiago, bringing along a provisional engineer battalion which had just been organized in V Corps. The convoy steamed eastward for three days through the Windward Passage, between Haiti and Cuba, and on toward Puerto Rico. On 22 July Miles informed the commander of his naval escort that the objective had been changed. Nevertheless, the convoy maintained course for Cape

San Juan until the night of 24-25 July.

Late on the 24th the expedition was north of Puerto Rico, about 50 miles northwest of San Juan. For most of the previous four days, the little fleet averaged only five or six knots, fairly common for merchantmen of the day. When the change of course was ordered, west, then south through Mona passage, speed was increased to about eight knots, maximum speed for most of the ships. Meanwhile a cruiser continued on to Cape San Juan. Its primary mission was to inform the reinforcement convoys of the change in plans, but it was also to fire a "preliminary bombardment," thereby further pinning Spanish attention to the eastern end of the island.

The convoy arrived off Guanica at about 0520 hours on 25 July. The invasion began at 0845 hours.

The armed yacht USS *Gloucester*, which had already reconnoitered Guanica on the 20th, stood in toward the harbor at 0845. Firing several rounds from her 6-pounders, she received no reply, and pressed on, entering the port. Within a short time a detachment of marines and sailors was put ashore, the customs house seized, and the stars and stripes run up the flagpole. A small contingent of Spanish troops—probably local militiamen from the *8th Volunteer Battalion*—opened fire. The marines set up a Colt machine gun and the bluejackets opened up with rifle fire, while *Gloucester* contributed a few 6-pounder rounds. The action lasted only a few minutes before the volunteers fled, leaving four of their number behind dead. There were no American casualties. Additional marines and sailors soon landed, and by 1000 hours the port area was secured. Miles came ashore shortly afterward, as his troops—2,500 infantrymen in Brig. Gen. G.A. Garretson's brigade, plus about a thousand artillerymen, engineers, and recruits—began landing.

Under Miles' personal supervision, the landings went smoothly, greatly facilitated by the capture of ten lighters. By noon most of the 3,500 troops were ashore, and Garretson's brigade had already moved out to secure the rest of the town and establish a defensive perimeter. Aside from a brief, bloodless skirmish in the mid-afternoon, local Spanish forces were inactive. By nightfall the troops had established a rough trench line around the town and were settling in for the night.

It was a quiet night, and the Spanish were inactive. But the troops were green and nervous. A few stray cattle wandering in the woods panicked pickets of the 6th Massachusetts, who opened fire. For a time there was widespread shooting all along the front, with rounds flying in all directions—some of the ships offshore were even hit by stray rifle fire—but Garretson and staff officers soon got the troops in order.

At dawn on 26 July Garretson moved out to the northeast, toward Yauco, about six miles away, taking with him six companies of the 6th Massachusetts and one of the 6th Illinois, plus some artillery. As the column approached Yauco, they fell in with elements of the Puerto Rican *8th Volunteers*, who subjected the column to harrasing fire. Deploying for action, Garretson pressed forward about a mile, where a little skirmish developed along a ridgeline. Although some mounted Puerto Rican troops attempted to intervene, the defenders soon drew off. The fight was short, and U.S. casualties light, only four wounded, while the Spanish seem to have suffered four killed. It could easily have turned out disastrously for Garretson, for some elements of the 6th Massachuetts panicked once again, with men even leaving the firing line. Despite this, Garretson pressed on, to occupy Yauco, which elements of the Spanish *25th Rifles* evacuated after attempting to sabotage the local rail terminus. The way was now open for an advance on Ponce, the army's immediate objective and the largest city in Puerto Rico. Miles came up with Maj. Gen. Guy V. Henry, commanding the Provisional Division, I Corps, to which Garretson's brigade belonged. While the people of Yauco were giving the *Norteamericanos* an enthusiastic reception, Miles and Henry conducted a quick investigation of the 6th Massachusetts, with the result that the regimental commander, the lieutenant colonel, a major, and a captain were relieved of duty for being absent from their troops. The four had not been with the regiment since the previous evening, having spent the night aboard their transports.

On 27 July, the rest of the 6th Illinois came up and Garretson resumed his advance. Meanwhile, a convoy carrying Maj. Gen. James H. Wilson, commanding 1st Division, I Corps, had arrived off Guanica with some 4,000 men, directed there by the cruiser which Miles had sent on to Cape San Juan. Rather than land Wilson's men at Guanica, Miles ordered them to Ponce, 20 miles to the east, intending to have Garretson attack it from the west on the 28th while Wilson landed at the port, some two miles from city proper.

On the afternoon of 27 July, the auxiliary cruiser USS *Dixie*, crewed by naval militiamen from Maryland, entered the harbor accompanied by two smaller vessels. They met no resistance, for the regular Spanish forces there, the *25th Rifles*, under Lt.-Col. Rafael Martinez Illecas, had been pulled out, leaving behind 300 volunteers to hold the town. With the help of the British and German consuls, the ship's skipper entered into prolonged negotiations with the commander of the *9th Volunteers*, whose men were already drifting away (in fact the company stationed at the port of Ponce had flatly refused to take up arms). Finally, at about 1730 hours on the 28th, an agreement was reached that brought honor all around, and a detachment of marines and sailors landed to take control of the port. Brig. Gen. G.H. Ernst's brigade (c. 3,500) began landing at 0700 hours the next morning, followed by Wilson and the staff of I Corps. Shortly afterward Miles and Garretson marched into Ponce. Losing no time, Miles had the two brigades form a defensive perimeter about the city and port, in the process of which there was some bloodless skirmishing with the rearguards of the *25th Rifles*.

The capture of Ponce and its port were of inestimable value to the invading army. Not only were the port facilities adequate for any volume of traffic needed to support the invasion, but the city was the economic and administrative heart of southwestern Puerto Rico. In addition, it possessed cable connections with Jamaica and the West Indies, putting Miles back in direct communication with Washington for the first time since he had left Santiago, a situation causing concern in the capital, albeit much to Miles' satisfaction. A further benefit of taking Ponce was that it was a major center of anti-Spanish feeling. As a result, when they entered the city the Americans were given a tumultuous welcome by the town's numerous *yanquífilos*. In a formal ceremony arranged by the mayor, Miles took possession of the city. At its conclusion, Miles proclaimed:

The chief object of the American military forces will be to overthrow the armed authority of Spain, and to give the people of your beautiful island the largest measure of liberty consistent with this occupation.

If anyone among the cheering multitude noted that the general was saying he intended to replace the "armed authority of Spain" with that of the United states, it has not been recorded.

With Ponce in hand, the invading army had established a firm lodgement in Puerto Rico. Using Ponce as a base, the army could then proceed to the reduction of the rest of the island. Over the next few days the city became the center of intense activity, as Miles pressed preparations for resuming his advance. There was much to be done. Additional troops had to be landed, much equipment had yet to be brought ashore, and rations and munitions had to be stockpiled. Miles had no intention of having the army in Puerto Rico suffer the fate of that in Cuba, and advance without having established a proper base.

The landing of reinforcements was comparatively easy. On 31 July Brig. Gen. Theodore Schwan's 2,850 strong brigade of Regulars came ashore at Guanica, while elements of I Corps (c. 7,000), under Maj. Gen. John R. Brooke arrived at Puerto de Ponce. Miles ordered Schwan to concentrate at Yauco while holding Brooke with about half his command (c. 3,500 men, including Brig. Gen. Peter G. Hains' brigade) aboard their transports for two days, before ordering them to land at Arroyo, some 60 miles east of Ponce. They were to concentrate on the nearby town of Guayama, and landing the balance at Ponce. The landing of men and equipment was greatly facilitated by the capture of 70 lighters in the port. In addition, when a contingent of professional stevedores failed to arrive from the U.S. to help with the offloading, representatives of the Porto Rican Commission, who had accompanied Miles, organized the local dock workers and boatmen to do the work. The offloading of equipment and supplies was complicated by the fact that 36 of the first 40 transports unloaded lacked bills of lading, having been loaded in excessive haste. This made it almost impossible to determine what was in a ship until it was at least partially unloaded. As a result, there were momentary shortages of some supplies and equipment. Although the situation was by no means as disastrous as that at Santiago, Brooke did spend a few anxious days at Arroyo without some of his artillery and transport wagons. Considering the amount of materiel to be unloaded—over two million rations alone—the business was handled quite well, due to determined management and the availability of the ports at Ponce and Guanica.

In another contrast with the Santiago Campaign, Miles had to contend with the civil administration, which in Cuba had been tended to by the revolutionary government. On 29 July Miles proclaimed limited martial law, as far as matters directly affecting military operations. In all other situations, Spanish civil law was to prevail, except where it conflicted with American constitutional practice or military necessity. Local officials were confirmed in office if they accepted the authority of the United States. He also agreed that the army would make no requisitions, but would pay for everything at prevailing prices. These arrangements greatly eased the adjustment of the populace to the American presence, with the result that the local people continued to harbor warm regards toward the invaders. Indeed, friendly relations were the norm. The Porto Rican Commission had no difficulty recruiting volunteers to serve the U.S. Army in the field, and by the end of the campaign some 2500 men were serving in the "Porto Rican Scouts" or the "Porto Rican Guards," armed and uniformed and under military discipline. Meanwhile the people of Ponce organized a hospital for the army, while inviting soldiers into their homes. Romance flowered. One young *ponceña*, Esperanza Bages, aged 16 and widely regarded as the most beautiful woman in Puerto Rico, was enthusiastically courted by whole regiments, despite the fact that she was already promised to a young man of the town, whom she later married. Another young woman waved the American flag so enthusiastically that her balcony began to collapse; fortunately she was rescued by an American lieutenant who soon afterward married her.

While all of this was going on, of course, Miles was planning a quick resumption of the offensive. His basic plan was a vast sweeping maneuver. Four reinforced brigades would advance against the enemy, pushing him toward San Juan. On the left, to the west, Schwan's brigade would advance northward along the coast, while a few miles further east Garretson's brigade would advance northward from Ponce along Whitney's trail through Utuado to Arecibo on the north coast, where it would await Schwan. After effecting a juncture, the two brigades under Maj. Gen. Guy V. Henry would proceed eastward along the north coast toward San Juan. Meanwhile Maj. Gen. James H. Wilson with Ernst's brigade and supporting arms would advance eastward across country from Ponce along the military road, one of the best in Puerto Rico. Hain's brigade, under Brooke, would advance northward from Guyama. Hains and Ernst would effect a junction at Cayey, and from there move north through Caguas against San Juan under Brooke's overall direction. As they became available, additional forces would be added to each of the columns, so that by the time they arrived before San Juan, probably around the beginning of September, Miles would have available some 30,000 men plus a considerable siege train. On paper the plan had a certain elegance, as the columns swept the enemy toward San Juan. But in practical terms it was somewhat risky. Miles was dividing his forces in the face of the enemy. He may, of course, have presumed a certain lethargy or timidity on the part of the Spanish. Or perhaps assumed that the war would be ending soon, since he was aware that very tentative negotiations were already in progress between the U.S. and Spain through the French. But such assumptions were potentially dangerous. At El Caney the Spanish had been neither lethargic nor timid. An energetic Spanish commander might be able to concentrate superior forces to ambush one of his columns, inflicting if not a defeat at least a bloody nose. And armistice negotiations could easily hve fallen through.

Miles' offensive was to begin on 7 August. In anticipation of this, several preliminary moves were made. Brooke moved up from Arroyo to Guayama on 3-5 August. In the process, his troops had several skirmishes with Spanish outposts, during one of which there was a momentary panic in C Company, 4th Ohio, a matter quickly handled but which served to remind everyone that most of the troops were recent volunteers. Brooke was also still having serious problems with his transport, for not all of his wagons had been landed and he was forced to rely on local carters. At the same time, Henry's command had already begun marching northward for Adjuntas, the southern terminus of Whitney's trail, carrying with it an enormous amount of engineering equipment in order to turn the track into a practicable road, a necessity given that the summer rains were already upon them. Meanwhile, at Yauco, Schwan was preparing his brigade for movement, but was forced to contribute some detachments of his precious regulars to support the other columns. Finally, at Ponce, Wilson was able to exchange the old Springfields which equipped his infantry with Krags, and had pushed his outposts some way up the military road to occupy the large town of Juana Diaz on 7 August.

Surprisingly, when Wilson's men entered Juana Diaz they not only encountered no resistance, but they also found it already under American control. Sort of. It seems that several days earlier, Stephen Crane and Richard Harding Davis, two of a host of correspondents who had accompanied the troops to Puerto Rico—arguably the most over-reported campaign in military history—had decided that since military events were not exactly producing scintillating copy, they would make some news on their own by heading into enemy territory ahead of the troops. When their preparations were completed, Crane, already famous as the author of *The Red Badge of Courage*, double crossed his partner, giving him the slip on 4 August, and headed for Juana Diaz through the Spanish lines. As it turned out, the Spanish had pulled out of the town by the time he arrived, and the local people took him to be the advanced guard of the American army. So Crane spent three days in relative luxury, being entertained by the local dignitaries, until Wilson's men showed up to end the party. Davis, who arrived with Wilson, pretended to take Crane's double cross in good spirits, but secretly vowed revenge. Meanwhile, Miles was ready to kick off his offensive. Almost everything was in readiness. Schwan was at Yauco, Henry was already at Adjuntas beginning his road, while Wilson was at Juana Diaz, and Brooke, despite his lack of transport, was at Guayama.

Wilson's Column, 7 - 13 August

Wilson had some 2,700 men and 16 guns at Juana Diaz on 7

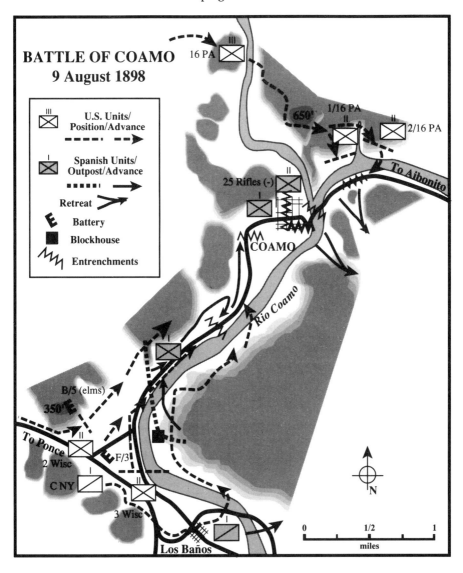

BATTLE OF COAMO
9 August 1898

16 PA

650'

1/16 PA

2/16 PA

To Aibonito

U.S. Units/
Position/Advance

Spanish Units/
Outpost/Advance

Retreat

Battery

Blockhouse

Entrenchments

25 Rifles (-)

COAMO

Rio Coamo

B/5 (elms)

350

To Ponce

2 Wisc

F/3

C NY

3 Wisc

Los Baños

N

0   1/2   1
miles

August. His immediate objective was Aibonito, a small town about 25 miles to the east, just where the military road passed into the mountains that form the spine of Puerto Rico. Intelligence gathered by Brooklyn's C Troop, New York Cavalry, as well as from Puerto Rican informants and Spanish deserters indicated that the enemy had about 2,000 men and some artillery entrenched at Aibonito, on highly defensible terrain.

On the afternoon of the 7th, Wilson moved his troops to the Rio Descalabrado, about seven miles east of Juana Diaz, and then gave them a good rest. Toward evening he moved them out, taking advantage of the cooler night air. With C Troop scouting about two miles ahead, the column made very good time, reaching the vicinity of Coamo, a small town some eight miles from Aibonito, shortly before sunset.

Coamo was set in a gorge. The Spanish had fortified the approaches to the town with trenches and some blockhouses. Preliminary reconnaissance suggested that the place was quite strong. Rather than undertake a precipitous assault, Wilson rested his troops on the 8th, while he sent patrols to scout out the area. Lt.-Col. John Biddle, of the engineers, soon brought in some useful information. There was a rough but practicable trail which led to the rear of the town, running through the mountains to its west. Wilson, a Civil War veteran, decided to turn the position. He selected the 16th Pennsylvania Volunteers, an understrength (it had only two battalions) but well-trained unit, for this mission. On the evening of the 8th it went on its way with orders to advance several miles then bivouac until dawn, in order to resume its advance to be in position to arrive in the rear of Coamo at about 0700 hours on the 9th. The balance of Wilson's command—the 2nd and 3rd Wisconsin, plus a battery each from the 3rd and 5th Artillery, and Troop C—would attack the town and its supporting positions from the front to fix the enemy's attention, thereby permitting the 16th Pennyslvania to fall on his right rear.

Lt.-Col. Raphael Martinez-Illecas had about 500 men in and around Coamo. The natural strength of Martinez's position was increased by the construction of several entrenchments and the conversion of a number of outlying agricultural structures into strongpoints. Martinez' command comprised three rifle companies and the mounted guerrilla company of his *25th Rifles*, about half the battalion, considerably more men than Wilson believed were present. He put one company into an outpost line about a third-of-a-mile to the southwest of the town, holding small posts and several blockhouses. The other two rifle companies were deployed in and about Coamo proper. The guerrilla company—composed of regular troops armed and equipped for

A contemporary engraving of the capture of a blockhouse during the final moments of the Battle of Coamo, 9 August 1898. The Wisconsin volunteers are wearing the Army's standard blue flannel shirt and toting the "trapdoor" Springfield.

reconnaissance, skirmishing, and irregular operations—held the village of Los Baños, on a converging road about two miles to the south, flanking the probable American line of approach. A battalion of infantry with artillery was available about a day's march to the rear.

Wilson's main body got into position at about 0600 hours on the 9th. The 2nd Wisconsin deployed astride the military road, directly confronting the Spanish outpost line, while the 3rd Wisconsin marched off to its right to advance along a converging road. The gap between the two regiments was to be covered by some of the artillery, while the balance of the guns opened fire on the blockhouses, including one which dominated the junction of the military road and the converging road. Meanwhile, C Troop was to cover the rear and flank of the 3rd Wisconsin from any threats from Los Baños.

The artillery opened up at 0700 hours. Meanwhile, C Troop scouted toward Los Baños, while the infantry opened fire. The

Spanish replied in kind, and a hot if less than decisive firefight began. The two Wisconsin regiments pressed forward at a leisurely pace, crossing the tiny Rio Coamo. Things seemed to be going well, but as the action continued, the 16th Pennsylvania failed to make its presence known in the enemy's rear. A seasoned veteran, Wilson remained calm and kept up the action. By about 0740 the sustained smoky fire of B Battery, 5th Artillery, had set the main blockhouse on fire, causing the defenders to flee. It was not until about 0800 hours that Wilson became concerned. Unbeknown to him, the advance of the 16th Pennsylvania had been more arduous than anticipated. Some of the hills it had to cross peaked at 650 feet, about 250 feet above the valley floor. It had lost its way in the predawn twilight and emerged from the mountains a few miles further north than planned. Doubling back by a rough track, the regiment was still too far off to influence events when the engagement began at 0700. Hearing the distant firing, the regimental commander had sent a single company on ahead to make the best time it could. By 0800 hours, this company had just reached a ridgeline overlooking the military road behind the town. As it approached the road, which lay across a shallow stream along the foot of the ridge, the company received fire from Spanish troops posted to cover the rear of the Coamo position. Sounds of this fight heartened Wilson and his men, but the lone company was not of itself strong enought to influence the outcome of the battle. So while in front of Coamo the Wisconsin regiments continued their leisurely advance. To the rear of the town the detached company engaged in a firefight with the Spanish rearguard. After a short while, the balance of the 16th Pennsylvania came up. The regiment quickly deployed along the ridgeline on a two-battalion front. As soon as it was in position, the 1st Battalion, on the right, opened a sustained fire. Under cover of this fire, the 2nd Battalion, on the left, advanced about a half-mile to the left, then advanced down the ridge and across the stream to a position enabling it to enfilade the right flank of the Spanish defenders. Shortly before 0900 hours, the 2nd Battalion attacked. The Spanish, greatly outnumbered, held for a time, but, as officers were wounded or killed, began to waver. Finally they broke, some streaming off to the rear while others attempted to surrender.

Apprised of the threat to his rear, Lt. Col. Martinez had already begun to fall back, committing the bulk of his forces against the 16th Pennsylvania, with only a thin rearguard to hold his front. Thus, there soon was only one company holding in front of Coamo, where the American main body had increased its efforts against the entrenched defenders. Meanwhile, C Troop, having ascertained that there was no threat from the direction of Los Baños (the Spanish troops posted there having abandoned the place, apparently without orders), doubled back toward the American right as the two Wisconsin regiments finally united at the road junction. Then, with C Troop on their right, the two regiments advanced directly on the town. By this time the 25th Rifles was pulling out of Coamo in good order. But then, at about 0930 hours, with C Troop poised to enter Coamo itself, Martinez was killed. Almost immediately his second in command also fell. The demoralized Spanish broke, many fleeing over the rugged hills which surrounded Coamo. By 0940 the action was over; Wilson had taken Coamo at a cost of one dead and about ten wounded, most from the 16th Pennsylvania, while inflicting six dead and 35 wounded on the Spanish and collecting 167 prisoners. One reason for the disparity in casualties was Wilson's artillery fire, to which the Spanish could make no reply.

The action at Coamo was intelligently conducted, taking advantage of the American superiority in numbers without using that superiority as mere cannon-fodder. Wilson, a regular with continuous service since the Civil War, never let the battle get out of his control. When the 16th Pennsylvania did not appear in the enemy's rear at the expected time, he merely continued his leisurely attack, deliberately stalling for time while occupying the enemy's attention. The reduction of the principal blockhouse, actually a rather stoutly-constructed wooden farm building surrounded by wired-in trenches, required 40 minutes and 66 rounds of artillery ammunition. In addition his troops had performed well, even better than had the Rough Riders in their first action; they had been on active duty longer, which had honed the skills many had acquired from years in the National Guard.

Almost as soon as the action at Coamo was over, C Troop began advancing toward Aibonito, with the dual mission of harrying the retreating Spanish and preventing destruction of the numerous bridges and culverts which carried the military road through the rugged countryside. The Brooklyn cavalrymen were quite successful; the Spanish being able to destroy only one bridge, which spanned a ravine about four miles east of Coamo. Within another mile or so, however, the troopers came under fire from Spanish artillery posted at Aibonito Pass, a deeply cut gorge between two steep hills about a mile below the town of Aibonito. Wilson ordered the troop to hold until relieved and hurried his infantry up to reinforce them.

Meanwhile, back at Coamo, the troops discovered that the press had once again beaten them to their objective. Richard Harding Davis, getting his revenge on Stephen Crane, had entered the town during the battle, infiltrating through both the American and Spanish lines to do so. But for Davis, revenge was something less than sweet. In contrast to the avid reception given Crane at Juana Diaz, the people of Coamo proved decidedly less enthusiastic about Americans. Wilson established his headquarters in Coamo, but a number of unpleasant encounters between townsfolk and American troops convinced him to post most of his men out of town. Although the bulk of his troops were positioned on the front where C Troop had encountered resistance from the Spanish, Wilson set up pickets in all directions, lest the enemy infiltrate troops through the mountains. Coamo itself remained unfriendly, and even after civil administration had been restored relations between the invaders and the townsfolk remained distant.

Wilson remained relatively inactive before Aibonito Pass for three days. It was a wise move. Occupying positions along the hills on both sides of the pass were some 1,300 Spanish troops, mostly regulars, with two guns under the command of Brig. Gen. Ricardo Ortega y Diez. Wilson spent the time well, sending out patrols on the 10-11 August. These confirmed that all direct approaches to the Spanish position were impractical, every one of them being well covered by entrenchments. Deliberating upon his options, Wilson therefore resolved to attempt a repetition of his successful maneuver at Coamo three days earlier.

Two of his regiments would undertake a march of about five miles around the Spanish right, while his third regiment, the artillery, and his cavalry would hold their attention in front. Since insufficient time had been allocated for the flank march at Coamo, and aware that the enemy was considerably stronger in the Aibonito position than he had been at Coamo, Wilson proposed to begin his operation earlier.

On 12 August Wilson essayed a reconnaissance by fire. At 1325 hours F Battery, 3rd Artillery, opened up. Within minutes the Spanish replied with artillery and rifle fire. The two sides exchanged fire for about a half-hour before the Spanish broke off the action. Although the Americans believed they had silenced the Spanish guns, it appears that Ortega had decided to conserve ammunition. In fact, his troops had suffered few casualties, for most of the American shells had been overs, which fell behind the Spanish lines. Nor had the Americans suffered greatly from the exchange, as Spanish aim was thwarted by the thick smoke from the black powder used by the American artillery. But, under cover of this exchange, the 2nd and 3rd Wisconsin, earmarked for the turning maneuver, had begun their march. By nightfall they had occupied the town of Barranquitas in the rear, off the Spanish right. Everything was ready for an attack early on 13 August. That morning, however, Wilson received word that an armistice was imminent. He ordered the operation postponed. Shortly after the attack was to have begun, he received definite word that an armistice had been concluded.

Schwan's Column, 7 - 13 August 1898

All of Brig. Gen. Theodore Schwan's troops were Regular Army, although, to be sure, some of the enlisted men were little more than recruits. In addition to his 2,850 Americans, Schwan had a contingent of the Porto Rican Scouts. At Yauco on 7 August, his ultimate objective was to unite with Henry's column at Aguado, on the north coast of Puerto Rico, but his immediate goal was the city of Mayaguez, some 45 miles up the west coast. The town, which had over 22,000 inhabitants, was garrisoned by the regular *24h Rifle Battalion* and the *6th Volunteer Battalion*, with the *7th Volunteer Battalion* posted in towns and villages to the southeast. Schwan marched out of Yauco on 9 August, his departure having been delayed by having to send all but two companies of the 19th Infantry to undertake occupation duties or bolster other columns, which also reduced his effectives to only about 1,500, but he did have eight pieces of artillery and four Gatling guns. Despite extreme heat and considerable humidity, the column made 12 miles on its first day, to a small town named Savana Grande. While the troops made camp, Schwan sent out his Puerto Rican Scouts to gather information.

Schwan delayed breaking camp on the 10th to ensure that all of the troops had been properly fed, and that all of his scouts had returned. When they finally did break camp, several hours march through the steamy countryside brought them to San German, about a dozen miles further on, at about noon. There Schwan learned that the *7th Volunteers* had been ordered to Mayaguez (The battalion was considered so unreliable that the captain general had ordered them disarmed days earlier; indeed one hostile tradition suggests that all but one man of the battalion deserted before the armistice—matters about which Schwan was, of course, unaware.). Schwan camped his troops at San German, where the residents proved quite friendly, even establishing an infirmary to care for troops suffering from heat and fever. One Spanish-speaking regular, Pvt. Karl S. Hermann, observed, "It was the popular impression... that every American soldier was a millionaire," going on to note that many people could not believe that the weary, ragged, dirty troops in ill-fitting flannel uniforms were the genuine article. Their confidence in American wealth was restored when the troops began to buy refreshments, but the troops didn't get a chance to spend very much. After only a short time in San German, Schwan's scouts brought word that the Spanish, about 1,200 men, were concentrating at Hormigueros. Rather than rest the troops, Schwan decided to press on, hoping to catch the enemy unawares. With A Troop, 5th Cavalry in the lead, the brigade marched out of San German about an hour after it had arrived.

Spanish Col. Julio Soto Villanueva, the military commander of Mayaguez, had available approximately 1,000 men of the *24th Rifle Battalion* under Lt.-Col. Antonio Oses Mozos, plus Puerto

Rican volunteers and two guns in the vicinity of Hormigueros. Soto had posted five rifle companies and the two field pieces on the Height of Silva, a considerable ridge dominating the broad boggy valley through which the road ran. The troops occupied several hundred yards of front more or less parallel to the road to a point opposite where an iron bridge brought the road across the Rio Grande, a modest stream which meandered across the floor of the valley, making it marshy in some places. A sixth company occupied the town of Hormigueros itself, at the southern end of the ridge, while a company of mounted guerrillas was thrown out on picket duty still further to the south.

At about 1500 hours, while advancing through a narrow valley just short of Hormigueros, A Troop came under fire from Soto's outposts. The troopers attacked, scattering guerrillas in the direction of Hormigueros and pursuing them right into the town, situated to the right of the road, while the Spanish abandoned it. Dispatching messengers to Schwan, the troopers then set up a dismounted defensive perimeter behind a railroad embankment just west of the town. The embankment itself was just under the ridge along which most of Soto's men were posted. There followed a lull in the action, as Schwan's advanced guard, his remaining two companies of the 19th Infantry, and the main body, the entire 11th Infantry plus his artillery, came up and Soto reshuffled his troops on the ridge in light of the withdrawal of his sixth company and the guerrillas.

At about 1600 Schwan's advance guard came up the main road behind the cavalry position. The two companies of the 19th Infantry advanced up the valley without receiving any fire until they reached a bridge across a small brook, one of the tributaries of the Rio Grande, which more or less separated the Americans and the Spanish. The two companies deployed there, about 400 yards from the Spanish lines, and began trading fire with the enemy, some of whom were outposted along the river. Meanwhile Schwan's main body came up. Schwan formed the 11th Infantry on a broad front about 1200 yards from the Spanish position, attempting to fill the substantial gap between Troop A on his right and the advance guard on the left. With the artillery and Gatling guns following behind, the 11th Infantry advanced more or less frontally toward the Spanish lines. About 800 yards

A platoon of Battery B, 5th Field Artillery, serving as infantry at Ponce, in Puerto Rico, apparently taken after the Armistice. They are wearing the Army's standard blue flannel shirts and brown trousers, with felt campaign hats, and are armed with Krag rifles.

from the main Spanish position, the regiment began to receive fire. Schwan then deployed the regiment into a firing line astride the road, somewhat obliquely to the Spanish positions, while sending two field pieces and his Gatlings to support the advanced guard, and posting his remaining six field guns on higher ground directly behind the main body. These dispositions being completed rather quickly, Schwan prepared to attack. His plan was simple, the main body would hold the attention of the Spanish while the advance guard and cavalry attacked on the flanks.

The advance guard supported by the Gatlings and field pieces rushed an iron bridge over the Rio Grande and succeeded in seizing it from the small contingent of Spanish troops posted to cover it, and then pressed on northwestward toward the Spanish left. At the same time the men of A Troop resumed their mounts, advanced through Hormigueros and passed over the heights, coming around behind Soto's left flank, causing the Spanish troops to fall back in confusion. Meanwhile the 11th Infantry, supported by the artillery, advanced to the Rio Grande. Although there was some confusion in one company as the regiment moved up, it succeeded in crossing the Rio Grande by various small bridges and reached the foot of the ridgeline. That was enough. With his left driven in, the American infantry pressing on his front, and his right threatened by further movement of the advanced guard, Soto pulled back, first to the reverse slope of the ridge, and then across the plain beyond. At a cost of one man killed and sixteen wounded—one mortally— Schwan had improvised a double envelopment to turn the enemy out of a very strong position while inflicting three dead and six wounded and collecting 136 prisoners, mostly deserters from the volunteers. The action was also an impressive testimony to the character of the American Regulars, who had marched some two dozen miles and fought a considerable engagement all in one day.

Schwan occupied the positions on the ridge which the Spanish had just abandoned and made camp there. He got his men up early on 11 August and put them on the road to Mayaguez, about a dozen miles to the north. The column reached Mayaguez without incident at about 0800 hours, to find it clear of defenders, Spanish regulars and volunteers having pulled out. By 0930 Schwan was setting up his headquarters, to an enthusiastic reception by the mayor and townsfolk. While his cavalry and scouts probed to the north and northeast, the bulk of Schwan's brigade camped just to the north of the town to be ready to resume the advance. Within hours Schwan's scouts came in with word that the Spanish rearguard was only about five miles from the town, to the northeast on the road to Lares. With his men exhausted (having marched about 45 miles in three days and fought a hot little battle in the bargain), Schwan ordered that contact be maintained with the retreating enemy, while ordering a reconnaissance in force for the next meeting. As a result, Schwan's infantrymen and artillerymen passed the night in camp, while his cavalrymen and Puerto Rican scouts remained in the field. During the night transports arrived at Mayaguez, bearing the overstrength 3rd Battalion, 1st Kentucky, which Miles had presciently shipped up from Ponce. The five companies landed shortly after dawn on 12 August. As they were equipped with the black powder Springfield, Schwan could only make limited use of them, and ordered only one company to take part in his renewed advance.

At about 1030 hours on 12 August six companies of the 11th Infantry plus one of the 1st Kentucky moved out on the road to Lares to the northeast, accompanied by artillery and cavalry, while other elements of both regiments moved northward up the coast to secure Añasco and the surrounding towns. The road to Lares was almost impassable, having been turned into a muddy track as a result of intermittent rains over the last few days. By sunset after some ten hours on the march, the troops had made but ten miles, much of it in drenching rain. The men bivouacked along the road, rising at dawn on 13 August to resume the advance at 0530 hours. On they plodded. Then, at about 0730, scouts brought word that the *24th Rifles* was just ahead, attempting to ford the swollen Rio Prieto near Las Marias.

Schwan deployed his men rapidly, and they quickly opened a devastating fire. Despite the heroic efforts of Col. Soto and his second-in-command, Lt.-Col. Antonio Oses y Mozos, the Spanish were unable to organize a coherent defense. The troops, numbering only 200-250—the balance of the battalion had retired northward, or deserted—began to flee. It was all over in less than a half hour. At no cost to themselves Schwan's troops had slain three of the enemy and taken 56 prisoners, including 27 wounded as well as both senior officers, while the *24th Rifles* had ceased to exist. With their prisoners, the tired troops camped on the field that night. The next day they learned that an armistice was already in force when they fought the action at Las Marias.

Brooke's Column, 7 - 13 August 1898

Maj. Gen. John R. Brooke's command was concentrated at Guayama in southeastern Puerto Rico by 7 August. Nevertheless, Brooke, a Civil War veteran commanding nearly 4,000 men with some 20 guns, was in a difficult position, because of a shortage of transport. His objective was to advance along the Cayey road and effect a juncture with Wilson, advancing from the southwest, at the town of Cayey proper. As a result, he was not able to get moving until 12 August, when his transport problems cleared up. He spent the intervening period profitably, employing his two cavalry troops—H Troop, 6th Cavalry and the Philadelphia City Troop—to scout out the enemy's positions. He was confident that the only troops confronting him were 500 men of the *6th Provisional Battalion*, a regular unit raised for garrison duty in Puerto Rico, and the *1st Guerrilla Flying Column*, one of the better volunteer units, with two guns, attached to Brig. Gen. Ricardo Ortega y Diez's command, the bulk of which was actually facing westward to confront Maj. Gen. James H. Wilson's column at Aibonito Pass. The Spanish troops were deployed along the forward edge of the rather steep Heights of Guanimani, north of Guayama. Their mission was to delay Brooke's advance as long as possible to facilitate the bringing forward of Ortega's 1,000 available reserves, some six or seven miles in the rear at Cayey proper. The two forces had skirmished inconclusively several times, most notably on 5 August, when Brooke's troops had suffered five wounded, one mortally, and on the night of 8-9 August, when two companies of the 4th Ohio suffered four men wounded in a brief firefight.

Brooke's plan for this operation was simple. On 12 August the 4th Ohio was sent on a flank march around some ridges and hills to the west, while the bulk of his command—the 3rd Illinois and 4th Pennsylvania, plus four batteries—pinned the Spanish attention to their front. The intention was for the artillery to open the fight on the morning of the 13th, with the 4th Ohio falling on the Spanish flank after they had become heavily engaged to their front. The attack never took place. In one of the more dramatic moments in the war, a courier handed word that an armistice had been concluded to Brooke literally seconds before the artillery was to open fire. Realizing that if he attempted to shout an order to stand down, the gunners, already on edge, might fire anyway, Brooke stepped in front of the guns. Having gotten the men's attention, he announced that an armistice was in force.

Henry's Column, 7 - 13 August 1898

Maj. Gen. Guy V. Henry's column, the bulk of which comprised Brig. Gen. G.A. Garretson's brigade (2,500) reinforced with regulars of the 19th Infantry, was at Adjuntas on 7 August, when Miles' offensive was to begin, having advanced there from Yauco over the previous few days. Although burdened with considerable construction equipment needed to turn Henry

Whitney's trail from Adjuntas to Utuado into a practicable road, the column made surprising progress. In six days it had advanced ten miles across the difficult mountainous spine of Puerto Rico, despite heavy rains. Of course, Henry and his troops were fortunate in not encountering any Spanish troops, but it was hardly a "walk in the sun." Carl Sandburg, a private in the 6th Illinois, observed that he lost eight pounds in those few days and would later write "the shovel is brother to the gun," in reference to his experiences as a road-building soldier in Henry's column. The armistice found them at Utuado.

The Armistice

When the armistice took effect at 0700 hours on 13 August, the military situation in Puerto Rico was by no means settled. To be sure, over 15,000 American troops had landed and had succeeded in occupying about a third of the island, while some 4,000 more men were scheduled to land within two or three days and an additional 18,000 more were preparing to embark for the island. Nor had the Spanish been successful in any significant engagement. But no clearly decisive action had yet been fought. The Spanish, adhering to their operational design had fallen back as intended each time they were confronted by the Americans. Although the action at Las Marias had turned out badly, the bulk of the 8,000 regular Spanish troops in Puerto Rico had not been enagaged by the invaders. As the Spanish pulled back, of course, they had discovered that the volunteers had a disturbing tendency to desert. But the hard core of regulars was holding together well, and as they fell back they would be concentrating, thereby improving their chances in a general engagement. Had the armistice not intervened the campaign would have unfolded in interesting ways.

Schwan, advancing from his victory at Las Marias, would have encountered the remnants of the *24th Rifles*, the whole of the regular *4th Provisional Battalion*, and whatever volunteers might have been concentrated, perhaps 2,000 men, at Lares. Schwan might have been able to secure support from Henry, his immediate superior advancing from Utuado. However, Henry's objective was the north coast at Arecibo. Schwan might have had to fight at Lares on his own, against forces more or less equal in number to his own.

The actions planned by Wilson at Aibonito and Brooke at the Heights of Guanimani both involved troops under Brig. Gen. Ricardo Oretga y Diez. Ortega commanded about 3,000 men, with four pieces of artillery, his combined opponents had some 7,000 men and 36 pieces of artillery. Given the odds, Ortega would have been forced to fall back, probably after a brisk rearguard action. On the map, the fortress of San Juan appears to be only about 20 miles to his rear, but he would cetainly have fallen back along the military road, the other roads in Puerto Rico being muddy trails in the rainy season. This would have permitted him to essay another rearguard action at Caguas, in the hills about 15 miles northeast of Aibonito, and again at Guayambo, in the hills about ten miles northwest of Caguas, before falling back the last dozen miles to San Juan. That city was already garrisoned with two regular battalions, plus various fortress troops as well as the *1st Volunteer Battalion*, the *Tiradores de San Juan* ("Sharpshooters of San Juan"), the best of the volunteer units, well-equipped and numbering well over a thousand, most of whom had strong ties to the Spanish authorities. A difficult siege would have been necessary.

Of course, at best the Spanish could not hope to do more than force the Americans to pay dearly for their conquest of Puerto Rico. Strategically the island was lost as soon as the Spanish fleet was sunk off Santiago. As it was, the conquest of Puerto Rico cost the U.S. nine men killed or mortally wounded and 46 less seriously wounded, including casualties resulting from naval operations. Spanish losses were 28 killed or mortally wounded and about 125 less seriously wounded, including casualties from the naval bombardment of San Juan on 12 May.

The period between the armistice and the final Spanish evacuation of Puerto Rico on 18 October passed quietly. A high degree of cooperation and courtesy prevailed between the Spanish and American officers and troops. Despite this, there were a number of untoward incidents. Several members of the *Guardia Civil*, the Spanish national police, attempted to seize Aguadilla and hold it for Spain, but were quickly brought to order by a show of force and the direct intervention of the departing Spanish authorities. In addition, some of the demobilized volunteers, mostly members of the local middle class which had benefitted from Spanish rule, attempted a guerrilla resistance in the name of Alfonso XIII, while a few other discharged volunteers tried to go into the bandit business. Some rural areas required patrolling for a while, and a few skirmishes took place more on the order of police work than military operations. With the cooperation of the local citizens, some 2,500 of whom were shortly in U.S. service as members of various volunteer groups, these matters were quickly cleared up, with few casualties. In later years Puerto Rican nationalists claimed that these incidents were actually part of a nationalist uprising, brutally supressed by imperialist Americans. Meanwhile, the bulk of the army was kept involved in busy work, safely ensconced on higher—and healthier—ground.

As the occupation proceeded, the troops began to look for ways to divert themselves. Although most of them were volunteer farmboys from staunchly religious backgrounds, prostitutes in the larger towns did a thriving business. American troops may not have been millionaires, but they certainly were better paid than their Spanish opponents! Some of the troops displayed open contempt for the people of Puerto Rico, their institutions, and their culture. A number of abuses occurred, which were generally covered up. While most Puerto Ricans quickly realized that they had merely exchanged Spanish domination for American, most did not find themselves unhappy about the change.

Militarily, the campaign is of interest for several reasons. Certainly the campaign strongly suggests that had Nelson A. Miles been given greater control over operations the war might have proceeded more efficaciously. In addition, the relative efficiency with which the operation was undertaken is a valuable demonstration of the learning capacity of the U.S. Army: the beginning of the Puerto Rican Campaign (25 July) was just 33 days after the start of the Santiago Campaign (22 June). The increased skill of America's volunteer soldiers underscored the country's ability to raise and train large armies relatively rapidly, a trait already demonstrated in the Civil War, albeit that European powers once again failed to take note.

The Press

Long before 1898 the press was an enormous force in American life. Nevertheless, its role in bringing about the war has been exaggerated. To be sure, the constant stream of atrocity tales, derived mostly from Cuban revolutionary sources, stirred strong feelings in the American public. But this alone did not cause the war. Indeed, most Americans did not support war with Spain. That took the destruction of the USS *Maine*, and even then war did not come for more than two months, after the Spanish government rejected any possible resolution involving independence for Cuba.

Once the war began, of course, the press wanted to report it. Journalists swarmed to the area of conflict. A remarkable 89 newspapermen accompanied V Corps when it sailed from Tampa, about one for every 180 men, and nearly as many more arrived during the few weeks the expedition remained in Cuba, making it the most over-reported military operation prior to the 1980s, when it was surpassed by the Grenada operation of 1982 (one journalist for every 62 troops).

Irresponsible journalists several times revealed information which could have been of great value to the enemy. Details of the Puerto Rico expedition, including the planned landing site, were reported in the press days before it actually sailed, a situation which prompted General Nelson A. Miles to change his objective once his troops were at sea.

Newspapermen even got in the way of operations. For example, when Captain Joseph H. Dorst made his first attempt to land supplies in Cuba from the steamer *Gussie* near Cabañas on 12 May 1898, two tugboats loaded with journalists came along for the fun. When the landing was disrupted by Spanish troops, Dorst found the reporters on the beach a hindrance to the safe withdrawal of his men. In a bit of poetic justice, the only American injured in the action was James F.J. Archibald, a reporter for the San Francisco *Post*, who was lightly wounded.

On several occasions reporters violated the rules of war, by taking an active part in the fighting. At Las Guasimas, both Richard Harding Davis, star war reporter, and Edward Marshal, of the Hearst New York *Journal*, apparently traded rounds with the Spanish. In fact Marshal was so seriously wounded that his life was despaired of, although he survived. And, of course, the antics of Stephen Crane and Richard Harding Davis at Juana Diaz and Coamo in Puerto Rico, while amusing, had little to do with journalism, and might easily have created serious security problems if the Spanish had captured either one and pumped him for information.

During the Civil War there had been a number of serious breaches of security due to overzealous reporting, leading several generals—including William Tecumseh Sherman—to ban journalists from their commands. By 1898 neither the Army nor the Navy had a system for dealing with journalists to allow them to do their job without spilling information to the enemy. The problem was never resolved, then or later.

Chapter VII

The Philippines

On the morrow of his smashing defeat of the Spanish fleet off Cavite, Commodore George Dewey found himself in an odd situation. Militarily his victory had made him master of Manila Bay and, arguably, of the Philippines. But his mastery was more theoretical than real. Dewey's squadron dominated the waters off the archipelago, but he had little ability to influence events ashore. His first priority was to communicate with his superiors in Washington, nearly half a world away. On the evening of 1 May, as the squadron lay anchored off the the Paseo de Luneta, he had notified the Governor-General, Basilio Augustin Davila, that he would refrain from bombarding the city so long as the Spanish did not fire upon the squadron with their shore batteries, an arrangement which was found mutually satisfactory. Dewey also informed the Governor-General that he would not sever the city's cable link with Hong Kong if he were permitted to use it. On 2 May, while awaiting a reply, Dewey decided to shift the squadron to Cavite. The town and naval base there lay on a conveniently defensible peninsula just seven miles southeast of Manila, and he planned to make it his base. The Spanish garrison—a battalion of the *74th Regiment* plus the sailors of the naval base—initially proved unwilling to yield, arguing that the white flag raised on the previous day signaled only a truce, not a surrender. When Dewey threatened to blow the naval base to pieces, the garrison quickly evacuated. A party of Marines and sailors occupied it, raising the Stars and Stripes. Since the Spanish had not anticipated abandoning the town, the base fell almost intact into American hands. With its machine shops and stores, including coal, the base proved very useful to the squadron over the next few weeks. With the base his, Dewey sent the cruisers *Raleigh* and *Baltimore* to Corregidor, which surrendered quietly. Dewey now had both a base and controlled the mouth of Manila Bay.

Meanwhile Governor-General Augustin informed Dewey that he would not be permitted to use the cable, whereupon Dewey ordered it cut, which was promptly done. He then sent the Revenue Cutter *McCullough* to Hong Kong with dispatches for the Navy Department. Although in cutting the cable Dewey believed he was also cutting the garrison of Manila off from communication with the outside world, in fact there was another cable link of which he appears to have been unaware. Of course, word of the battle at Manila Bay had already been spread worldwide by the Spanish. Despite the favorable "spin" which they put upon it, it was clear that Dewey had won a substantial victory. Even as Washington awaited an official communication from him, the Navy Department began taking steps to reinforce him. As early as 2 May the Navy had already discussed with the Army the need for troops for the Philippines. On 7 May *McCullough* brought word from Hong Kong that Dewey had just been promoted rear admiral, and that the cruiser *Charleston* and the armed merchantship *City of Pekin* would shortly sail from San Francisco with ammunition, supplies, and troops, "unless you telegraph otherwise." Dewey responded by indicating that he needed at least 5,000 men, based on his calculations that the Spanish had about 10,000 at Manila. He also observed that there were some 30,000 insurgents under arms, commanded by Emilio Aguinaldo.

The Philippine Republic

By 1898 the Philippines had been under Spanish rule for nearly four centuries. That rule had not always been benevolent, and was not usually very efficient either. Not until the 1870s had Spanish authority reached Jolo in the far south. The four centuries had been punctuated by occasional insurrections or uprisings. But the ethnic diversity of the native population precluded coherent opposition to Spanish control. There were some 80 different languages spoken in the islands, and while Spain had brought Catholicism to the northern and central areas, Islam was strong in the south, while in many areas animism prevailed. By the late nineteenth century a considerable native middle class had developed, particularly among the Tagalog-speaking majority on Luzon. Prosperous, educated, Catholic and hispanicized, they looked to Spain as the "mother country" and thought of themselves as Spanish. Unfortunately, the Spanish saw differently. As in most colonial empires, the "natives" were distinctly second-class, regardless of how enthusiastically they embraced the mother country. Filipinos were generally excluded from the public life of the colony. Surprisingly, considering their policies in other parts of the empire, in the Philippines not even the Church, which controlled enormous estates, was open to the indigenous people beyond the lowest ranks of the clergy.

In the 1880s a liberal movement began, notably among Filipinos educated in Spain, a small group of intellectuals known as the *Ilustrados*, of whom the most notable was José Rizal. The *Ilustrados* sought not nationalist liberation but rather the assimilation of Filipino people into the Spanish world, so that they could benefit from increased opportunity. In 1892 Rizal organized the *Liga filipina*, which urged peaceful progress towards the fullest integration of the archipelago into the Spanish Empire. In classic shortsightedness typical of authoritarian regimes, the Spanish banished Rizal to Mindanao, leaving the expression of Filipino dissatisfaction to more extreme elements. At the time Rizal was being banished—tradition says on the very same day, 7 July 1892—a more radical movement was founded, the *Katipunan* (Society of the Sons of the People). The *Katipunan* favored outright warfare against the Spanish overlords. With a vaguely socialist platform, it promised land to the landless, equality to the races, and justice for all in a Filipino republic. By early 1896 the *Katipunan* claimed 100,000 members, but the actual number was probably no more than 30,000. Most of the members were Christian Tagalogs, largely from the peasant class, although the leadership came from the working class and the middle class. Andres Bonifacio, a night watchman,

Emilio Aguinaldo y Famy, in his uniform as President and Dictator of the "Republic of the Philippines." Although a naturally talented commander, Aguinaldo lacked the skill to create an effective political foundation on which to build a revolutionary movement.

became the organization's president on 1 January 1896 and immediately began plotting an insurrection which would be characterized by a simultaneous rising in all parts of the Philippines, so that the tiny Spanish garrision (6,000 troops, about a third of them Filipinos) would be overwhelmed. The plot was uncovered in August, long before preparations had been completed, and Bonifacio fled into the mountains near Manila. From there he issued the *Grito de Balinawak*, an insurrectionary manifesto calling for revolution against the Spanish. The *Katipunan* began a desultory guerrilla war.

The insurrection caught the Spanish by surprise. Although the rebels met with only modest success, Governor-General Ramon Blanco y Erenas—the same who would command in Cuba in 1898—requested reinforcements. Strained by the demands of the Cuban insurgency, the government in Spain nevertheless complied. Meanwhile the rebels met with a general lack of success in the field. Their most effective commander proved to be a young man of mixed Filipino and Chinese descent, Emilio Aguinaldo. On 8-9 November 1896 Aguinaldo inflicted a sharp defeat on the Spanish in two clashes. This brought him considerable attention and increased influence in the leadership of the insurgency, so that he quickly rose to commanding general of the insurgent forces. By the end of 1896, during which there had been 20 serious clashes with the insurgents, there were about 25,000 Spanish troops in the islands, and a new Governor-General, Camilo de Polavieja. Polavieja initially blundered badly, when he had the innocent José Rizal shot, thereby alienating that portion of the Filipino middle class seeking closer ties with Spain. However, militarily he was much more effective and began serious counter-insurgency operations against the rebels, operations which bore considerable fruit.

Dividing Luzon into five military districts, Polavieja provided each with a fixed garrison plus a mobile command. The garrision was responsible for the defense of towns and vital installations, while the mobile command was charged with relentless pursuit of the insurgents. He unleashed his offensive in January of 1897. The result was a hard, wearing campaign conducted with great ferocity on both sides. The next four months saw numerous clashes between Spanish troops and the insurgents, 57 by one reckoning, of which 28 were serious enough to be called battles. In most of these the rebels came off second-best, and by April they were clearly on the run. This led to serious tensions within their leadership. On 20 April Emilio Aguinaldo—whose elder brother Crispulo had been killed in action on 3 March—staged a coup, unseating Bonifacio as leader of the insurgents. Shortly afterwards Bonifacio was tried by court martial and shot, along with a brother and several others. Meanwhile, despite his success in the field, just five days later, on 25 April 1897 Palovieja was replaced as Governor-General by Fernando Primo de Rivera, the Marquess de Estella, a brilliant, politically adept officer. By this time the insurgents had been reduced to small guerrilla bands. Aguinaldo withdrew them to the mountains of Bulacan province, north of Manila, making his headquarters in Biyak-na-Bato. There he attempted to reorganize the rebel forces. To strengthen the insurgency's political base, Aguinaldo issued the "Program of Biyak-na-Bato," a political manifesto which demanded land reform, restructuring of the ecclesiastical hierarchy, racial equality, and autonomy within the Spanish Empire, a long step back from independence. The program attracted some attention, but did little to strengthen the insurrection (although some Japanese officers volunteered for service on the principle of "Asia for the Asiatics"). The leadership of the insurgency was largely Tagalog, urban, hispanicized, and from Luzon. This, plus its failures in the field and the death of Bonifacio, alienated many who might otherwise have supported the movement. Indeed, throughout the whole insurrection the Moslem regions of the far south, which had only been brought under Spanish control during the previous quarter-century, remained quiet. By mid-1897 Spanish forces had virtually destroyed the rebel forces. With Aguinaldo and the other leaders of the insurgency pinned down by a small force at Biyak-na-Bato, Primo de Rivera offered to negotiate. A truce was established, during which the Spanish actually supplied rations to the rebels. The negotiations were long and tedious. In the end, a deal was struck. On 14 December 1897 Primo de Rivera and Aguinaldo agreed to the "Pact of Biyak-na-Bato." In return for an indemnity of 800,000 gold Mexican pesos (to be paid half down and the balance in two installments depending upon developments), another 900,000 to be paid to the injured, an amnesty, and a promise of reform, Aguinaldo and 27 other rebel leaders agreed to leave the Philippines. Neither side was particularly sincere about the deal. Realizing that the rebellion had been crushed in the field, Aguinaldo saw the pact as a way of filling the rebel coffers, while Primo de Rivera saw it as a quick, and relatively cheap way to end the rebellion immediately, with little intention of instituting major reforms.

Aguinaldo's departure from the Philippines (he landed in Hong Kong on the last day of 1897), did not bring complete peace to the islands. To be sure, most of the surviving rebel troops laid down their arms, so that Primo de Rivera paid the second installment of the indemnity and issued a general amnesty. But unrest continued, and there was sporadic fighting throughout the first months of 1898, so that the final installment of the indemnity was never paid. Even as Primo de Rivera took ship for Spain in March, Aguinaldo and his colleagues plotted a renewal of the insurrection. Rising tensions between the United States and Spain over Cuba suited them quite well. Indeed, representatives of the Filipino insurgents had several times approached American consular officials in various Asian cities with requests for support, which had been met with a certain lack of interest. However, by March 1898 the possibility of war between the two countries resulted in an increased American interest in talks with the Filipinos. Negotiations began and Aguinaldo met several times with Commander Edward P. Wood of the USS *Petrel*. Precisely what was said to whom by whom will forever remain unknown. Aguinaldo claimed that Wood said the U.S. had no interest in the islands, and merely wanted to assist him in securing the liberation of the Philippines from Spain. Wood's account of the meetings was much different, suggesting a far more casual series of discussions about common interests. In subsequent meetings between Aguinaldo and the U.S. consul at Singapore, E. Spencer Pratt, the Filipino leader agreed to cooperate with Dewey and stated that the Filipinos would be happy with independence under American protection. Aguinaldo later claimed that Pratt agreed to this. Pratt, however, reported to Washington that he had informed Aguinaldo that he had no authority to discuss the political future of the Philippines. Charges of mendacity and conspiracy fly freely in discussions of these negotiations, but the most likely explanation is that neither side knew precisely what it wanted from the other, and that both heard what they wanted to hear. In any case, on 16 May Aguinaldo boarded the revenue cutter *McCulloch* at Hong Kong, and landed at Cavite three days later.

Even before Aguinaldo landed in the Philippines the rebel leaders Dewey deposited ashore on 30 April had begun their work. Despite defeat in the field and the "Pact of Biyak-na-Bato" insurgent bands were at large, living a fugitive life and often behaving no better than bandits. And the infrastructure of the *Katipunan* remained intact. As a result, shortly after Aguinaldo landed at Cavite the insurgents began large scale operations again.

The Spanish Army in the Philippines

When Dewey sailed into Manila Bay the Spanish had 45,000 troops in the Philippines. The bulk of these troops were stationed on Luzon. Of 28 regular infantry battalions in the archipelago, 24 were on Luzon, and nine of those were in Manila. With the capital under the guns of an American squadron, Governor-General Basilio Augustin Davila undertook a number of measures to strengthen his political position. On 4 May he created an advisory council to give the government a semblance of popular participation, hinting at greater autonomy in the future. An appointed body of 17 notable Filipinos, some of them closely identified with the *Katipunan*, it did not meet until the end of the month. In fact, the assembly was a matter of "too little, too late." Had such a measure been taken earlier, before the threat of war had become reality, it might have been seen as a logical outgrowth of the "Pact of Biyak-na-Bato." Almost immediately denounced by Aguinaldo, the council never exerted any influence over either the colonial authorities or the people. On 4 May Augustin also authorized the creation of a popular militia. Recruiting for this force proved satisfactory, and perhaps as many as 20,000 men joined. However, many of these men proved to be rebel sympathizers, who deserted as soon as they had arms and equipment. Both of these measures demonstrated that Augustin, in common with most Spaniards, was laboring under the misconception that many Filipinos were loyal to Spain. In fact even some of the men he appointed to the new colonial assembly were rebel sympathizers; several shortly were leading Aguinaldo's new insurgency.

Militarily Augustin also made a number of serious errors. He initially had about 9,000 troops in the vicinity of Manila. When hostilities began he called in only a handful of the forces from the provinces, apparently 3,000-4,000 or so. Control of Manila was the key to military control of the Philippines. Had he concentrated more forces in the capital he would have made more difficult an American attempt to capture the city. To be sure, pulling in the regional garrisons—or even just the mobile forces—would have left the provinces undefended. However, as several Spanish historians have observed, if most of the Filipino people were loyal to Spain the garrisons were superflous, whereas if they were disloyal, as was to prove to be the case, there would not be enough strength available to fight both the Americans and the rebels at the same time. The optimal course would have been to pull most of the troops into Manila retaining small garrisons in the larger towns. A large enough force concentrated at Manila might inflict a defeat on the Amerians. With Manila secure, the army could have been returned to the provinces to resume counter-insurgency operations.

Manila was a highly defensible city. Although it sprawled on both sides of the mouth of the Pasig River, its core was an historic walled district on the south side of the river. The *Intramuros* was designed to resist assault from both land and sea. In anticipation of a naval bombardment, Augustin sent all the women and children out of the *Intramuros* to the suburbs. With care food and ammunition stocks in the city could last some months, and the city's water supply was well protected. The southwestern corner of the defenses was the most critical. An attack there could be conducted by both land and sea, and it was only 1.5 miles through lightly built-up suburbs to the southern face of the *Intramuros*. An old fort there, San Antonio de Abad, was strengthened and provided with additional artillery. From there, a line of entrenchments and blockhouses— hold-overs from the 1896-1897 insurgency—stretched in a five to six mile arc around the eastern side of the city, encompassing the principal suburbs. These positions were strung along waterlines as much as possible. They were generally composed of earthworks and heavy timbers, and were protected by barbed wire. Many of the posts were connected to central headquarters by telephone. On the seaward side, the beachfronts to the north and south of the *Intramuros* were provided with strong points and trenches, lest the Americans attempt a landing there. These constituted the inner defenses of Manila. Augustin also gave some thought to securing a larger area. Beyond the inner defensive line, he established an outpost line based on farms and villages. He thus provided Manila with three lines of

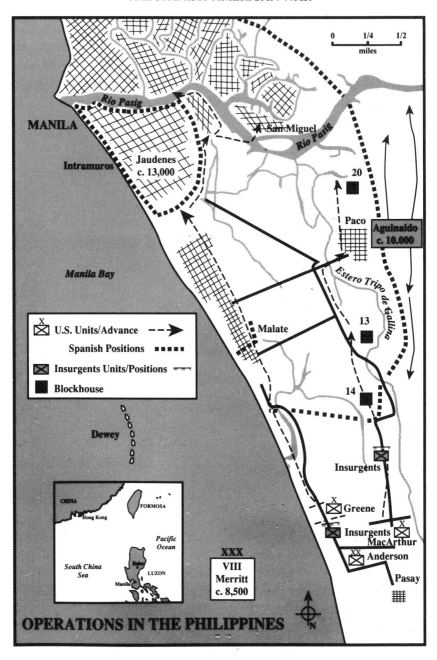

OPERATIONS IN THE PHILIPPINES

(Map labels:)

MANILA

Intramuros

Jaudenes c. 13,000

Rio Pasig

San Miguel

Rio Pasig

20

Paco

Aguinaldo c. 10.000

Manila Bay

Estero Tripo de Gallina

X U.S. Units/Advance

Spanish Positions

Insurgents Units/Positions

Blockhouse

Malate

13

14

Dewey

Insurgents

Greene

Insurgents

MacArthur

Anderson

Pasay

CHINA

FORMOSA

Hong Kong

Pacific Ocean

South China Sea

LUZON

Manila

XXX VIII Merritt c. 8,500

N

defenses: the outpost line, the inner line, and the *Intramuros*. Although Cavite was in American hands, held by Marines

272

and bluejackets from Dewey's squadron, Augustin tried to retain control of most of the rest of the province. A defensive line was established between the towns of Zapote and Bacoor in the area between Laguna de Bay, a large lake in the interior, and the coast just west of Cavite. The line was lightly manned, a problem created by the fact that Augustin left most of his troops in garrison across Luzon.

While he was making his preparations, Augustin was also in communication with his superiors in Madrid via a little known cable that went through the Visayas. His principal request was for reinforcements, in particular enough ships to defeat the American squadron. It was this request which set in motion the movement of Rear Admiral Manuel de Camara's 2nd Squadron from Cadiz to the east. Dewey's victory at Manila Bay caught the Spanish government and naval leadership completely by surprise, both having failed to consider the possibility that the Americans might attack the Philippines despite being over 7,000 miles from a friendly base. For more than a month they dithered as to what action to adopt. Not all of Spain's major warships had sailed with Cervera's 1st Squadron. Spain's two most powerful vessels, the battleship *Pelayo* and the armored cruiser *Carlos V*, were not yet ready for sea when Cervera sailed, the former just completing a refit and the later only just completing her fitting out. In the end, it was decided that these ships should be sent to the Philippines, rather than be used as a strategic threat to American sea power in the Atlantic. On 15 June the Ministry of Marine ordered Rear Admiral Manuel de Camara, commanding the 2nd Squadron at Cadiz, to prepare to sail for the Philippines. Camara sailed the next day, with *Pelayo*, *Carlos V*, the auxiliary cruisers *Patriota* and *Rapido*, and the destroyers *Audaz*, *Osado*, and *Prosepina*, escorting the transports *Buenos Aires* and *Panay*, carrying 4000 troops, plus four colliers, each laden with some 5000 tons of coal. Given time, Augustin would have his reinforcements. Meanwhile, Dewey's squadron continued to lay out in Manila Bay and the insurgents were becoming increasingly active.

Manila Invested

For Dewey and the officers and sailors of his squadron each day was one of anxious waiting. From its base at Cavite, which proved immensely valuable, they engaged in a routine of patrols and exercises, all the while wondering when reinforcements would arrive, so that they could complete the work of conquest. Unbeknown to all but Dewey, help was on the way. Their victory and Dewey's request for reinforcements had caused considerable stir in Washington. Despite slow communications between the squadron and Washington—it required two days to steam to Hong Kong, the closest available cable station—the Army and Navy had proceeded as quickly as possible. On 22 May the cruiser *Charleston* sailed from San Francisco with a cargo of ammuntion, Dewey's supply being desperately short. Meanwhile, orders were going out to concentrate troops at San Francisco under the command of Maj. Gen. Wesley Merritt, a Civil War veteran. The first convoy for the Philippines sailed on 25 May. It was three weeks *before* the Santiago Expedition got underway. The voyage was long, 7,600 miles. The ships, albeit fast for their day, could sustain little more than 8 knots for so long a trip, and so it would take about a month for them to reach the Philippines. Meanwhile Dewey would have to make do with what he had.

One of Dewey's primary concerns was relations with the Filipinos. Without political guidance, he had to move carefully. Although he encouraged Aguinaldo to recreate the insurgent army, he refrained from making any political commitments. Relations with the insurgents were at first quite good. Dewey provided some arms for the rebels and permitted them to land additional equipment procured by American consular officials using the Mexican pesos which had been supplied to Aguinaldo by the Pact of Biyak-na-Bato. By 24 May Aguinaldo had restored his control over the insurgents, proclaiming himself "dictator" of the revolutionary movement until an elected government could be established. He also went out of his way to say nice things about the United States. By late May the insurgents had a substantial force under arms again, perhaps 30,000 men, of whom but two-thirds were on Luzon. Not all of these troops were well equipped, but there were enough weapons between those which had been procured abroad, those hidden after the Pact of Biyak-na-Bato, and those brought over by deserters— perhaps as many as 15,000 of them—from the Spanish militia to resume operations against the Spanish. Although there were outbreaks in several parts of the Philippines, including some of the southern islands, the principal focus of the insurgency was once again in the Tagalog-speaking areas of Luzon.

The first real offensive move was against the Bacoor-Zapote Line, which Augustin had created in an attempt to secure control of Cavite Province. Thinly held, the line broke readily when Aguinaldo pressed it with about 10,000 rebels. The insurgents quickly swept the Spanish out of the province. Then they pressed on to the outer defenses of Manila. Once again, they readily broke through, as the Spanish fell back on their inner line. The success of these opeations greatly strengthened Aguinaldo's hand. It is difficult to believe that had Augustin pulled more troops into the Manila area the rebels would have obtained such success. As it was, Aguinaldo 's forces in the Manila area were outnumbered by Augustin's, some 10,000 insurgents against about 13,000 Spaniards. As a result, since the Spanish troops were committed to fixed defenses, the number of men available was always inferior to the number that Aguinaldo could concentrate for his attacks. Had the Spanish been able to put more troops into action at the critical points the Filipinos would have had a far more difficult task. The troops who might have made the difference had been left at garrisons all over Luzon. In the weeks which followed Aguinaldo's investment of Manila some 7,000 Spanish troops were captured by the insurgents as they overran many of the smaller garrisons in the islands, while many thousands of others languished in isolated posts under occasional harassment from the rebels.

Meanwhile, Aguinaldo imposed a blockade on Manila. Dividing the front into four sectors, each under a subordinate commander (the rebel army had "an abundance of generals"), he had his men build earthworks and trenches. It was the best he could do, given his manpower and equipment. Had Dewey supported him with naval gunfire Aguinaldo would probably have been able to storm the city. However, by the end of May

Dewey had received his first political instructions. Although Secretary of the Navy Long gave him considerable latitude, he concluded by saying, "It is desirable, as far as possible, and consistent with your success and safety, not to have political alliances with the insurgents or any faction in the islands that would incur liability to maintain their cause in the future." In Dewey's view, his instructions precluded assisting the insurgents in the capture of Manila. Nevertheless, Dewey did not wholly withdraw support from the Filipinos. As he saw it, their success would save American lives when his reinforcements finally arrived.

Aguinaldo was fully aware that his political situation was precarious. As quickly as possible he took steps to strengthen his position. On 12 June he proclaimed the independence of the Philippines, followed within days by a series of decrees establishing a civil administration, a cabinet, and a judiciary. He also addressed some attention to formalizing the military forces of the new republic, proclaiming a universal military service obligation for all men aged 18 to 35 (with provision for buying exemption from conscription). Despite this, relations between Aguinaldo and Dewey remained warm, indeed, the admiral seems to have had some personal liking for the young nationalist leader. There were other reasons as well, for each side still needed the other. Particularly after a new player appeared on the scene.

German Interlude

In the military practice of the day, it was not uncommon for a non-belligerent to send observers to a theater of war. Observers would study the conduct of operations, monitor the maintenance of blockades, and occasionally serve as "honest brokers" in negotiations between the belligerents. The Spanish-American War was no different from any other conflict in this regard. HMS *Linnet*, a British gunboat, had turned up on 2 May after following Dewey from Hong Kong. Three days later the French armored cruiser *Bruix* was there. The rules of war provided for certain formalities with regard to the presence of third party observers in a combat zone. As a result, the captains of both ships made formal requests of Dewey—the man in charge—for permission to enter Manila Bay. Dewey granted this and indicated appropriate anchorages for each ship. But when the German cruiser *Irene* turned up on 6 June, her skipper ignored the rules, failing to acknowledge Dewey's authority in the situation, and anchoring as he saw fit. Later that very same day the German transport *Darmstadt* arrived, loaded with several hundred replacements for the German naval squadron in the Far East. And she too ignored all the rules. At the least it was an exercise in bad manners. However, many of those present, Britons and French as well as Americans, considered that the German action might be even more deliberate. German-American relations were by no means smooth. Tensions had existed over the status of Samoa, claimed by both powers, and it was widely known that Germany had offered to purchase some of Spain's colonies. There had been talk of war on several occasions and both powers had actually prepared plans for such a contingency. Dewey sent polite notes to the captains in question, who returned non-committal responses. On 7 May the British armored cruiser *Imortalité* arrived, proceeding according to the rules. The next day the small German cruiser *Kormoran* arrived and, true to form, failed to request permission to enter the bay or to anchor, even ignoring a warning shot fired across her bow by the cruiser *Raleigh*, an incident not recorded in the latter's log. Two days later the Japanese protected cruiser *Itsukushima*, an unusually powerful vessel, arrived, requested permission to enter the bay, and was assigned an anchorage. And on 12 May the senior German naval officer in the Far East arrived aboard the cruiser *Kaiserin Augusta*, which also ignored the formalities. So by 12 May there were two British warships in Manila Bay, plus one French and one Japanese, as well as four German warships and a transport carrying several hundred men. Moreover, German Rear-Admiral Otto von Diederichs had a problem with Americans, reaching back a decade to the Samoan crisis. The presence of the German squadron caused Dewey considerable concern. Over the next few weeks the Germans maintained a constant presence in Manila Bay, consistently ignoring protocol. By mid-June Dewey was urging the Navy Department to hasten the dispatch of the monitors *Monterey* and *Monadnock* from San Francisco to Manila, already under orders to sail in response to the threat posed by Camara's squadron. Meanwhile the German problem grew; on 20 June the old battleship *Kaiser* arrived in company with the cruiser *Prinzess Wilhelm*. One German warship having meanwhile sailed, this still left five German ships in Manila Bay, which taken together were more powerful than Dewey's own squadron, which had still not been reinforced.

Meanwhile, Diederichs took every opportunity to challenge Dewey's authority; his ships entered and left Manila Bay, changed their anchorages without securing permission, and refused to obey instructions of American officers. When Dewey questioned his actions, Diederichs argued about fine details of international law, despite the fact that the senior British officer present, Captain Edward Chichester, consistently supported Dewey's position, based on the British understanding of the rules of blockade. The presence of the Germans even began to concern Aguinaldo. The Germans had several times made unauthorized landings on Philippine soil. A party of seamen had even landed at Maraviles, on the southern tip of the Bataan peninsula, occupied the customs house, and conducted infantry drill. On 7 July the German cruiser *Irene* landed a party of sailors on Isla Grande at Subic Bay. Isla Grande was a Spanish outpost, a naval station which was under blockade by the insurgents. Reluctant to challenge the Germans to a fight, Aguinaldo quickly passed word of the incident to Dewey, who dispatched the cruiser *Raleigh* and a transport with 1,300 troops. As soon as *Raleigh* and her consort reached Subic Bay, *Irene* departed. Fearful of surrendering to the investing Filipinos, the Spanish troops on Isla Grande had apparently been negotiating a surrender to the Germans. The two American ships took them aboard, and they were subsequently turned over to the insurgents. Things came to a head on 10 July.

One of Diederichs' aides visited Dewey to respond to a series of protests that Dewey had submitted to the German admiral on 7 July. Dewey listened quietly at first. Then the officer, Commander Paul von Hintze, began making complaints about American actions, arguing that *Irene* had been lawfully engaged on 7 July, and that *Raleigh* had possessed no right to interfere in her actions. Dewey angrily responded, "Does Admiral von Diederichs think he commands here or I? Tell your admiral if he wants war, I am ready." Although the outburst might easily have provoked an international incident, in fact it had precisely the opposite effect. At the time it was believed by many that Diederichs' behavior was inspired by Berlin. In fact, his instructions were to keep Germany's options open, and keep an eye on what everyone else was doing. His bad manners, in fact, appear to have been merely a manifestation of his personal animosity towards Americans. When confronted with the potentially dire political consequences of his actions, his manners improved considerably. But then, Dewey's military situation was also improving.

The Philippine Expedition

The debate about how quickly to reinforce Dewey was short but acrimonious. There was no question but that an expedition would be sent, nor even much about its size. But there was considerable debate about its composition. On 12 May Major General Wesley Merritt was appointed to command an expedition to the Philippines. A Civil War veteran, the second-ranking man in the Army and commander of the Department of the East, Merritt quickly discarded Dewey's suggestion that 5,000 men be sent, requesting nearly three times as many (over 14,000 men) including 6,000 Regulars and 8,000 Volunteers. Reviewing his request, General Miles upped the figure to nearly 15,000, but changed the ratio between Regulars and Volunteers to 3,000 and 12,000. Merritt objected, much preferring Regulars. Unkind words were said, notably by Merritt, but retracted (by means of blaming the press). In the end 20,000 men were assigned to what was shortly designated VIII Corps. There were to be several convoys. The first convoy sailed from San Francisco on 25 May, the second 21 days later on 15 June, the third ten days after that on 25 June, the fourth 20 days later on 15 July, and the fifth eight days later on 23 July. Additional convoys followed. Meanwhile, the Navy was also sending reinforcements, the cruiser *Charleston* departing San Francisco as an escort to the first convoy, the monitor *Monterey* with a small escort on 11 June, and the

The first convoy bearing troops for the Philippines is given a tu-
multuous sendoff as it sails from San Francisco, 25 May 1898, three
weeks before V Corps took ship for Cuba. Escorted by the protected
cruiser **Charleston,** *the three transports carrying Brig. Gen.*
Thomas K. Anderson's 2,500-man brigade landed at Cavite on 30
June, after nearly 36 days at sea.

monitor *Monadnock* on 4 July.

The first reinforcements to reach Dewey arrived on 30 June, 36 days out from San Francisco. The cruiser *Charleston* and three transports landed some 2,500 men (elements of the 14th Infantry, plus the 1st California and the 2nd Oregon), plus tons of equipment at Cavite, along with Brig. Gen. Thomas M. Anderson. It had been an arduous voyage. The Army knew little about the trans-oceanic movement of troops, and the vessels were crowded and poorly managed. They quickly became dirty, the food was poor, and the men ill-housed. Surprisingly everyone came through the experience well. En route, the ships stopped briefly at Honolulu, and *Charleston* had stopped off at Guam to seize the island from a tiny Spanish garrison that was not even aware of the war. The voyages of the two follow-up convoys

The Astor Battery moving up to the front in the Philippines. A unique unit, the battery was the personal contribution of millionaire John Jacob Astor to the war effort. He provided a blank check to the War Department and told it to "buy a battery." The War Department turned the job over to Peyton March, a young artilleryman, who did so good a job that the battery was in action in the Philippines by the end of the war.

were equally hard, they too making the short landfall at Honolulu. The second convoy left San Francisco in three transports on 15 June to arrive at Cavite on 17 July, bringing nearly 3,600 men (elements of the 18th and 23rd Infantry Regiments, plus the 1st Colorado, 1st Nebraska, and 10th Pennsylvania Volunteers and two batteries from Utah) under Brig. Gen. Francis V. Greene, one of the most experienced officers in the army. The third echelon—"convoy" is not quite the correct word—departed San Francisco 25-29 July and reached Cavite on 25-31 July. Its seven ships brought over 4,800 men (the balance of the 18th and 23rd Infantry Regiments, a battalion of the 3rd Artillery, and a company of engineers, Regulars all, plus the 1st Idaho, 1st North Dakota, and 13th Minnesota Volunteers, a battalion of the 1st Wyoming, and the Astor Battery) under Brig. Gen. Arthur MacArthur, a Civil War hero, along with Maj. Gen. Wesley

Merritt, commanding the VIII Corps. Two additional convoys were already en route, with nearly 5,000 more men.

As the troops arrived, Dewey and the generals began delicate negotiations with Aguinaldo. The first of these was held on 1 July, the very day after General Anderson landed. It was clear that the arrival of American ground troops was not pleasing to the Filipino leader. He had hoped to take Manila with his own forces, assisted by the U.S. Navy. Now he would have to deal with the U.S. Army as well. Dewey's influence on the negotiations was considerable. He convinced Anderson that no attempt should be made to interfere with any of Aguinaldo's military or political acts, but that these should not be directly supported either, thereby keeping a free hand. Meanwhile Anderson's troops, and Greene's when they arrived, were held in the relative safety of Cavite, kept busy training, preparing campsites, and handling supplies. By that time Merritt had arrived, American ground strength in the Philippines was nearly 11,000 officers and enlisted men, with 22 pieces of artillery.

Of course in Manila, Governor-General Augustin could not but be aware of the arrival of the American ground forces. His own hope of reinforcement had long since passed. Camara's reinforcing squadron had departed Cadiz on 16 June. On the advice of his professional staff, Secretary of the Navy Long decided that the best way to counter the Spanish movement was to threaten Spain itself, a decision on which Dewey concurred. On 18 June Admiral Sampson was informed that as soon as Camara passed through the Suez Canal he was to form the "Eastern Squadron." This was to be composed of two battleships, an armored cruiser, and several auxiliary cruisers drawn from the fleet off Santiago. Under Commodore John C. Watson, the Eastern Squadron was to raid the Spanish coast in order to force the recall of Camara for home defense. Secretary Long cabled Dewey about the decision to form the Eastern Squadron on 27 June, giving him a list of the ships involved and adding that the same information was being leaked to the Spanish. Camara passed Suez on 5 July. The news caused some consternation both in Washington and Manila Bay. With two monitors Dewey would have a good chance against the heavier ships of the Spanish squadron. Just one monitor would help even the odds considerably. However, by various calculations it was determined that Camara could reach Dewey as early as 1 August, a few days before the monitor *Monterey* did, while *Monadnock* could not possibly arrive before mid-August. As a result, Dewey contemplated several alternative plans. He might seize Manila immediately with whatever troops were at hand, then use its coast defense batteries to support his own squadron. Alternatively, he could take his squadron out to meet *Monterey* on the high seas east of the Philippines, and then return to try conclusions with the Spanish. A third possibility was to hide his squadron somewhere in the numerous bays and inlets of the Philippines and ambush Camara, in the hope of catching him off guard. Neither course proved necessary. On 7 July—in the wake of the Spanish naval defeat at Santiago—the Minister of Marine ordered Camara to return immediately to Spain. If the news was pleasing to Dewey, it was disastrous for Augustin.

Although Manila was strongly held, without reinforcements the ultimate fall of the city was inevitable. Morale began to sag badly. With proper management, the food supply should have sufficed for several months, but shortages had begun to develop. Aware that negotiations were already underway between the United States and Spain, Augustin requested permission to conclude a truce rather than subject the city to a possible assault on the eve of peace. He was refused.

Meanwhile negotiations between the Americans and the Filipinos continued. In order to bring U.S. troops into action against the Spanish it would be necessary for them to take over a portion of the insurgents' lines of investment about Manila. Fearful of committing the U.S. to even implied recognition of the Filipino government, Merritt decided to avoid any direct dealings with Aguinaldo, and assigned Brig. Gen. Francis V. Greene. Aware of the slight, Aguinaldo deputized General Mariano Noriel commander of the southeastern sector of the lines of investment about Manila. In the end a simple arrangement was made. On the night of 29-30 July the insurgents withdrew their troops from about 1000 yards of their lines between the sluggish backwater Estero Tripa de Gallina and Manila Bay, about a half-mile south of the Spanish lines, directly facing Fort San Antonio de Abad. They left only a small detachment on the coast. Into this position General Anderson began moving his troops. Greene's brigade entered the lines first. The Americans settled in easiliy. The next day Dewey tested the defenses of Fort San Antonio de Abad, and a noisy but bloodless exchange of fire ensued. By this time aware that the lines in that sector had been taken over by U.S. troops, the Spanish prepared a little reception for the newcomers. On the night of 31 July-1 August the Spanish began harassing the American lines with both rifle and artillery fire. The Americans, mostly men from the 10th Pennsylvania and the 1st California, responded in kind, though rather more wildly than the better disciplined Spanish. The result was several hours of heavy firing, with 14 Americans killed or mortally wounded, plus an additional 41 less seriously injured. Spanish casualties were believed by the Americans to number "200 killed and 300 wounded," but were actually much less, a handful killed and several more wounded. As the troops grew accustomed to the hardships of life in the trenches, Merritt pressed preparations for an assault on the city. Finding the insurgents' trenches inadequate, Greene had the troops construct new positions, particularly after a second skirmish on 5 August resulted in additional casualties. Meanwhile MacArthur's brigade began entering the lines, taking the right side. By 7 August, when MacArthur's troops had completed landing, there were some 8,500 Americans occupying over a thousand yards of recon-structed trenches, with their left on the sea and their right on the marshy banks of the estero. Even as the troops were entering the lines Dewey was trying to negotiate a deal with Augustin, in the hope of avoiding an assault. Merritt frankly believed his efforts would prove fruitless, and pressed him to support an immediate assault, but Dewey persisted, even after the monitor *Monterey* arrived on 4 August. At the same time, tired of Augustin's pessimistic communications, the Spanish government sacked Augustin, replacing him with General Fermin Jaudenes y Al-varez, in the hope that the new Governor-General might pro-long the defense until peace negotiations had been concluded.

Sensing a chance, on 6 August Dewey and Merritt issued a demand that the city be surrendered. Jaudenes ignored it. Three days later the two American commanders tried again, more politely, observing that the city's situation was hopeless and that honor had certainly been satisfied. Jaudenes convened a council of war of his 14 seniormost commanders. A vote to begin surrender negotiations or to continue resistance came up a tie. Jaudenes decided to do both, by spinning out negotiations as long as possible. He informed Dewey and Merritt that he had no authority to surrender, and asked for time to communicate with his superiors. The Americans rejected his message. But at the same time, Dewey remained in clandestine contact with Jaudenes through several channels. One was the Belgian consul, Edouard C. André, who had the right to pass through the lines freely. On 10 August a deal was made through André. Jaudenes hinted that he might agree to surrender after a sham battle, provided the insurgents were kept out. After a brief discussion, Dewey and Merritt acceded to Jaudenes' proposal. Some quick negotiations followed to iron out the details. Dewey was to bombard Fort San Antonio de Abad for a short while, and it would then surrender upon demand. It was a simple arrangement, designed to assuage Spanish honor. Merritt was not sure it would work, fearing that some Spaniards might insist on fighting to the end, and was troubled by the possibility of a clash with Filipinos. As a result, he made his preparations as if for a real battle. He arranged for the Filipinos to withdraw from their remaining positions on the right of the American lines in front of Blockhouses 13 and 14. This permitted him to attack on a two-brigade front without having to directly assault Fort San Antonio. He assumed that if the Spanish offered serious resistance he would let Dewey's ships pound their defenses into rubble before attacking, but if they surrendered immediately the troops would quickly move to occupy the city, with the aid of six companies of the 2nd Oregon Volunteers, which would land from a transport directly against the *Intramuros*, so that the inner city would be occupied before the insurgents had any chance of reaching it through the suburbs. To ensure that the insurgents understood his intentions, on 12 August he notified Aguinaldo that insurgent troops were not to enter the city.

The Fall of Manila

The morning of 13 August 1898 was humid and somewhat misty in Manila Bay. At 0845 hours the American ships began taking station off the city of Manila. The cruisers *Baltimore*, *Boston*, and *Charleston* positioned themselves directly opposite the Luneta batteries. The cruiser *Concord* stationed herself off the mouth of the Pasig River to cover the batteries on the north side of the city. The main body of Dewey's squadron took station directly opposite Fort San Antonio de Abad, with the cruisers *Olympia* and *Raleigh*, the gunboat *Petrel*, and the gunboat *Callao*, captured from the Spanish at Cavite and put into U.S. service, supported by the Revenue Cutter *McCulloch*, with the powerful monitor *Monterey*, which had arrived as scheduled on 4 August, moved close inshore. Although the senior officers of all of the ships were aware that only a demonstration was to be made, the junior officers and enlisted men believed a general action was in the offing. Much to their surprise, when firing began at 0935, only *Olympia*, *Raleigh*, *Petrel*, and *Callao* opened fire. A desultory bombardment of Fort San Antonio ensued. Much to everyone's surprise, the fort, armed with nine mostly obsolete field pieces, made no reply. The bombardment lasted almost an hour. During it, several of the foreign warships present changed station to secure a better view of the events. As the British ships moved after the German vessels, the legend arose that Captain Edward Chichester, believing Rear Admiral Otto von Diederichs was attempting to interfere in the bombardment, had interposed his ships between the Germans and the Americans, saying "Blood is thicker than water." In fact, the movements by both German and British ships were wholly innocent. The legend developed because of Diederichs' earlier bad manners and increasing American and British concern about German power. At the time, no one recorded anything unusual during the bombardment. The firing by Dewey's vessels ceased at 1025 Hours. General Anderson immediately ordered his troops to attack.

Greene's brigade, on the left, advanced first, assaulting Fort San Antonio de Abad, which proved unoccupied, and was quickly overrun. Greene pressed on. As his men entered the town of Malate they came under fire from some entrenched

Brigadier General Arthur MacArthur, in full dress, wearing the Medal of Honor he won in the Civil War. MacArthur's services in the war with Spain were surpassed by those during the Philippine Insurrection, during which he trained many of the officers who would rise to high command during the First World War.

Spanish troops. The Americans responded and a short fight ensued, with light casualties on both sides, before the Spanish drew back. Greene's men pressed on, against virtually no resistance. The firing to his left was MacArthur's signal to advance, and his troops quickly came under fire from Spanish troops entrenched around Blockhouse Number 14. The action became heated, but the blockhouse did not fall until about 1120 hours. MacArthur's men advanced northwards along the Pasay-Manila Road, overrunning Blockhouse Number 13 and entering the suburb of Singalong. There they became involved in a fight with Blockhouse Number 20 for nearly two hours before overcoming resistance and pressing on to occupy the suburb of Paco and reach the Pasig River, thereby cutting the town off from the Filipino insurgents. While MacArthur's men were relatively heavily engaged (they suffered five killed and 38 wounded), after their brief skirmish at Malate, Greene's men found themselves virtually unopposed (they had one man killed and 54

A company of Filipino troops, in a photograph taken between the end of the Spanish-American War and the beginning of the Philippine-American War. Some of the men appear to be wearing odds and ends of Spanish uniforms. The officers, in front, appear unarmed, as do several of the men. The rest appear to be equipped with versions of the Spanish Mauser, including at least one carbine.

wounded) as they pressed on through the inner suburbs of the city and crossed the Pasig River to occupy the districts of San Miguel and Binondo, thereby preventing Filipino access to the *Intramuros* from that quarter. The day had cost the United States six men killed and 92 wounded; Spanish losses were reported as 150 killed and 300 wounded, but these figures probably include losses incurred over the previous few days as well. Most of the day's fighting was unnecessary. Even before MacArthur's troops had succeeded in overruning Blockhouse Number 14, Manila had already surrendered.

Having completed the "bombardment" of Fort San Antonio at about 1025, Dewey had ordered *Olympia* to steam northward two miles to a position off the Paseo de Luneta. At 1100 hours he ordered hoisted the "DWHB," international flag signal for "Do you surrender?" Anxious minutes passed as every eye on the ship—Dewey would later say there were "fifty people looking"—tried to spot any sign of surrender. Then Dewey himself spotted it, on the south bastion of the Luneta. Two officers, Merritt's aide Lt. Col. Charles A. Whittier, and Dewey's aide Lt. Thomas M. Brumby went ashore to arrange terms. Arrange-

Officers of the 20th Kansas, in dress uniform, posing under the walls of the **Intramuros,** *at the northwestern corner of Manila, where the Pasig River empties into Manila Bay. The regiment was at sea when the Armistice was concluded, and thus did not see combat in the war with Spain, but saw considerable service during the Philippine Insurrection.*

ments went quickly, and by 1430 Brumby was back reporting that a formal agreement had been reached. Merritt landed and signed a preliminary agreement with Jaudenes. Then the 2nd Oregon Volunteers landed to take up security duties in the *Intramuros.* At 1743 hours the Spanish flag came down, and Brumby hoisted the Stars and Stripes.

Meanwhile problems were developing between the U.S. and Filipino forces. As the fighting proceeded, General Anderson reiterated his previous message to Aguinaldo, informing him that he was not to let his troops enter the city without American permission, and that they would come under fire if they did so. Aguinaldo chose to press the issue, though cautiously. As Greene's and MacArthur's troops moved northwards, he sent about 4,000 of his own men—General Noriel's division and some others—in behind them, and by the afternoon of 13 August they were in occupation of Malate, Paco, and Ermita, while other troops occupied the more outlying districts on the northern side of the Pasig River.

Unbeknown to those present, armistice negotiations in Paris had borne fruit. By evening Manila time, an armistice had been concluded. Had Governor-General Jaudenes been kept better informed by Madrid, he could easily have postponed any deals with Dewey and Merritt, preserving the city under Spanish control, thus rendering it a useful card in subsequent peace negotiations. Unfortunately for Spain, the government proved as inept at the end of the war as it had been at its beginning. Word of the armistice did not reach the Philippines until 16 August. By that time American and Spanish officers had formalized the details of the surrender of Manila. Although Jaudenes subsequently objected to certain of the terms, on the grounds that the final capitualtion had occurred after the armistice, he was really in no position to argue, and the agreement remained unchanged.

The American expedition to the Philippines was a surprisingly successful operation. Indeed, of the three overseas expeditions mounted by the United States in the war, it was the most well-managed, and that despite the fact that it actually was the first to depart American shores. The first ships bound for the Philippines sailed from San Francisco on 25 May, while the Santiago expedition did not get to sea until 14 June. Cooperation between the Army and Navy was quite good, there were no serious shortages of supplies or equipment, no epidemics. With surprisingly little loss, about 20 men killed and fewer than 150 wounded, the United States acquired a vast, rich territory.

José Profansio Rizal y Alonso

José Profasio Rizal y Alonso (1861-1898) came from a prosperous, thoroughly hispanicized Filipino family. He had the benefit of a very fine Jesuit education and, although trained in medicine, from an early age proved himself a talented writer, winning a drama prize at the age of 17. In 1882 he went to Spain to complete his education, taking an M.D. and a Ph.D. in literature by 1885. While in Spain he joined with other young Filipinos in seeking political, social, and economic reforms for the islands within the Spanish Empire. From 1885 to 1890 he traveled extensively in Europe, the U.S., and Asia, while churning out a surprising number of poems, zarzuela librettos, plays, and novels, and supporting himself as a journalist. After two years in Hong Kong, in 1892 Rizal returned to the Philippines, but was shortly exiled to Mindanao for political agitation. While in Mindanao he joined the *Katipunand*. In 1896 he was sent to Spain, but upon his arrival was almost immediately returned to the Philippines, where he was tried by court martial and shot, despite the fact that he had never actually borne arms against Spanish rule.

Emilio Aguinaldo y Famy

Emilio Aguinaldo y Famy (1869-1964) was born into a prosperous Tagalog-speaking family in Cavite Province, on Luzon. Of mixed Filipino and Chinese ancestry, Aguinaldo was well educated, and as a young man had served for a time in the Cavite militia. Inspired by liberal and nationalist ideas, he joined the *Katipunan* revolutionary movement. Joining the Philippine insurrection of 1896, he showed himself to be a naturally gifted commander, quickly rising to prominence among the rebel leaders, a rise aided by a certain ruthlessness in disposing of potential rivals. On conclusion of the Pact of Biac-na-Bato (December 1897), which ended the insurgency in return for a substantial bribe, he went to Hong Kong with the other rebel leaders.

On the outbreak of the Spanish-American War, Commodore Dewey arranged for Aguinaldo to be landed in the Philippines by the Revenue Cutter *McCulloch*. He promptly proclaimed the Republic of the Philippines, with himself as president and dictator. Aguinaldo cooperated reluctantly with the Americans, recognizing that there would almost certainly be a showdown after the Spanish were disposed of. It is probable that the initial clashes between American and Filipino troops occurred at his instigation, resulting in the U.S.-Philippine War.

Aguinaldo's attempt to fight the U.S. Army in a conventional war proved disastrous, and within a very short time he proclaimed a guerrilla war. However, he was never able to inspire broad-based support for his republic, the political and military leadership of which was overwhelmingly Tagalog, to the exclusion of the numerous other ethnic groups in the Philippines. Captured on 28 March 1901 (the day after his 37th birthday!) in a daring operation conducted by Frederick Funston, Aguinaldo shortly took an oath of allegiance to the United States, effectively ending the war. He lived quietly thereafter. During World War II Aguinaldo gave tacit support to the Japanese-sponsored "Republic of the Philippines." Taken into custody by U.S. forces upon the liberation of the islands, he was cleared of any charges of collaboration. Never completely reconciled with American rule, until the independence of the Philippines in 1946 Aguinaldo wore a black bow tie.

The Philippine Army

The Philippine insurgents were not as successful in organizing an army as the Cuban rebels had been. Even during the 1898 campaign their organization remained rudimentary. Although there was a central command, comprising 15 generals and their staffs, the army was essentially organized on a provincial basis. The commanding general of each province was required to maintain between one and six companies, depending upon population. On paper, companies were to be of 113 officers and men, a figure never attained. Four companies constituted a battalion, which had a staff of five. Higher formations were mostly ad hoc.

Although the insurgents procured some arms abroad, the largest source of supply was the Spanish Army. Between captured weapons and arms brought in by deserters from the militia, about half of the 30,000 men Aguinaldo had under command at the time of the Manila Campaign appear to have been armed. They did have some artillery, mostly *lantacas*, improvised wooden cannon. The few field pieces which they managed to secure, through capture from the Spanish, were beyond their skills, and so they impressed Spanish prisoners into service, a practice which continued even during the Filipino-American War.

The insurgents were determined though usually unskilled fighters. Their great failure was that they resorted to conventional warfare against the Spanish in 1896-1897 and against the Americans in 1899-1900, rather than irregular operations.

Wesley Merritt

Wesley Merritt (1834-1910) was born in New York City, but raised in Illinois. Graduating from West Point in 1861, he was commissioned in the Dragoons. His Civil War service was considerable, and varied. He served as an aide-de-camp to Maj. Gen. Philip St. George Cooke, and later took part in Maj. Gen. George Stoneman's raid towards Richmond during the Chancellorsville Campaign in the spring of 1863, meanwhile rising to captain. On the eve of the Gettysburg Campaign he was one of three cavalry captains promoted to brigadier generals in the volunteer army; the other two were Elon Farnsworth, killed in action leading a brigade at Gettysburg 3 July 1863, and George Armstrong Custer, killed in action at the Little Big Horn, 25 June 1876. Merritt commanded under Maj. Gen. Phil Sheridan during Grant's 1864 Virginia Campaign and the subsequent Petersburg Campaign and the Appomattox Campaign in April of 1864, meanwhile rising to major general of volunteers and lieutenant colonel in the regular army.

After the Civil War Merritt became lieutenant colonel of the 9th Cavalry, a black regiment, transferring to the 5th as its colonel in 1876, while seeing extensive service in the Indian Wars. After serving as superintendent of West Point 1882-1887, he was promoted to brigadier general in the regular army and held various departmental commands, while rising to major general. When the war with Spain broke out he was commander of the Department of the East, from which post he was sent to San Francisco to take command of the VIII Corps for operations in the Philippines.

Merritt served less than two months in the Philippines. He arrived at Manila Bay on 26 July, with the first contingent of VIII Corps, organized the capture of Manila on 13 August, and served about two weeks as military governor before being ordered to join the American negotiating team at the Paris peace conference. By December Merritt was back in his old post as commander of the Department of the East, from which he retired in 1900.

A talented cavalryman, Merritt's diplomatic skills were also considerable, as demonstrated by his negotiations with the Spanish to stage a virtually bloodless capture of Manila, while avoiding a direct confrontation with the Filipino nationalists. How he would have performed against the Filipinos was another matter entirely.

Arthur MacArthur

Arthur MacArthur (1845-1912) volunteered for Union service in 1862, at the age of 17, and was appointed second lieutenant in the 24th Wisconsin. He had a distinguished record during the Civil War, fighting in the Western theater and earning a two grade promotion to major for leading his regiment up the slope at Missionary Ridge (25 November 1863), a feat subsequently also rewarded with a Medal of Honor. He commanded the regiment in the Army of the Cumberland during the Atlanta Campaign and at Franklin (30 November 1864), where he was severely wounded, and for which he was promoted to colonel early in 1865, though not yet 20.

Upon being mustered out of the Volunteer Army in 1865, MacArthur was commissioned as a second lieutenant in the Regular Army. He rose to captain by mid-year, a rank in which he spent the next 24 years, mostly on frontier duty in the southwest. In 1898, by which time he was a lieutenant colonel in the adjutant general's department, MacArthur was made a brigadier general of volunteers and sent to command a brigade in the Philippines, where he took part in the capture of Manila on 13 August, for which he was

cited for bravery and promoted to major general of volunteers. Subsequently heavily involved in the suppression of the Philippine Insurrection, MacArthur was promoted to brigadier general in the Regular Army in 1900, and was shortly named military governor of the Philippines. During his tenure in this post (1900-1901), he instituted local elections while being promoted to major general in the Regular Army. He later served in various administrative posts in the U.S., was an observer with the Japanese Army during the Russo-Japanese War, and retired as a lieutenant general in 1909.

He died on 5 September 1912, having just completed a speech to the veterans of his old outfit, the 24th Wisconsin, thereby becoming the last Civil War officer to die at the head of his regiment. General of the Army Douglas MacArthur was his son. They are the only father and son to have both won the Medal of Honor.

Frederick Funston

Frederick Funston (1865-1917) spent a footloose youth in middle America. Drifting from odd job to odd job, by 1890 he had managed to spend two years at the University of Kansas. In that year he landed a job with the Department of Agriculture. Funston participated in government expeditions to Death Valley and the Yukon. In June of 1896 he attended a rally at Madison Square Garden in support of the Cuban Revolution. A

fiery speech by Maj. Gen. Daniel Sickles, a former Civil War general who had lost a leg at Gettysburg, accumulated an impressive record as a rake, and managed to avoid conviction on numerous charges of corruption over many years, prompted Funston to join the rebels. Two days later he dropped in on Sickles and secured a letter of introduction to Tomas Estrada Palma, leader of the Cuban junta in New York. On the strength of having once watched a cannon being fired—or so he said—Funston was sent to learn the operation of the 12-pounder Hotchkiss breech loading field gun, the use of which he imparted to Cuban volunteers, all without once having fired the piece. After numerous "cloak and dagger-type" adventures, Funston landed in Cuba with the rank of captain, commanding the artillery of the revolutionary army.

Funston served for 18 months, participating in numerous engagements and rising to lieutenant colonel. Early in 1898, when a Spanish-American war seemed imminent, Funston returned to the U.S. and began agitating for a volunteer commission. In May he was made colonel of the 20th Kansas in the Volunteer Army, and shortly thereafter shipped out for the Philippines. Funston arrived in the islands after the armistice with Spain, but was soon heavily engaged in the suppression of the Philippine Insurrection. He took part in several notable actions, winning a Medal of Honor for the Battle of Calumpit (27 April 1899), and was promoted to brigadier general of volunteers. Despite this, by late 1900 it was clear that he was not going to be offered a commission in the Regular Army. To rectify the situation, acting on some intelligence garnered from captured documents, in March of 1901, together with a small party of Filipino and American troops, he undertook a daring special operation which succeeded in capturing Emilio Aguinaldo, and secured for himself a commission as brigadier general in the Regular Army.

Funston's peacetime career was impressive. Commanding the Department of California at the time of the San Francisco earthquake and fire in 1906, his prompt dispatch of troops had much to do with preserving order and life in the devastated city. He later commanded U.S. troops which occupied Vera Cruz, Mexico, in 1914, and along the Mexican border in support of the Pershing Expedition in 1916-1917, dying while still on active duty. Some historians have speculated that had he lived he would have played an important role in the American Expeditionary Force during World War I.

Funston was one of a rare breed, the amateur who turns to soldiering rather late in life with considerable success.

The Siege of Baler

One of the many Spanish garrisons isolated in the Philippines by the failure of the Governor-General to concentrate his forces at Manila, gave one of the most heroic defenses in modern history at Baler, a small town on the east coast of Luzon, about 115 miles northeast of Manila. It was held by 57 men of the *2nd Expeditionary Rifle Battalion.* Commanded by Captain Enrique de las Morenas y Fossi, a native of Puerto Rico, the detachment had been established at Baler in February and was virtually isolated from the start. At the time it was well provided for, with over 14,000 rations on hand and plenty of ammuntion.

Baler was first invested by Philippine insurgents on 1 July 1898. Thereafter, for the next 336 days, there were never fewer than 200 Filipino troops, and often as many as a thousand, with six cannon, five of them *lantacas* and one a proper field piece. At first the defenders managed to secure a relatively large perimeter encompassing many of the buildings around the town's main square, the church, the city hall, and the *Guardia Civil* barracks. This was a rather long line for so few troops, and gradually the perimeter was contracted to include only the church, some of its outbuildings, and a portion of the churchyard. Although the defenders beat off numerous assaults, their losses were surprisingly light. Five men were killed in action, including Captain de las Morenas, and three disabled by wounds, in contrast to the 300-350 dead and wounded admitted by the local Filipino commander. An-

other 13 of the defenders died of disease, and six men deserted. There were an unknown number of civilians with the defenders as well, and about 20 of these died, mostly of disease, including the local priest. Towards the end of the siege the Filipino lines were in some places as close as 40 yards to the Spanish.

Several times during the siege short truces were arranged, and as a result of one of these the defenders learned that Manila had fallen to the Americans. Captain de las Morenas was killed on 22 November and command devolved upon 2nd Lt. Saturnino Martin Cerezo. By February 1899 the troops were down to about 200 grams of hard tack a day, starvation rations. Still they held out, fearful of being captured and hopeful that they would be relieved by American forces. In fact, their heroic defense was not widely known, the Filipinos prefering to keep the matter quiet. Not until April—after the outbreak of the Filipino-American War—did the U.S. authorities learn about the matter. The gunboat *Yorktown* was dispatched to effect a rescue, but when she arrived off shore on 21 April insurgent troops prevented a landing. So the siege continued.

By the end of May 1899 the garrison was literally out of food. Lieutenant Martín Cerezo called for a parlay. The besieging Filipinos proved amenable, and on 2 June 1899 the garrison laid down its arms. Only then did they learn that Spain had given up the Philippines, and "this little bit of earth which we had defended even unto madness, was no longer ours." The garrison received surprisingly good treatment, a fate not usually accorded prisoners of the Filipino guerrillas. They were taken across Luzon and turned over to the Americans near Manila.

Lieutenant Martín and his men returned to Spain on 4 September 1899 to a tumultuous welcome. There were promotions and rewards all around. Captain de las Morenas received a posthumous promotion to major, plus the Cross of San Fernando, both of which greatly increased his wife's pension. Martin Cerezo, a reserve officer, received a promotion to captain in the regular army, plus a San Fernando. The company's medical officer was also promoted and decorated, and all of the men, living and dead, were awarded a Cross of Military Merit, plus a small monthly pension.

Frederick Funston, who knew something about heroism, called the defense of Baler one of the most heroic feats in military history, and counted himself honored to have met Martín Cerezo and his men.

The Annexation of Hawaii

Through the nineteenth century Hawaii maintained a precarious independence under the House of Kamehameha, cautiously treading its way between the claims and demands of greater powers. In the early 1890s the monarchy had been overthrown by an internal revolt, led by American expatriates, and abetted by the U.S. Navy. A plea for annexation to the United States fell on deaf ears, and a republic was established. This too had a precarious existence, with the desire of some for annexation to the U.S. prompted by fear that Japan would acquire the islands.

On 16 June 1897 another attempt was made to secure annexation by means of a bill introduced into the Senate by a friendly legislator. This languished in committee. Then the Spanish-American War broke out. The pro-American Hawaiian government was technically neutral, but immediately violated its status on a grand scale, offering material support, including a battalion of volunteers. When U.S. warships and convoys landed at Honolulu en route to the Philippines, the government of Hawaii provided entertainment and refreshments for the sailors and troops at its own expense. Meanwhile, interest in the annexation of Hawaii revived. On 4 May a joint resolution was introduced in Congress to annex the islands. Although opponents of the move, including the Speaker of the House, were able to delay it, the measure began moving through the legislative process. The bill passed the House by a vote of 209 to 91 on 15 June, and the Senate by 42 to 21 on 6 July. The measure was signed into law by the President on 7 July.

To effect the annexation of the islands, on 6 August the 1st New York was extracted from a convoy bound for the Philippines and ordered ashore. It took up occupation duties, and conducted the ceremonial assumption of control on 12 August. The regiment remained in Hawaii until November.

The acquisition of Hawaii was part of a spate of annexations implemented by the U.S. in the period during and immediately following the war with Spain. In addition to Hawaii and the territories acquired from Spain the U.S. took control of Midway Island, Wake, and a number of smaller places in the Pacific to which it had some claim, mostly through discovery by American mariners.

Chapter VIII

"A Bully Fight"

Peace negotiations had begun between the United States and Spain almost as soon as the war broke out. They were essentially an outgrowth of the prewar efforts by several powers to bring about a peaceful solution to the Spanish-American crisis. As early as 8 May, just a week after Dewey's victory at Manila Bay, the British government made informal inquiries as to what terms the U.S. would accept for peace. This feeler—originating from Joseph Chamberlain, colonial secretary and noted proponent of close ties between Britain and America—was passed to the State Department by John Hay, U.S. ambassador to Britain who had first entered public service as secretary to Abraham Lincoln. The State Department waited to reply until 3 June, after Cervera's squadron had been blockaded at Santiago, a development greatly strengthening America's strategic position. The terms were simple:

1. Cuban independence, after a short period of U.S. administration.
2. Cession of Puerto Rico to the U.S. in lieu of an indemnity.
3. Cession of a base to the U.S. in the Philipppines, which would remain Spanish.
4. Cession of a base to the U.S. in the Marianas, which would remain Spanish.

The first item, of course, was the principal American war aim, since the status of Cuba had been the primary cause of the war. Although the terms were modified on 14 June to reflect a possible alteration of the status of the Philippines with regard to the insurgents, they essentially remained the American program

Theodore Roosevelt wearing his uniform as colonel of the 1st Volunteer Cavalry, the "Rough Riders," in a photo taken shortly after the war, which propelled him into the White House within three years. Roosevelt's uniforms, provided by Brooks Brothers, were tailored with additional inside pockets so that he could carry extra eyeglasses, of which he brought a dozen pairs with him to Cuba.

for ending the war. These terms were quietly imparted to Spain by Britain through Austrian channels. There was no response from Madrid. On 15 June, Spain suggested that Manila be placed under international control in an obvious attempt to prevent the U.S. from taking the city. Save for Austria, native land of the Spanish queen, and Germany, all of the great powers objected strongly to this initiative since it was a violation of their neutrality. The matter was dropped. For a time it seemed as though nothing would occur. But after the defeat of Cervera's squadron at Santiago on 3 July, Spanish prime minister Sagasta began taking some small steps towards opening negotiations. He polled various military commanders as to their belief in the necessity of making peace at this point in the war, finding most of them opposed to the idea, but committed to obeying orders. Meanwhile, of course, negotiations began between Shafter and Toral over the possible surrender of Santiago de Cuba. Sagasta's plans became more evident on 14 July when he suspended various constitutional guarantees, notably freedom of the press, in an apparent attempt to curb public opposition to peace proposals. By this time negotiations for the surrender of Santiago were well advanced. Four days later Spain presented its first formal offer. Through the French foreign ministry, the Spanish proposed peace on the basis of independence for Cuba. Unfortunately, a series of coincidences prevented the message from getting through. The president of France was out-of-town and the foreign minister was ill, while the principal energies of most of the foreign ministry staff were focused on arrangements for a major reception. This did not ecome known until 20 July. Finally, on 22 July French minister Jules Cambon was asked to deliver a message from the Queen Regent of Spain to President McKinley, asking for his terms. A further delay ensued because the message was sent in code and the Spanish consulate in Montreal had to supply the key to the French mission in Washington. McKinley finally received the message on 26 July.

Over the next few days McKinley conferred with his cabinet, senior members of Congress, and other dignitaries, while closely perusing the press to ascertain public opinion. There was considerable debate as to what terms to offer. Meanwhile operations in the Philippines and Puerto Rico went forward, prompting the Spanish to later charge that the President had deliberately delayed his response to gain the greatest negotiating advantage. In fact, he was seriously concerned about securing the best possible terms without creating further problems for the U.S. or for his political future. His response came on 30 July and essentially reiterated the terms offered on 3 June. When the Spanish objected, the President observed that the terms were the same as those offered earlier, when Spain's situation had been far better than was presently the case. There were a few more qibbles, but by 4 August broad agreement on the basis for negotiations had been arranged. McKinley offered only two concessions: To assuage Spanish pride, the negotiations would take place in Paris rather than Washington; and, to the mutual satisfaction of both the U.S. and Spain, representatives of the Filipino insurgents would be excluded. Over the next few days details were ironed out, and on 12 August the U.S. and Spain concluded an agreement to hold negotiations, and established an armistice to take hold the next morning. The fighting was over.

Negotiations for a formal end to the war began in Paris in late September. They dragged on for weeks. There was much debate about numerous issues, mostly small matters. Yet the only major issue turned out to be the status of the Philippines, which was, in fact, a matter of much domestic debate in the U.S. Ultimately McKinley insisted on annexation. Although anti-imperialists scoffed at his claim to have sought guidance in prayer, he actually was deeply troubled by the question of the Philippines. The islands could not in good conscience be returned to Spain. Letting them go their own way—a popular idea among some Americans, provided the U.S. retained a naval base—seemed a dangerous course, given evident German and Japanese interest in the islands. In the end, annexation seemed the least bad of several bad options.

The treaty of peace was initialed on 10 December 1898. There were seventeen articles, but the basic terms were independence for Cuba after a short period of American occupation, annexation of Puerto Rico in lieu of an indemnity, annexation of Guam, and annexation of the Philippines, for which the U.S. would pay Spain $20 million in compensation. A few Americans opposed the treaty on the grounds that it was imperialistic. Some of these people were motivated by high ideals, such as Mark Twain, while some feared that control of distant areas such as the Philippines would involve the U.S. in conflicts with other powers; still others were concerned that the annexation of areas inhabited by non-whites would have a polluting effect on America. Nevertheless, despite considerable acrimony the treaty passed the Senate by a comfortable margin. And so the U.S. became a global power.

The consequences of the Spanish-American War were manifold. For Spain it was a humiliation which only added to the country's long decline from global mastery during the "Golden Century." Although defeat in the war led to the literary and artistic flowering of the so-called "Generation of '98," including Ortega y Gassett and Unamuno, it also led to a worsening of civil-military relations. The two decades prior to the war had been largely free of acrimonious civil-military disputes. This began to change in 1895 with the outbreak of revolution in Cuba and the Philippines. Then came the devastating defeat at the hands of the United States. The disaster of 1898 sensitized Spanish political leadership to the pressing need for military reform and particularly to the necessity for a drastic reduction in the size of the officer corps. However, in the decade following the Spanish-American War the political leadership was unable to develop a consistent military policy or effect serious military reform, while the army became highly politicized as a result of perceived threats to its integrity. Added to Spain's inability to establish a stable political system, the rapid industrialization of the country and humiliation of the ill-conceived Moroccan adventure of 1909-1927, this ultimately helped bring about the civil war of 1936-1939.

For the U.S. the consequences of the war were equally significant. The Spanish-American War established the United States as one of the great powers. Hitherto only peripherally involved in world affairs, after the war the U.S. became an increasingly active player on the global scene. The war also increased the professionalism of the armed forces to an enormous extent. The Army saw its structure entirely revamped, including the creation of the post of chief-of-staff over the staff bureaus and the institution of a war college. Reform of the Army during the post-war years was the most noticeable, if only because the failures—or perceived failures—of the Army were greater by far than those of the Navy, nevertheless, the Navy underwent major changes as well, particularly in its command structure and provisions for realistic training, particularly in gunnery. The structure of the armed forces which emerged from the military reforms of the decade following the war remained essentially intact until after World War II.

But if the war led to significant improvements in the American armed forces, in many ways the military achievements of the United States during the war were overlooked by other powers. During the war the U.S. had accomplished more than any other major power ever had. In a matter of four months it had raised, trained, equipped, and sent into action large armies on distant fronts with considerable success. To be sure there had been problems, serious problems. But even Britain had problems when, only a year later, it found itself having to send an army to South Africa to fight the Boers. European powers were

Philadelphia welcomes the troops home. Most American cities staged elaborate celebrations for their returning boys. Note the elaborate columns and arch, which formed a "Court of Honor," with city hall in the background.

wont to judge military potential on the basis of standing forces, and of these the U.S. had few, even after the expansion of the armed force engendered by the necessity of securing the country's newly won foreign empire. Germany certainly overlooked the American ability to quickly create effective armies, though perhaps not wholly professional, a matter which proved of some consequence in 1917.

The U.S. also had to face serious political consequences of the war. The war created an American empire with the acquisition of the Philippines, Puerto Rico, and Guam, to which were shortly added Hawaii, portions of Samoa, and the Panama Canal Zone, not to mention *de facto* protectorates over Cuba and other small Caribbean countries. It was the annexation of the Philippines which had the greatest political consequences for the United States, however—this over the objections of Aguinaldo and many of the Filipinos, with the "Philippine Insurrection" breaking out in February of 1899 and dragging on into 1902. Costing over four thousand U.S. lives (only a quarter in battle) and many thousands more Filipino lives, it was a hard, brutal affair (albeit by no means as brutal as has sometimes been claimed), with victory ultimately the result of the failure of the insurgents to effectively broaden their political base. For the most part, the rebellion remained largely confined to the Tagalog-speaking regions. But even as the "pacification" of the Philippines was in progress, serious questions were being raised about the wisdom of the acquisition. Having taken the Philippines the United States became responsible for them, and thus was increasingly drawn into the politics of the Far East, with consequences which would echo through the twentieth century.

It had indeed been, in Theodore Roosevelt's words, "A bully fight," and one with a global impact.

Some Notable Spanish-American War Alumni

Aside from a few generals and heroes who garnered headlines in the Spanish-American War, as in the case of all wars, most of the men who served did so anonymously. Yet some of those faceless men went on to achieve prominence in later life.

The Americans

Captain Trasker Bliss, military attache in Madrid when the war broke out, served as a staff officer in Puerto Rico and Cuba, later helped implement the Root reforms of the Army, served as chief-of-staff early in World War I, and then as the American representative to the Allied Supreme War Council. The last American officer to hold a brevet in the rank of full general, he retired as a permanent major general in 1920.

Edgar Rice Borroughs, a young journalist, was turned down by the Rough Riders because the rolls were full. He later went on to become the author of notable adventure tales, including *Tarzan of the Apes*.

Smedley Butler, a 16 year old high school student, was rejected by the Army as too young, lied about his age and joined the Marines, who commissioned him a second lieutenant. He served at Guantanamo, and later aboard the armored cruiser *New York*. Discharged after the war, he reentered the Corps as a first lieutenant in April 1899. An effective if controversial officer, he served in numerous "Banana Wars" before retiring as a major general in 1931, having been three times nominated for, and twice awarded, the Medal of Honor, not to mention garnering a nomination for a Victoria Cross.

Benjamin O. Davis was commissioned a second lieutenant in the 8th Volunteer Infantry, an "immune" regiment, in July 1898. Mustered out in March 1899, he enlisted in the 9th Cavalry, served in the Philippines, won a commission, and began rising through the army. After retiring in 1941 as a colonel, he was promptly recalled to duty as a brigadier general and retired in this grade in 1947. He was the first black general in the U.S. Army, and the only black officer in the Regular Army from 1916 to 1936, when his son graduated from West Point.

Charles Dick, an Ohio politician who served in Cuba as lieutenant-colonel of the 8th Ohio, later entered Congress and was the author of the Dick Act of 1903, which established a federally regulated National Guard.

Robley D. Evans, skipper of the battleship *Iowa*, was one of the few senior naval officers in the war to go on to greater things, commanding the "Great White Fleet" for the first half of its world cruise in 1907-1909.

William S. Graves, a second lieutenant in the 7th Infantry, spent the war as a staff officer in the U.S. He afterwards saw combat in the Philippines as a captain in the black 24th Infantry, and rose to command the U.S. expeditionary force in Siberia during the Russian Civil War, 1919-1921.

Thomas C. Hart, Annapolis '97, was a passed midshipman in the battleship *Massachusetts*. By 1939 he was an admiral in command of the Asiatic Fleet, based in the Philippines, where he served with some distinction during the opening months of World War II and later on the Navy's general board until he was appointed to fill a senate vacacny from Connecticut.

Ernest J. King, in his first year as a midshipman at Annapolis, saw service in USS *San Francisco* during the war. During World War II he served as chief-of-naval operations, going on inactive service in 1945 as a fleet admiral.

Walter Kreuger left high school to enlist as a private in the 2nd Volunteer Infantry, an "immune" regiment, rising to sergeant major before being mustered out early in 1899. He promptly reenlisted, won a commission, and during World War II commanded the Sixth Army under Douglas MacArthur in the Pacific, retiring as a full general in 1946.

Frank Knox, a lawyer, joined the Rough Riders, and saw action in Cuba. After the war he returned to law, became prominent in Republican party circles, and was named Secretary of the Navy by President Franklin Roosevelt, in which post he served until his death shortly before the end of World War II.

Fiorello LaGuardia, a 16-year old newspaper correspondent at Tampa during the concentration of V Corps, saw his hopes of going with the troops to Cuba dashed when his father, a regular army bandmaster, became gravely ill. He later beame mayor of New York, generally regarded as the most successful in the city's history.

William D. Leahy, Annapolis '97, was a passed midshipman in USS *Oregon* throughout the war, and retired from the service as an admiral in 1939. Recalled to active duty during World War II, he was President Roosevelt's personal chief of staff, U.S. ambassador to Vichy France for a time, and chairman of the joint chiefs, retiring as a fleet admiral in 1949.

Peyton March, a recent graduate of the Artillery School, was offered command of the Astor Battery at the outbreak of the war and provided with a blank check to pay for recruiting, equipping, and training the battery, a feat which he accomplished with considerable skill and not a little cleverness (Being a devotee of the old saw, "If it stays in the army it ain't stealing."). After the he rose steadily, and by 1917 he was a brigadier general commanding the artillery in the American Expeditionary Force in France, from which post in early 1918 he was named chief-of-staff of the Army, a task which he performed with considerable skill. He retired in 1921.

John A. McIlheny, of Louisiana, served as a second lieutenant in E Troop of the Rough Riders, survived a serious bout of fever, and returned to his native parish to go into the tabasco business. Another Rough Rider who went back to the family business was **William Tiffany**, who had served as a sergeant.

William "Billy" Mitchell entered the service as a volunteer private in the 1st Wisconsin in April, and was shortly made a second lieutenant in the Volunteer Signal Corps. Remaining in the service, he eventually became a brigadier general and an advocate of air power, destroying his career when his enthusiasm turned into fanaticism.

John J. Pershing, a lieutenant in the 10th Cavalry, went on to command the American Expeditionary Force during World War I.

Damon Runyon, the author, served in the 1st Colorado Volunteers, seeing action in the Philippines.

Carl Sandburg, the poet and biographer, served in Puerto Rico with the 6th Illinois. After the war he attempted to secure an appointment to West Point, was rejected, and turned to literature. His most famous biography was that of Lincoln, another young man from Illinois who had once gone to war and seen no action, but came away profoundly influenced by his experience.

Joshua Slocum completed the first solo 'round-the-world voyage a few weeks after his encounter with *Oregon.* He covered 43,000 miles in three years, two months, and two days, on his sixth trip around the world under canvas. In 1909 the old salt (born in 1844) took a new wife, and they set out once more in *Spray* to sail around the world. After making their last landfall in November, they were never heard from again.

Charles Young, a black West Point graduate, spent the Spanish-American War as commander of the black 9th Ohio Battalion. After the war he reverted to his regular army rank, first lieutenant in the 9th Cavalry, held a variety of posts, commanded an advisory group in Liberia, and in 1916 was forcibly retired from the army as a full colonel, ostensibly for high blood pressure and age, but possibly because the brass were reluctant to promote a black man to brigadier general.

The Spaniards

As the Spanish Army was primarily composed of conscripts, and as it was possible for wealthier people to buy exemption from the draft, virtually all of the Spanish veterans of the war who attained some distinction in later life were professional soldiers. In fact, of the 84 generals on active duty in the Spanish Army on the eve of the civil war of 1936-1939, 78 were already in the army by 1897, and 28 were veterans of the war with America.

Damaso Berenguer Fuster, a captain serving as a staff officer at Holguin in Santiago Province, rose to a major generalcy in the Moroccan Wars, retiring in the 1920s to become a distinguished military historian.

Alberto Castro Girona, first lieutenant in the *36th Infantry* in Santa

Clara Province, went on to a distinguished career, becoming known as the "Spanish Lawrence" for his exploits during the Moroccan Wars and accumulating seven promotions by merit. A lieutenant general awaiting retirement in 1936, he escaped from a Republican prison to join the Nationalists.

First Lieutenant Rogelio Caridad Pita of the *75th Infantry* made the long march from Manzanillo to Santiago with Escario, afterwards rose to brigadier general, and in 1936 was shot after leading Republican resistance to the Nationalists at La Coruña.

Mariano Gamir Ulibarri, a first lieutenant with the *19th Rifle Battalion*, made the long march with Escario to reinforce Santiago, and afterwards attained some distinction in the Moroccan Wars; during the Spanish Civil War he rose to command an army group in the Republican Army before fleeing into exile.

Manuel Gonzalez Carrasco, a second lieutenant in the *13th Rifle Battalion* in Santiago Province, later rose to a major generalcy. One of the principal Nationalist conspirators in 1936, he bungled the uprising in Valencia, so that the Republicans easily overcame his forces. Fleeing to France, he ended his days in exile, condemned to death by both sides.

Gonzalo Gonzalez de Lara, a first lieutenant with the *11th Infantry* during the battle for Santiago, later rose to brigadier general. Deposed from command of a brigade by the Republicans in 1936, he escaped, helped raise Guadalajara for the Nationalists, but was recaptured and shot.

Pio Lopez Pozas, a major in the *10th Infantry* at Vequita in Santiago Province, eventually became the seniormost officer on active duty with the Spanish Army in 1936 before being shot on the outbreak of the civil war by the Republicans, apparently on general principles.

José Rodriquez Casademunt, a captain with the *9th Expeditionary Rifle Battalion* in the Philippines, was also a lieutenant general by the outbreak of the Spanish Civil War, when, like Lopez Pozas, he was arrested and shot by the Republicans on general principles.

First Lieutenant José Sanjuro Sacanel served with the *8th Infantry* in garrison at Vequita in Santiago Province. He afterwards attained great distinction in the Moroccan Wars, was imprisoned and then exiled for attempting a coup against the Spanish Republic in 1932, and was killed in an airplane accident while returning from exile to assume command of the Nationalist forces.

Luis Polo de Bernabé, who succeeded Dupuy de Lomé as Spanish minister in Washington, but requested the return of his passports when Spain broke relations with the U.S., later became the Spanish minister in Berlin, and when the U.S. went to war with Germany in 1917 accepted responsibility for American interests in Germany, a task which he performed with considerable skill.

Miguel Primo de Rivera, a lieutenant colonel, was the nephew and aide-de-camp of Fernando Primo de Rivera, Captain General of the

Philippines until the eve of the war. For a short time after the signing of the Spanish-Filipino settlement in December 1897, he served as a hostage until the promised "indemnity" was paid to Aguinaldo and his comrades. In later years he rose to prominence during Spain's Moroccan wars (1909-1927) and was dictator of Spain (1923-1930). He was the father of José Antonio Primo de Rivera, the founder of Spanish fascism. Undoubtedly the most notable Spanish alumnus of the war.

An Other

Winston Leonard Spencer Churchill, a recent graduate of the Royal Military College at Sandhurst, spent several weeks as a journalist with the Spanish Army in Cuba in 1895 before reporting to his regiment in India. In violation of his status, he served as an officer and was several times under fire. Churchill later achieved some distinction as a soldier on the Northwest Frontier at Omdurman in the Boer War, and in World War I, as well as in political life.

Spain's Strategic Options

Given the imbalance of resources, it seems quite unlikely that Spain could have won the war with the United States. Ultimately, whatever Spain did the outcome was likely to have been the same: defeat and the loss of the remnants of her empire. However, there were measures which could have been adopted which might have prolonged the war, and perhaps salvaged something from the struggle, if only in terms of securing an honorable—rather than a disastrous—defeat.

The shattering defeats inflicted upon the Spanish fleet at Manila and Santiago were both avoidable. Had the squadron in the Philippines been dispersed, rather than concentrated at Cavite, Commodore Dewey would not have secured so signal a victory at the very outbreak of the war. With some seven thousand islands to hide among, Montojo's aging vessels could easily

have posed a threat—a "fleet in being"—to the safety of an American expedition to seize Manila. Dewey would have found the task of searching all those potential hiding places tedious, time consuming, and potentially dangerous, yet necessary despite the relative worthlessness of the Spanish ships in question. It would certainly have taken months to winkle out the last of the Spanish fleet. Of course, the Philippines were a sideshow. The critical theater was the Atlantic.

It is difficult to disagree with the belief of Admiral Cervera and other Spanish naval officers that their government had given little thought to strategic planning beyond the notion of sending the fleet westwards in order to lose it in a "Trafalgar" so that the war would end quickly. There was an optimal strategy for Spain, one which Cervera more or less suggested. The U.S. could not safely invade Cuba until the Spanish fleet had been neutralized. Cervera's proposal was to keep the fleet concentrated in the Canary Islands. There it would continue to pose a threat to American maritime movements and at the same time be available to intercept possible American raids on the Spanish mainland. Spain's resources were adequate for this strategy. At the start of the war Spain had four major warships in commission, three *Maria Teresa* class armored cruisers plus the new armored cruiser *Cristobal Colon*, albeit that she lacked her single 10-inch main gun. These were the ships which formed the core of the squadron that Cervera took to Santiago. Two other major warships which became available almost immediately, the battleship *Pelayo*, completing a refit, and the armored cruiser *Carlos V*, a very powerful vessel just entering service, could easily have been added to this squadron.

Even had they remained relatively inactive, these six heavy ships concentrated in the Canary Islands and supported by the available cruisers and various lighter warships could easily have proven extremely worrisome to the United States Navy. From the Canaries, one or two of the armored cruisers and some of the half dozen or so smaller cruisers could have been sent to raid U.S. maritime commerce and threaten the populous East Coast, which was already experiencing something of a panic even before Cervera's squadron actually sailed. Such a strategy would have prolonged the war in several ways.

The U.S. Navy would have been forced to divert resources from the Caribbean to chase after the Spanish commerce raiders and to guard the Atlantic coastline. A descent upon Cuba or Puerto Rico would have been delayed, due to the shortage of escorts. Given that the U.S. Army was extremely concerned about the danger of operating in the Caribbean during the fever season, a landing in Puerto Rico or Cuba might easily have been delayed until the fall, assuming a decision was made to undertake one at all, given the potential danger from the Spanish fleet in the Canaries. Indeed, precisely what the U.S. would have done in such circumstance is difficult to determine. An expedition against the Canaries was actually considered, but only after Cervera's defeat, and primarily as a means of preventing Spain from attempting to reinforce the Philippines. Moreover, it seems unlikely that the U.S. Navy could have done much more than undertake a massive raid, lacking the logistical train to support a more serious expedition at such distance from North America.

Assuming that Cervera's squadron was sent to the Caribbean, the Spanish Navy could have supported it by creating a new fleet in being. Even as Cervera was sailing westwards, the Ministry of Marine had ordered the concentration of the 2nd Squadron of the fleet at Cadiz. Comprising the refurbished battleship *Pelayo*, the new armored cruiser *Carlos V*, two auxiliary cruisers, and three destroyers under Vice Admiral Manuel de la Camara, this squadron was supposed to escort several troop transports to the Philippines in order to wrest control from George Dewey's little squadron. Had this force instead been concentrated in the Canaries after

Cervera's departure from the Cape Verdes, it would have limited the U.S. Navy's flexibility to cope with the latter when he turned up in the Caribbean. As it was, the potential use of Camara's squadron in the Atlantic caused the U.S. Navy some concern until 15 May. At that point intelligence confirmed that it was bound for the Philippines, whereupon the Navy began spreading rumors of imminent raids on Spanish soil in order to convince the Spaniards to retain Camara for the defense of the homeland.

Even the success of the American V Corps in overrunning the outer defenses of Santiago on 1 July, in the battles of El Caney and San Juan Hill, were not necessarily decisive. If, instead of essaying a sortie, Cervera had been permitted to remain in Santiago, and committed all his manpower and whatever weapons and ammunition that could have been landed, the defense of the city might have been prolonged. As it was, the final days of the siege of Santiago saw something of a race between the American ability to keep the place invested in the face of increasing disease and privation and the Spanish ability to hold out.

Of course Cervera did sortie. But even the loss of Cervera's squadron did not mean that Spain retained no further options. Her army in Cuba remained virtually intact despite the loss of Santiago, and the Cuban guerrillas did not pose a significant threat. Most Spanish officers in Cuba believed they could deal with an American expedition against Havana, particularly given that, following the disastrous collapse of the victorious U.S. V Corps due to fever, such an undertaking would certainly be postponed for several months. While their optimism may be questioned (after all, the American blockade of Cuba would only grow tighter, and the garrison's food supply was heavily dependent on imports), there is some validity to their logic. A defeat—or even a serious reverse—before Havana might result in greater American willingness to seek less than total victory.

Of course, ultimately Spain lost the war. Nevertheless, by prolonging the war, American patience would have been tried, particularly given long casualty lists from disease. A more favorable international climate might have arisen, one in which the Great Powers might have lent their good offices to a negotiated settlement. Cuba would certainly still have been lost, but the Philippines and Puerto Rico might have been salvaged. Even more, of course, might have been saved had the Spanish government paid heed to Cervera's suggestion that a diplomatic settlement be reached. Cuba would have been the price, but that would still have left Spain with the Philippines and Puerto Rico, without loss of many lives and the pride of her navy.

Battles, Combats, and Skirmishes

Battles, Combats, and Skirmishes of the Spanish-American War

Date	Location	Type of Action	Casualties (D/W/M) U.S.	Spain
27 Apr	Matanzas	Ships vs batteries	0/ 0/0	??
29 Apr	Cienfuegos	Naval skirmish	0/ 0/0	??
1 May	Manila Bay, P.I.	Naval battle	0/8/0	167/214/0
4 May	Guanojay	U.S. landing party	0/ 0/0	0/ 3/0
6 May	Havana	Ships vs batteries	0/ 0/0	??
6 May	Santiago	Ships vs batteries	0/ 0/0	??
7 May	Havana	Ships vs batteries	0/ 0/0	??
9 May	Havana	Ships vs batteries	0/ 0/0	??
10 May	Havana	Ships vs batteries	0/ 0/0	??
11 May	Cardenas	U.S. landing party	5/ 5/0	??
11 May	Cienfuegos	Ships vs batteries	2/ 14/0 ??	
12 May	Cabañas	U.S. landing party	0/ 1/0	??
12 May	Punta Arbolitas	U.S. landing party	0/ 0/0	??
12 May	San Juan, P.R.	Naval bombardment	4/ 7/0	6/ 50/0
14 May	Havana	Naval skirmish	0/ 0/0	??
18 May	Santiago	Ships vs batteries	0/ 0/0	??
18 May	San Juan, P.R.	Ships vs batteries	??	??
31 May	Santiago	Ships vs batteries	0/ 0/0	0/ 0/0
3 Jun	Santiago	*Merrimac* Affair	0/ 0/7	7/ 36/0
6 Jun	Santiago	Ships vs batteries	0/ 0/0	9/ 63/0
7 Jun	Guantanamo Bay	Skirmish	0/ 0/0	??
6 Jun	Guantanamo Bay	Marine landing	0/ 0/0	??
10-14 Jun	Guantanamo Bay	Skirmishes & Battle of Cuzco	6/ 9/0	??
10 Jun	Havana	Naval skirmish	0/ 0/0	??
11 Jun	Fisher's Point	U.S. landing	6/ 16/0	??
13 Jun	Havana	Ships vs batteries	0/ 0/0	??
14 Jun	Santiago	Ships vs batteries	0/ 0/0	0/ 7/0
16 Jun	Santiago	Ships vs batteries	0/ 0/0	2/ 18/0
16 Jun	Havana	Ships vs batteries	0/ 0/0	??
21 Jun	Santiago	Ships vs batteries	0/ 0/0	0/ 3/0
22 Jun	Santiago	Ships vs batteries	1/ 8/0	0/ 3/0
22 Jun	Aguadores	Bombardment	0/ 0/0	0/ 7/0
22 Jun	Siboney-Daiquiri	U.S.landing	0/ 0/0	1/ 6/0
22 Jun	San Juan, P.R.	Naval skirmish	0/ 0/0	2/ 0/0
23 Jun	Havana	Blockade runners escape	0/ 0/0	0/ 0/0
24 Jun	Las Guasimas	Battle	16/ 49/0	12/ 24/0
25 Jun	Aguadores	Skirmish	0/ 0/0	0/ 3/0
26 Jun	Santiago	Ships vs batteries	0/ 0/0	0/ 8/0
26 Jun	Sevilla	Skirmish	0/ 0/0	??
29 Jun	Rio San Juan	Attempted U.S. landing	1/ 6/0*	??
30 Jun	Tayabacoa	Attempted U.S. landing	??	??

313

Date	Location	Type	U.S.	Spanish
30 Jun	Manzanillo	U.S. Navy raid	0/ 3/0	2/ 13/0
1 Jul	Manzanillo	U.S. Navy raid	0/ 0/0	0/ 0/0
1 Jul	Havana	Ships vs batteries	0/ 0/0	??
1-3 Jul	Santiago	Battle	223/1374/0	215/375/200
1 Jul	Aguadores	Skirmish	2/ 10/0	??
2 Jul	Santiago	Ships vs batteries	0/ 0/0	1/ 32/0
2 Jul	Cape Tunas	Ships vs batteries	0/ 0/0	??
3 Jul	Santiago	Naval battle	1/ 1/0 323	151/1720
4 Jul	Santiago	*Reina Mercedes* affair	0/ 0/0	??
10-11 Jul	Santiago	Naval bombardment	0/ 0/0 6	48/0
10-11 Jul	Santiago	Skirmish	2/ 12/0	1/ 17/0
18 Jul	Manzanillo	Naval engagement	??	3/ 14/0
19 Jul	Havana	Ships vs batteries	0/ 0/0	??
23 Jul	Rio Manimani	U.S. landing	3/ 8/0	??
25 Jul	Guanica, P.R.	U.S. landing	0/ 4/0	4/ ?/0
26 Jul	Yauco, P.R.	Skirmish	0/ 0/0	3/ 13/0
26-27 Jul	Caimanera U.S.	Navy minesweeping	0/ 0/0	??
28 Jul	Ponce, P.R.	Skirmish	0/ 0/0	0/ 0/0
30 Jul	Manila, P.I.	Shipsvs batteries	0/ 0/0	??
31 Jul-1 Aug	Manila, P.I.	Skirmish	14/ 41/0	??
5 Aug	Guayamo, P.R.	U.S. landing	1/ 4/0	1/ 2/0
5 Aug	Cape San Juan, P.R.	U.S. landing party	0/ 0/0	0/ 0/0
5 Aug	Manila	Skirmish	5/ 20/0	??
8-9 Aug	Guayamo-Cayey, P.R.	Skirmish	0/ 4/0	0/ 0/0
9 Aug	Coamo, P.R.	Battle	1/ 10/0	6/ 35/167
9 Aug	Cape San Juan, P.R.	U.S. landing party	1/ 0/0	0/ 0/0
10 Aug	Hormigueras, P.R.	Combat	2/ 15/0	3/ 6/136
12 Aug	Havana	Ships vs batteries	0/ 0/0	??
12 Aug	Aibonito Pass, P.R.	Skirmish	2/ 5/1	0/ 0/0
12 Aug	Manzanillo	U.S. Navy attack	0/ 0/0	6/ 31/0
13 Aug	Las Marias, P.R.	Ambush	0/ 0/0	3/ 27/56
13 Aug	Manila, P.I.	Battle	6/ 92/0	150/300/12000

All known engagements between American and Spanish forces during the war have been listed, including those which resulted in no casualties on either side. Unless otherwise indicated, actions are in Cuba: P.I., Philippines; P.R., Puerto Rico.

D/W/M = *deaths from combat/wounded in combat/missing or prisoner.*
* *U.S. casualties include Cubans.*
+ *Includes the fighting for El Caney and the Heights of San Juan on 1 July, and the skirmishing which followed over the next two days.*

Cuban casualties for the three days amounted to about 150 men killed, wounded, or missing.

The published total of U.S. war dead was 345 men, a figure which cannot be reconciled with the reported deaths from individual actions, which total 302, because the official figure includes men who died of wounds after the close of hostilities. In fact, V Corps suffered 243 men killed in action or mortally wounded. The average battle loss per month was actually higher than that in the American Revolution (50) or the War of 1812 (62), and the same as that for the Mexican War (86, based on the official figure for battle deaths).

Naval Gunnery Effectiveness

During the Spanish-American War neither side displayed spectacular accuracy in gunnery. Indeed, American accuracy was poor, and Spanish worse, as the accompanying tables will illustrate. It is important to realize that there is some uncertainty as to the precise number and caliber of hits in almost all cases. In addition, at Santiago American shooting was certainly better than the figures would seem to suggest for two reasons. Although an attempt was made to survey the wrecks of the Spanish ships, it was not possible to determine the number of hits aboard *Quendo* and *Vizcaya* in the areas of their hulls and superstructures which were heavily damaged by internal explosions. Also, hits on *Pluton* and *Furor* are not included, although both were subject to fire by several of the heavier ships, and were the targets of virtually all the 1,369 rounds fired by *Gloucester*. Despite this, however, even assuming that American gunnery accuracy was twice as good as the figures suggest, it is worth noting that it was still greatly inferior to the accuracy of the Chinese Navy at the Battle of the Yalu against the Japanese just two years earlier: the Chinese fired 197 12-inch rounds, of which 10 hit, approximately 5 percent, while of 484 smaller rounds fired, down to 4.7-inch, 48 hit, nearly 12 percent.

Manila Bay, 1 May 1898
U.S. Ships

Caliber	Fired	Hits	Percent
8"	157	10	6.4
6"	635	8	1.3
5"	622	26	4.2
6 pdr	2124	31	1.5
3 pdr	689	?	?
1 pdr	1632	?	?
Undetermined	67		
Total	**5859**	**142**	**2.4**

Of the "undetermined" hits, 33 were estimated to have been caused by 5-inch, 6-inch, or 8-inch shells, making the accuracy for these pieces 77 rounds out of 1414 fired, or 5.5 perecnt. The other 44 were probably 1-pounder, 3-pounder, or 6-pounder, making the accuracy for these pieces 72 out of 4445 rounds fired, 1.6 percent.

The Naval Battle of Santiago
U.S. Ships

Caliber	Fired	Hits	Percent
13"	47	0	0
12"	39	2	5.1
8"	319	12	3.8
6"	171	3	1.8
5"	473	11	2.3
4"	245	14	5.7
6 pdr	6553	77	1.2
3 pdr	780	?	?
1 pdr	466	3	0.6
Smaller	330	?	?
Total	**9433**	**122**	**1.3**

Hits by Spanish Ships

Caliber	Fired	Hits
11"	??	0
8"	??	0
6"	??	5(actually 5.9")
5.5"	??	2
4.7"	??	3
6 pdr	??	16
Smaller	??	0
Total		26

Ammunition expenditure cannot be determined for the Spanish ships, and thus accuracy cannot be determined. However, it is known that Cristobal Colon fired 184 rounds of 6-inch ammunition and 117 of 4.7-inch, and Vizcaya apparently fired 223 rounds of all types. Even ignoring ammunition expended by the other ships, this gives an overall accuracy rating of less than 5 percent.

The Medal of Honor

The only decoration that existed for members of the U.S. armed forces at the time of the Spanish-American War was the Medal of Honor. Created during the Civil War, the circumstances under which the Medal of Honor (in different versions for the Army and the Navy) could be award were broad. The Navy medal (for which Marines were also eligible, but not officers nor members of the Revenue Cutter Service) could be awarded for courageous acts in the face of life threatening danger not only in combat but also including shipboard accidents and rescues at sea. The Army medal could be awarded for distinguished performance of one's duty, usually, but not always, in direct combat. As a result, the Medal of Honor was awarded rather generously.

During the Spanish-American War 109 men received the Medal of Honor.

Medal of Honor Awards

Date	Location	Awards
1 May	Manila Bay	1
11 May	Cienfuegos	52
11 May	Cardenas	3
21 May	Cavite: accident, USS *Concord*	3
28 May	Santiago: accident, USS *Vixen*	2
3 Jun	Santiago: *Merrimac* affair	8
14 Jun	Cuzco	2
24 Jun	Las Guasimas	1
30 Jun	Tayabacoa	4
30 Jun	Manzanillo	1
1 Jul	Santiago: The Heights of San Juan	13
1 Jul	Santiago: El Caney	9
2 Jul	Santiago: Skirmishing	2
3 Jul	Santiago: Naval Battle	1
20 Jul	Santiago: accident, USS *Iowa*	2
23 Jul	Manimani	1
26-27 Jul	Caimanera	4

Every enlisted man who took part in the cable cutting party at Cienfuegos and in the attempt to scuttle the collier *Merrimac* at Santiago received the Navy Medal of Honor, although only three of the men involved in the action at Cardenas did. Since the Navy Medal of Honor could not be awarded to members of the Revenue Cutter Service, on 3 May 1900 Congress authorized a large (3.125-inches to be precise) plaque for each of the men involved. The "Cardenas Medal of Honor," came in three grades, gold for Lt. Newcomb of the USRC *Hudson*, silver for his officers, and bronze for his enlisted men.

Ten of the Medals of Honor went to black soldiers, all of the 10th cavalry, four for the action at Tayabacoa, during which a party of Company H engaged in landing supplies for the Cuban insurgents was ambushed by Spanish troops, and the balance for San Juan Hill.

Only eight of the Medals of Honor went to officers, and one of these not until 1933, when President Franklin D. Roosevelt awarded one to Rear Admiral Richmond Pearson Hobson for the *Merrimac* affair. This was because the normal reward for officers performing distinguished service was a brevet—honorary—promotion.

Most of the awards to soldiers were made for rescuing the wounded under fire. None of the awards was posthumous.

Warships—General Information

US Ships	Type	Class	Displacement Light	Full	Engines HP	SP	Coal Norm-Max	Crew
Indiana	BB1	Indiana	10,288	11,688	9.0	15.0	400-1640	636
Iowa	BB1		11,410	12,647	11.0	16.0	626-1795	654
Massachusetts	BB1	Indiana	10,288	11,688	9.0	15.0	400-1640	636
Oregon	BB1	Indiana	10,288	11,688	9.0	15.0	400-1640	636
Maine	BB2		6,682	7,180	9.0	17.0	400-896	374
Texas	BB2		6,135	6,665	8.6	17.0	500-850	500
Amphitrite	BM	Amphitrite	3,990		1.6	12.0	250-270	191
Miantonomoh	BM	Amphitrite	3,990		1.6	12.0	250-270	163
Monadnock	BM	Amphitrite	3,990		3.0	11.6	250-386	191
Monterey	BM		4,084		5.3	13.6	230-	218
Puritan	BM		6,006		3.7	12.4	410-	270
Terror	BM	Amphitrite	3,990		1.6	12.0	250-270	163
Brooklyn	CA		9,215	10,068	16.0	20.0	900-1753	581
New York	CA		8,200	9,021	16.0	20.0	750-1290	566
Vesuvius	CD		929		3.2	20.0	152-	70
Atlanta	CP1	Atlanta	3,189		3.5	13.0	340- 490	284
Baltimore	CP1		4,413	5,436	10.8	19.0	400-1144	386
Boston	CP1	Atlanta	3,189		3.5	13.0	340-490	284
Charleston	CP1		3,730	4,200	7.7	18.9	328-758	300
Chicago	CP1		4,500	4,864	5.0	14.0	593-831	450
Cincinnati	CP1	Cincinnati	3,183	3,339	10.0	19.0	350-460	320
Columbia	CP1	Columbia	7,375	8,270	21.0	21.0	730-1670	477
Minneapolis	CP1	Columbia	7,375	8,270	21.0	21.0	730-1670	477
New Orleans	CP1		3,769	4,011	7.5	20.0	512-747	366
Newark	CP1		4,083	4,592	8.5	18.0	400-800	384
Olympia	CP1		5,865	6,558	13.5	20.0	400-1093	450
Philadelphia	CP1		4,324	5,305	9.0	19.0	400-1031	384
Raleigh	CP1	Cincinnaiti	3,183	3,339	10.0	19.0	350-460	320
San Francisco	CP1		4,088	4,583	10.5	19.0	350-627	384
Katahdin	CR		2,155	2,383	5.1	16.0	175-202	97
Detroit	CU	Montgomery	2,094	2,235	5.4	17.0	200-340	274
Marblehead	CU	Montgomery	2,094	2,235	5.4	17.0	200-340	274
Montgomery	CU	Montgomery	2,094	2,235	5.4	17.0	200-340	274
Badger	CX		4,784		3.2	16.0	836-	235
Buffalo	CX	Yankee	6,888		3.8	14.5	1000-	282
Dixie	CX	Yosemite	3,800		3.8	16.0	1371-	285
Harvard	CX	Harvard	13,000		20.6	21.8	2656-	407
Panther	CX		4,260		3.2	13.0	475-	198
Prairie	CX	Yankee	6,888		3.8	14.5	1000-	297

US Ships	Type	Class	Displacement Light	Full	Engines HP	SP	Coal Norm-Max	Crew
St. Louis	CX	St. Louis	14,910		20.0	22.0	2677-	377
St. Paul	CX	St. Louis	14,910		20.0	22.0	2677-	381
Yale	CX	Harvard	13,000		20.6	21.8	2656-	407
Yankee	CX	Yankee	6,888		3.8	14.5	1000-	282
Yosemite	CX	Yosemite	3,800		3.8	16.0	1371-	285
Annapolis	GB	Annapolis	1,000	1,153	1.0	12.0	100-324	150
Bancroft	GB		839		1.2	14.5	100-139	148
Bennington	GB	Yorktown	1,710	1,921	3.4	16.0	200-370	200
Castine	GB	Machias	1,177	1,318	1.9	15.5	125-290	154
Concord	GB	Yorktown	1,710	1,921	3.4	16.0	200-370	200
Dolphin	GB		1,486		2.3	16.0	265-	152
Helena	GB	Wilmington	1,397	1,689	1.9	15.0	100-277	195
Macias	GB	Machias	1,777	1,318	1.9	15.5	125-290	154
Marietta	GB	Wheeling	1,000	1,170	1.1	13.0	120-231	140
Nashville	GB		1,371	1,719	2.5	16.3	150-395	180
Newport	GB	Annapolis	1,000	1,153	1.0	12.0	100-235	150
Petrel	GB		867		1.0	11.4	125-200	138
Princeton	GB	Annapolis	1,000	1,153	1.0	12.0	100-235	150
Topeka	GB		2,372		2.2	16.0	273-394	152
Vicksburg	GB	Annapolis	1,000	1,153	1.0	12.0	100-235	150
Wheeling	GB	Wheeling	1,000	1,170	1.1	13.0	120-231	140
Wilmington	GB	Wilmington	1,397	1,689	1.9	15.0	100-277	195
Yorktown	GB	Yorktown	1,710	1,921	3.4	16.0	200-370	200
Hudson	RC		120		?	12.0	?	11
McCulloch	RC		1,280	1,280	?	17.5	?	100
Cushing	TB		116	116	1.6	23.0	35.4	22
Du Pont	TB	Porter	165		3.2	27.5	76	24
Ericsson	TB		120		1.8	24.0	35.4	22
Foote	TB	Foote	142		2.0	25.0	44	20
Porter	TB	Porter	165		3.2	27.5	76	24
Rodgers	TB	Foote	142		2.0	25.0	44	20
Winslow	TB	Foote	142		2.0	25.0	44	20
Dorothea	Yct		594		1.6	15.0	90	69
Eagle	Yct		434		0.9	15.5	64	64
Gloucester	Yct		786		2.0	17.0	94	94
Hornet	Yct		425		0.8	15.0	55	55
Mayflower	Yct		2,690		4.7	16.8	171	171
Scorpion	Yct		850		2.8	17.9	111	111
Vixen	Yct		806		1.3	16.0	82	82
Wasp	Yct		630		1.8	16.5	55	55

Spanish Ships	Type	Class	Displacement Light	Full	Engines HP	SP	Coal Norm-Max	Crew
Pelayo	BB1		9,745		8.0	16.7	800-	630
Numancia	BB2		7,190		???	13.0	740-1050	590
Almirante Quendo	CA	Maria Teresa	6,890		13.7	20.2	1050-	497
Cristobal Colon	CA		6,800	7,900	14.0	20.0	1050-	543
Emperador Carlos V	CA		9,090	9,800	18.5	20.0	1200-2040	590
Infanta Maria Teresa	CA	Maria Teresa	6,890		13.7	20.2	1050-	497
Vizcaya	CA	Maria Teresa	6,890		13.7	20.2	1050-	497
Alfonso XIII	CP1	Reina Regente	4,725		11.6	20.4	1285-	420
Lepanto	CP1	Reina Regente	4,725		11.6	20.4	1285-	420
Isla de Cuba	CP2	Isla de Luzon	1,045		2.2	14.0	164-200	156
Isla de Luzon	CP2	Isla de Luzon	1,045		2.2	14.0	164-200	156
Marquess de2.2								
la Enseñada	CP2	Isla de Luzon	1,045		2.2	14.0	164-200	156
Alfonso XII	CU	Alfonso XII	3,090	3,900	4.1	0.0	500-720	380
Aragon	CU	Aragon	3,312		4.4	14.0	460-	389
Castilla	CU	Aragon	3,312		4.4	14.0	460-	392
Conde de Venadito	CU	Velasco	1,150		1.5	14.0	240-	180
Don Antonio de Ulloa	CU	Velasco	1,150		1.5	14.0	240-	180
Don Juan de Austria	CU	Velasco	1,150		1.5	14.0	240-	180
Infanta Isabel	CU	Velasco	1,150		1.5	14.0	240-	180
Isabel II	CU	Velasco	1,150		1.5	14.0	240-	180
Navarra	CU	Aragon	3,312		4.4	0.0	460-	389
Reina Cristina	CU	Alfonso XII	3,090	3,900	4.1	0.0	500-720	380
Reina Mercedes	CU	Alfonso XII	3,090	3,900	4.1	14.0	500-720	380
Velasco	CU	Velasco	1,150		1.5	30.0	240-	180
Audaz	DD		400		7.5	28.0	96-	65
Furor	DD		370		6.0	30.0	100-	67
Osado	DD		400		7.5	30.0	96-	65
Pluton	DD		400		7.5	30.0	96-	65
Prosepina	DD		400		7.5	28.0	96-	65
Terror	DD		370		6.0	11.5	100-	67
Elcano	GB		540		0.6	11.5	80-	95
General Concha	GB		540		0.6	11.5	80-	95
General Lezo	GB		540		0.6	13.0	80-	95
Jorge Juan	GB		935		1.1	11.5	228-	160
Magellanes	GB		540		0.6	10.0	80-	95
Marques del Duero	GB		492		0.6	23.0	89-	98
Destructor	TGB		348		3.8	20.0	37-93	45
Galicia	TGB		562		4.5	20.0	100-130	110
Marques de Molina	TGB		562		4.5	20.0	100-130	110
Martin Alonzo Pinzon	TGB		562		4.5	20.0	100-130	110

Spanish Ships	Type	Class	Displacement Light	Full	Engines HP	SP	Coal Norm-Max	Crew
Nueva España	TGB		562		4.5	20.0	100-130	110
Rapido	TGB		562		4.5	20.0	100-130	110
Temerario	TGB		562		4.5	20.0	100-130	110
Vicente Yañez Pinzon	TGB		562		4.5	20.0	100-130	110

Key to Ship Table

The table lists the principal vessels involved in the war, plus minor vessels named in the text. Both fleets had many other vessels of lesser importance, which played no role in the war. Ships are arranged by type, and then listed alphabetically, regardless of class.

Type:

BB1 Battleship, 1st Class

BB2 Battleship, 2nd Class: More lightly armed and armored than a 1st Class Battleship, more or less similar to an Armored Cruiser, but slower.

BM Monitor: A ship slower and smaller than a battleship, with poor seakeeping qualities, but with the same main battery and considerable armor protection.

CA Armored Cruiser: A cruiser provided with an armored belt, and enhanced protection; In the Spanish fleet they were rated as 2nd Class Battleships.

CD Dynamite Cruiser, an unsuccessful experimental type

CP1 Protected Cruiser, 1st Class: A cruiser provided with an internal armored deck, with sloping sides coming down to just below the waterline. 2nd Class Protected Cruisers had light protection; 3rd Class Protected cruisers are here included as gunboats.

CR Ram, an unsuccessful experimental type.

CU Unprotected Cruiser: A cuirser with no armor whatsoever

CX Auxiliary Cruiser: A fast merchantship given an improvised cruiser-scale armament.

DD Destroyer: In this period, more properly Torpedo Boat Destroyer, small, fast vessels designed to hunt torpedo boats, and to serve as a torpedo boat.

GB Gunboat: A vessel of limited speed and seakeeping capabilitites, varying in size from that of a cruiser (hence some were rated as 3rd Class Protected Cruisers 2nd), to quite small.

RC Revenue Cutter: A relatively small, lightly armed vessel for coast guard duties.

TB Torpedo Boat: Small, fast vessels designed with torpedoes as their principal armament

TBG Torpedo Gunboat: A slow vessel, heavily armed with torpedoes

Yct Yacht: A unarmed luxury yacht, serving as an auxiliary gunboat, used because they were usually fast, and had good seakeeping qualitites.

Class: Given were applicable

Displacement: The "weight" of the ship in tons in terms of the water it displaces.

Light Displacement with only normal equipment and stores

Full Displacement with full wartime allocations of everything, not always known for some ships.

Engines: Indicates maximum Horse Power and Speed in knots.

Coal: Bunkerage in tons.

Crew: Normal complement.

Warships—Statistical Profile

US Ships	Flotation	Mobility	Firepower	Value
Indiana	104	14	68	134
Iowa	115	14	52	124
Massachusetts	104	14	68	134
Oregon	104	14	68	134
Maine	67	15	32	81
Texas	62	15	22	68
Amphitrite	40	11	22	53
Miantonomoh	40	11	20	51
Monadnock	40	10	22	52
Monterey	41	12	25	58
Puritan	61	11	34	75
Terror	40	11	20	51
Brooklyn	93	18	42	106
New York	82	18	30	89
Vesuvius	9	18	0	23
Atlanta	32	12	17	45
Baltimore	44	17	24	63
Boston	32	12	17	45
Charleston	37	17	18	53
Chicago	45	13	31	66
Cincinnati	32	17	15	48
Columbia	74	19	14	70
Minneapolis	74	19	14	70
New Orleans	38	18	16	53
Newark	41	16	22	59
Olympia	59	18	27	74
Philadelphia	43	17	22	61
Raleigh	32	17	15	48
San Francisco	41	17	22	60
Katahdin	22	14	0	26
Detroit	21	15	12	38
Marblehead	21	15	12	38
Montgomery	21	15	12	38
Badger	48	14	8	
Buffalo	69	13	6	
Dixie	38	14	18	
Harvard	130	20	10	
Panther	43	12	9	
Prairie	69	13	18	
St. Louis	149	20	5	

US Ships	Flotation	Mobility	Firepower	Value
St. Paul	149	20	8	
Yale	130	20	0	
Yankee	69	13	13	
Yosemite	38	14	13	
Annapolis	10	11	5	21
Bancroft	8	13	4	21
Bennington	17	14	11	34
Castine	12	14	7	27
Concord	17	14	11	34
Dolphin	15	14	2	24
Helena	14	14	7	27
Macias	12	14	7	27
Marietta	10	12	5	22
Nashville	14	15	7	28
Newport	10	11	5	21
Petrel	9	10	7	22
Princeton	10	11	5	21
Topeka	24	14	7	33
Vicksburg	10	11	5	21
Wheeling	10	12	5	22
Wilmington	14	14	7	27
Yorktown	17	14	11	34
Hudson	1	11	0	12
McCulloch	13	16	2	24
Cushing	1	21	0	22
Du Pont	2	25	0	26
Ericsson	1	22	0	23
Foote	1	23	0	24
Porter	2	25	0	26
Rodgers	1	23	0	24
Winslow	1	23	0	24
Eagle	4	14	0	16
Gloucester	8	15	0	20
Hornet	4	14	0	16
Mayflower	27	15	3	32
Scorpion	9	16	0	21
Vixen	8	14	0	19
Wasp	6	15	0	18

Spanish Ships	Flotation	Mobility	Firepower	Value
Pelayo	98	15	40	104
Numancia	72	12	21	68
Almirante Quendo	69	18	29	81
Cristobal Colon	68	18	26	78
Emperador Carlos V	91	18	28	92
Infanta Maria Teresa	69	18	29	81
Vizcaya	69	18	29	81
Alfonso XIII	47	18	20	62
Lepanto	47	18	20	62
Isla de Cuba	11	13	7	25
Isla de Luzon	11	13	7	25
Marquess de la Enseñada	11	13	7	25
Alfonso XII	31	0	13	29
Aragon	33	13	15	44
Castilla	33	13	10	40
Conde de Venadito	12	13	5	23
Don Antonio de Ulloa	12	13	5	23
Don Juan de Austria	12	13	5	23
Infanta Isabel	12	13	5	23
Isabel II	12	13	5	23
Navarra	33	13	10	40
Reina Cristina	31	0	13	29
Reina Mercedes	31	0	13	29
Velasco	12	13	5	23
Audaz	4	27	0	29
Furor	4	25	0	27
Osado	4	27	0	29
Pluton	4	27	0	29
Prosepina	4	27	0	29
Terror	4	25	0	27
Elcano	5	10	3	16
General Concha	5	10	3	16
General Lezo	5	10	3	16
Jorge Juan	9	12	5	21
Magellanes	5	10	3	16
Marques del Duero	5	9	1	12
Destructor	3	21	1	24
Galicia	6	18	3	23
Marques de Molina	6	18	3	23
Martin Alonzo Pinzon	6	18	3	23
Nueva España	6	18	3	23

Spanish Ships	Flotation	Mobility	Firepower	Value
Rapido	6	18	3	23
Temerario	6	18	3	23
Vicente Yañez Pinzon	6	18	3	23

Key to Ship Table

Profile: A statistical evaluation of various capabilities of each vessel. In each case, the larger the number, the better the rating.

Flotation: A numerical rating of the resilience of the vessel, combining armor protection, dimensions, and interanl subdivisions, which are otherwise not shown. This has been ometted for Auxiliary Cruisers and Yachts, since they tended to be very vulnerable.

Mobility: The speed and maneuverability of the vessel.

Firepower: The ability to "dish it out."

Value: An overall evaluation of the ship's relative worth, incorporating flotation, mobility, and firepower. Not given for merchant cruisers and yachts.

Warships—Armament

US Ship	Main		2nd		3rd		Other Armament						Torpedo Tubes	
	#	cal	#	cal	#	cal	#	cal	#	cal	#	cal	#	size
Indiana	4	13	8	8	4	6	20	6pdr	6	1pdr			6	18"
Iowa	4	10	8	8	6	4	20	6pdr	4	1pdr			4	14"
Massachu-setts	4	13	8	8	4	6	20	6pdr	6	1pdr			6	18"
Oregon	4	13	8	8	4	6	20	6pdr	6	1pdr			6	18"
Maine	4	10	6	6			7	6pdr	8	1pdr			4	14"
Texas	2	10	6	6			12	6pdr	6	1pdr			4	14"
Amphitrite	4	10	2	4			2	6pdr	2	3pdr				
Miantonomoh	4	10					2	6pdr	2	3pdr				
Monadnock	4	10	2	4			2	6pdr	2	3pdr				
Monterey	2	12	2	10			6	6pdr						
Puritan	4	12	6	4			6	6pdr						
Terror	4	10					2	6pdr	2	3pdr				
Brooklyn	8	8	12	5			12	6pdr	4	1pdr			5	18"
New York	6	8	12	4			8	6pdr	4	1pdr			3	14"
Vesuvius							3	15pneu	3	3pdr				
Atlanta	2	8	6	6			2	6pdr	2	3pdr				
Baltimore	4	8	6	6			4	6pdr	2	3pdr	2	1pdr		
Boston	2	8	6	6			2	6pdr	2	3pdr				
Charleston	2	8	6	6			4	6pdr	2	3pdr	2	1pdrd		
Chicago	4	8	14	5			2	6pdr	2	1pdr				
Cincinnati	1	6	10	5			4	6pdr	2	1pdr			4	18"
Columbia	1	8	2	6	8	4	8	6pdr	4	1pdr			4	18"
Minneapolis	1	8	2	6	8	4	6	6pdr	4	1pdr			4	18"
New Orleans	6	6	4	4.7			6	6pdr	8	1pdr			3	18"
Newark	12	6					10	6pdr	4	3pdr	2	1pdr		
Olympia	4	8	10	5			4	6pdr	6	1pdr			6	'8"
Philadelphia	12	6					14	6pdr	4	3pdr	2	1pdr		

US Ship	Main		2nd		3rd		Other Armament						Torpedo Tubes	
	#	cal	#	cal	#	cal	#	cal	#	cal	#	cal	#	size
Raleigh	1	6	10	5			4	6pdr	4	1pdr			4	18"
San Francisco	12	6					8	6pdr	4	3pdr	2	1pdr		
Katahdin							4	6pdr						
Detroit	9	5					6	6pdr	2	1pdr			3	18"
Marblehead	9	5					6	6pdr	2	1pdr			3	18"
Montgomery	9	5					6	6pdr	2	1pdr			3	18"
Badger	6	5					6	3pdr						
Buffalo	2	5	4	4			1	15pneu	6	6pdr				
Dixie	10	6					6	6pdr						
Harvard	8	5					8	6pdr						
Panther	6	5	2	4			6	3pdr						
Prairie	10	6					6	6pdr						
St. Louis	4	5					8	6pdr						
St. Paul	6	5					6	6pdr	6	3pdr				
Yale							4	6pdr	4	3pdr				
Yankee	10	5					6	6pdr						
Yosemite	10	5					6	6pdr						
Annapolis	6	4					4	6pdr	2	1pdr				
Bancroft	4	4					8	3pdr	1	1pdr			2	18"
Bennington	6	6					4	6pdr	2	3pdr	4	1pdr		
Castine	8	4					4	6pdr	2	1pdr				
Concord	6	6					4	6pdr	2	3pdr	4	1pdr		
Dolphin	1	6					2	6pdr	4	47mm				
Helena	8	4					4	6pdr	4	1pdr				
Macias	8	4					4	6pdr	2	1pdr				
Marietta	6	4					4	6pdr	2	1pdr				
Nashville	8	4					4	6pdr	2	1pdr				
Newport	6	4					4	6pdr	2	1pdr				
Petrel	4	6					2	3pdr	2	1pdr				
Princeton	6	4					4	6pdr	2	1pdr				

US Ship	Main		2nd		3rd		Other Armament						Torpedo Tubes	
	#	cal	#	cal	#	cal	#	cal	#	cal	#	cal	#	size
Topeka	8	4					2	6pdr	4	3pdr	2	1pdr		
Vicksburg	6	4					4	6pdr	2	1pdr				
Wheeling	6	4					4	6pdr	2	1pdr				
Wilmington	8	4					4	6pdr	4	1pdr				
Yorktown	6	6					4	6pdr	2	3pdr	4	1pdr		
Hudson							2	3pdr						
McCulloch	4	3												
Cushing							3	6pdr					3	18"
Du Pont							4	1pdr					3	18"
Ericsson							4	1pdr					3	18"
Foote							3	1pdr					3	18"
Porter							4	1pdr					3	18"
Rodgers							3	1pdr					3	18"
Winslow							3	1pdr					3	18"
Dorothea							4	6pdr	2	3pdr	4	1pdr		
Eagle							4	6pdr						
Gloucester							4	6pdr	4	3pdr				
Hornet							3	6pdr	2	1pdr	2	37mm		
Mayflower							12	6pdr						
Scorpion	2	5					6	6pdr						
Vixen							4	6pdr	4	1pdr				
Wasp							4	6pdr						
Spanish Ships														
Pelayo	2	12.5	2	11	9	5	3	57mm	13	37mm			17	17.7"
Numancia	4	7.9	3	6.2	14	5.5	12	47mm	2	37mm			2	17.7"
Almirante Quendo	2	11	10	5.5			8	12pdr	10	37mm			8	17.7"

Spanish Ship	Main		2nd		3rd		Other Armament						Torpedo Tubes	
	#	cal	#	cal	#	cal	#	cal	#	cal	#	cal	#	size
Cristobal Colon	2	10*	10	6	6	4.7	10	57mm	10	37mm			5	17.7"
Emperador Carlos V	2	11	8	5.5	4	3.9	2	12pdr	4	6pdr	4	1pdr	6	17.7"
Infanta Maria Teresa	2	11	10	5.5			8	12pdr	10	37mm			8	17.7"
Vizcaya	2	11	10	5.5			8	12pdr	10	37mm			8	17.7"
Alfonso XIII	4	7.9	6	4.7			6	6pdr					5	14"
Lepanto	4	7.9	6	4.7			6	6pdr					5	14"
Isla de Cuba	6	4.7					4	6pdr					3	14"
Isla de Luzon	6	4.7					4	6pdr					3	14"
Marquess de la Enseñada	6	4.7					4	6pdr					3	14"
Alfonso XII	6	6.4					8	6pdr	6	3pdr			5	14"
Aragon	6	6.4	2	3.5	4	3							2	14"
Castilla	4	5.9	2	4.7	6	3.5							2	14"
Conde de Venadito	4	4.7					4	6pdr					2	14"
Don Antonio de Ulloa	4	4.7					4	6pdr					2	14"
Don Juan de Austria	4	4.7					4	6pdr					2	14"
Infanta Isabel	4	4.7					4	6pdr					2	14"
Isabel II	4	4.7					4	6pdr					2	14"
Navarra	4	5.9	2	4.7	6	3.5/3							2	14"
Reina Cristina	6	6.4					8	6pdr	6	3pdr			5	14"
Reina Mercedes	6	6.4					8	6pdr	6	3pdr			5	14"
Velasco	2	6	2	3									2	14"
Audaz							2	14pdr	2	6pdr	2	1pdr	2	14"

Spanish Ship	Main		2nd		3rd		Other Armament						Torpedo Tubes	
	#	cal	#	cal	#	cal	#	cal	#	cal	#	cal	#	size
Furor							2	14pdr	2	6pdr	2	1pdr	2	14"
Osado							2	14pdr	2	6pdr	2	1pdr	2	14"
Pluton							2	14pdr	2	6pdr	2	1pdr	2	14"
Prosepina							2	14pdr	2	6pdr	2	1pdr	2	14"
Terror							2	14pdr	2	6pdr	2	1pdr	2	14"
Elcano	2	4.7	1	3.5									1	14"
General Con-cha	3	4.7											1	14"
General Lezo	2	4.7	1	3.5									1	14"
Jorge Juan	2	6.2	2	3										
Magellanes	3	4.7											1	14"
Marques del Duero	1	6.4	2	4.7										
Destructor	1	3.5					4	6pdr	2	3pdr			5	15"
Galicia	2	4.7					4	3pdr					4	15"
Marques de Molina	2	4.7					4	3pdr					4	15"
Martin Alonzo Pinzon	2	4.7					4	3pdr					4	15"
Nueva España	2	4.7					4	3pdr					4	15"
Rapido	2	4.7					4	3pdr					4	15"
Temerario	2	4.7					4	3pdr					4	15"
Vicente Yañez Pinzon	2	4.7					4	3pdr					4	15"

Key to Ship Table
Armament: Weapons carried, given as number (#) and Caliber, the later usually in inches
Main: Principal armament
2ndly.....3rdly: Other heavy guns carried (ships in this period notoriosly carried a great variety of heavier guns).
Smaller Guns: given usually in pounderage or millemeters, plus the pneumatic guns on several vessels which proved a failure; omitting machineguns
Torpedoes: Number and size of tubes carried.

Order of Battle: The SANTIAGO CAMPAIGN

U.S. FORCES	Strength	Losses K / W
V Army Corps		
HQ & Staff	17	0 /0
1st Sqn, 2nd Cavalrly	c. 265	0/ 1
C & E, Engineer Battalion	c. 200	0 / 1
Detachment, Hospital Corps	c. 275	0 /1
Detachment, Signal Corps	c. 90	0 /1
1st Division	11	0 /0
1st Brigade	12	2 /1
6th Infantry	c. 510	12 /115
16th Infantry	c. 675	14 /115
71st New York Volunteers	c. 970	15 /68
2nd Brigade	14	0 /0
2nd Infantry	c. 640	8 /57
10th Infantry	c. 455	5/40
21st Infantry	c. 470	6 /32
3rd Brigade	5	1 /0
9th Infantry	c. 470	5 /27
13th Infantry	c. 465	18 /91
24th Infantry	c. 540	7 /83
2nd Division	8	0 /0
1st Brigade	11	0 / 0
8th Infantry	c. 510	6 /46
22nd Infantry	c. 500	9 /35
2nd Massachusetts Volunteers	c. 930	5 / 44
2nd Brigade	13	0 / 0
1st Infantry	c. 450	0 / 2
4th Infantry	c. 465	9 / 35
25th Infantry	c. 530	8 / 30
3rd Brigade	20	0 / 0
7th Infantry	c. 915	33 / 99
12th Infantry	c. 585	8 / 37
17th Infantry	c. 505	8 / 40
Independent [Regular] Brigade	11	0 /0
3rd Infantry	c. 485	0 / 3
20th Infantry	c. 600	1 / 15

Independent [Volunteer] Battalion	4	0 / 0
9th Massachusetts Volunteers	c. 840	0 / 0
8th Ohio Volunteers	c. 1100	*
33rd Michigan Volunteers	c. 1000	2 / 10
34th Michigan volunteers	c. 640	0 / 0
Cavalry Division	13	0 / 0
1st Cavalry Brigade	9	0 / 0
3rd Cavalry	c. 455	3 / 15
6thCavalry	c. 450	2 / 57
9th Cavalry	c. 220	3 / 20
2nd Cavalry Brigade	10	0 / 3
1st Cavalry	c. 540	20 / 55
10th Cavalry	c. 495	8 / 54
1st Volunteer Cavalry	c. 595	23 / 104
Artillery Battalion	1	0 / 0
E, 1st Artillery (?) (8-inch mortar)	82	0 / 0
K, 1st Artillery (Grimes) (3.2-inch)	80	1 / 0
A, 2nd Artillery (Capron) (3.2-inch)	82	2 / 8
F, 2nd Artillery (Parker) (Gatling)	79	0 / 3
G, 4th Artillery (Best) (3.2-inch)	55	0 / 0
H, 4th Artillery (Parkhurst) (3.2-inch)	66	0 / 0

Only forces which were before Santiago prior to its surrender have been included. Numbers refer to the strength of the units at the time of their arrival, with figures on the division and brigade lines referring to staffs. Casualty figures are given as K (killed or mortally wounded) and W (wounded). The 8th Ohio (*) sent a good many of its troops to strengthen some of the other units, including several of the batteries, and losses among them, if any, appear to have been included in the totals of the units to which they were attached.

Commanders have been given for the artillery because it was common to refer to batteries by the commanding officer's name. Changes in command among the other units were quite common.

SPANISH FORCES   Strength

IV Army Corps (Part)

Santiago Division (Part)

    1st Brigade

1st Provisional Battalion of Puerto Rico	c. 600
1st Bn., Regiment of San Fernando, No. 11	c. 750
1st Bn., Regiment of the Constitution, No. 29	c. 600
1st Bn., Regiment of Asia, No. 55	c. 1000
1st Bn., Regiment of Cuba, No. 65	c. 900
2nd Bn., Regiment of Cuba, No. 65	c. 1100
4th Talavera Peninsular Battalion	c. 900
1st Bn., Regt. of Simancas, No. 64 (elements)	c. 125

Manzanillo Division (Part)

Escario's Brigade

3rd Alcantara Peninsular Battalion	c. 750
19th Puerto Rico Rifle Battalion	c. 650
1st Bn., Regiment of Andalucia, No. 52	c. 700
1st Bn., Regiment of Isabel la Catolica, No. 75	c. 600
2nd Bn., Regiment of Isabel la Catolica, No. 75	c. 600

Attached

1st Tercio of Guerrillas	c. 1250
2nd Tercio of Guerrillas	c. 1400
1st Cavalry Regiment	c. 250
6th Btty, 10th Fortress Artillery Battalion	c. 301
6th Btty, 4th Mounted Artillery Regiment	c. 53
1st Btty., 5th Foot Artillery Regiment	c. 47
19th Tercio of the Guardia Civil	c. 200
Engineers and sappers	c. 550
Administrative Corps of the Army	c. 110
Medical Corps	c. 130
Miscellaneous Personnel	c. 150

The organization of the Spanish forces at Santiago was less fixed than that of the U.S. V Corps. Linares, and later Toral, shifted units around between the various provisional brigades which they had organized. Numbers are estimated, and omit about a thousand sailors landed from Cervera's squadron, and approximately 475 more who were attached to various ships and installations in Santiago proper. The distribution of casualties is unknown.

Order of Battle: THE PUERTO RICO CAMPAIGN

	Strength
U.S. FORCES, by Date of Arrival	
Troops Landing 25 July at Guanica	
Expeditionary Force (Miles)	c. 50
Provisional Division (-) (Henry)	c. 185
Garretson's Brigade	c. 50
6th Massachusetts Volunteers	c. 1250
6th Illinois Volunteers (-)	c. 875
Attached	
F, 3rd Artillery (3.2-inch)	c. 120
B, 4th Artillery (3.2-inch)	c. 250
Engineer Bn	c. 250
(Detail, Engineer Corps)	
(H, 1st D.C. Volunteers)	
(A, 1st Illinois Volunteers)	
Provisional Battalion of Recruits	c. 275
Troops Landing 27 July at Ponce	
1st Division, I Corps (-) (Wilson)	c. 300
1st Brigade (Ernst)	c. 75
16th Pennsylvania Volunteers (1st & 2nd Bns.)	c. 850
2nd Wisconsin Volunteers	c .900
3rd Wisconsin Volunteers	c .950
1st Bn. (+), 1st Kentucky Volunteers	c. 550
D&M, 6th Illinois Volunteers	c. 175

Troops Landing 31 July at Guanica

Independent Regular Brigade (Schwan)	c. 75
11th Infantry	c. 1100
19th Infantry	c. 1400
A, 5th Cavalry	c. 100
C, 3rd Artillery (Gatling)	c. 75
D, 5th Artillery (3.2-inch)	c. 110

Troops Landing 31 July to 5 August at Ponce and Guayama

I Corps (Brooke) (-)	c. ?
2nd Brigade, 1st Division (Hain)	c. 50
3rd Illinois Volunteers	c. 1100
4th Ohio Volunteers	c. 1200
4th Pennsylvania Volunteers	c. 1150
Attached	
F, 6th Infantry	c. 120
H, 6th Cavalry	c. 100
A&C, New York Volunteer Cavalry	c. 200
Philadelphia City Troop, Pennsylvania Volunteer Cavalry	c. 100
Provisional Artillery Battalion	c. 900
(B, Pennsylvania Volunteer Artillery)	
(27th Indiana Volunteer Battery)	
(A, Illinois Volunteer Artillery)	
(A, Missouri Volunteer Artillery)	
(U.S. Dynamite Battery)	

Only forces present in Puerto Rico as of the armistice of 13 August have been shown. Medical and signal personnel have been included with headquarters staffs.

SPANISH FORCES

	Strength
Headquarters, Staff, and Services	c. 300
Regular Army and Police Forces	
24th Rifle Battalion, Alfonso XIII	c. 1100
25th Rifle Battalion, de la Patria	c. 1100
3rd Puerto Rico Provisional Battalion	c. 950
4th Puerto Rico Provisional Battalion	c. 950
6th Puerto Rico Provisional Battalion	c. 950
Prince of Asturias Regular Volunteer Battalion	c. 800

12th Fortress Artillery Battalion	c. 800
14th Tercio of the Guardia Civil	c. 780
Public Order	c. 210
Puerto Rico Telegraph Company	c. 210
Medical Brigade of Puerto Rico	c. 40
Volunteer Forces	
1st Volunteer Battalion (San Juan)	c. 1200
2nd Volunteer Battalion (Bayamon area)	c. 550
3rd Volunteer Battalion (Rio Piedras area)	c. 550
4th Volunteer Battalion (Arecibo area)	c. 650
5th Volunteer Battalion (Aquadilla area)	c. 550
6th Volunteer Battalion (Mayaguez)	c. 650
7th Volunteer Battalion (Maricao area)	c. 450
8th Volunteer Battalion (Saban Grande area)	c. 450
9th Volunteer Battalion (Ponce)	c. 750
10th Volunteer Battalion (Coamo area)	c. 550
11th Volunteer Battalion (Guayama area)	c. 650
12th Volunteer Battalion (Hato Grande area)	c. 550
13th Volunteer Battalion (Humacao area)	c. 550
14th Volunteer Battalion (Utuado area)	c. 550
Vieques Volunteer Company (Vieques Island)	c. 50
Governor's Escort Squadron (San Juan)	c. 50
Ponce Cavalry Squadron (Ponce)	c. 50
Public Order Vounteers (Yauco)	c. 50

All figures are approximate. The *1st, 2nd* and *4th Provisional Battalions of Puerto Rico* were on duty in Cuba, the *1st* taking part in the battles of Las Guasimas and the Heights of San Juan. In addition to the volunteer units shown, each of the island's six counties or districts supported a mounted guerrilla company, these forming two "flying guerrilla" colums. The best of the volunteer battalions was the *1st*, the *Tiradores de San Juan*. In addition to the normal four companies, it had a mounted guerrilla company (c. 40 man), a coast artillery detachment (c. 50 men) and a bicycle platoon (c. 20), which performed yeoman service during the American naval bombardment of the city on 12 May: The young cyclists carried more than 85 messages in the course of the action.

Order of Battle: THE MANILA CAMPAIGN

	Strength
U.S. FORCES by Date of Arrival	
Troops Landing 30 June at Cavite	
Anderson' Brigade	c. 2,500
14th Infantry (A,C,D,E, & F)	
1st California Volunteers	
2nd Oregon Volunteers	
A&D, California volunteer Artillery (Elements)	
Troops Landing 17 July at Cavite	
Greene's Brigade	c. 3,600
18th Infantry (-)	
23rd Infantry	
1st Colorado Volunteers	
1st Nebraska Volunteers	
10th Pennsylvania Volulnteers	
A & B, Utah Artillery	
Troops Landing 25-31 July at Cavite	
MacArthur's Brigade (+)	c. 4,800
18th Infantry	
23rd Infantry	
1st Idaho Volunteers	
1st North Dakota Volunteers	
13th Minnesota Volunteers	
1st Bn., 1st Wyoming Volunteers	
Astor Battery	
A, Volunteer Signal Corps	
3rd Bn., 3rd Artillery	
A, Engineers	

Only units in the Philippines as of the armistice of 13 August have been included, but the Hospital Corps has been omitted. Details of unit strengths are unavailable. As of the armistice there were not quite 11,000 U.S. troops in the Philippines, with 5,000 more in two further convoys which arrived within a few days.

SPANISH FORCES
Military District of Luzon

1st Bn., Regiment of Magellan, No. 70
2nd Bn., Reiment of Magellan, No. 70
1st bn., Regiment of Visayas, No. 72
1st Bn., Regiment of Jolo, No. 73
2nd Bn., Regiment of Jolo, No. 73
1st Expeditionary Rifle Battalion
2nd Expeditionary Rifle Battalion
3rd Expeditionary Rifle Battalion
4th Expeditionary Rifle Battalion
5th Expeditionary Rifle Battalion
6th Expeditionary Rifle Battalion
7th Expeditionary Rifle Battalion
8th Expeditionary Rifle Battalion
9th Expeditionary Rifle Battalion
10th Expeditionary Rifle Battalion
11th Expeditionary Rifle Battalion
12th Expeditionary Rifle Battalion
13th Expeditionary Rifle Battalion
14th Expeditionary Rifle Battalion
15th Expeditionary Rifle Battalion

All Spanish troops on Luzon have been included. In the event, of course, most of these troops saw no action against Americans. However, the possibility of a relief column reaching Manila, much as Escaio reached Santiago, was an ever present concern during the campaign.

Guide for the Interested Reader

*F*or those interested in pursuing the history of the Spanish-American War further, there are a host of resources. What follows is intended to be more of a guide, suggesting further references and resources, rather than a full bibliography.

Books

Histories and Technical Treatments. The most detailed recent general history of the war, including political and diplomatic aspects, is David F. Trask's *The War with Spain in 1898* (New York: 1981), but Frank E. Chadwick's two volume *The Relations of the United States and Spain* (New York: 1911) is still extremely valuable, and much more detailed. A very good treatment of the diplomacy of the war is John L. Offner's *An Unwanted War: The Diplomacy of the United States and Spain over Cuba* (Chapel Hill, NC: 1992).

The most detailed account of operations in Cuba remains Herbert H. Sargent's three volume *The Campaign of Santiago de Cuba* (Chicago: 1914). A good look at the campaign drawn from soldier's memoirs and letters may be had in A. B. Feuer's *The Santiago Campaign of 1898* (Westport, CT: 1993).

Graham Cosmas' *An Army for Empire: The United States Army in the Spanish-American War* (second edition, Shippensburg, PA:

1994) is the best discussion of the Army in the war, albeit somewhat hostile to the National Guard and volunteers. Also of interest on the Army are Perry D. Jamieson's *Crossing the Deadly Ground: United States Army Tactics, 1865-1899* (Tuscaloosa: 1994) and *Crucible of Empire: The Spanish-American War and Its Aftermath*, edited by James C. Bradford (Annapolis: 1993) includes a number of essays examining unusual apects of U.S. military operations in the period. Jack Shulimson's *The Marine Corps' Search for a Mission, 1880-1898* (Lawrence, KS: 1993) provides a valuable discussion of the development of amphibious warfare, and has a useful treatment of the Guantanamo operation.

The best recent treatments of the Filipino-American War are Russell Roth's *Muddy Glory: America's "Indian Wars" in the Philippines, 1899-1935* (West Hanover, MA: 1981) and Brian McAllister Linn's *The U.S. Army and Counterinsurgency in the Philippines War, 1899-1902* (Chapel Hill: 1989). Donal H. Dyal's *Historical Dictionary of the Spanish American War* (Westport, Ct: 1996) is quite useful, as is *The War of 1898 and U.S Intervention 1898-1936*, edited by Benjan R. Beedes (NY: 1994), despite its political correctness and some errors of judgment.

The most readily accessible reference on the ships involved in the war is *Conway's All the World's Fighting Ships, 1860-1905* (New York: 1979). For those with a really serious interest in the subject, however, nothing beats the materials available in *Warship Inernational*, a naval interest quarterly (5905 Reinwood Dr., Toledo, OH, 43613), but it is not indexed. The most useful popular treatment of the naval war is A.B. Feur's *The Spanish-American War at Sea* (Westport, CT: 1995). The controversy over the destruction of the USS *Maine* is covered in Hyman Rickover's *How the Battleship Maine Was Destroyed* (Annapolis, 1976), Michael Blow's *A Ship to Remember: The Maine and the Spanish-American War* (New York: 1992), and Peggy and Harold Samuels' *Remembering the Maine* (Washington: 1995).

Of popular histories there is a surfeit, most of which are not very good. However, the recent *The Spanish War: An American Epic, 1898*, by G.J.A. O'Toole (New York: 1984) and Joseph Smith's *The Spanish-American War: Conflict in the Caribbean and the Pacific, 1895-1902* (New York: 1994) are pretty good. Walter

Millis's *The Martial Spirit* (Cambridge, Ma: 1931) wholly misses the effectiveness of U.S. mobilization and the significance of the war in terms of the development of the modern U.S. armed forces.

Two very interesting and at times useful contemporary treatments of the war are *The Story of Our Wonderful Victories* (Philadelphia: 1899), edited by J.R. Jones, and *Behind the Guns with American Heroes* (Chicago and Philadelphia: 1899), edited by the notorious J. W. Buell. These contain excerpts of original letters, portions of official reports and documents by Dewey and other heroes, journalistic accounts, newspaper stories, and much more, including songs and poetry. While not always reliable, the material is usually lively and often quite valuable.

There are very few useful accounts of the war in Spanish. The most valuable by far remains Severo Gomez-Nuñez' five volume *La Guerra hispana-americana* (Madrid: 1899-1902), by the former chief of the personnel section of the Inspector General of Artillery in Cuba during the war. For the brief campaign in Puerto Rico there are two very good works in Spanish: Angel Rivero Mendez's *Cronica de la Guerra hispana-americana en Puerto Rico* (Madrid: 1922) and Carmelo Rosario Natal's *Puerto Rico y la crisis de la Guerra hispana-americana (1895-1898)* (Hato Rey, P.R.: 1975). Otherwise the field is barren.

Christopher H. Brown's *The Correspondents' War: Journalists in the Spanish-American War* (New York: 1967) is an amusing treatment of that aspect of the war, although he fails to realize the extent to which the conflict was overreported.

Memoirs. The war is treated in a host of memoirs, the more interesting of which are, of course, Theodore Roosevelt's *The Rough Riders* (several editions), as well as Russell A. Alger's *The Spanish American War* (New York: 1901), Richard Harding Davis' *The Cuban and Porto Rican Campaigns* (New York: 1898), James H. Wilson's *Under the Old Flag* (New York: 1912), Karl Stephan Herrmann's *From Yauco to Las Marias* (Boston: 1899), and Nelson A. Miles' *Serving the Republic* (New York: 1909). Frederick Funston's *Memories of Two Wars* (New York: 1911) is a very useful account of his service with the Cuban insurgents and in the Philippine Insurrection.

Spanish memoirs are numerous as well, but have mostly not

been translated into English. Two notable exceptions are José Muller y Teijeiro's *Battle and Capitulation of Santiago de Cuba* (Washington: 1898) and Saturnino Martin Cerezo's *The Siege of Baler* (Kansas City: 1909)

Regimental Accounts. There are numerous regimental histories, which often contain interesting material, albeit they often cover up unfortunate events. See particularly Frank Edwards' *The '98 Campaign of the 6th Massachusetts, U.S.V* (Boston: 1899), Anthony Fiala's *Troop "C" in Service* (Brooklyn: 1899), Ernest MacPherson's *History of the First Regiment of Infantry, the Louisville Legion, and Other Military Organizations* (Louisville, Ky: 1907), and Thomas J. Stewart's *The Record of Pennsylvania Volunteers in the Spanish-American War* (Harrisburg: 1900), and the official *New York and the War with Spain* (Albany: 1903).

Fiction. Although the war made its way into numerous works of fiction, none of them are of particular value either as literature or as documents. The most recent efforts are *Fenwick Travers and the Years of Empire* (Novato, CA: 1993) and *Fenwick Travers and the Forbidden Kingdom* (Novato, CA: 1994) by Raymond M. Saunders, dealing amusingly, but not very accurately, with the war in Cuba and the Philippine Insurrection respectively.

Places to Visit

None of the original battle sites of the war are preserved, or worth visiting, urban sprawl having overwhelmed all of them. However, there are numerous relics of the war which can be visited with some profit. The most notable of these is the cruiser *Olympia*, preserved in Philadelphia. The only survivor of the numerous vessels that took part in the war, she is a typical specimen of the warships of the period, down to the extensive use of wood paneling, in total disregard for the threat of fire. Portions of the ill-fated *Maine* are preserved, including a mast at the Naval Academy and another at Arlington National Cemetery. Two of the ship's 10-inch guns were formerly incorporated in a monument in Cuba, but this was demolished by the current dictator, and the pieces apparently scrapped.

The lack of a museum of U.S. military history in the Smithsonian complex ought to be a national scandal, but there are a surprising number of small military museums around the country, on military bases, national parks, and in state capitals, which often have excellent exhibits on the Spanish-American War. Notable among them are the West Point museum and the Navy and Marine Corps Museums in the Washington Navy Yard, but even smaller facilities, such as the Harbor Defense Museum, at Fort Hamilton, Brooklyn, New York, have some interesting exhibits. There are relics of the war in the most unlikely places. For example, the silver service of the armored cruiser *Brooklyn* is at Brooklyn College.

Simulation Games

Although there have been only a handful of wargames dealing with the Spanish-American War, these have been uniformly good. *Remember the Maine!*, which appeared in *Strategy & Tactics Magazine*, No. 108 (July-August 1986), is a good treatment of the war on both a strategic and operational level. *Rifle and Saber* (Simulations Publications, c. 1972), which simulated tactical combat in the late nineteenth century, included several scenarios drawn from the war, notably El Caney. *Fire When Ready* (Metagaming, 1982), a game of tactical naval combat, included scenarios for Manila Bay and Santiago. Currently in progress is *San Juan Hill*, by Simulations Workshp, Inc, a tactical level wargame of the fighting before Santiago in late June and early July 1898.

Film

The Spanish-American War has been part of a surprising number of motion pictures and some television programs (even an episode of the old *Rawhide* series), but none have ever proven of value as historical treatments. The most recent, *Posse*, suggested enormous casualties at Santiago inflicted by Gatling guns, the Spanish never had.

It is, however, worth noting that there is presently in progress a documentary in the style of the notable Public Television *Civil War* series, although a perusal of a list of the editorial consultants for the series does not inspire confidence, military historians being notable by their absence.

Index

Aguinaldo, Emilio, 264, 266, 267, 268, 269, 270, 274, 276, 278, 282, 283, 289, 290-291

Alger, Russell A., 77, 83, 107, 115, 206, 207, 208, 211, 231

Anderson, Thomas, 280 , 284, 286

Augustin Davila, Basilio, 263, 264, 270, 271, 273, 275, 282, 283, 284

Bagley, Worth, 73-74

Barton, Clara, 210, 220

Bates, John C., 122, 133

Biddle, John, 246

Black, Wilson, 68

Blanco y Erenas, Ramon, 37, 118, 171, 172, 195, 209, 266

Brooke, John R., 233, 256

Camara, Manuel de, 168, 273, 282, 283, 311, 312

Cape Verde Islands, 58, 67, 77, 78, 79, 80

Capron, Allyn K., Jr., 126, 127

Capron, Allyn K., Sr., 133, 135, 136

Castillo Duany, Demetrio, 122, 123

Cervera y Topote, Pascual, 58, 59, 60, 78, 79, 80, 83, 84, 85, 86, 87, 88, 90, 107, 118, 147, 159, 169, 171, 172, 175, 178, 184, 188-189, 311, 312

Chadwick, French E., 120

Chaffee, Adna R., 133

Chamberlain, Joseph, 299

Chickamauga (Camp Thomas), TN, 62, 100, 197, 198

Cisneros Betancourt, Salvador, 33

Cleveland, Grover, 31, 32, 35

Crane, Stephen, 162, 163, 244, 250, 261

Cuba, 24, 37, 39, 44, 57, 67, 70, 71, 83, 230, 302

Cuba, towns, cities, and features
Aguadores River, 131, 132
Bayamo, 25, 75
Cabañas, 76, 121
Camaguey Province, 33
Camino Real, 125, 129, 130, 203
Cardenas, 73
Cienfuegos, 72, 86
Daiquiri, 118, 121, 123, 129, 166
El Caney, 119, 131, 133, 135, 136-137, 191, 193
El Pozo, 129
El Viso, 133
Fisher's Point, 74
Guam, 302

Guantanamo Bay, 159, 160-163, 192
Havana, 39, 40, 58, 68, 166, 200-201
Havana Harbor, 42
Holguin, 25, 192
Las Guasimas, 123-130
Mantua, 29
Manzanillo, 74, 192
Mariel, 33, 77
Matanzas, 71
Oriente Province, 25, 39, 75, 116, 121
Pinar del Rio Province, 33, 75
San Juan Heights, 131, 135, 137-147, 191
San Juan River, 120, 129, 131, 137
Santa Clara Province, 72
Santiago, 84, 86, 87, 108, 116, 118-120, 131, 156, 159, 163, 165, 169, 173, 185, 191, 192, 205, 210, 231
Siboney, 121, 122, 123, 129, 166, 202, 203
Zanjon, 26
Cuban Insurrection 1868-1878 (Ten Years' War), 25, 26, 27
Cuban Revolutionary Party (Partido revolucionario cubano), 27, 31

Davis, Richard Harding, 140, 143, 244, 250, 261
Dewey, George, 15, 17, 22, 23, 48, 66, 67, 68, 69, 263, 264, 273, 274, 276, 278-279, 282, 283, 284, 285, 290
Diederichs, Otto von, 277, 279, 286
Dorst, Joseph H., 75, 143
Duffield, Henry M., 131, 133
Dun Loring, VA, 197

Dupuy de Lome, Enrique, 41, 132

Escario Garcia, Federico, 137, 153-154, 192, 195

Fish, Hamilton, Jr., 126, 127
Funston, Frederick, 294-295, 297

Garcia y Iñiguez, Calixto, 75, 120, 191, 197
Garretson, G.A., 238-239, 257
Gomez, Maximo, 27, 28, 29, 30, 33, 39, 49, 50-51
Greene, Francis V., 283, 284, 286, 287, 289
Gridley, George V., 20, 22

Haiti, 40
Hanna, Philip C., 229
Hawaii, 297-298
Hay, John, 299
Hearst, William R., 31, 41
Henna, Julio José, 228
Henry, Guy V., 239, 243, 257
Hobson, Richmond P., 156-157, 158, 159, 202, 208
Hong Kong, 23, 67, 68, 264, 274, 276
Hostos, Eugenio Maria de, 228
Howell, John A., 81
Huntington, Robert T., 160, 161

Jacksonville, FL, 197, 201
Jaudenes y Alvarez, Fermin, 284, 285, 289, 290

Kent, Jacob F., 138, 140
Key West, FL, 81

Lawton, Henry W., 122, 123, 131, 133, 135, 136, 146
Lee, Fitzhugh, 38, 39, 101, 201, 214

Linares Pombo, Arsenio, 116, 118, 129, 132, 137, 144, 146, 147, 151-152, 169, 171, 172, 191
Long, John D., 41, 65, 66, 77, 83, 87, 108, 155, 168, 208, 231, 276

MacArthur, Arthur, 281, 284, 287, 289, 293-294
Maceo, Antonio, 27, 29, 33, 34-35, 52-53
Maceo, José, 28, 34, 53
Macias Casado, Manuel, 235-236
Mahan, Alfred T., 64, 65, 80, 82, 108, 206, 231
Maria Cristina, Queen Regent of Spain, 37, 44
Martí, José, 27, 28, 51-52
Martinez Campos, Arsenio, 26, 28, 29
Martinez-Illecas, Raphael, 246, 249
McKinley, William, 36, 38-39, 42, 43, 45, 63-64, 67, 70, 83, 107-108, 115, 206, 231, 232, 233, 301, 302
Merritt, Wesley, 274, 279, 281-282, 283, 284, 285, 289, 290, 293
Midway Island, 298
Miles, Nelson A., 62, 66, 77, 82, 83, 96-97, 107, 108, 115, 201, 207, 208, 209, 230, 231, 232, 233, 236, 240, 242, 260, 279
Mobile, AL, 62, 100
Montojo y Pasaron, Patricio, 17, 19, 21, 22, 48-49, 69

Naval vessels, American
    Amphitrite, 71, 166
    Baltimore, 16, 21, 69, 264, 286
    Boston, 16, 17, 20, 21, 23, 69, 171, 286
    Brooklyn, 90, 121, 168, 172, 173, 174, 175, 176, 178, 180, 181, 182, 185

Callao, 286
Charleston, 264, 274, 279, 280, 286
City of Pekin, 264
City of Texas, 210
Columbia, 203
Concord, 16, 17, 20, 23, 69
Dixie, 168, 240
Dolphin, 162
Florida, 76
Gloucester (originally *Corsair*), 66, 174, 179, 180, 183, 238
Gussie, 75, 76
Harvard, 85, 184, 185, 203
Hudson, 73, 74
Indiana, 71, 81, 116, 174, 176, 178, 180
Iowa, 81, 155, 168, 174, 175, 176, 177, 178, 179, 180, 182, 183, 185
Maine, 39, 40, 42, 46-47, 89, 127, 159
Marblehead, 40, 72, 73, 88, 160
Massachusetts, 71, 155, 173
Mayflower, 155
McCullough, 16, 17, 69, 264, 269, 286
Merrimac, 157, 158
Minneapolis, 169
Monadnock, 168, 277, 279, 283
Monterey, 168, 277, 279, 283, 286
Montgomery, 41
Nashan, 17
Nashville, 70, 72
New Orleans, 155, 166, 173
New York, 71, 81, 132, 166, 171, 175, 181, 182, 184
Newark, 173
Olympia, 15, 20, 21, 23, 69, 286, 288
Oregon, 66, 67, 71, 81, 82, 93-

96, 168, 174, 176, 177, 178,
180, 182
Panther, 160
Petrel, 16, 23, 269, 286
Porter, 155
Puritan, 71, 81
Raleigh, 16, 17, 264, 277, 278,
286
St. Louis, 86, 184
St. Paul, 89, 159, 166, 167,
169, 170
Segurança, 115, 120, 129
Solace, 184
Suwanne, 133
Terror, 71, 81, 166
Texas, 163, 174, 175, 178, 180,
181, 182, 183
Vesuvius, 165-166
Virginius, 25
Vixen, 174, 176, 181
Wasp, 75
Wilmington, 73
Windom, 72
Winslow, 73, 74
Yale, 203
Yankee, 160, 168
Yosemite, 166, 168
Yucutan, 114
Zafiro, 17
Naval vessels, British
Fame, 68, 69
Imortalité, 277
Linnet, 276
Naval vessels, French
Bruix, 276
Naval Vessels, German
Darmstadt, 277
Irene, 277, 278
Kaiser, 278
Kaiserin Augusta, 277
Kormoran, 277
Prinzess Wilhelm, 278
Naval vessels, Japanese
Itsukushima, 277

Naval Vessels, Spanish
Almirante Quendo, 58, 78, 80,
169, 170, 172, 173, 176, 178-
179, 180
Antonio Lopez, 167
Audaz, 273
Buenavista, 70
Buenos Aires, 273
Castilla, 23, 69
Cristobal Colon, 78, 80, 89-90,
155, 169, 172, 173, 176, 177,
179, 180, 181, 182, 184, 311
Don Antonio de Ulloa, 23
Emperador Carlos V, 58, 59,
167, 168, 273, 311
Furor, 80, 85, 171, 172, 173,
176, 179, 180
General Concha, 166, 167
Infanta Maria Teresa, 78, 80,
85, 170, 172, 173, 176, 177,
178, 179, 182
Isabel II, 166, 167
Isla de Cuba, 21
Isla de Luzon, 21
Osado, 273
Panay, 273
Patriota, 273
Pelayo, 58, 59, 167, 168, 273,
311
Pluton, 80, 158, 171, 172, 173,
176, 180
Ponce de Leon, 167
Prosepina, 273
Rapido, 273
Reina Cristina, 21, 22, 23
Reina Mercedes, 158, 191, 195
Restormel, 89, 170
Terror, 80, 85, 166, 167, 179
Tornado, 25
Vizcaya, 41, 58, 78, 83, 85, 158,
169, 170, 172, 176, 179, 180,
181, 183
Naval War Board, 108
New Orleans, LA, 62, 100

New York, NY, 41
Noriel, Mariano, 283, 289

O'Neill, William, 122, 142
Ortega y Diez, Ricardo, 250, 257
Oses y Mozos, Antonio, 252, 255

Pershing, John J., 98, 127
Philippine insurgents, 263, 265-
  267, 269-270, 273, 274-275, 276,
  283, 285, 288, 289, 292, 296, 301
Philippine Insurrection, 54, 287,
  295, 304-305
Philippine Islands, 57, 302, 312
Philippine Islands, towns, cities,
  and features
    Baler, 296-297
    Bataan Peninsula, 15
    Boca Grande Channel, 15, 16
    Caballo Island, 15, 16
    Cañacoa Bay, 17
    Cavite Peninsula, 17, 19, 58,
      70, 263, 274
    Corregidor Island, 15
    El Fraile Island, 15, 16
    Luzon Island, 15, 270
    Manila, 17, 19, 264, 270, 271,
      275, 283, 286, 288
    Manila Bay, 15, 70, 273, 276
    Sangley Point, 17, 20
    Subic Bay, 69, 70
Polavieja, Camilo de, 267
Polo de Bernabé, Luis, 42, 45
Pratt, E. Spencer, 269
Primo de Rivera, Fernando, 267,
  268, 269
Primo de Rivera, Miguel, 50
Puerto Rico, 37, 57, 67, 70, 71,
  82, 108, 201, 227, 230, 231-232,
  233, 235, 302, 312
Puerto Rico, towns, cities, and
  features
    Aguado, 251
    Aibonito, 245, 250, 251

Barranquitas, 251
Cape San Juan, 230, 236, 237
Cayey, 256
Coamo, 246, 247, 248, 250, 251
Fejardo, 236
Guanica, 237, 238
Hormigueros, 252, 253, 254
Juana Diaz, 244
Los Baños, 247, 249
Mayaguez, 251, 255
Ponce, 239, 240
San Juan, 38, 71, 82, 84, 85,
  166, 227, 259
Pulitzer, Joseph, 31

Rabí, Jesus, 121
Rizal, José, 265, 267, 290
Roosevelt, Theodore, 43, 66, 80,
  113-114, 116, 122, 125, 126, 127,
  130, 142, 143, 145-146, 211, 212,
  228, 300
Rowan, Andrew S., 75
Rubin, Antero, 118, 125, 127,
  128, 129

Sagasta, Praxides Mateo, 37, 38,
  79, 209, 300
Sampson, William T., 67, 71, 81,
  87, 108, 115, 120, 129, 130, 155-
  156, 165, 166, 168, 173, 175, 186-
  187, 192, 197, 208, 282
San Francisco, CA, 197
Sandburg, Carl, 193, 237, 258
Schley, Winfield S., 67, 81, 87, 89,
  155, 168, 171, 175, 180, 187-188
Schwan, Theodore, 251, 252, 253,
  254, 255, 258
Shafter, William R., 76, 77, 97-98,
  108, 109, 115, 120, 121, 123, 128,
  129, 130, 131, 132, 135-136, 137,
  146, 191, 193, 195, 196, 197,
  202, 205, 207, 208, 209, 211, 212,
  300
Sicard, Montgomery, 65, 77, 108

Sigsbee, Charles D., 39, 89, 159, 166
Sims, William S., 66, 167, 168
Soto Villanueva, Julio, 252, 253, 255, 256
Spain, 57-59, 302-303
Spain, towns, cities, and features
  Cadiz, 59, 78, 167
  Canary Islands, 59
Sumner, Samuel S., 138, 142, 145

Tampa, FL, 62, 76, 100, 109, 110-112, 197, 198
Teller, Henry M., 44
Todd, Roberto, 228, 230
Toral Vasquez, José, 118, 172, 191, 193, 195, 205, 207, 208, 210, 215, 300

United States, 60
Units, American
  Navy, 59, 64-65, 82, 303
  Naval Militia, 81
  Revenue Cutter Service, 82
  North Atlantic Fleet, 168
  First North Atlantic Squadron, 168
  Second North Atlantic Squadron, 168
  Asiatic Squadron, 17, 66, 67
  Auxiliary Naval Force, 81
  Eastern Squadron, 168, 233, 282
  Flying Squadron, 67, 81, 86, 88, 89, 115, 171
  North Atlantic Squadron, 67, 68, 81, 115, 181
  Northern Patrol Squadron, 81
  Marines, 72, 73, 163, 238
  1st Marine Battalion, 159, 160, 161-162
  Army, 61, 82, 98-101, 104-105, 303

Military Information Division, 75, 228
I Corps, 101, 201, 239
II Corps, 101, 198, 201
III Corps, 101, 201
IV Corps, 101, 201
V Corps, 76, 101, 103, 104-105, 108, 109, 115, 120, 121, 123, 129, 146, 191, 196, 201, 202, 203, 211, 212-213, 232, 237, 312
VI Corps, 201
VII Corps, 101, 201
VIII Corps, 101, 279, 282
1st Division, 138
1st Brigade (1st Division), 141, 143
2nd Brigade (1st Division), 138
3rd Brigade (1st Division), 141, 142
2nd Division, 122, 133, 138
1st Brigade (2nd Division), 133
2nd Brigade (2nd Division), 135
3rd Brigade (2nd Division), 133
Independent Brigade, 122, 133
Cavalry Division, 138, 139, 140
1st (Cavalry) Brigade, 125, 141
2nd (Cavalry) Brigade, 124, 140
1st Cavalry, 124, 125, 127, 128, 140, 143
2nd Cavalry, 132, 133, 196
3rd Cavalry, 141, 143, 144
5th Cavalry, 252, 254
6th Cavalry, 141, 143, 256
9th Cavalry, 63, 125, 127, 128, 141, 143

10th Cavalry, 76, 98, 122, 124, 125, 127, 140, 143, 146
1st Infantry, 75-76
2nd Infantry, 114
3rd Infantry, 136
6th Infantry, 141, 145
9th Infantry, 141
11th Infantry, 105, 253, 254, 255
12th Infantry, 136
13th Infantry, 141
14th Infantry, 280
16th Infantry, 141, 145
18th Infantry, 281
19th Infantry, 105, 252, 253, 257
20th Infantry, 136
22nd Infantry, 110
23rd Infantry, 281
24th Infantry, 141
25th Infantry, 113, 136
National Guard, 61-62, 98-101, 104
1st Volunteer Cavalry (Rough Riders), 80-81, 105, 109, 113-114, 122, 124, 125, 127, 128, 130, 140, 142, 143, 145, 150-151, 300
New York Volunteer Cavalry, 245, 246, 249, 250
Philadelphia City Troop, Pennsylvania Volunteer Cavalry, 256
1st California Volunteers, 280, 284
1st Colorado Volunteers, 281
1st Idaho Volunteers, 281
3rd Illinois Volunteers, 257
6th Illinois Volunteers, 239, 258
20th Kansas Volunteers, 289
1st Kentucky Volunteers, 255
6th Massachusetts Volunteers, 105, 239

33rd Michigan Volunteers, 131, 132, 196
34th Michigan Volunteers, 132, 196
13th Minnesota Volunteers, 281
1st Nebraska Volunteers, 281
71st New York Volunteers, 114, 140, 141, 142, 145
3rd North Carolina Volunteers, 198
1st North Dakota Volunteers, 281
4th Ohio Volunteers, 243, 257
2nd Oregon Volunteers, 280, 285, 289
10th Pennsylvania Volunteers, 281, 284
16th Pennsylvania Volunteers, 246, 248, 249
2nd Wisconsin Volunteers, 246, 247, 251
3rd Wisconsin Volunteers, 246, 247, 251
1st Wyoming Volunteers, 281
1st Artillery, 133, 138
2nd Artillery, 138
3rd Artillery, 246, 251, 281
4th Artillery, 139
5th Artillery, 246, 248, 253
Astor Battery, 281
Artillery, 105
African-American troops, 63, 220-224
Women in medical service, 224
Units, Cuban
I Corps, 121
Castillo Duany's brigade, 122, 124
Black troops, 225
Units, Puerto Rican
Porto Rican Scouts, 251, 252, 255

Units, Spanish
  Army, 102-104, 105-106
  V Corps, 116
  artillery, 116
  cavalry, 71
  1/11th Infantry Regiment ("San Fernando"), 138
  1/29th Infantry Regiment ("Constitution"), 133, 136
  65th Infantry Regiment ("Cuba"), 76
  74th Infantry Regiment, 263
  1st Talavera Peninsular Battalion, 121, 137, 144
  2nd Expeditionary Rifle Battalion, 296
  24th Rifle Battalion ("Alfonso XIII"), 251, 256
  25th Rifle Battalion ("de la Patria"), 239, 240, 246
  Guardia Civil, 76, 116, 259
  1st Provisional Battalion of Puerto Rico, 138, 144
  4th Provisional Battalion of Puerto Rico, 258
  6th Provisional Battalion of Puerto Rico, 257
  1st Volunteer Battalion (San Juan, PR), 259
  6th Volunteer Battalion (Mayaguez, PR), 251
  7th Volunteer Battalion (Maricao, PR), 252
  8th Volunteer Battalion (Saban Grande, PR), 239
  9th Volunteer Battalion (Ponce, PR), 240
  Tiradores de San Juan, 259
  1st Guerrilla Flying Column, 257
  Cuban volunteers, 119
  Galician volunteers, 72
  Guerrilla companies, 246

Vara del Rey y Rubio, Joaquin, 118, 133, 135, 137, 152
Villaamil, Fernando, 85

Wake Island, 298
Watson, John C., 282
Weyler y Nicolau, Valeriano, 29-30, 32-33, 35, 49-50
Wheeler, Joseph, 123, 124, 127, 138, 148, 208
Whitney, Henry H., 229, 237
Williams, Oscar F., 68, 69
Wilson, James H., 236, 243, 244-245, 246, 248, 249, 250
Winslow, Cameron, 72, 73
Wood, Edward P., 269
Wood, Leonard, 113, 125, 126, 127, 129, 142, 149-150, 191, 202, 212
Woodford, Stewart L., 37, 44

Yellow fever, 206, 207, 210-212, 312
Young, Samuel B.M., 123, 124